W9-BKR-852

Tibet Wild

Tibet Wild

A Naturalist's Journeys on the Roof of the World

George B. Schaller

Washington | Covelo | London

Library of Congress Cataloging-in-Publication Data

Schaller, George B.
  Tibet wild : a naturalist's journeys on the roof of the world / George B. Schaller.
    p. cm.
  Includes bibliographical references and index.
  ISBN 978-1-61091-172-6 (cloth : alk. paper) — ISBN 1-61091-172-5 (cloth : alk. paper) 1. Natural history—China—Tibet Autonomous Region. 2. Tibet Autonomous Region (China)—Description and travel. 3. Tibet Autonomous Region (China)—Environmental conditions. I. Title.
  QH181.S35 2012
  508.51'5—dc23

                            2011049249

Printed on recycled, acid-free paper ✦

Manufactured in the United States of America
10 9 8 7 6 5 4 3 2 1

Keywords: Island Press, Tibet, China, Afghanistan, conservation, international conservation, wildlife conservation, naturalist, snow leopard, chiru

For my companions on these many journeys into the wild

This center of heaven
This core of the earth
This heart of the world
Fenced round with snow
The headland of all rivers
Where the mountains are high
And the land is pure
— Tibetan poem, eighth–ninth century

Whatever happiness is in the world has arisen from a wish for the
    welfare of other beings.
Whatever misery there is has arisen from indulging in selfishness.
    — Buddhist precept

The World is sacred,
    It can't be improved.
If you tamper with it,
    You will ruin it.
If you treat it like an object,
    You will lose it.
    — Laozi, Chinese philosopher, sixth century BCE

I am myself and
    What is around me,
And if I do not save it,
    It shall not save me.
    — José Ortega y Gasset, Spanish philosopher, twenty-first century

The chestnut by the eaves
In magnificent bloom
Passes unnoticed
By man of this world.
    — Basho, Japanese poet, seventeenth century

Contents

Introduction

For nearly four decades my wife, Kay, and I have lived on North America's East Coast beside a forest of maple and pine. Our house is a converted barn once used to stall cattle and dry tobacco. One half of the house consists of a huge, high room with the original barn beams still in place. It is our living room and the loft in it is lined with bookshelves crammed with travelogues, memoirs, histories, and expedition accounts about countries in which I have worked. But mainly it is a room of artifacts, of casual items acquired for their beauty, interest, or merely because they resonate in our hearts, each a memento of exploration and desire.

Wooden masks from the Congo and Nepal hang on a wall, as does a Masai shield of buffalo hide from Tanzania. A Dayak headhunting knife from Sarawak is suspended from a beam beside an intricately woven basket from Laos used for collecting edible plants, land crabs, and other items for a meal. A shelf holds a stone adze from Brazil, a chunk of dinosaur bone from Mongolia, and a walrus tusk from Alaska with scrimshaw of seals and a polar bear. Against a wall stands a carved wooden chest from Pakistan's Swat Valley. A brass bucket from Afghanistan holds firewood, and there is a lamp with a bronze base from India, and a photograph of Marco Polo sheep that reminds me of my studies in Tajikistan.

Of all the countries in which I've worked, I spent far more years on projects in China than anywhere else. In 1980, I was invited to join a team of Chinese scientists in a four-year study of giant pandas, a venture arranged by World Wildlife Fund. After the conclusion of that project, I began field research on the high Tibetan Plateau of western China, and I continue with it still, drawn to the luminous landscape, the wildlife, and the Tibetan culture. Tibetan rugs cover the floor of our room. A large *thangka*, a scroll painting of Tara, the deity of loving kindness and compassion, covers part of one wall. Seven lacquered *tsampa* bowls, lovely in shape and design, used for storing barley flour, cover one table. On a shelf rests a prayer wheel, a tiny temple bell with crystalline sound, a cup for butter tea, and an incense box with two carved snow lions, their turquoise manes flowing, reminding us of Tibet's snowy mountains. A large black-and-white photograph, taken over a hundred years ago, shows the Potala, the Dalai Lama's former home, on its hill overlooking fields and mountains beyond Lhasa.

The Tibetan Plateau has infected me, particularly the Chang Tang, the great northern plain. Chang Tang. The name enchants. It conjures a vision of totemic loneliness, of space, silence, and desolation, a place nowhere intimate—yet that is part of its beauty. Even years before my first visit, I had long wanted to explore its secrets and, intrigued by the accounts of early Western travelers, I traced and retraced their journeys with a finger on a map. The Chang Tang was forbidden to foreigners, devoid of roads, and almost uninhabited; its inaccessibility enhanced its allure. In 1984 I finally had the opportunity to penetrate its vastness, an area which covers not just the northern part of the Tibet Autonomous Region, but also western Qinghai Province, and the southern rim of the Xinjiang Uygur Autonomous Region. By 2011, I had made twenty-six journeys to the Chang Tang for a total of about forty-one months, not counting wildlife surveys I've also made in eastern Tibet and the Pamir Mountains of southwest China.

Though drawn to remote and little-known places by inclination, I also knew that the Chang Tang in northern Tibet and other parts of the Tibetan Plateau harbored a variety of large mammals, none of them studied, their lives still a mystery. Years of political turmoil had decimated China's wildlife, as I had noted during the panda study, and I wondered about the current status of various other species. Mainly I wondered how certain species of the Tibetan Plateau had fared.

I wanted to delve into the lives of the Tibetan antelope (or chiru), the Tibetan wild ass (or kiang), the wild yak, and other members of the unique mammal community on these uplands. Initially the State Forestry Administration (called the Ministry of Forestry at the time) in Beijing suggested that I survey the distribution of snow leopard. This I did, but soon my attention shifted to chiru. The species intrigued me with its wanderings, here today and gone tomorrow. To know about the movements of an animal is a first step in protecting it. Little did I realize how many years it would require, at what cost in comfort and funds, and how many miles of uninhabited terrain we would have to traverse to obtain even a general idea of the chiru's migratory patterns.

I approached the project as a scientist, more specifically as a biologist focused on conservation. This involved collecting facts, many of them, because they are the only reliable tool of science, and it is upon facts that conservation must ultimately be based. I do not mistake numbers and measurements and statistical detail for meaning, but I hoped to collect enough scattered facts to discover from them certain patterns and principles which underlie the Chang Tang ecosystem. But nothing remains static, neither a wildlife population nor a culture, and I knew my efforts would represent just a moment in time, a record of something that no one has seen before and never would again. My information offers the landscape an historical baseline, drawn over a three-decade period from which others working in the future can reclaim the past and compare it to their present. Because the Tibetan Plateau is being rapidly affected by climate change, the accumulation of such basic knowledge has now become especially timely and urgent.

To learn as much as possible about chiru became a personal quest, almost an indulgence, and it gave direction and coherence to much of my work on the Tibetan Plateau. To save one of the last great migrations of a hoofed animal in Asia, surpassed in number only by the million Mongolian gazelles on the eastern steppes of Mongolia, is important for itself, as well as to China and the world. And no one else at the time had devoted themselves to the task. By happy coincidence the chiru offered me an opportunity to explore terrain which few had ever seen and at the same time to study a

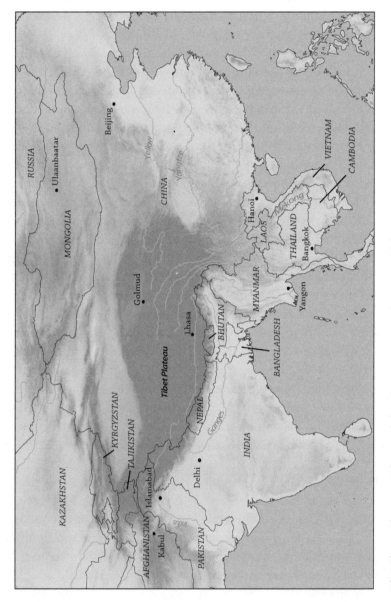

The Tibetan Plateau in China and the adjacent countries where our wildlife conservation work was done.

little-known species. I am less a modern field biologist devoted to technology and statistics than a nineteenth-century naturalist who with pencil and paper describes nature in detail, though with little desire to collect specimens, as was then in vogue; instead I strive to observe species and protect them.

To become familiar with an area that is still healthy, productive, and diverse, one still unspoiled by humankind, has a special appeal. It is not a matter of surveying the last orangutans in Sarawak or searching for saola in Laos, as I have done, but of conserving vigorous populations of all animal and plant species in an ecosystem. Conservation has in recent decades focused on rain forests with their great diversity of species, whereas attention to rangelands, which cover 40 percent of the earth's land surface, has languished. Yet rangelands too display biological treasures in beauty, variety, and uniqueness. The Serengeti savanna or Mongolian steppe offers an unsurpassed sense of place; it invites a feeling of empathy for the landscape, including the pastoral cultures of the people who dwell there. Here in the Chang Tang was a neglected area of over 300,000 square miles, a third of them uninhabited, an area twice the size of California, or the size of France and Italy combined. Here one could address the conflicting demands of conservation, development, and the livelihood of its pastoral people, and here conservation would not need to be confined to a protected area of modest size but could involve a vast landscape, one larger than many countries. Good management options persisted and solutions to problems could be applied based on solid science, sound policy, and local support, drawing on the knowledge, interests, and participation of the area's communities.

Changes in the Chang Tang, already under way in the 1980s when I first visited, have been accelerating with more roads, more households, more livestock, and more fences, which, together with new land-use policies, have had a major impact on the land and its wildlife. As economic conditions have improved, most families have settled into permanent houses instead of nomadic tents, and have exchanged horses for motorcycles. Livestock is often kept in fenced private plots instead of herded on communal pastures, leading to overgrazing and hindering the movement of wildlife. The conservation goal now, as before, is to manage the rangelands, livestock, and wildlife in dynamic stability, to maintain ecological wholeness. Changes over recent decades have made this more difficult. My perceptions and actions have had to change as well. As the human population grows there as elsewhere, one has to confront the necessity of limits, of regulating the use of the landscape. Some parts should be wholly protected, closed to human intrusion, where plants and animals can seek their destiny. Much of the northern Chang Tang is such a place, one still mostly devoid of people, and it requires such full protection. Other parts need to be managed in cooperation with the local communities, limiting livestock to sustainable numbers, managing wildlife to reduce conflict, strictly regulating development, and the like. When I now return to the Chang Tang, I can still see the past in the present because relatively little land has so far been degraded by human action. My mission, indeed my passion, is to help the Chang Tang endure for decades and centuries to come in all its variety and beauty through careful, intelligent management.

My dream is that communities will learn to treasure and manage their environment for no reason other than to keep it healthy and beautiful. How can I graft my knowledge and feelings onto the beliefs, emotions, and traditions of others? As His Holiness the Dalai Lama said: "Ultimately, the decision to save the environment must come from the human heart." The Buddhist religion stresses love and compassion toward all living beings, and this predisposes its followers to be receptive to an environmental message, more there than elsewhere. Humans seem to have a kind of mental glaucoma as they obsessively destroy nature, tearing it apart, even while seeing the ever-increasing damage that threatens their future. Conservation remains an ideological and psychological minefield through which everyone who hopes to preserve something must blunder. Nevertheless I see progress on the Tibetan Plateau and keep a positive spirit.

Conservation is a long journey, not a destination, something to which my years in and around the Chang Tang can attest. Chinese expeditions had done important initial work by making lists of species and plotting their distribution, but my Han Chinese and Tibetan coworkers and I came with a different agenda. We came not just to learn but also to inform and inspire, to reveal the richness of the Chang Tang and other places in this region of the world. We became witnesses who tried to alert those around us to what was being lost. We promoted the establishment of nature reserves, more accurately termed conservation areas because pastoralists with their livestock live in most of them. Much of the Chang Tang area is now officially protected in such nature reserves, a glowing achievement for China. We alerted the government to the mass slaughter of chiru for their fine wool in 1990, and this has led to much better protection of the species. Above all, the environment of the Tibetan Plateau has become a major concern of the government at all levels, of nongovernmental organizations, and of many communities. I had only a small part in this, but I have been an admiring observer, and have remained active in further conservation efforts there.

"But what has been has been, and I have had my hour," wrote the seventeenth-century poet John Dryden. Indeed I have. But I hate to acknowledge this. I cannot resist returning to the solitude of these vast uplands. With each expedition, I slough off my past like a snake skin and live in a new moment. Marooned in mind and spirit, I have no idea when my work there will end; I continue to plan new projects. But like all good ventures it will end someday without heroics.

In recent years, I have neglected to publish much on our work. There have been occasional scientific papers and popular articles, mostly in Chinese publications such as *Acta Zoologica Sinica* and *China's Tibet*. My two most recent books are the popular *Tibet's Hidden Wilderness* (1997) and the scientific *Wildlife of the Tibetan Steppe* (1998), both also available in Chinese translation. But so much has been learned since then. I have made annual trips to China, to the Chang Tang, to southeast Tibet, and to the Pamir mountains of western China and adjoining countries.

This book, built on these explorations, is part observation and part evocation. Eight of the fourteen chapters deal with the Chang Tang, a number of them devoted primarily to chiru. By the mid-1990s, when I wrote my previous books, I had failed to find any calving grounds of the migratory chiru populations, a principal goal and a critical one in their conservation. Ultimately we reached two of them, and the travails of travel and the exultation of finding the newborns deserve accounts. In these chapters, I have tried to bring out not just the discoveries and excitements of fieldwork, but also what happens in the day-to-day course of our work. I thus emphasize some of the difficulties, of vehicles bogging down in July mud time after time and digging them out at 16,000 feet, of snowstorms in summer, of winter temperatures in a frost-encrusted tent at −30°F, and the daily tedium of moving camp for weeks on end. I could only view my Tibetan, Han, and Uygur companions on the various journeys with respect for their fortitude and dedication under such conditions.

A struggle for conservation all too often confronts greed, and so it was with the chiru, whose fine wool, when woven into shahtoosh shawls, had by the late 1980s become a fashion statement of the world's wealthy. The slaughter of this species and its consequent decline, the developing effort to protect it, and its subsequent slow recovery, is a tale of desecration and redemption. My chapter on this shows how a species' circumstances can almost overnight change from seeming security to being threatened with extinction. It is a lesson that nothing is ever safe, that if a country treasures something it must monitor and guard it continually.

Of the 150 or so mammal species on the Tibetan Plateau, I studied the chiru in greatest detail. I had also wanted to make more observations on the rare wild yak, the ancestor of the abundant domestic yak; to me the presence of wild yaks sanctifies the Chang Tang as wilderness. But chiru drove me on, either to places where yaks have been exterminated or to habitat unfavorable to them. I have, however, written here about three other species of the Chang Tang. The small and endearing pika, whose presence is so vital to the ecosystem yet is being widely poisoned, is the subject of one chapter. Another is on the powerful and uncommon Tibetan brown bear, which has come into increasing conflict with humans. And a third chapter is on the snow leopard, ever present but seldom revealing itself, whose enigmatic presence has haunted me over the decades.

We have also conducted wildlife surveys in the southeastern part of the Tibetan Plateau. With its maze of forested mountains and the world's deepest canyon, eastern Tibet is wholly different from the Chang Tang, and it fascinated me by its contrasts. There I experienced the close attentions of leeches in the humid warmth and learned about the hidden land of Pemako, sacred in Buddhist geography. We trekked through the region on two lengthy trips to check on the status of wildlife and evaluate it as a possible reserve.

An uncommon animal on the Tibetan Plateau is the Tibetan argali sheep. I saw it seldom and learned little about its life but much about its death. Trophy hunters have an inane desire to kill rams with the longest possible horns, and I tell a story, in which I played but a minor part, of what happened when four American hunters returned home with their trophies: it turns into a cautionary tale, a sordid saga of sloppy science, deception, and political intrigue that damages the credibility of various persons and institutions.

The Tibetan Plateau is often considered the Roof of the World, and the Pamirs to the west are, in effect, its veranda. The precipitous terrain of the Karakoram and Kunlun Mountains between the Tibetan Plateau and the Pamirs has affected the distribution of wildlife. The snow leopard ranges throughout these mountains and Tibetan people once did, too. Kiang, chiru, and Tibetan gazelle failed to reach the Pamirs. Tibetan argali inhabit the Tibetan Plateau, whereas a unique argali subspecies, the Marco Polo sheep, lives in the Pamirs. This magnificent animal, the grandest of all wild sheep, roams across several international borders. To protect and manage it requires cooperation between Pakistan, Afghanistan, Tajikistan, and China, something best achieved by the creation of a four-country International Peace Park or Trans-Frontier Conservation Area. My efforts to promote this goal after working in each of the four countries, some of them politically volatile, provide me still with some useful lessons, about patience and persistence above all.

For a naturalist there is conflict between a life of comfort, companionship, and security at home, and one of hardship among mountains and plains. Observing undisturbed Marco Polo sheep fills me with delight, and waves of pleasure surge through me. Hearing that a government has protected an area that I had recommended is a balm to the soul, giving meaning to my life. But I renounce so much by seeking wilderness—a settled life, friends, and contact with those I love. There is usually no one other than my wife, Kay, in the field in whom I can truly confide during days of adversity. For years my family was with me in the field: first only Kay in the Congo, then also our two children in India, Tanzania, and Pakistan, and, when these had grown up, only Kay again in China and Mongolia. She was not just my coworker and one who greatly enjoyed camp life, but she also edited my manuscripts (including this one), raised our two sons, of whom I am immensely proud, and contributed in innumerable other ways. But Kay did not join me on most of the journeys described in this book, except in my heart, because her health did not permit it. I missed having her with me, always helping, encouraging, renewing my excitement in the work, and sharing memories. Love is the only bridge connecting us during lengthy separations. There is the knowledge that my return is awaited, a gift of happiness from someone who is part of myself. We each carry a different burden of hardship when separated. Nevertheless our lives keep going, round and round, together and apart, a mandala of love and compassion.

The various projects described in the chapters that follow have depended on many persons and institutions for support since the mid-1990s, and with deepest gratitude I acknowledge their generous assistance. Most are in China, the focus of this book, and I owe that nation an immense debt for hosting me so generously over the years. I particularly would like to mention the splendid cooperation of director Abu and Drolma Yangzom in the Forestry Department, Tibet Autonomous Region; of director Li Sandan and Zhang Li[1] in the Forestry Department, Qinghai Province; and of director Zhu Fude and Shi Jun of the Forestry Department, Xinjiang Uygur Autonomous Region. I also refer to my work in a number of other countries, particularly those bordering China, among them Afghanistan, Tajikistan, India, Bhutan, Nepal, Myanmar, Mongolia, Vietnam, and Laos. I thank all countries collectively, and extend my special

---

[1] Throughout this book, Han Chinese names are given in their traditional manner with the family name first and then the given name.

appreciation to the many individuals, from herder to farmer and from government official to scientist, who so graciously extended their hospitality to us. Most of the individuals who took direct part in our journeys since the mid-1990s are mentioned in the text.

The support of three institutions has been critical. For over half a century I have been affiliated with the Wildlife Conservation Society in New York; WCS also has an office in Beijing directed by Xie Yan. William Conway and John Robinson, among others at WCS, gave me the freedom to fulfill my dreams in the world's wilderness, doing work on behalf of conservation that enriched my life. In 2008 I also joined Panthera, a nongovernmental organization devoted to the conservation of the world's wild cats that is directed by Alan Rabinowitz, an old field colleague of mine. I have in addition an adjunct position with the Center of Nature and Society at Peking University in Beijing, which is directed by Lu Zhi. All research in China was done with the full cooperation of the State Forestry Administration in Beijing. The Tibet Plateau Institute of Biology and the Tibetan Academy of Agricultural and Animal Sciences in Lhasa also provided fruitful collaboration.

The project has in recent years depended for any success on various foundations and individual donors, and I am deeply indebted to all for their faith in our efforts. Among these are the Liz Claiborne-Art Ortenberg Foundation, the Armand Erpf Fund, the Judith Mc-Bean Foundation, the Patagonia Company, the John D. and Catherine T. MacArthur Foundation, the Hoch Charitable Lead Trust, and the National Geographic Society. The European Union-China Biodiversity Programme, through the Wildlife Conservation Society, funded a project in Tibet in which I took part. Edith McBean, Anne Pattee, and Darlene Anderson, among others, also helped us generously.

Three individuals have accompanied me on several journeys, and they deserve special mention for their valuable contribution to the projects, as well as for their companionship, dedication, adaptability, and tenacity, often under most difficult conditions. Kang Aili, a co-worker on six of my trips during the past decade, is affiliated with the Wildlife Conservation Society–China office and coordinates its field program in western China with great ability and persistence.

Lu Zhi, director of both Peking University's Center for Nature and Society and the Shan Shui Conservation Center, a nongovernmental organization, has with initiative and deep insight established several community conservation projects on the Tibetan Plateau. We worked together on two trips in the Chang Tang and two in southeast Tibet, and she also supervises the Tibetan brown bear program. Beth Wald, a photographer, added outstanding value to two expeditions in Afghanistan and two in Tajikistan by documenting the mountains, wildlife, and local people in glorious detail, something that greatly helped to promote our work and raise awareness of these areas.

With exceptional editorial skill, insight, and interest, Jonathan Cobb meticulously edited the manuscript on behalf of Island Press, and I owe him a great debt of gratitude for improving it so much. I also extend my deep appreciation to Kathy Zeller for preparing the maps, and to Michael Fleming for superbly copyediting the manuscript. Most persons who contributed to my conservation efforts are mentioned in the text, but, in addition, I thank Luke Hunter, David Wattles, Rebecca Martin, Margarita Trujillo, Lisanne Petracca, Sun Shan, and Donna Xiao.

This is a personal book of science, conservation, and exploration based on my observations, experiences, and feelings. Sometimes I sound churlish and at other times exhilarated. My companions would no doubt write somewhat different accounts. But I want to stress that we worked as congenial teams. No matter what tribulations confronted us, we surmounted them and returned in good health, with solid information, and with many bonds of friendship intact.

George Schaller
Roxbury, Connecticut
December 22, 2011

A Note on the Text

I have used the English system of weights and measures in this book. The conversions into the metric system are as follows:

1 inch = 2.54 cm
1 foot = 0.305 m
1 mile = 1.6 km
1 square mile = 2.59 km^2
1 ounce = 28.35 g
1 pound = 0.45 kg

✳ CHAPTER 1 ✳

A Covenant with Chiru

W E'RE TRAVELING SOUTH on the highway from the city of Golmud in Qinghai Province on a bitter October day in 1985
when I see chiru (Tibetan antelope) in the distance, mere specks in
the immensity of white, and ask our driver Ma Shusheng to stop the
Land Cruiser so I can get out. Snow covers plains and hills to the
edge of vision, and a veil of luminous cloud shrouds the sky. One
hill floats like an iceberg on a low layer of fog. I plow through the
snow adrift in space, the chiru and I the only visible life, bound to
each other by the desolation. In front of me a herd of male chiru
plods mutely past in single file through knee-deep snow, the animals imposing in their black-and-white nuptial coats and with their
long, slender horns rising almost straight up from the head. I am in
a dream landscape of unicorns, of Tibetan horsemen with lances, of
antelopes from the Serengeti plains transported high into winter.
Here is a place to give wings to the imagination.

This, my first meeting with chiru, comes only five days after a
blizzard has covered this part of Qinghai with a foot of snow, the
heaviest such snowfall in years. We have just completed a snow leopard survey in the north of the province, and we have come to check
on the status of wildlife along the highway, not realizing the serious-
ness of conditions in the storm's wake. The highway from Golmud
winds over the Kunlun Mountains and crosses the eastern edge of
the Chang Tang before continuing into Tibet. Our leader is Guo
Gieting, a pleasant, low-key official from the Forestry Department,

in his early fifties. Qiu Mingjiang and Ren Junrang, two biologists in their early twenties, have also joined me, as they did during previous research work.

We are traveling in a Toyota Land Cruiser and a pickup truck across the desert of the Qaidam Basin and up into the hills, climbing steadily past sharp-edged peaks until, after eighty-seven miles, we surmount Kunlun Pass at 15,600 feet and descend into rolling plains beyond. I have seen a pair of ravens, for me a good omen.

In the evening I write into my field journal:

A crystal-clear space so vast needs a place to rest the eye. We scan ahead and to the sides and see black dots scattered in clumps and singly. Under binocs and scope they become wild ass [kiang]. We count, drive on a little and count others. In one sweep of the scope resting on the hood of the Toyota I count 262 asses. Further on are more herds, most standing in the snow half a mile or more from the road, sometimes seen only in silhouette and others with a golden tan in the lowering sun. A few near the road are skittish and trot off when our two cars stop to photograph.

Then I see some chunky tan antelopes: female Tibetan antelopes, the first I've ever seen. For 20 km we are always within sight of animals, so easily visible against the snow that I can spot them at 2 km or more. We casually count about 525 asses and as many as 700 antelope. . . . A wonderful wildlife afternoon; for once reality lives up to anticipation and hope.

I write these notes in a mud-walled room in Wudaoliang where we stay overnight, a desolate cluster of buildings at 15,000 feet, a truck stop with a few small restaurants, shops, and a military post. The room has hard beds, each with two folded quilts, and a stove we crowd around and constantly stoke with sheep droppings from a bucket.

The Land Cruiser does not start the following morning, even though it is only −5°F, probably because of water in the gasoline, but a pull from the pickup gives it life. Continuing south we encounter little wildlife, only a few herds of chiru and kiang and several forlorn gazelles struggling through the snow. The kiang, powerful and horse-sized, expose grass with such vigorous sweeps of a foreleg that they've abraded the back of each foreleg into a bare, bloody patch. The chiru also paw craters in search of grass tufts. None of the species here have broad hooves like caribou have, adapted for walking on snow. Usually they don't need them, because winter winds tend to expose the ground quickly after a storm, but this time it is unusually calm and cold and the snow deeper than the usual inch or two. Walking through snow and digging again and again to obtain just a few stalks of coarse, dead grass expends the valuable energy an animal needs to conserve for the long, harsh winter months ahead. A Tibetan man sits on a kilometer stone, bicycle beside him, rifle in hand, watching four gazelle drift closer. We halt and chase the gazelle away. In the afternoon we reach Tuotuohe on the banks of the upper Yangtze River, another truck stop. We rent a room in a government barracks where we spend more noisy nights than we anticipated hearing trucks arrive and being started at intervals to keep the engines from freezing.

Tuotuohe with its transitory population of a few hundred reminds me of a small Alaskan community on a winter morning with stovepipes emitting plumes of smoke into an ice fog of glittering crystals. But rather dissimilar are the Tibetan pilgrims crowded in the backs of open trucks headed for the holy sites of Lhasa, swaddled like mummies in thick sheepskin *chubas* and almost hidden by piles of bedding and sacks of belongings. Truckers heat their diesel tanks with blow torches and build fires with wood splinters beneath the engines to warm them. Flocks of horned larks and rufous-necked snow finches searching for food hop over exposed ground and packed snow tinged with urine and blood from slaughtered animals. A goat eats a cardboard box. We report ourselves to the local community leader, who tells us that livestock are starving and that most of the nomads remain isolated in scattered households and will need outside help. The snow is too deep for us to drive cross-country in our vehicles to survey wildlife, and horses cannot be used because there is no fodder for them.

Mingjiang, Junrang, and I walk away from the settlement to observe chiru. We see many of them stream northeast in ragged lines, some consisting only of males and others only of females and young. I tell my companions that I want to continue alone to photograph.

A dip in the terrain provides cover after my careful approach and I kneel there. About 600 chiru are scattered over the plain. A herd of males gathers near me, a veritable forest of horns. When looked at from the side, the horns blend so that the animal appears to have only one horn like a unicorn. The anthropologist Toni Huber has noted that the name *chiru* may have come from the Tibetan *bse ru* (pronounced "siru"), meaning "rhinoceros," perhaps because the horns of both species are used for medicine; they certainly are not similar in appearance. Another herd wanders to within 150 feet of me. Two males face each other with lowered heads, rapier horns ready for conflict. Then they clash. I wonder why they waste energy on testing dominance when their survival in this deep snow is at stake. Clouds suddenly engulf us, everything vanishing in a white-out, and I stand there in driving snow as ghost creatures pass, still drawn toward the northeast. Where have they come from and where are they going?

"We know too little of high Tibet to be able to draw maps of the occurrence of big game and its wanderings with the seasons." So wrote the Swedish explorer Sven Hedin in his book *Southern Tibet*, published in 1922. More than sixty years later, we still don't know. What a challenge for us, especially now, with wildlife drastically re-duced and the chiru and several other species listed as threatened with extinction!

Before the snowstorm engulfs me, I look west with longing to-ward Tibet, over 150 miles away, the direction from which the chiru are coming. Subconsciously I have made a covenant with the species to help it by unraveling its mysterious life—its travels, its numbers, its habits. Whenever I do research in an area, I select a totem animal in which my heart can rest, an animal of beauty and interest and in need of conservation, such as the mountain gorilla, the tiger, or the giant panda. Here in the Chang Tang the chiru will be that totem. When plains and hills emerge again from the clouds, I admire the chiru and look at their tracks scribbled in the snow like a script of their own, and then head back elated.

The drivers Ma Shisheng and Xao Rijie cook mutton soup for breakfast. It is a chilly −13°F, the road is icy, and fog imprisons us until ten o'clock. Again we drive south, our surveys confined to the highway. Many pikas, the tiny relatives of rabbits weighing a mere four ounces or so, sit on the snow, puffed up fur balls with dark eyes. Waiting to feast on unwary pikas are upland buzzards, saker falcons, and ravens perched on mounds and telephone poles. A Tibetan hare, a species unique to this plateau, sits in the snow drawn deeply into itself, then hops off slowly as we approach on foot to take a photograph. As it reaches the highway, a passing truck suddenly stops, the driver leaps from the cab and grabs the hare by the ears in anticipation of a meal. Mingjiang quickly retrieves the weak animal from the driver, and we return it to the plains to die in peace. I regret that we disturbed it. Nearby is the carcass of a kiang female with hindquarters chopped off for its meat, and beyond her lie three gazelle someone has killed, gutted, and dragged to the road. Farther on, we come across signs of the desperate leaps of animals in the snow, along with splattered blood, shell casings, and the drag marks of five bodies toward the road. A little distance away is a female chiru, dead for at least a day, with snow partly drifted over her. We weigh her—forty-eight pounds—and examine her viscera. There is not a trace of fat; no doubt she starved to death.

As we drive north from Tuotuohe for a day-trip the following morning, I spot a raven hacking at something, a dead female chiru. It has been ten days since the blizzard and more animals are dying from starvation. This female had reclined in the brutal cold, her body melting enough snow to create a bare patch around her, and then she died lying on her side, her legs twitching and scrabbling in the snow. She weighs fifty-five pounds and is lactating. Near her body is another female with two young pawing in the snow. She barely pauses in her digging to look at me as I approach, her long eyelashes glimmering with snow. When she moves away only one of the young follows her; the other drifts away alone. A chiru herd suddenly bolts and bunches up, a mastiff dog at its heels. The dog grabs a lagging calf and shakes it. As we draw near the dog flees, leaving its victim dead and bloody with lacerated throat and neck.

When we return to Tuotuohe that evening, Guo Gieting informs us that the governor of Qinghai, Song Rui Xiang, wants to see us. He is here to look into the snow emergency, and we meet him at the military post. A forceful person, he gives orders and queries those around him about the situation. We suggest that illegal hunting of wildlife along the highway be stopped. He tells us that instead he will have hay put along the highway for the wildlife and send helicopters to kill wolves. I demur, and Guo Gieting later explains that these are political decisions about which we can do nothing. To check on the condition of the nomads and the wildlife, the People's Liberation Army, we are told, will send a truck and tractor-pulled wagon filled with food and fuelwood, and we are invited to go along.

The vehicles are expected imminently. Three days pass. We eat in huts adorned with deep-blue flags out front proclaiming that they are restaurants with names like "Sichuan Flower." Inside each one is a table or two, and on the table is a tin can with wooden chopsticks and perhaps a pot of ground red pepper. On the menu is a sole dish of noodles, rice soup, or meat and vegetable soup, depending on the place. Minjiang, Junrang, and I decide to take more walks to observe wildlife. Driver Ma is surly, wanting to go back to Golmud, just as driver Xao has done with the pickup, and not ferry us around when requested. When I inquire of Mingjiang why a driver can determine our work, he replies: "Ma is on the same level politically as Guo. Therefore, Guo is in no position to give orders." But the waiting, cold, and altitude are affecting us all. Junrang is more withdrawn than usual, Mingjiang wanders off alone without informing us, and my temper has become short.

It is −30°F as we once again head into the whiteness, the crusted snow crunching underfoot. We see chiru just standing, backs hunched, too weary now even to dig through the hardened snow. Ahead are several dark mounds and near them two dogs, very shy as we draw near. Of the four chiru bodies, two have shredded throats and two have starved. We look for more bodies in order to collect such vital statistics as weight, sex, and age based on tooth wear. We crack open a long bone and look at the marrow. If the marrow is a thick, fatty white, the animal still had some body reserves; if it is a bloody jelly it meant all reserves were depleted. By afternoon our body count is ten, seven killed by dogs. When we report this to the community leader, he exclaims, "*Leng*" ("Wolf"). After we convince him otherwise, he notes that these dogs belong to a nearby road camp. When Guo Gieting adds that driver Ma has a shotgun, the leader suggests that we shoot dogs that are killing wildlife. We stop at the road camp to ask its headman to please tie up the dogs. A lone brown-headed gull flies over as we return to our Spartan room.

Driver Ma agrees to drive us along the road to look for more dead animals to autopsy. Just north of Tuotuohe two large black mastiffs and a half-grown pup sit by four chiru they have killed. Ma shoots the two adults but permits the pup to flee toward some nearby huts. I understand the killing lust of these dogs when prey, usually so fleet and shy, is suddenly defenseless. In general, carnivores will kill far more than they can eat when given an opportunity, as I have observed in the Serengeti with spotted hyenas and lions. Wolves, lynx, and snow leopards enter corrals where they may kill a dozen or more domestic sheep where one would do. And of course there are ample published accounts of trophy hunters mindlessly shooting and shooting when given a chance. I feel dejected—my heart is with the chiru in their struggle for survival. Four more dog-killed chiru and more bodies are in sight, but just then the long-awaited army truck and tractor pass us and we return to Tuotuohe. Yaks are being slaughtered because there is no fodder for them. The air is heavy with the steam of their bodies and the odor of blood.

Our counting of bodies, no matter how seemingly morbid, does produce useful information of a kind not usually obtained. In a sample of twenty-two dead chiru there were nine young, six adult females, two yearling (one-year-old) females, and five yearling males. Of these, thirteen were killed by dogs and nine died of malnutrition. Since our counts of living chiru showed that there are over twice as many females as young; the young were proportionately more vulnerable than the others. No adult males are among the dead. Their large size enables them to dig more easily for forage and to plow through snow with less energy than others. A large male has a lower metabolic rate and lower nutritional requirements per unit weight than a female and especially a calf. In addition, males have stored much fat while lounging around during summer, whereas females enter the winter lean from months of pregnancy and then lactation.

It is now October 31, and we are ready to start our cross-country trip into the white void in an old red tractor with wide treads pulling a wagon and an army truck with worn tires and a large red-and-white sign proclaiming in Chinese characters: "To Contribute to the Rescue Work." We carry eight barrels of diesel fuel, a pile of firewood, and a pile of army coats and boots to hand out. The team members include four soldiers and several Tibetans from Tuotuohe; of the latter two are community doctors and one a mathematics teacher. One of the Tibetans, Zhi Mai, is the leader. He wears a fox-skin hat and carries a .762 rifle. I join the Tibetans in the open wagon so that I can count the wildlife along our route. An hour after leaving, the truck breaks through the ice of a shallow pond hidden beneath the snow. After we laboriously unload the truck, the tractor can finally pull it out and we continue at our modest pace of about four miles per hour. The sun vanishes shortly after six o'clock and winter asserts its grip. We stop in darkness at eight o'clock and erect one tent of heavy green canvas, large enough for us all. With two blowtorches roaring, the Tibetans melt snow and prepare instant noodles and tea. It is −30°F inside the tent at night. I am chilled through and my feet numb, in spite of wearing all my clothes inside the sleeping bag.

In the morning, the inside of the tent is thick with frost as we have tea and a frozen bun for breakfast. The tractor has idled all night to keep from freezing. The truck again does not start, and even when pulled by the tractor its wheels will not turn. The all-purpose blowtorches are then used to heat the engine and wheel bearings so we can get under way. As we travel, I take notes on wildlife within 300 m on each side of our route—one male gazelle, six male chiru, three female chiru, and two young chiru. By noon we reach a tent surrounded by bloody sheep hides laid out to dry, a pile of sheep heads, and viscera dragged onto the ice of a nearby stream. The soldiers leave armloads of wood and several pairs of shoes for the family, though I doubt that they need this. The inhabitants are dressed more warmly than we are, and mounds of yak dung near the tent provide ample fuel. With 1,500 sheep, this family is quite wealthy. But sixty have so far died, and many more will probably starve too. We pass another tent, cross a low pass, and enter a broad valley with a jagged range ahead. The tractor breaks through the ice of a shallow lake, but by ramming the ice again and again it finally reaches shore.

To warm my feet, I walk ahead on the lake, crossing a vast bed of ice flowers gleaming in the last lingering light, until I come upon a female gazelle lying in this great emptiness, awaiting death. Even when I pass within six feet she does not move. Ahead, at the base of a hill, are four tents. It is dark when we reach them.

Zhi Mai, Mingjiang, and I are invited to stay in a small family tent. Our host is a young man wearing sunglasses, his eyes sore from a touch of snow blindness; he and his wife and two girls, aged five and seven, are all wearing thick sheepskin *chubas*. A baby has been so tightly wrapped in a quilt and stuffed into a yak-skin basket that it can only follow life inside the tent with its eyes. We crowd the large iron stove. Near it hang two massive horns of wild yak, used as milk pails. Our dinner is noodle and mutton soup with butter tea—a hot, nourishing meal. We sleep on the floor in a corner of the tent, grateful for this family's hospitality. Our hostess rises early to start a fire; the two girls remain hidden in their nest of sheepskins but I can hear them giggle. A porridge made of *tsampa* mixed with tea is our breakfast.

Guo Gieting comes by and says, "*Jintian xiuxi*" ("Today rest"). We then join the others in a large tent. Blue sheepskins serve as rugs. Posters on the walls show Buddhist deities, lamas, and Chairman Mao. I write notes by the stove while others play cards, chat, and drink endless cups of butter tea. All told, there are four families here, including seventeen children. Collectively they have 3,100 sheep of which 200 have died so far since the storm, and none from wolf predation this year, I'm told.

When the Russian explorer Nikolai Przewalski traveled through this region in 1872, it was uninhabited and storms were just as severe. He wrote in his 1876 book *Mongolia, the Tangut Country, and the Solitudes of Northern Tibet*:

> There is no regular road anywhere in the Tibetan deserts, nothing but the tracks of wild animals in all directions. The caravans take a straight course, guiding their march by the salient features of the country. . . . In February 1870, a caravan which left Lhasa 300 strong, with 1,000 beasts of burden, in a violent snow-storm, followed by severe cold, lost all the animals and fifty men besides.

The following day we come to another tent. As usual, the Tibetan men greet each other by first shaking hands and then touching right cheek to right cheek. We leave some firewood and two pairs of boots and continue. While crossing low hills, we spot two argali sheep, a young male and female, fleeing in panic. A female gazelle lies dead near our route. We stop and I weigh her at twenty-nine pounds, an unusually light and lean animal. The next household has two tents, one of which it generously vacates for our night's stay. The soldiers with us—Li, Wang, Jing, and Dai—work hard and are uncomplaining, no matter how miserable the situation. They take the truck to haul some yak droppings back from a distant site for the family. Later, I sit by the tent and watch a trusting groundpecker pulling bits of fat from an old sheepskin near my feet. As at Tuotuohe, flocks of small birds seek food near human habitation. Suddenly there is a fusillade of shots. Li and one of his companions, back from their errand, are bored and the birds offer target practice. Their bag: one injured groundpecker—a small light-brown bird with a curved bill—and one dead snow finch. I protest but words from a foreigner are considered irrelevant.

We continue on our way. I shiver in the open wagon and try to burrow further into the baggage. The others, too, are mute and disengaged, trying to ignore the cruel situation. Many pikas are here and vanish into the snow as we pass. By a marmot burrow a manul cat is curled up in the sun. Built like a squat house cat but with a pug-like face and long, grizzled hair, the manul is rare and seldom seen. One of the Tibetan doctors, Qin Mei Dao Ji, picks up his rifle and motions the tractor to halt. "*Bu*, no!" I yell, waving my arms. The cat vanishes into the marmot burrow, and Qin mutters something. "The cat was resting so peacefully in this beautiful land that it was not the right moment to die," I say calmly, but my scowl conveys my feelings. At a small range broken by rock pinnacles are three stags, donkey-sized and dark brown with large ivory-colored antlers. They are MacNeill's deer, a subspecies of red deer, the first I ever encountered, surprisingly far from their usual home in the forests to the east. By a rock outcrop are several small herds of blue sheep and I learn from one of the Tibetans that a few snow leopards persist in the area. Seeing these animals revives my spirit—until we reach the next tent, a slaughterhouse. I count seven blue sheep males, five kiang, two chiru, and one gazelle. Eight dogs are tied up, hunting dogs used to chase blue sheep onto a cliff where they are cornered while the hunter shoots at leisure. Nearby is another tent with an old man, an old woman, two young women, and several children. The belongings in the tent are worn and scant, and the fire is almost out. Wood from our wagon soon warms us and we brew hot tea. I have sympathy for this poor family and do not begrudge them the wildlife they kill for subsistence. With the death of their sheep this winter they will be destitute. We erect our tent nearby. It is at least −40°F in the night; the thermometer will not register any lower. I have a sore throat and the others sniffle and cough, not surprising given our closeness and the habit some of them have of spitting and blowing their noses almost anywhere.

November 5 is memorable because the truck, in which I am riding that day, suddenly sinks into wet ground beneath the snow. The driver guns the engine, the wheels spin, and the truck sinks deeper. The tractor has gone ahead to another encampment and we have no way to contact it. The wheels quickly freeze solidly into the ice. We huddle together in the truck like hibernating marmots, covered with army coats. For dinner we gnaw on chunks of frozen bread. The tractor carries all the fuel and so we cannot even make a fire for hot tea. The others return at noon the next day after a three-hour drive from the encampment where they had spent the night. Junrang reports that he saw two MacNeill's deer and a cluster of twelve dead Tibetan gazelle along the way. Before leaving again for the encampment of the previous night, the team tries to dig around the wheels of the truck and the tractor repeatedly yanks it with a cable but it does not budge. We prepare to spend a second night here. We make a smoking dung fire and soon have hot tea to replenish our dehydrated bodies. From a frozen sheep carcass we've bought from a household, we cut slivers of meat, impale them on a wire, and roast kebabs. Usually one relishes a hard life afield even while complaining of discomforts such as the cold and the wet. Here we have too great a measure of both. However, in future years I may well recall this journey with a touch of nostalgia.

The tractor returns at noon the next day. There is some desultory digging, more out of principle than expectation, and then the soldiers, all good mechanics, discover that something in the gearbox is broken. The truck cannot continue. Three Tibetans will stay with the truck while the rest of us head west to the highway for help: the rescue team has to be rescued. A kiang lies dead in the snow and another stands beside it as if guarding the body. At our approach it does not flee but merely circles its dead companion.

The next day we see trucks ahead moving south, seemingly adrift on snow. We are nearing the highway. There has been little wild-life along our eight-day route, a meager 154 animals, mostly gazelle, chiru, and kiang. Where have the large herds of chiru gone? In the 250 miles or so of our travel, we've passed a mere dozen households. So far only 3–4 percent of the sheep have starved, according to what families have told us, but the future looks grim. Some animals are already being slaughtered for cash so that new ones can be bought in spring. Interestingly, only one household has lost sheep to wolves this year, a mere three animals, and we have not spotted a single wolf in our travels. The helicopter wolf hunt the governor proposed may not achieve much, fortunately.

The beginning of our study of chiru and other wildlife in the Chang Tang has been depressing. But the days have also provided an invaluable lesson in showing how just a single and rare weather event may have a drastic impact on the wildlife in this harsh and high land, no matter how well the animals are protected from the depredation of humans. Now, whenever I rejoice that a species is increasing in number, I am also apprehensive that a catastrophe can wipe out any gains.

We finally reach the highway with the last glimmer of sun. Tuo-tuohe is twenty miles to the south, several hours by tractor. Eager to get back, we flag down a truck and the driver agrees to take four of us. We climb into the back of the covered truck only to face two kiang carcasses. With perverse luck we are in the one truck among hundreds which collects bodies along the highway for converting to glue. Two more bodies are added to our count. I sit on the back of a frozen kiang as we return to Tuotuohe, our three-week survey completed.

A year later, in November 1986, we returned for ten days to the Tuotuohe area to check on the fate of the wildlife and that of the pastoralists and their livestock. Two-thirds of the sheep and goats and half of the yaks had died for lack of fodder, we were informed, and many households face extreme hardship still. Compared to the previous year, there was little wildlife near the road. However, the plains were almost free of snow and we could drive anywhere in search of them. One of our routes was upriver from Tuotuohe, where chiru had been so abundant just after the blizzard. This time they were still present—but as mummified bodies encased in brittle hides. We tallied 193 carcasses.

In his book *Across Tibet*, the explorer Gabriel Bonvalot wrote that, while crossing the Chang Tang on January 12, 1890, he found "a valley strewn with the bones of animals," including argali, kiang, and chiru—probably a situation similar to the one we came across now. To the north, away from the road, were scattered chiru herds—we saw a total of 1,380 animals—with the males in rut, displaying by strutting and bellowing to the females. Few females were accompanied by a youngster, probably because after having been in such poor physical condition the previous winter, they failed to conceive, or aborted, or produced weak newborns that soon died. In addition to the chiru, our counts showed 465 kiang, 83 gazelle, and 14 wolves, including a pack of eight. These were among the survivors which would replenish the Chang Tang, and I looked forward to meeting them and their descendants in the years ahead.

We had been witness to the extremely harsh conditions which the Chang Tang can offer chiru and other species, as well as the human intruder. Rare natural events such as the blizzard of 1985 may have a varied and long-lasting impact on life at these high altitudes, a valuable lesson for me. More than ever, my mental compass was focused westward toward the Chang Tang in Tibet with its vast blank on the wildlife map. Any quest such as ours ends with more questions to answer than it began with. I wondered, for example, about the chiru's annual migrations, not just movements driven by hunger, as I had witnessed. Like the chiru, I now also wandered, making annual visits to the Tibetan Plateau, to the northwest part in Qinghai, the southern rim in Xinjiang, and finally also to Tibet, trips I described in *Tibet's Hidden Wilderness*. Each trip added useful fragments of knowledge about the chiru's faraway life, but I needed to know much more, especially about the chiru's secret calving grounds. The search for these and my efforts to protect them and the chiru's future spurred me on in the years ahead.

CHAPTER 2

Riddle of the Calving Ground

IN 1988, I BEGAN FIELD WORK in Tibet's Chang Tang, the vast region that extends from the western border of Qinghai about 550 miles westward past the magnificent basin with the lakes Aru and Memar Co (*co* means "lake" in Tibetan) toward the border with India. By 1994 I had made seven wildlife surveys in that region alone with staff of the Tibet Forestry Department and the Tibet Plateau Institute of Biology. Kay often accompanied me, and range ecologist Daniel Miller joined us on two journeys to evaluate pasture conditions. Except for occasional forays north into the desolate desert steppe, much of which lies at 16,000 feet and higher, our research concentrated in alpine steppe at somewhat lower elevations (around 14,500 feet), the broad band of grassland where chiru, kiang, Tibetan gazelle, and other species are most common, and pastoralists with their livestock are permanently settled. However, my eyes roamed ever northward across plains and snow-capped ranges toward uninhabited terrain.

Our observations, coupled with information from herdsmen, indicated that chiru generally spent the period from autumn to spring on alpine steppe, often near livestock. Most female chiru disappeared sometime in May toward the north to a mysterious place where they gave birth. No one could tell me where they went, only that in late July or August they reappeared with their calves. The males did not travel with the females but hung around the winter area or only wandered short distances, as if waiting for everyone to get back together in November and December to rut. Naturally, I was intrigued. Here was the challenge of solving a scientific mystery and of exploring places in the Chang Tang so remote that not even the nomads had been there. Around the world, similar species, such as caribou, wildebeest, and Mongolian gazelles also calve at certain sites, but, unlike chiru, the males migrate to the same sites as well. Every species has adapted itself to a unique combination of ecological conditions, and I couldn't even guess what specific forces had shaped this aspect of chiru society. Over the course of our early travels in the region, we had found evidence of three more or less distinct migratory chiru populations in Tibet, which I called the East, Central, and West Chang Tang populations, each with its distinct calving ground; I also became aware of another population in Qinghai.

It's fun to unravel a problem of natural history such as the female chirus' migratory destinations, and it's satisfying to gain new insights into the life of a species. But instead of the leisurely quest I might have expected, it had suddenly become urgent to find out as much as possible about the chiru. In the late 1980s and early 1990s the animals were beginning to be massacred, but I had no idea about the driving force behind this slaughter. Finally in 1992, I discovered that the animals were being killed for their fine wool, which was then smuggled to India to be woven into expensive shahtoosh shawls, as I will recount in a later chapter. Even after the Chang Tang Nature Reserve was established as a protected area in 1993 by the Tibet Autonomous Region, and in 2001 made a national reserve covering an area of about 115,000 square miles, almost as large as Germany, poaching of chiru continued. This was not surprising because at that time around 4,000 families lived in the reserve (many more do now), access by vehicle from towns was easy, and the financial gain from the illegal trade was great. The region is so vast that there were not enough vehicles, personnel, and funds to sustain antipoaching efforts, especially not in uninhabited terrain.

To be saved, the migratory chiru populations must be protected on their winter range, along their migratory routes, and, importantly, on the calving ground where they are concentrated and most vulnerable. Concerning the last two points we knew little or nothing. Our task was more difficult and frustrating than I had anticipated.

No aircraft was available to count and follow animals, as was done in Africa. The snows and rains of summer often delayed our travels. Finding and studying the calving grounds would turn out to be an exercise in persistence. It would last seventeen years.

Scientific reports present facts neatly arranged and tabulated, marching from concept to conclusion in a wonderfully linear manner. But that is not the reality of fieldwork. In the Chang Tang, for instance, it included endless days of snowstorms, icy winds, bogged-down vehicles, impassable terrain, creative disinterest of some co-workers, and vanishing chiru, but on occasion sparkling encounters with wildlife as well. I've tried to capture here something of the messy way in which information is actually gathered, erratically and haphazardly, with the solving of everyday logistical problems, and sometimes even with mere survival as the most immediate concern. Patience is perhaps the most valuable commodity. Yet somehow, in the end, one often does gain the kind of information upon which conservation can be based.

To locate the calving grounds of the three migratory chiru populations in Tibet required at least two expeditions each, the task made particularly difficult because the females give birth in late June, when travel in the Chang Tang is at its worst. Here I pick up the story of our 1994 search for the calving grounds of the East Chang Tang population.

Many chiru tracks lead north and northeast past the huge, glaciated Purog Kangri massif near Shuanghu, an administrative center in the eastern Chang Tang. In a valley ahead is a herd of about 300 chiru females, walking rapidly, focused on some distant goal. Today, May 30, 1994, we are at the tail end of the migration and all we have to do now is follow these animals of the East Chang Tang population to the calving ground.

There are many streams and gravel outwashes from Purog Kangri, relatively easy for our Land Cruisers to cross, but not always easy for a heavy truck. Our team of ten, including rangeland ecologist Daniel Miller, comes to one such place; Liu Wulin of the Tibet Forestry Department suggests we establish a base camp here and just use the Land Cruisers. We are too far from any calving ground, and I obstinately insist on going on. One driver, Ba Bu, looks at the site

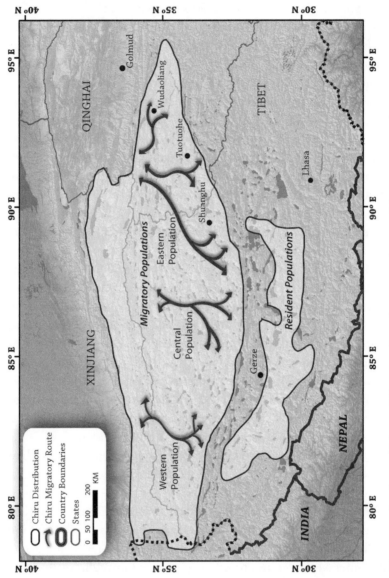

The current distribution of chiru or Tibetan antelope, showing travel routes of the migratory populations.

and proclaims, "*bu xing*" ("not possible"), a refrain we hear so irritatingly often that we refer to him as Bu Xing. Now a ritual ensues, one often seen on this and other trips. Everyone stands around indecisively, looks, stamps a foot to test the ground, and throws pebbles into the water but no one offers a decision. Liu Wulin, our nominal leader, explains his pragmatic philosophy: "I let the drivers decide the route and then they will be glad to dig us out when we get stuck." Or to put it less diplomatically, if you make a decision and bog down then it's your fault. At any rate, we cross this stream easily.

On the north side of Purog Kangri is Dogai Coring, a lake about thirty miles long. Travel is difficult because of the many streams flowing into the lake. We go eastward but cannot find chiru tracks. Assuming that the chiru have headed north around the west side of the lake, we go in that direction. We spend several days in search of the migration but it has vanished completely. Hundreds of chiru are there but all are males obviously using this area for their summer vacation. We head still further north toward a high peak, the Rola Kangri, on the slope of which we find a female brown bear digging for pikas, her broad forepaws shoveling geysers of dirt behind her. Five feet away is an elegant wolf, light tan in color, hoping to snatch an escaping pika. And nearby lies a very large male bear—it is courting season—the sun shining on his rich-brown coat. When the female bear walks off, the wolf is right behind her, and the male bear brings up the rear, as strange a procession as I have seen.

The chiru females could only have gone eastward, I now realize, through the foothills of the Purog Kangri and across the nearby border into Qinghai. Why, I wonder, use that difficult route when the basin of Dogai Coring offers much easier travel? At the end of the last ice age, lakes like Dogai Coring were much larger, as shown by old beach lines high on the surrounding slopes. With the retreat of glaciers and evaporation of lake water under intense sun, the lakes shriveled. Perhaps the chiru have simply maintained their ancient migration route to circumvent a lake that once lapped the base of the hills. After a month of searching we return to Shuanghu in late June. It has been a useful trip, but the female chiru have eluded us.

Various explorers had traveled through the part of the Chang Tang where we were searching for the chiru, and all encountered problems—though problems very different from ours. But there was one expedition of particular interest to me: the last foreign expedition to cross this area prior to our visits. I had avidly read various accounts of the few foreigners who had penetrated the northern Chang Tang to compare with what I saw in 1994, whether it be a mountain peak or a herd of wild yak, in effect searching for a bridge to the past. But for the twentieth century there was no one alive to fill the gap between Sven Hedin's 1908 exploration of this part of the Chang Tang and the present—except the American Frank Bessac and his White Russian companion Vasili Zvanzov, who crossed the Chang Tang in 1950. Introduced by Daniel Miller, I visited Frank Bessac and his wife Suzanne in 1992, and again in 2004, in Missoula, where he had been a professor of anthropology at the University of Montana. Frank Bessac is tall and thin, with a short, patchy white beard. His unfocused eyes stare upward, almost blind from glaucoma, and he answers my questions about his wildlife observations in a low, precise voice. The original notes of his journey remain Top Secret with the CIA, inaccessible even to Bessac after nearly half a century. When I applied for them through the Freedom of Information Act, I received a highly edited typescript. In 2006 Bessac and his wife published their own book-length account, *Death on the Chang Tang*. (Frank Bessac died in 2010 at the age of eighty-eight.)

Bessac went to China in 1945 with the OSS, the precursor of the CIA. Afterward, as a Fulbright scholar in Beijing, he became interested in the Mongolian culture. Moving westward in 1949 as far as Tihwa, now called Urumqi, he met Douglas Mackiernan, American consul and CIA agent. With the advance of Mao Zedong's army, the two fled to southern Xinjiang, accompanied by three White Russians who had escaped the turmoil in their own country. In March of the following year, the five men headed south into the mountains with camels and horses, and were aided by Kazakh guides for the first part of their route. What is now Xinjiang's Arjin Shan Reserve, they found "lousy with antelopes," Frank Bessac told me, and "yak would come and walk toward us"—wildlife evidently more abundant and less fearful than now. They continued south past the Mustagh massif into Tibet. Mackiernan used a radio to keep in contact with the U.S. State Department, asking them to notify Lhasa of their coming. In his book Bessac notes about Mackiernan, "I think he had a Geiger counter with him," a strangely indefinite statement. There has been suspicion that Mackiernan was looking for minerals —specifically uranium.

Mackiernan kept a journal, and it ends abruptly on April 25. From that point on we have only Bessac's account. On April 29 they saw a scatter of tents, their first contact with people in Tibet, and also six armed men, part of a Tibetan border patrol. Bessac went off to visit a nearby nomad family. As he returned, to quote his journal, he observed "four men with hands above the head left tent . . . and approached the Tibetans who also approached our men. Just before the two groups met two shots, Mac's shout, 'Don't shoot,' and another shot were heard. Three men fell to the ground. The fourth was running to the tent. A fusillade of shots was heard . . . the left leg of the person doubled under him, but he managed to make it to the tent."

Mackiernan and two White Russians were killed, the third was wounded. Bessac and Zvanzov were taken prisoner, robbed, and escorted southward. Not until May 3 did a messenger arrive from Lhasa ordering all border guards to assure the expedition safe passage. The State Department had been lax in notifying Lhasa: the messenger arrived five days too late to forestall the killings. Bessac and Zvanzov were released eventually and made their way to Lhasa and on to India.

After our unsuccessful effort to trace the migration of the East Chang Tang population in 1994, we try once more in 1997. Our goal this time is to intercept the migration after it leaves Tibet and enters Qinghai, and then to follow it to the calving ground. Our logic is impeccable but the reality of our travel will turn out differently.

On June 1 we drive north from the Tibetan town of Nagqu toward Golmud, crossing the Tanggula Pass into Qinghai and on to Tuotuohe, the base of our winter days in 1985. North of Tuotuohe we turn off the road into the Kekexili region, and head west toward the Tibet border, an endless horizon before us. There are eleven of us, including drivers, a cook, and Xi Re of the Forest Police, in two Land Cruisers and two trucks. Liu Wulin is again team leader, and Zhang Hong, also of the Tibet Forestry Department, is along as well. Lu Zhi, later the director of the Center for Nature and Society and the Shan Shui Conservation Center at Peking University, is collaborating with the research. She spent years working on a masterful study of giant pandas, which gave her a good background for dealing with this rough environment of mountains and snow.

The Tibetan deities of the Chang Tang are not kind to us even at the beginning of this journey, each day bringing such foul weather that every mile is a struggle. The driver Lo Te tries to appease the deities by starting a yak dung fire and burning a sliver of argali horn we have found, a reddish piece signifying the sun. But to no avail—day after day we are lashed by snow driven by ferocious east winds. When the snow melts, as it often does at midday, every rivulet turns into a waterfall and every hillside and valley into a quaking and quivering morass. My field notes give some indication of our daily life at the time:

> *June 4. Left at 0830 and within a few km truck got bogged down on sandy embankment, though a better route was pointed out to driver Lo Te. . . . It took two hours to get out, carrying rocks, digging, jacking up wheels. A little farther on, a muddy ravine. It is easy to circumvent at base of hill above a spring. Instead of following our car trail, truck took shortcut and sank into soft ground on slope.*
>
> *June 9. On ridge above 7 yaks, including 3 tiny ones. . . . It is after 0900 and frozen ground is getting soft from sun. Mostly clear day but icy wind. In hills we see a bear, and nearby a female with a yearling, and then a fourth bear. Two Tibetan sand fox follow one bear which has been digging for pikas. Near crest of hill, in a ravine, both trucks get stuck. Turf quakes even underfoot. It's only 1015. . . . We have to wait for ground to freeze at night.*

We decide to establish a base camp, park the trucks, and continue only with the Land Cruisers. On June 12 we set off toward the west, heavily loaded with food, camp gear, and extra gasoline, only to sink into sucking mud within sight of camp. It takes the whole team to extract us. Near the eastern edge of a large lake, Xijir Ulan Hu, we come upon several herds of female chiru, totaling about 400 animals. We continue westward to the Tibet border, near where we were in 1994, to find out where these females might have come from, but we find only male chiru. After three days we turn back toward the base to prepare for a survey to the north. Within sight of the tents, though, both Land Cruisers again get bogged down. It is the sort of day that makes me question my devotion to this region. The truck drivers want to return home. They are worried about meeting Muslim gold prospectors, whose pits we have seen. Deadly fights over land claims, they tell us, have recently occurred between Tibetan nomads and the intruders. Besides, Lhasa Tibetans are used to a more comfortable life and fear the harsh Chang Tang.

The sand looks deceptively dry, but the Land Cruisers sink in deeply—eight times in a little more than a mile—requiring seven hours of exhausting work to get them out. The next day, heading north toward another large lake, the Hoh Xil Hu, we see a herd of about 500 female chiru, very shy, flowing up a slope streaked with snow. We feel that surely we are near the calving ground. The lake is still frozen, a desolate place with only nine chiru adrift in the vast space. Snow and wind pound the tents all night and by morning drifts are up to two feet deep, preventing onward travel that day. It does not look like spring, but a purple-flowered *Oxytropis*, a white *Ajuga*, and a yellow saxifrage tell us otherwise.

Sven Hedin passed Hoh Xil Hu in 1901. I do not envy his months on horseback in dismal weather, at least we have the warmth of a car. He was unusual among explorers in that he reveled in the solitude of the Chang Tang. Remarkably, he always completed his year-long journeys of mapping unknown terrain accompanied only by local crews. Less commendable was his crass determination to gain accolades for his travels upon returning to Europe, a quest that earned him the enmity of many when he sought these in Germany during the 1930s and 1940s. It is from reading one of Hedin's books as a boy in Germany, though, that I first learned of Tibet. His vivid and alluring descriptions and his excellent sketches of nomads wrapped in sheepskin, of strange creatures like the chiru, and of the uninhabited uplands took me on pleasurable mental journeys. Years later, after I had crossed and recrossed Hedin's tracks in the Chang Tang, and read many of his other books, such as *Trans-Himalaya* (1908), I felt a bond with his attitude toward this land. He, too, seemed to realize that the uniformity of the Chang Tang is not sameness and that there is beauty in absence.

Here, for example, are two exuberant descriptions from his books:

Those who imagine that such a journey in vast solitude and desolation is tedious and trying are mistaken. No spectacle can be more sublime. Every day's march, every league brings discoveries of unimagined beauty. . . .

It was a delicious feeling to know that we were the first human beings to travel these mountains, where existed no path, where there never had been a path, and where there was not a footprint visible, except those made by the hoof of yak, antelope, or kulan [kiang]. . . .

We notice the chiru head east from the vicinity of Hoh Xil Hu over a snow-covered range toward a lake, Zonag Co, using a route too difficult for us to follow by car. We instead loop north where there is less snow, and into a valley leading to that lake. Black curtains of snow shroud the horizon. The vehicles bog down. Liu Wulin, Lu Zhi, Zhang Hong, and I climb a nearby hill, hoping to spot herds of chiru ahead. There is a only a lone male gazelle. The migration route must be somewhere else.

The following morning, about to start on our way back toward base, I have an interesting experience. I drink a mug of hot orange juice, made from a powdered concentrate (Tang), break into a sweat, and faint. I wake up, flat on the ground, and look up into a circle of worried faces. I get up, feeling fine (but have never touched Tang since). On a pass leading from Hoh Xil Hu, we meet about ninety chiru moving east like the others. Nearby is a wolf kill, a female with full-term fetus. Later that day, June 23, we again have problems, as my field notes indicate:

> *The valley ahead is a terrible morass. Lu Zhi and I suggest one route (a good one it later turns out). Zhang Hong, to whom the driver So La for some reason always listens, suggests a shortcut—and both cars get deeply mired in liquid mud. It is 11 o'clock. The two drivers in rubber boots work in the mud for hours, hands cold, jacking up the wheels. We carry tons of rock, it seems, to put under the wheels and on top of the quaking mud. Car advances a meter or two and sinks in again. . . . I go off to look at some Kobresia turf by a small lake nearby. It is a major wolf latrine. I check 44 scats for content—mostly chiru, pika, and marmot. As so often, a raven comes to investigate. Two ruddy shelducks fly by calling. . . . By evening the cars are both on rocks amidst the mud. The hope is to drive them out in the morning when the ground is frozen. Instant noodles again: it's our only meal.*

From our many sightings of chiru and their tracks it seems clear that most chiru are arriving directly from the south and are part of a Qinghai migratory population. These animals winter upriver from Tuotuohe, as we discovered during a survey a year earlier. We have traced them now seventy-five miles north and east toward the calving ground in the Zonag Co area. But where is the East Chang Tang population? We have seen many tracks coming from Tibet into Qinghai determinedly heading north, and we suspect that these belong to our missing animals. Possibly they calve somewhat to the east of us, around another lake, the Lixioidian Co. Thus at least two migratory populations may calve in this general region.

We reach our base on June 25 and prepare for a general retreat. The weather does not allow further work. The drivers walk ahead to select a potential route, but since they neither mark it nor follow in each other's vehicle tracks we are stuck as often as before, once eleven times in a single day. When we drive a whole mile without bogging down it is cause for jubilation. Blue poppies are in bloom. A lone female chiru is reluctant to flee, and our driver spots her newborn. It is June 30 and we have found a calving ground—of one.

It has taken five days to travel a half-day's distance. Lo Te should have burned more argali horn to placate the deities. The trucks cannot continue. We set up tents and glumly dig a trench around each. Should all of us walk out, or should the Toyotas drive to the highway and arrange for a powerful Mercedes truck to pull out the underpowered Dong Feng trucks? (*Dong Feng* means "East Wind" but they are at best an "East Breeze.") We argue back and forth. It is finally decided that the two truck drivers and Xi Re of the Forest Police, a solid, hard-working person, will stay with the trucks and the rest of us will drive out. We have no satellite phone, and even if we could make contact there is only a small chance that anyone would consider sending a rescue team.

We leave on July 4 in bright sunshine. Muchung, a local Tibetan and former gold miner who has come with us as guide, says he knows the quickest way to the nearest nomad camps, even though he was last here twenty-one years previously. Soon we are lost and we have to camp. A herd of wild yak has passed nearby and a count of tracks shows fifty-four animals, including thirteen calves. The following day we meander onward, the vehicles sinking into mud so often that we have to abandon them too and walk to the highway for help.

We each carry a pack with sleeping bag, air mattress, extra clothes, bowl and spoon, notebook, and camera. Two small tents, a kettle, some food, and a blowtorch complete our basic camping gear. Breakfast consists of hot water and dry biscuits. A violent hailstorm comes through and we huddle under a tarp, the Tibetans together in one cluster and the rest of us in another. The hills are now white with *Arenaria* cushions in flower. I enjoy walking across wild topography such as this; the desolation calms, it does not intimidate. It gives a sense of scale. A seemingly nearby hill may take two hours to reach. I feel connected to the landscape, it ignites the senses, and I feel a bond with the horned lark and the hamster colony. However, I must admit, right now I would rather scoot across the terrain in a Land Cruiser. It is a tough hike for everyone. At first I worry about Lu Zhi: beneath her helmet of hair and soft, round face with its charming smile, she seems rather fragile. But she is as tough as any of us.

The following day, Muchung says that nomads live south of here. We soon spot eight yaks far ahead, and Muchung notes that wild yaks do not occur here anymore; our binoculars reveal patches of white on some animals, a sure sign that they are domestic. By evening two white dots appear in the distance, and these eventually resolve into nomad tents. Perhaps tomorrow we can rent yaks to carry our loads. While our Tibetan crew tries to find help, we wander around, content with some leisure hours in the warm sunshine. Nearby are several rocky outcrops. One niche has a saker falcon nest with a large chicks, and another niche only fifteen feet away has a ruddy shelduck nest. The duck seems to derive protection from the proximity of this pair of large white-and-grey falcons, even though the ducks could be easy prey.

In late afternoon three horses and two yaks arrive, led by a nomad. Muchung takes one horse, Liu Wulin and Lu Zhi alternately ride the other, and I walk the five miles to camp. It is home for a hospitable family with 6 children, 950 sheep, and 30 yaks. There are nomad encampments here from both Tuotuohe and across the border in Tibet, now competing for grazing land—no one lived here before the mid-1950s—and last year there were fights between them. I suggest that the drivers go back and retrieve the Land Cruisers. The weather has been fairly good and most of the route is now dry enough. Liu Wulin agrees, but, as he points out, the drivers are Tibetan; he can't order them and they don't want to go. Besides, So La is the driver for a party secretary. If something goes wrong, it is his story that will be believed. Lu Zhi adds that any blame for anything gone wrong will fall on me, the foreigner, even though I don't make decisions. Such are the group dynamics.

Yogurt is served for breakfast, a delicious change. Three yaks carry our baggage, unruly and untrained animals, bucking and dashing off, scattering their burdens. Shortly after noon we reach an encampment with three tents and seventeen persons. It is a wealthy family with 1,200 sheep, 210 yaks, and 15 horses. Aja, the encampment leader, agrees to take us to Tuotuohe the following day. The trek over this fine steppe is a welcome change from digging vehicles out of mud, but I have looked in vain for a vista with wildlife. Since heading back toward Tuotuohe, my notebook shows a total of only nine gazelles, eleven chiru males, and one kiang. Some in Tuotuohe "have become rich" from killing chiru, nomads tell us, and outsiders poach for meat to sell or to survive on while digging for gold. Little wildlife now remains in many thousands of square miles.

The following day, July 12, Tuotuohe lies ahead. Our host camps two miles from town, but two of his yaks carry our baggage for us the rest of the way. A bus will take the cook He Zhangbao, Zhang Hong, Lu Zhi, and me to Lhasa. The others will take the next bus to Nagqu, where they will arrange to have our vehicles retrieved with the generous help of the People's Liberation Army.

Months later, I unexpectedly receive a bill for $42,235 from the Forestry Department, a request for extra payment because, it is claimed, trucks and staff were marooned in the Chang Tang for several weeks. In fact, the military rescued the expedition within days. When confronted, Liu Wulin readily admits that much of the bill was bogus. "When staff cheats foreigners on behalf of our department, we get praised by the leaders," he explains succinctly; "if we cheat for personal gain, we get criticized." I pay the small legitimate fraction of the bill, and our cooperation continues.

To trace Tibet's East Chang Tang population to its calving ground in Qinghai was our goal in 1994 and 1997. Instead we came across the approximate location of another migratory population, one based in Qinghai, and we only suspected the route of the Tibet animals from their tracks. The riddle of this calving ground remained. Chiru migrations in that region were far more complex than I had imagined—and as later work revealed. In the meantime, there were also the chiru migrations in the western and central Chang Tang to follow and the calving grounds to discover.

CHAPTER 3

The Longest Walk

THE SEARCH FOR THE CALVING GROUNDS of the West Chang Tang population began in August 1988 when Kay and I were members of a team entering Tibet from the west. We crossed the snow-capped Aru Range and descended into a basin. The tranquil twin lakes, Aru Co and Memar Co, are found there, and on the hillsides wild yak and a few chiru and gazelle grazed peacefully. We were, as far as we knew, the first Westerners to behold this basin since 1903. Our visit was brief, but I was determined to return. When we did so next, in July 1990, the basin was full of idle male chiru and only a rare female. Then on August 11, at the northern rim of the basin, I saw a strange pinkish mass. Groping for a memory, I visualized flamingos on a lake in the Chilean Andes. But what I was seeing here, we soon discovered, were female chiru with their month-old young, about two thousand animals crowded into a dense herd. It appeared to be the vanguard of a major migration heading south. I knew almost nothing about this western chiru population. I would have to return earlier in the year, I realized, and try then to follow the animals to their calving ground. North of the Aru basin my map showed a large plain, labeled Antelope Plain, a name given to it by the explorer Henry Deasy in 1896 after he encountered great herds of female chiru with small calves there. Was this a calving ground?

JUNE 1992

On our return to the region two years later, we bypass the difficult route through the Aru basin and head directly east toward the Antelope Plain from the nearest road, hoping to intersect the route of the migrating chiru females. The plain is a bleak desert with scant vegetation, and now, in early June, there is not a hint of green, To the south is the great glacial massif of Toze Kangri, 21,160 feet high. Only a few chiru are in sight, looking forlorn. Snow and wind lash us almost nightly, leaving the ground so sodden that vehicles often cannot travel. Our large team includes interpreter Ding Li; Liu Yujun from China Central Television, here to make a chiru documentary; Chi Doa and Gu Binyuan from the Tibet Plateau Institute of Biology; and others. They play cards and chat. Kay and I wander widely on foot, as do truck driver Dawa and cook Wen Bin, the two most interested and energetic team members, hoping to find the elusive migratory route. Finally, with great relief after much searching, we locate it, a narrow route that funnels animals between Toze Kangri and a small lake. We exult as we watch herd after herd move north, not tarrying on the Antelope Plain, as they head toward another snow mountain. We move camp near the base of that mountain to make it easier to follow the migration.

Exploring this new area, we come upon a saker falcon nest on a cliff with two large young. Near the nest, blending into the rocks so well that at first we do not see it, is a lynx, the color of cream and with long cheek whiskers. The lynx is resting, utterly calm, its golden eyes placid, innocent of humans. Searching for wildlife in the foothills of the snow mountain, Dawa and Wen Bin are bluff-charged by a Tibetan brown bear, they observe three wolves eating a chiru, and they find several female chiru with newborns, as well as a herd of three hundred still striving northward. It is June 26, and at least some females have evidently failed to reach their intended goal before giving birth.

We move camp again, this time to the base of a ridge with the tracks of many chiru leading upward. Dawa and I follow on foot until the terrain falls away and we see below us a huge basin with three massive volcanoes bordering its far edge. Beyond are the giants of the Kunlun Mountains. Descending into the basin to the shore of a large lake, Heishi Beihu, we follow chiru tracks northward across a desolation of naked soil and frost heaves. The tracks lead toward low hills that mark the Xinjiang border, beyond which we have no permission to go. The chiru have outwalked us.

JUNE 2001

Nine years passed after we failed to reach the calving grounds in 1992 while I focused on projects in Mongolia, Laos, and Russia, among others, as well as different parts of western China, including Tibet. My conscience nagged me about having failed the West Chang Tang chiru population, of having left an important conservation task undone. I knew approximately where these chiru gave birth, and I only had to confirm the site. This time I would not follow the migration over the long, arduous route in Tibet, but approach from the north across Xinjiang's Kunlun Mountains.

On May 27, I fly from Xinjiang's capital Urumqi south to Hetian (Hotan), an oasis town at the southern rim of the Taklimakan Desert, where the team is waiting. Jon Miceler, then a trekking tour operator (and now with World Wildlife Fund), has already bought twenty donkeys and two camels from various villages as pack animals, accumulated food and equipment, and hired as translator Iskander, a university student, and as cook Aziz from the Kashi Mountaineering Association. Jon has organized a small trekking group to explore a little-known corner of the Kunlun Mountains, one that includes the probable chiru calving ground, and I am invited to go along. It is an unusual trip for me because I am involved neither in planning nor organizing the expedition. Jon and I were together on a wildlife survey in eastern India the year before, but I have not met the other three, all Canadians. There is Pat Morrow, filmmaker and well-known mountaineer, who has ascended the highest peak on all seven continents, and his wife, Baiba, as well as Jeffrey Boyd, an emergency surgeon in Banff. All are young, in their forties and early fifties, more fit than I, and widely traveled.

We drive east through gray, stony desert interrupted by occasional sand dunes, and through villages with flat-roofed, mud-brick

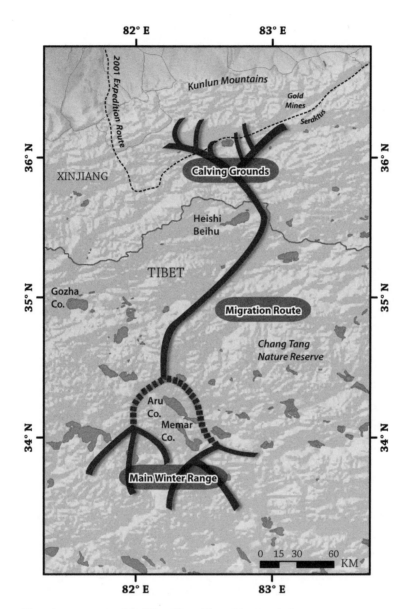

The migratory route of the West Chang Tang chiru population.

houses and streets lined with tall, thin poplars. At Minfeng (Niya) we turn south toward the Kunlun Mountains hidden in dusty haze, and up an endless gradual slope over a barely perceptible track. At 8,000 feet, a river has gnawed into the desert and we note some shrubby vegetation there before we climb into the foothills. They open into a river valley and the village of Dawantue, where we will await our pack animals. We follow a suggestion by a villager to camp in the river flats, but toward midnight a deluge of rust-red water floods our tents and we move to higher ground.

The donkeys arrive as an uncontrolled mob, braying, bucking, kicking, biting, mounting. Four Uygurs and one Kyrgyz start to load them. A donkey can carry about 80 to 90 pounds and a camel 350 pounds, except that now after a long winter the animals are malnourished. I give the crew a weighing scale but it is ignored. I can see that we have far too much gear, including dead weight such as a basket of squash and four cases of tinned eggplant, army rations that expired five years ago according to the label. Much should be discarded; instead it is piled on the animals and another donkey is bought. I stand back and let the crew sort it out.

We leave in the early afternoon, taking a path across the hills because the shorter route along the river is flooded. Many wild iris are in bloom. Progress is slow as our caravan totters along on trails three inches deep with dusty silt. Loads slide off the donkeys, and tired animals lie down and must be unloaded before they can get back up. There is a village somewhere ahead, within half an hour, or maybe it's within five hours—estimates vary. When it gets dark we use flashlights to find our way. It is close to midnight when we reach Pokurma Aghiz. A generous family gives us tea, flat *naan* bread, and refreshing yogurt. The next day we buy more donkeys and discard unnecessary stuff. Two courageous locals hack open a tin of eggplant, taste it, and violently spit it out.

Ahead of us is the Serak Tus (Aktash) Valley, fifty miles long, slicing diagonally through the Kunlun as if cut by a cleaver. This rift-like valley, formed by movements of the earth's crust, offers easy access to the Tibetan Plateau. Captain Deasy wrote of having ascended the Serak Tus in 1897 during one of his surveying trips through the region. Camel driver Gumana Hun tells me that thirty years ago he was with a Polish mapping expedition in the upper valley and later helped two Japanese climbing expeditions.

The river has several channels and we go from gravel bar to gravel bar, wading through ice water. The donkeys are troublesome, exasperating, and obviously lacking in team spirit. Males roar at each other with teeth bared and ears laid back, and slash with a foreleg. Animals suddenly stop, or head back down the trail, or veer to one side. The donkey drivers always yell, chase them, and whack them with a heavy stick to drive them ahead. When not able to follow along the river, we ascend to high terraces and then scramble through ravines until we stop for the night. The donkeys are turned out to graze on meager grass and scattered sage. We are now at 11,000 feet, the sun warm, the setting peaceful. I feel a sense of exhilaration at being on foot and on the move. I can imagine us as a small trading caravan of a century ago, a thought of quiet atavistic pleasure.

Aziz is an experienced cook—he worked in a restaurant—and serves small, round loaves of fresh bread and fried eggs for breakfast. Our morning starts are slow because it takes two to three hours to load the pack animals. I walk ahead of the others with the hope of finding wildlife. A marmot sits hunched and I note that its hindquarters are weak when it stumbles to its burrow. Bubonic plague, transmitted by fleas, affects marmots and people in Xinjiang. At the mouth of a creek are abandoned gold diggings and the usual refuse associated with them. On a nearby hillside Chinese characters created with white pebbles read "Long live Chairman Mao's Communist Party." We switch companions while hiking and chat, Pat describing his climbs in the Antarctic and on other continents, Baiba recounting her partnership with Pat, and Jeff reporting on his travels in Chile and Nepal and his recent visit to Medog in southeast Tibet, where I have been the previous year. It snows as we camp that evening at 13,000 feet and a cold wind blows up-valley. I crawl into my sleeping bag while Aziz prepares an elaborate dinner of potato-vegetable stew, rice, noodles, and scrambled eggs. We have neither the food nor the gas cylinders for many such banquets, though. The following day it snows so heavily and the wind is so cutting that we stay mostly in our tents. The donkeys find little to eat except the stubbly tips of *Ceratoides* shrub and the camels lie and shiver, almost naked from their spring molt.

Striding ahead of the caravan the next day, I come upon a few yearling and adult female chiru. We cross a divide and camp by a small lake in a snowstorm that continues all night. By morning snowdrifts are piled against the tents and the camels, and there is no indication that the weather will soon improve. I go to the cook tent for some tea, and, warming my hands on the hot cup, return to my tent, remaining isolated beneath its yellow dome. Later, I see six ruddy shelducks on the lake, cheerful spots of color.

On June 8 we reach a large basin with a salt lake, the Shar Kul (*kul* means "lake" in Uygur). On our right, to the north, are the snow peaks of the Kunlun. On his 1897 map, Deasy labeled the basin "barren and waterless," and indeed we walk for hours over a barren gravel outwash. However, the lake has a margin with grass, a procumbent *Myricaria* shrub with tiny pink blossoms, and a fine spring with clear, sweet water. A camel and a donkey skeleton here are reminders that our pack animals need ample food; we have some hay as supplement but far too little, given the heavy burden the animals carry each day.

Hiking west with Pat and Baiba, I count 232 female chiru, and feel certain that we are in the general calving area. What possible benefit is there for the chiru to expend so much energy by traveling 200 miles from the good grazing in the south to this desolate place? We cross over a low divide into another basin, the Ser Kul. Some gnarled skeletons of juniper stand in the sand, as if reminders of a more congenial age. We veer up a red-rock canyon into rolling hills. About 450 female chiru are here, many of them pregnant but not quite ready to give birth, judging by their belly size. We then descend into the broad valley of the Keriya River, which like all rivers here flows north to vanish in the sands of the Taklimakan Desert. I feel tired and barely drag along. I would like to spend a week in these hills to study the chiru on their calving ground, wherever it is, but the pack animals are growing weaker and we can afford neither detours nor much extra time. Gumana Hun says there is better grazing to the west. In unusually fine weather we find a valley with lush pastures; no chiru are here, but a herd of thirty-eight wild yaks, including three newborns, flee when Pat and Baiba try to film them. On the other side of the pass are chiru males grazing singly and in small herds. The calving grounds must be somewhere behind us, then; we have failed to confirm their exact location and we are too early to record any births.

After another day of travel, a magnificent valley opens before us with a glacier range on one side crowned by Qong Muztag, 22,800 feet high, a peak first climbed the previous year by a Japanese team. At camp that evening I learn that two of the donkeys have refused to continue and so have to be abandoned. We follow the base of the snow range all the following day until we come upon a startlingly green oasis with *Kobresia* turf around several springs. Tomorrow we must reorganize and discuss how best to get out of the region; the route back is long but easy, whereas the one ahead is shorter but difficult. Pat and Baiba would like to film chiru and I would like to observe them, but Jeff and Jon want to move ahead and complete a circuit. All morning, at lunch, and at dinner, we discuss our options, including splitting the team in two. I finally tell them to decide. Jon later comes to my tent and says we shall continue ahead together. Later, I learn that Jon is also anxious about his health, that he has pains in the abdomen, which, when examined by Jeff, turn out to be two small hernias. Observations on a calving ground have again eluded me, and now I can relax and just be a tourist, receptive to anything during the days ahead.

Our route lies westward over hills to another basin, the Aqik Kul, and down the gorge of the Aqsu (White Water) River. There is good grazing but little wildlife. It rains or snows and the streams roil, half submerging the donkeys and baggage when we have to cross. Sadek falls into the river. Did a donkey push him in retaliation for being repeatedly whacked so hard on head and legs with a heavy stick? On one crossing the soil is like quicksand, the donkeys sinking to their belly. Even unloaded, they require much effort to push and pull them out to prevent their becoming tomorrow's fossils. The snow does not stop. I get a cup of cocoa and boiled potato for breakfast and wait much of the day in the tent. Moving on, we see a bicycle track and find a chemical hand warmer and lens cap. Pat tells me that a lone cyclist named Mark Newcombe had come this far up the Aqsu and then turned back, a rather quixotic venture.

On July 19 we reach a 17,300-foot pass, and stop to take a group photo, realizing that with the Aqik Kul ahead the trip is almost over. We come to patches of eroded road leading into the Aqik Kul with its two lakes. In 1949 the People's Liberation Army started to build a road up the Aqsu gorge for access to Tibet, using prisoners from Chiang Kai Shek's Kuomintang army as labor, but the road was quickly washed out and covered by landslides. Under a leaden sky, a lone shaggy wolf bounds past our camp in pursuit of a male chiru; it's a race where neither gains and the wolf gives up. By checking wolf scats along our route for content, we note from the hair, teeth, and bone splinters that in this region most prey consists of Tibetan woolly hare and chiru, but also of such species as yak, blue sheep, marmot, pika, and an occasional snowcock. Wildlife observations have been so meager this trip that we rejoice even to find scats.

After a night of snow, we set off into a gloomy morning and past brooding volcanic cones toward a distant pass that will lead us into the Aqsu canyon. A black sky signals a serious storm. Instead of camping, Jeff and Jon push far ahead and we can only follow. For two hours the storm roars and lashes, caking everything with wet snow while we trudge along, heads lowered against the wind. I walk slowly, too slowly, the tracks of the caravan vanishing quickly in the weather's fury. Pat and Baiba return to check on me. Pat takes my pack and gives me a power bar to eat; I am deeply grateful.

It is still snowing the following morning and the fog is dense, yet we pack the sodden baggage and move on. A donkey has died during the night. Another donkey, a male, walks a few feet and stops even without a load. Iskander and I stay with him, and I speak gently as I stroke its gray-brown neck, saying, "Be a good donkey, you can do it." These are perhaps the only kind words this male has ever heard. Suddenly he turns, walks back over his trail and stands, rump upwind, ears back, head low. We have to leave. On the approach to the pass is a cache of food and hay left by a previous traveler. We take a little hay and leave behind a donkey-load of flour, potatoes, and other items. Another donkey refuses to continue, and I last see it as a black silhouette standing motionless in the immensity of white.

Snow is a foot deep around the pass. That evening we lighten our loads still more to help the remaining eighteen donkeys and two camels. The canyon has slopes of silt and brittle rock and is filled with boulders and a violent stream careening from side to side. The sun finally shines through, making the more than thirty stream crossings that day more tolerable. Boulders have to be moved for the camels, and the donkeys, never predisposed to following each other, flounder in deep pools and must be dragged out, pushed up inclines, unloaded, and loaded back up, our crew working tremendously hard. As we set up camp that evening, I hope that no flash flood will roar down upon us.

The next day the valley widens as we travel down it, but the gorge narrows so much that we have to traverse hillsides on vague trails. A yellow *Clematis* is in bloom, signaling a lower elevation. One camel cannot surmount a difficult part of the slope, and we leave it behind for Pat, Jeff, and Gumana Hun to retrieve after we find a campsite. On June 29, we meet a man and a boy on donkeys, the first people we've seen in nearly a month.

It has taken us five days to travel through the canyon. We're certainly not alone in our travails here. Captain Deasy in 1898 lost ponies, baggage, and a man. And the archaeologist-explorer Aurel Stein wrote of his 1908 trip in *On Ancient Central Asian Tracks* (1933):

> Last evening we reached the high plateau, 15–16,000 ft above the sea, after four somewhat trying days from Polu. I should not have thought much of the continuous scrambles in the narrow gorges half-filled by glacier-fed torrents, but to get all our baggage & supplies through safely was rather a business. There were continuous crossings & re-crossings of the tossing stream which our little donkeys had trouble to negotiate at all times. . . . The track whether winding amidst slippery boulders at the bottom of the gorge or along rock slopes above was impressively bad.

Within hours of emerging from the canyon, we find willows and poplars and fields of bright yellow rape in bloom, and then the village of Polu. It has a tea shop where we drink glass after glass and eat noodles. Chinese is not understood here, not even by the party secretary, who like everyone else speaks only Uygur. There is no telephone with which to alert the Kashi Mountaineering Association of our arrival, but a truck leaves for the town of Yutian the following day and we hitch a ride. We give the pack animals to our crew as reward for their loyalty and hard work.

As we bump over the rough track into the heat and dust of the Taklimakan Desert, I reflect that it has been a fine trip, a marvelous old-style trip with pack animals and good companions. But another expedition will be necessary to confirm the location of the chiru calving ground and make plans for its protection.

JUNE 2002

The team of four out of Lhasa is on its own in the northern Chang Tang. The men have driven north through the Aru Basin and now in the shadow of Toze Kangri massif, where in 1992 I began to follow the chiru migration, they too are on a quest to find the calving ground. Instead of using vehicles they will walk, each pulling a two-wheeled rickshaw loaded with about 250 pounds of food and equipment, enough for a month-long trek. It is an unusual team of elite high-altitude mountain climbers. Instead of ascending vertically to the summit of Everest or K2, which two of the team have done, they will travel horizontally nearly 300 miles through uninhabited terrain. Instead of a venture just to reach a mountaintop, they have an important conservation goal. Last year we failed to confirm the exact location of the calving ground, and now they plan to do so to help me promote the establishment of a reserve there for the chiru and other wildlife.

The team has taken on that challenge under the leadership of Rick Ridgeway. He works for the Patagonia Company, a manufacturer of outdoor clothing, whose founder, Yvon Chouinard, provides grants for environmental initiatives. Stimulated by a 1993 article of mine in *National Geographic*, Ridgeway contacted me about exploring in the Chang Tang. After a first ascent of a peak bordering the Aru Basin in 1999, he is back on behalf of the chiru. With him is Galen Rowell, the premier outdoor photographer and writer of his time. His book *In the Throne Room of the Mountain Gods* (1977) is a classic account of his expedition in Pakistan's Karakoram Range. I met him there in 1975 and we have stayed in contact since then. The other two members are Conrad Anker, a well-known climber who works with The North Face Company, and Jimmy Chin, who has been in the Antarctic with Anker.

Rick Ridgeway has asked me to join them on the trip. Looking at his powerful, muscular build, I know that I lack the strength. Walking several hundred miles with a modest pack is no problem, but pulling a loaded cart at 17,000 feet through snow and mud, and up and down steep slopes is probably beyond me. In his superb chronicle of the expedition, *The Big Open*, published in 2004, he quotes the following conversation:

"It's just too bad George isn't here with us."

"He didn't think he'd be strong enough to pull a cart," I reply.

"He probably could have done it," Galen says. "He's not even seventy yet." [Galen was 61 then.]

There is no irony in the tone of Galen's comment, so I know he regards it as a matter of fact. I consider how the comment is also a window into how Galen imagines the arc of his own life, and of the physical strength he expects to own when he is seventy.

"How old would you be," I say, quoting the baseball great Satchel Paige, "if you didn't know how old you was?"

Galen laughs, telling me he's going to remember that one.

The team heads across Antelope Plain along the chiru migration route, as I described it to Ridgeway. Yet only a few scattered chiru are there. The phone rings at my home in Connecticut and Kay answers it. It is Ridgeway on a satellite phone. The conversation is brief:

"Where are the chiru?"

"Keep looking," answers Kay. "They are there."

I was in Tajikistan at that time and could not have been more precise.

Finally on June 8 the team locates the migration route on a ridge on Heishi Beihu, the lake where, a year earlier, we had to abandon the struggle to follow the animals. This year the herds had traveled a little farther east than they had in 1992. The team members follow the lake northward and enter Xinjiang. They are now tracing the chiru over unknown paths in terrain never before seen by Westerners. Ridgeway describes the grueling work of pulling the rickshaws:

> There is a dull ache from my shoulder blades to the small of my back and I would like nothing more than to stop and stretch.
>
> Ahead we see what appears to be the top of the gulley, but the slope steepens even more, and we have to double-team the carts, one pulling and one pushing. The altitude is approaching seventeen thousand five hundred feet, and when at last we have all the carts on top, I sit on top of my rickshaw and try to recover from a fit of coughing.
>
> I remind myself that tenacity is easier when you have no choice.

The chiru are spread out, trails leading north, northwest, and northeast. The team toils on and descends a valley that becomes a narrow canyon, the Gorge of Despair, as they call it, boulder-strewn and almost filled by a stream. "Yesterday was annoying, "says Anker, sitting on a rock and emptying water from his boots, "but this is fun." Hemmed in by rock walls, they can only bulldoze their way downstream.

> This time we will have to triple-team the carts—one pulling and two pushing—while Galen and Jimmy, alternating take photos and video. Before we start we have to roll several large rocks aside to create clearance wide enough to get the rickshaw into the river. . . . We manage to advance it about ten feet downstream when our first obstacle, a rock four feet high, blocks us. . . . We shrug our shoulders and grab the cart by the wheel frames.
>
> "Okay," Conrad says, "one . . . two . . . three!"
>
> We lift the nearly two-hundred-and-fifty-pound cart on top of the rock and balance it while we catch our breath. Jimmy points the video camera at me and says, "Can you please explain to the audience how this rickshaw has come to be sitting on top of this big rock?"
>
> I shake my head, smile, and say, "No, I can't."

I greatly enjoy the vicarious expedition experience of reading Ridgeway's account, envious of the team's easy camaraderie based on understanding one another's humor, compulsions, and needs. It is a tightly knit group, not burdened by any uninterested coworkers and focused solely on achieving its goal. Yet I realize, as I did in the beginning, that I might have been a burden on these tough and tough-minded climbers, vertical or horizontal.

The Ridgeway team is short of food, so short that it hesitates to tarry anywhere for more than a day. They hungrily contemplate a few baby hares in a nest, and consider a granola bar a special treat. "If we can't have food, at least we can suffer," Anker notes. The canyon finally behind them, the four rickshaw wallahs at last reach Shar Kul, where in the hills to the south they see many chiru, just as we did the previous year.

> June 18. Galen leaves, and in a few minutes, as Conrad is serving the chocolate in our mugs, we hear Galen yell. "I've got a calf! I'm sure I saw a baby chiru."
>
> We scamper out of the tent. Galen is bent over his spotting scope, and he looks up when I rush to his side.
>
> "I'm sure it was a calf," he says. "Here have a look, see what you think."
>
> "Just a second. It still looks like a dot, but yeah, it's moving. There it goes. It's definitely moving. In fact, it's running. The dot . . . it's running . . . running to catch up to its mother."
>
> "This is like a summit day," Conrad says. "All the effort, all the time, all the expense, reduced to this moment."

During the following two days they find more newborns. They creep close to photograph them:

> "We're doing what our ancestors did," Galen says. "Stalking game animals. But the result is an image instead of a roasting carcass."
>
> "I'm beginning to favor the roasting carcass," I reply.

The team counts about 1,300 chiru females dispersed over a hundred square miles, and on June 20 they observe over twenty newborns. At last, the calving ground of the West Chang Tang population has been pinpointed.

On June 26, as the four descend the Serak Tus Valley, the rickshaws now easy to haul, they hear the hum of an engine. Impossible, they think, remembering my comment that the area is uninhabited and too dissected by ravines for vehicles. They come to a gold mine where a bulldozer has dammed two ponds and water is pumped to a sluice. It took the bulldozer twenty days to cut an access road, the foreman tells the team, and the mine has now been operating for three months.

The team continues down-valley after their success. At their last camp before vehicles will come to pick them up, Galen Rowell says that this trip "is in a class by itself when I think of everything together—the adventure, the team, the migration, the birthing grounds, the conservation component. I can see someday I might look back on this trip as the best of my life."

Two weeks after the team returned to the United States, on July 22, Kay and I met Rick Ridgeway at Galen and Barbara Rowell's home in Bishop, California. Galen and Barbara had moved there to live close to the Sierra and to open the Mountain Light Gallery in order to market his spectacular collection of photographs. Both Rick and Galen still looked very lean after their trek. We spent a wonderful day comparing the 2001 and 2002 information on the chiru migration, summarizing the valuable counts and other data which Conrad Anker in particular had collected, and just perusing maps and taking virtual trips. The news of the gold mine road up the Serak Tus bothered me greatly because it makes the calving ground easily accessible to motorized poachers. Hundreds upon hundreds of chiru females might be killed for their fine wool just as they are giving birth, as has happened in recent years in the Arjin Shan and Kekexili reserves. But even such thoughts could not dampen the feeling of contentment and enjoyment of that day.

The following morning Galen and Barbara would leave, he to teach a photography workshop in Alaska. We were never to see them again. A few weeks later they were homeward bound in a light aircraft, piloted by a friend, when it crashed at night near Bishop.

We published our scientific information from the calving ground jointly in a journal, and I submitted a report to the Xinjiang authorities with suggestions for protection of the area. Rick Ridgeway's 2003 article in *National Geographic* and his book *The Big Open*, both featuring Galen Rowell's photographs, raised international awareness of the chiru and the slaughter of the species for its fine shahtoosh wool.

Conservation is like crossing the Chang Tang on foot—one step at a time. The new road up the Serak Tus signaled how rapidly wilderness can be developed and destroyed. But some further steps on behalf of the chiru were soon to be taken. In 2004 a guard post was established in the Serak Tus, manned by Uygur staff during the calving season, with initial funds provided by the Patagonia Company and Wildlife Conservation Society. On November 20, 2004, the local government designated the Shar Kul Tibet Antelope Nature Reserve, five hundred square miles in size and encompassing most of the calving ground. To my colleagues and me, the reserve serves as a living memorial to Galen Rowell, symbolizing his dedication to the beauty of the natural world.

JUNE–JULY 2005

I had not as yet observed chiru on the calving ground and wanted to do so, not only for pleasure but also for the kind of information that could contribute to the conservation of the population. What, for example, was the mortality rate of females and young in a place with so little food and much snow during the birth season? Now that we knew the exact location of the calving ground we could go there directly at the right time in mid-June over the same route we had taken in 2001. Two of my valued coworkers on this trip were Kang Aili of the Wildlife Conservation Society, joining me for the first of several journeys to which she would contribute so much, and Liu Yanlin, then a graduate student at Peking University with whom I later collaborated on other ventures.

I presume that the new road up the Serak Tus Valley will make our trip to the calving ground quick and easy. We will use vehicles this time instead of undisciplined and obstructive donkeys as pack animals. The Forestry Department in the town of Hetian, which administrates the new chiru reserve, has generously provided two cars and a truck, as well as equipment such as tents and a gas stove.

We leave on June 8 to cross the hundred miles of desert to the foothills of the Kunlun. The mountains have evaporated in dusty haze and the sky is the color of skim milk. At the broken-down village of Ka Er Sane with its ruins of mud-brick walls and lounging men, staring at us indifferently, our old Toyota breaks down. The starter does not work, the gearbox grinds, and the engine stalls haphazardly—not useful traits for mountain driving. The car has to be returned to Hetian. Farther on, at a river's edge the truck breaks down, too, requiring another trip to Hetian for spare parts, and more lost days. Meanwhile a surge of chocolate-brown water floods the valley and maroons the truck in the river. Then a truck arrives from up-valley with prospectors who have been in the Shar Kul to look for gold and jade. We are able to rent that truck to transport our gear to Shar Kul, and, after our jeep returns from town, we finally are on our way again. There is much to be said on behalf of donkeys.

In mid-afternoon we reach Yalike, the new guard post, a three-room, flat-roofed stone hut. There are six guards, powerful men dressed in camouflage clothes. One of their duties is to check the permit of any vehicle driving up to the gold mines and beyond. A problem is that officials in town write the permits in Chinese characters, which none of the Uygur guards can read. Another problem is that the guard post is 125 miles from the calving ground—and the guards have no transport. Yesterday we met a geological survey team also en route to Shar Kul. Its leader mentions that another new road is being built, this one from Tibet over the Keriya Pass, just north of the Antelope Plain, into the region. Within four years the peace we and the chiru experienced in 2001 has been shattered by intrusive development.

Clouds rest on the ground and snow whips horizontally as we continue, when our truck sinks into mud and we are forced to camp. The next day takes us over the barren, bumpy outwash of the Shar Kul, on past the lake, where we see several herds of chiru, to the mouth of a canyon where we establish a base. Rick Ridgeway and his team struggled down this same canyon three years earlier. Nearby a big hole has been dug into the gravel in search of gold, leaving a campsite littered with refuse which we try to bury. We erect a yurt-like tent and a large cook tent, and Kang Aili, Liu Yan-lin, and I each have our own small tents. This will be our base until we leave in five weeks.

I remember the horrible weather of our 1997 journey in search of calving grounds in western Qinghai with its frequent snow-storms driven by furious winds and the dispiriting, sodden landscape into which our vehicles continually sank. The month here is just as good—except that we do most work on foot. To summarize simply and leave detail to the imagination, it snows or hails on nineteen of the twenty-eight days between June 10 and July 7, a period that includes the birth season. On six other days there are violent sand-storms. But three days are wholly pleasant, with blue skies and fluffs of white cloud sailing with the breeze.

We divide into two teams. One consists of the local staff under the leadership of Qi Jun, the demanding but dedicated manager for wildlife of the Forestry Department in Hetian; and the other team is made up of researchers, those devoted to wandering the hills in search of chiru. The latter includes Aili, Liu Yanlin, Cai Xinbin of the Forest Research Institute in Urumqi, and me. The chiru, we soon discover, are widely scattered and much on the move, present somewhere one day only to have deserted it the next, leaving the bleak hills empty to the horizon. Perhaps the animals simply have to shift around to find food. There is little to eat in the hills except the low shrub *Ceratoides*—with an average ground cover of only 2.5 percent—and a bit of dead grass, with the first green blades of spring just appearing.

On June 18, Aili and I search the hills under a stormy sky, she on one ridge and I on another. I see her coming toward me with jaunty steps, her ponytail bobbing and her face beaming. "I saw a baby," she says. We observe it from a distance, a small grayish mound on gray, gravelly sand, while its mother feeds nearby. Galen Rowell spotted the first newborn on the same date three years earlier.

The chiru are drifting westward and concentrating there in the hills. A few youngsters follow their mothers but they are too agile for us to catch. We particularly want to find newborns, still unsteady on their feet, to fit several with a tiny radio transmitter around the neck in order to help us trace migratory movements. We hike for hours and many miles until one day after returning tired to camp, one of our crew casually mentions that there is a newborn nearby. We see it crouched, neck and head extended along the ground, a mere bump on the open plain. I put on surgical gloves and rub these with aromatic *Ceratoides* leaves to hide my human scent from mother and calf. Coming from behind, I grab the newborn, which bleats and struggles briefly as I place it into a cloth bag to be weighed by Yanlin: 6.4 pounds. I check its sex—a female—slip the radio transmitter mounted on an expandable collar around her neck, and place her gently on the ground. I check my watch: the time elapsed from beginning to end is 1.5 minutes. We retreat quietly.

A valley projects south from the basin in the direction where the chiru are congregating. Our car takes us a short distance up this valley until we're halted by overflow river ice, *aufeis*. We then shoulder heavy packs and hike two hours to an upland plain. There, within sight of chiru, we camp by a stream, erecting our small tents. One challenge in traveling with coworkers in their twenties is their endless energy. Yanlin, tall and lean, is a particularly exuberant hiker, rushing up ridges just to be on top, crossing valleys to inspect some burrow, collecting scats and plants for identification. As I plod along, I envy him and think of my younger days when I ranged over landscapes from Alaska and Tanzania to India and Nepal, often just to feel the ground underfoot, open to anything that might come my way. We find two dead chiru calves, precise cause of death unknown; being born tiny and wet in a snowstorm and howling wind, though, is certainly a test of survival of the fittest. Xinbin waves to us and points—a newborn. As it attempts to stagger away, Aili snags it. Radio-collared, we later hear its signal from camp and know from the directional antenna that it has moved on with its mother.

The radio transmitters can also indicate activity. A slow beep-beep means that the animal is inactive, and fast beeps that it is alert or has moved. Aili is very interested and patient in recording activity, holding up the antenna and checking the speed of the pulse every fifteen minutes on the receiver. She spends hours on that, day and night. For example, signals from one youngster show active signals 25 percent of the time between 10:40 a.m. through the day and night until 4:25 a.m. early the next morning, and from another youngster it was 33 percent. During the first days of life, newborns spend most of the time lying quietly and sleeping.

While Aili monitors radio signals, Yanlin, Xinbin, and I try to learn as much as possible about chiru life and death on the calving ground. Research consists of repetition, of collecting the same kind of fact again and again, often a tedious occupation, and not uplifting here because we find so many dead chiru. And then there are many unanswered questions based on the facts. We note that many females do not seem to be pregnant, or at least that their bellies are not expanded. We find a female which died giving birth. I check her stomach contents and note that half of what she has eaten is *Ceratoides* and the other half grass. Why so much grass with leaves dead and not nutritious? Down south the grass is now tender and green yet the chiru have come here instead. In general, migratory ungulates, such as wildebeest, move with the seasons to places where food is growing and most nutritious, especially around the time of giving birth. By contrast, these chiru seemed to have abandoned good pastures for this desolate terrain. Why? Other hoofed animals avoid this place: we have seen only a lone kiang. Perhaps chiru reduce competition for forage with other ungulates and avoid predators and humans by coming here, two of several possible reasons.

The chiru move constantly, frustrating Aili because the radio-collared young vanish, their signals obstructed by hills. We make a brief trip to base camp for more supplies, and return to the high plain, content with the freedom to roam alone or together, each of us coming back in the late afternoon with new information. Crouched in the erosion gulley around our primus stove, waiting for a hot drink, we share experiences. A newborn stood up for the first time at fifteen minutes of age, I relate, suckled at thirty-eight minutes, and followed its grazing mother at one hour. Aili has seen a pair of red fox with two large pups.

When I look out of my tent in the morning of July 3, dense snow whips past and clouds have erased the mountains. When the weather improves the white plain is peppered with chiru. Yanlin and

I count: there are at least 2,300. Many lie in the snow, each distinctly separated from one another, even mother and offspring. They are curiously alone together instead of cuddling close for warmth and protection. Later we check that area and find nine dead young. Even having the world's finest and warmest wool cannot save them all. I see a disheveled piece of fur. Another dead newborn, I think. But the fur moves, a head pops up, and just as quickly ducks and is motionless, eyes half closed as if dead. One eye blinks. I disturb it no further and walk on.

At the end of the birth season, we summarize some of the information:

- Number of females in the area: about 4,000–4,500.
- Percentage of females that are yearlings and not due to give birth until the following year: 16.
- Percentage of adult females accompanied by calves: 40.
- Number of females found dead, and cause of death: 21 (childbirth, 6; wolf kills, 4; unknown, 11).
- Number of calves found dead, and cause of death: 42 (bird of prey, 2; red fox, 5; unknown, 35).

A car arrives at camp, able to reach us because melting river ice has opened a passage. Qi Jun has brought a delicious watermelon. We return to base with him to get more food for a final week with the chiru. Already during the first week of July many females have shifted southward as if impatient to begin the return migration, just as grass is greening and asters and wild dandelions are in bloom.

By July 13 the calving ground is deserted except for a few stragglers. Only one to three weeks old, the calves suddenly have to travel far and fast. Aili and Yanlin will follow the migration for two days to determine the route, while Xinbin and I wait in camp. The primus stove has expired and we cook a little on smoking *Ceratoides* twigs. Breakfast: one cup coffee, six cookies; lunch: one chocolate bar, a handful of nuts and dried fruit; dinner: the inevitable *fang bian*, instant noodles to which only hot water is added. When Aili and Yanlin return, they tell us that the chiru hurried south over a series of hills, up a valley and over a pass, and down a valley onto a plain.

The animals continued south and southeast in the direction of the Heishi Beihu basin where most had passed through as they moved north a mere month and a half earlier to give birth.

I feel a great sense of relief. As a Tibetan proverb states, "The goal will not be reached if the right distance is not traveled." After so many years, we have finally traveled the right distance on behalf of these chiru. So far poachers have not desecrated this calving ground with mass slaughter. We now have the information to prod the appropriate government department to provide more protection for the area. Our recommendations will include: greatly expanding the existing small reserve, especially southward to the Tibetan border, to prevent development along the migratory routes; making the calving grounds inviolate to human intrusion, in order to assure the animals a tranquil birth season; and upgrading the whole region to a provincial and ultimately a national reserve. We discuss these and other proposals as we pack at base camp, ready to leave these hills now so empty of chiru.

Constant snows and subsequent meltwater have turned the rivers into angry torrents, and roads are washed out and littered with boulders and landslides. Our retreat down the Serak Tus and the gorges of the Kunlun with our vehicles is an interesting experience lasting several days. Again, I would have preferred donkeys.

Through our reports and meetings with local and provincial officials, we not only made them aware of the calving ground and potential threat to its survival but also stressed the fact that this population, the West Chang Tang population, needed the cooperation of both Tibet and Xinjiang in conservation efforts. To our delight, the Xinjiang provincial government considered our recommendations and in 2007 established the West Kunlun Reserve, about 11,500 square miles, in size.

The previous year, the guards had established a tent camp at the edge of the calving area to better protect it—but the chiru failed to appear. So little snow had fallen during the past months that the hills were parched and there was virtually no forage for the animals. According to rumor, the chiru had turned westward in Tibet before reaching the Xinjiang border. Aili and I unfortunately have no further information about these chiru at their calving ground. The provincial government failed to provide the anticipated funds for the guard post and it closed in 2009.

With the new West Kunlun Reserve added to the existing Mid-Kunlun and Arjin Shan reserves, all chiru areas in Xinjiang were now officially protected. These reserves adjoin the Chang Tang Reserve across the border in Tibet and the Kekexili Reserve to the east in Qinghai, all of them together comprising a vast upland landscape of around 175,000 square miles, an area somewhat larger than California, where the main migratory chiru populations can still travel unhindered back and forth to their traditional calving grounds. To establish a reserve is a fairly straightforward political and administrative action; to protect and manage that reserve effectively is a long-term process, one never completed, because conditions change and new threats appear. But for the present the chiru can endure

❋ CHAPTER 4 ❋

A Deadly Fashion

O N FIRST ENCOUNTERING CHIRU in 1985, I admired their beauty and was eager to learn about their life in these bleak uplands of the Chang Tang. Then, as I grew to know them better, and become aware of the great chiru migrations, I realized that their travels defined the landscape. Protect the chiru, and all other species in the region, the whole ecosystem, would benefit. But by 1990 I realized, too, that Tibetan nomads were killing chiru not just for subsistence, something for which I have sympathy, but also for commercial profit by selling hides. What were the hides used for, and where were they sent? I had no idea. Slowly I discovered that chiru wool was smuggled to Kashmir in India to be woven into expensive shawls, sold under the name of *shahtoosh*. With the mass slaughter of chiru that began in the late 1980s, with so many guns against them, including those of poachers who lived far from the Chang Tang, I could no longer simply continue my peaceful studies.

Conservation now had priority. For more than two decades I have followed the decline and partial recovery of the chiru in China and have tried to raise awareness about the plight of the species in the rest of the world. Many others joined the campaign to inform the public that wearing shahtoosh kills. Conservation organizations, among them the Wildlife Protection Society of India, the Wildlife Trust of India, and the International Fund for Animal Welfare, have published valuable reports; television shows have aired depressing footage of the massacre, with heaps of chiru bodies and hides; and

Rick Ridgeway's *The Big Open* has covered the problem admirably, to name just a few sources. Nevertheless, chiru killing continues, though thanks to such efforts, it continues at a much reduced rate than in the 1990s; chiru wool still reaches Kashmir, and shahtoosh shawls are still widely available, especially in the Middle East and in Asia, in spite of ongoing efforts to stop the illegal trade by China and the international conservation community.

At first, most purchasers of shahtoosh shawls, scarves, and other products had no idea that the wool came from chiru or what the implications might be. In the early 1990s, for example, the New York department store Bergdorf Goodman advertised the shawls as follows:

> It is a long and hard process to collect and weave Shahtoosh wool. The source of the wool is the Mountain ibex of Tibet. After the arduous Himalayan winter is over, the Ibex sheds its down undercoat by scratching itself against low trees and bushes.
> A difficult process then commences as local shepherds, called Boudhs, from the region of Chang Thang, Tibet, climb into the mountains during the three spring months to search for and collect this matted hair.

The only thing accurate in this advertisement is the location.

But here was a shawl—exotic, luxurious, and expensive, a golden fleece collected by diligent nomads and later woven by local artisans. It was politically correct and virtuous to buy the shawls because this contributed to the livelihood of poor people without harming wildlife. This was nothing like the fashion rage for egret feathers to adorn hats in the early 1900s and the skins of leopard, jaguar, and other spotted cats to make garments in the 1970s and 1980s. No wonder the shawls became a favorite wrap of the world's wealthy.

Only slowly did awareness grow that the source of the wool is not an ibex, a species of wild goat devoted to rugged terrain, but the chiru, and that the animal is killed to obtain the wool. I wonder how often such misrepresentations were deliberate lies by traders and dealers rather than simply "just-so" stories about a little-known species in a faraway place. Regardless, the issue certainly has a long history.

The story begins in Leh, the capital of Ladakh, the western extension of the Tibetan Plateau in India. Leh was once a prominent center for trade in Central Asia, with caravans traveling east into Tibet as far as Lhasa and north to Hotan (Hetian), Kashgar (Kashi), and other cities in what is now the Xinjiang region of western China. Caravans of donkeys, horses, and mules left Leh for Tibet carrying grain, spices, tea, cloth, cooking oil, and other trading goods in demand by nomadic herders. They stopped along the route to trade in towns such as Rutog, Gerze, and especially in Gartok, site of an annual fair from August to October where goods and livestock were bartered and bought. After months on the trail, caravans headed back toward Leh with turquoise, gold, salt, butter, meat, and wool. Sheep were often driven back alive, each carrying saddle bags stuffed with up to thirty-five pounds of goods. The main trade item, however, was wool.

There are three main kinds of wool. One is the common and cheap sheep wool. Then there is the underwool or fleece from domestic goats, the animals in the cold highlands of Tibet that produce the finest and longest such fibers. Exported from Leh to Kashmir, the goat wool has long been woven there to produce cashmere shawls—light, durable, and warm. The finest quality of cashmere is known as pashmina, a term derived from *pashm*, which in Persian merely means "wool." And then there is a third kind of wool, rare and ultra-fine, called *tus, toosh*, or *asli toosh*.

Toosh has been a highly valued item for centuries. The earliest account I can find is that of the Buddhist monk Hiuen Tsang, variously known as Yuan Chwang, Hsuan Tsang, and Xuan Zang. Born in China's Hunan province in 603 during the Tang dynasty, he became a Buddhist monk at the age of thirteen and was fully ordained at twenty. In the year 629 he became a pilgrim and for sixteen years traveled widely through central and south Asia, crossing the Pamir and Altai Mountains with their "hard and dazzling sheets of ice" and visiting many Buddhist shrines in India. He returned to China to great acclaim, bringing with him 657 volumes of Buddhist texts which he worked on translating until his death in 664.

Hiuen Tsang's own writings were translated into English and published in 1906 as *Si-Yu-Ki: Buddhist Records of the Western World*. Hiuen

Tsang passed through Kashmir on his travels and noted "garments also made of Kien-po-lo (kambala) which is woven from fine goat-hair; garments also made from Ho-la-li (karala). This stuff is made from the fine hair of a wild animal: it is seldom this can be woven, and therefore the stuff is very valuable, and it is regarded as fine clothing."

The Moghul emperor Jahangir, who ruled from 1605 to 1628, wrote in his memoirs about "a Tus shawl which my revered father [Akbar the Great] had adopted as a 'dress' . . ." Soon thereafter, the Frenchman Francois Bernier, in 1646 the first European to visit "Kuchemire," wrote in his book *Travels in the Mogul Empire*:

> But what is peculiar and considerable in them, and which draws the trade and silver into the country, is that prodigious quantity of stuffs called *chales* [shawls], which they work there, and employ their little children in. . . . They make two sorts of them; one, of the wool of the country, which is finer than that of Spain; the other, of a wool, or rather of an [sic] hair, they call Touz, taken from the breast of a wild goat of the great Tibet. These latter are of a far greater price than the former; neither is there any *Castor* [beaver] so soft and delicate.

William Moorcroft, in 1812 the first British traveler to penetrate western Tibet, was in search of the source of *pashm*, the fine cashmere wool, on behalf of the East India Company, as he and George Trebeck described in *Travels in the Himalayan Provinces of Hindustan and the Punjab* (1841). In Ladakh from 1820 to 1822, he estimated that in that time about 120,000–240,000 pounds of *pashm* reached Kashmir annually, whereas only 1,000 pounds of *tus* did so. He noted that only two looms in Kashmir specialized in *tus* and the rest on cashmere and other wool. Moorcroft also believed that wild goats were the source of *tus* wool. "This article must always be high priced from the difficulty of procuring the animal that produces it, the wild goat rarely venturing within gun-shot during the day, and being obtained only by snares at night, when they come down the mountains to browse in the valleys."

Alexander Cunningham, who visited Ladakh two decades later, in 1846 and 1847, noted in *Ladak* (1854) that *tus* came from "Tibetan ibex," and he accurately described the long curving horns of that species and their craggy habitat. "They are killed for the sake of the soft under-fleece, which, in Kashmir, is called *Asli Tus*. This is an exceedingly fine and soft wool of a light brown colour, which is exported to Kashmir. . . . It is also woven into a very fine cloth, called *Tusi*, of a soft and delicate texture, which is much prized for its warmth."

The confusion of ibex with chiru by these early Europeans is understandable. They did not see the latter in the wild, nor did Kashmiri traders who only went as far as Leh. However, traders who went into Tibet as far as Gerze and beyond would have seen chiru or learned about them from the nomads. Janet Rizvi, who interviewed old Ladakhis and Kashmiris in the 1980s and 1990s about the early trades, wrote in her book *Trans-Himalayan Caravans* that "I have never in Ladakh or in Kashmir heard of *toosh* being produced by any animal other than the Tibetan antelope (chiru or stos)." Ibex occur in Tibet only rarely, in a small area of the southwest, and to my knowledge they have never provided enough wool for shawls.

That shahtoosh shawls were produced from chiru wool was obviously known widely in the region, yet dealers continued to spin fictions that ibex wool was plucked from bushes and even that Siberian goose down was the source of *tus*. Perhaps they were trying to avoid public protest by disguising the true source of this lucrative wool from an endangered species, or later eager to avoid government attention for dealing in a product that is illegal in India and China, as well as by international convention. Not just dealers but Kashmiri politicians were for years successful in pulling the wool over the eyes of the public.

When I began fieldwork on the chiru, I had never heard of shahtoosh. In 1985, when I first encountered chiru in the Chang Tang of Qinghai, no one collected the hides of the many chiru that died in the wake of the blizzard. A demand for chiru hides had obviously not yet reached Qinghai.

I first met chiru hunters three years later, in August 1988, south of the Aru basin in Tibet. Each of the two men carried a muzzle-loader and leg-hold traps. These traps are simple and efficient, and, judging by accounts of the 1800s, have been in use for centuries.

Toni Huber of the Humboldt University in Berlin describes the foot trap, or *khogtse*, as it is known locally, in a 2005 journal article of the Milan Science Museum:

> The khogtse is based on a plaited ring of dry grass stems mixed with the quills of geese. . . . This strong plaited ring, with a thickness of 3 cm, is bound around with yarn made of sheep wool and goat hair, and has an overall diameter of about 20 cm. An antelope horn must then be soaked in water to make it pliable for cutting into thin slivers. The dried slivers of antelope horn . . . with sharpened points are inserted at angles into the ring.

The trap is placed over a hole on an animal trail and concealed with grass; a rope attaches the trap to a stake hammered into the ground. When an animal steps through the ring, its leg drops into the hole and the prongs prevent it from withdrawing. There it struggles and then stands until the hunter comes for the kill.

Tibetan nomads hunt chiru for meat and they use the horns of males as tent pegs and to tether horses. Sven Hedin told of coming to a camp on his 1906 journey, and "in one of the huts lay the hides and meat of nine antelopes. The people lived almost exclusively on the game they caught in their snares." But this was entirely different from the commercial chiru trade I observed in 1990.

In August 1990, after another wildlife survey in western Tibet, we stopped for the night in the small town of Gerze, the same town that once was a major trading center of caravans to and from Ladakh. The following morning a Tibetan team member took me past the row of government buildings along the main street to the edge of town with its mud-brick huts, tents, and trash. Traders had spread their wares on a cloth in front of the tents—everything from shoes, clothes, and rope to dried apricots, rice, and potatoes. A Tibetan woman walked by as she plucked tufts of chiru hair and wool from a hide. Nearby, a Tibetan man sat on the ground pulling handfuls of hair and wool from a chiru hide. His two companions were Khampa traders from eastern Tibet, red wool yarn braided through their hair. I peered over the wall of a compound where a sign announced the Gang Di Si Mo No store. About twenty chiru hides were spread on the ground in the courtyard, and two open sacks were stuffed with chiru wool. When we inquired of an apparent caretaker about the hides, he told us that nomads and traders sell hides to this store. From here the sacks of hair and wool are exported to Nepal by Tibetan and Nepalese traders. More he did not know.

However, I did know that the chiru is fully protected by law, listed in Appendix I of the Convention on International Trade in Endangered Species (CITES) since 1979 and also a Class I protected animal by China's 1988 Wildlife Protection Law. Here in Gerze, though, an illegal commercial chiru trade flourished openly. I reported the killing and smuggling to the Tibet Forestry Department. Wondering for what purpose the wool was being exported to Nepal, I wrote to the World Wildlife Fund to ask if they knew. Receiving no reply, I was negligent in pursuing the matter at the time.

When I was again in western Tibet in December of the following year, I discovered more evidence of a trade in chiru. We came upon an isolated tattered tent. Nineteen yaks grazed nearby. Two chiru hides were pegged out to dry, and a dead hare was still in the foot trap in which it had accidentally been caught. Two young men in dirty *chubas* came from the tent as we drove up. I did not realize at first that this was a camp of commercial hunters, one of three in the area, the men told us. They had come from Gerze, over one hundred miles away. Covered with saddle blankets were twenty-two skinned and frozen chiru carcasses, their bloody bodies in striking contrast to the somber landscape. There were also fourteen chiru heads, all of them males with long, elegant horns. The two nomads were friendly and invited us into their tent. Chiru hides were neatly folded and stacked against one tent wall. I gave the nomads each a card. On one side is a drawing of Milarepa, an eleventh-century Buddhist monk and saint, surrounded by adoring wild animals and a kneeling hunter laying down his bow and quiver in submission, and on the other is an exhortation by the Buddha in Tibetan script:

> All beings tremble at punishment,
> To all life is dear.
> Comparing others to oneself,
> One should neither kill nor cause to kill.

After this was read aloud, there was general laughter at the appropriateness of the message; perhaps the men considering it a good joke on themselves, one perhaps tinged with guilt as well. But I was no closer to learning what chiru wool was used for.

A month later, on January 22, 1992, and back home in the United States, I received a letter from a Michael Sautman, general director of a company named Monamco (now California Cashmere Company). He wrote:

> My company, MONAMCO, specializes in the production and sale of rare animal fibers such as cashmere, camel wool and yak. . . . A client of ours, who owns one of the largest cashmere companies in the world, has expressed an interest in obtaining a supply of one of the rarest of all wools called Shahtoosh. As you might know, Shahtoosh is found mainly in Tibet where we believe it is derived [from] the animal Capra ibex. Others have stated that Shahtoosh is obtained from a Tibetan antelope. . . . It is brought into Nepal and Ladakh where it is bought by Kashmiri weavers who produce the famous Shahtoosh shawls.

Here, finally, must be the answer!

I informed Sautman of the connection between the illegal chiru killing and wool trade that I had witnessed in Tibet, and he replied that "based upon the information received from you, I have abandoned the Shahtoosh project and have advised my client and colleagues to do likewise." I wish that all traders had responded with such moral concern for wildlife.

Now that I had made the basic association between the chiru and shahtoosh, a brief search of the literature indicated that chiru wool, called *tsod-khulu*, was sold by nomads to traders, that weavers in Kashmir were the only ones able to handle the fine wool, and that India's Punjab state had once been a main market for the shawls. There, a shahtoosh—a word meaning "king of wool" in Persian—was a royal gift, a wedding dowry, an heirloom, one for which a family saved for years to buy. A shahtoosh shawl is so fine that it can be pulled through a finger ring, giving it the name "ring shawl." (However, a high-quality goat pashmina can also be pulled through a ring.) In the past, nomads hunted chiru for their meat, for subsistence, and the sale of wool was a small bonus. As usual, traders made the most substantial profits from the sale of wool, an estimated 600–1,000 percent today.

I still did not know much about shahtoosh but, based on what Sautman had written me, it was apparently now an international commercial product. To reduce this illegal trade would require three measures, I realized. China had to protect its chiru better, the weaving of shawls in Kashmir had to be suppressed, and the marketing and promotion of shahtoosh to consumers had to be stopped.

To state broad goals such as these is perhaps a useful exercise, but it did nothing to curb the chiru slaughter, which continued unrestrained and indeed accelerated though the 1990s. I had confirmation of this when I returned to Tibet during the summer of 1992.

A herder offered us any number of chiru hides for the equivalent of about twenty-five dollars each. In the Aru basin I met Chida, the headman of five families which had the previous year settled permanently in the basin for one reason only—to hunt chiru. Every person needs about four sheep as food per year and there were forty people in his group. With a total of only 600 sheep and 45 yaks there was not enough livestock to feed everyone without decimating the herd. Chiru meat preserves the lives of his sheep, and the sale of the wool brings much-needed cash, Chida emphasized. With increased income, Chida had bought a truck. But a truck requires gasoline, and unlike a horse it cannot be refueled by turning it out to graze. Indeed, just the day before, Chida's truck had left with fifty chiru hides to trade for gasoline. Feeling perhaps somewhat guilty, Chida told us that the previous winter officials from Gerze had come twice to hunt chiru. "If officials obey the law and stop hunting, we will too," he added.

The chiru massacre was an unanticipated shock to me when I realized its extent. The relentless and unchecked slaughter of the American bison from the 1860s through the 1880s came to mind. The railroad construction workers and the military needed meat, hides were in demand as blankets in urban areas, and tongues became a delicacy for the well-to-do. "The extermination of the herds became an organized industry," in the words of Martin Garretson in his 1938 book *The American Bison*. A few quotes illustrate this: ". . . in 1871, a firm in St. Louis bought 250,000 skins"; ". . . in one district alone 210,000 buffalo were slaughtered in two months"; and between December 1877 and January 1878 "more than one hundred thousand hides" were taken by hunters. "The railroads advertised buffalo hunting excursions. . . ." And "after the great slaughter, bones of buffalo literally whitened vast areas of the great plains. . . ." By the end of the century the millions of bison that had once roamed the American plains had dwindled to one small herd in Yellowstone National Park. It was a shameful chapter in American history. Would history repeat itself on the Tibetan Plateau?

Nomads, officials, truck drivers, the military, and others all killed chiru for quick profit. The most deadly were organized gangs of armed poachers in vehicles from distant towns—Golmud, Xining, Chamdo—who sought out chiru herds and often massacred the confused animals at night in the beam of headlights. An even more destructive practice was the slaughter on the calving grounds the poachers had discovered in Xinjiang's Arjin Shan Reserve and Qinghai's Kekexili Reserve, the latter of which we had tried to reach in 1997. Females were gunned down just before or after giving birth, killing the new generation as well, leaving bloody carcasses stripped of hides to rot and newborns abandoned to starve.

In September 1993 the Arjin Shan Reserve had been invaded illegally by over 50,000 gold miners, who contributed greatly to the decline of wildlife. How Man Wong, the head of the China Exploration and Research Society, which has done so much to help maintain the reserve, related in his field report: "In April this year, PSB [Public Security Bureau] at a neighboring asbestos mine doing [a] routine check of passing vehicles intercepted four trucks out of a 17-truck convoy and discovered 674 antelope skins en route to Lhasa. At Huatugou, they tracked down one group with 360 skins and at Ulan, another group with 300 skins." When biologist William Bleisch visited the reserve in 1998, he counted 1,003 skinned chiru

bodies strewn over the calving ground of a resident chiru population, and the following year he tallied "917 carcasses" there. Obviously protection of the reserve had not improved between 1993 and
1999.

Gold was discovered in the Kekexili (Hoh Xil) area of western
Qinghai in 1984, and soon about 30,000 miners, mostly Muslims
of the Hui minority, penetrated this remote and uninhabited area
to sift gravel for the precious metal. With the influx of miners, the
county government established in 1992 what it called the Western
Work Committee under the leadership of Jiesand Suonan Dajie, a
deputy party secretary. The committee went to check on the gold
mining but encountered so much chiru poaching that the committee changed its focus to wildlife protection and began patrolling the
region. Suonan Dajie was killed in January 1994 when he drew his
gun in a confrontation with one poacher and was shot by another.
Four of the poachers in this gang were later caught. But why not the
others, including the killer? The complete story remained to be told.
Seventeen years later, on December 28, 2011, the Chinese newspaper *Global Times* reported that one more of these poachers had been
arrested and six others had surrendered. "Police are still searching for
the last four members of the group, officials said." In the meantime,
Suonan Dajie had become a national hero. His patrol team, dubbed
the Wild Yak Brigade by the media, virtually ceased its antipoaching
activities when the area became the Kekexili Reserve in 1996 and
the government took over the patrol duties. The Wild Yak Brigade
kept no detailed records, but one former member told me they had
confiscated between 8,000 and 9,000 chiru hides. When in 1997
we struggled for days through mud and snow to reach the Kekexili
calving grounds and failed, we did not know that poachers had preceded us there. I am glad that we did not.

Two years after our Kekexili visit, in April 1999, the Forestry
Public Security bureaus of Qinghai, Tibet, and Xinjiang joined
forces in an antipoaching sweep that included over a hundred police. The Kekexili region alone yielded 71 poachers in 19 camps, 18
vehicles, 12,000 bullets, 1,754 chiru hides, and 545 chiru heads with
horns. When caught and convicted, poachers receive stiff prison
sentences. In 1998, for example, forest police in Tibet arrested 10

poachers with 461 hides, and the court sentenced them to prison for four to nineteen years.

How many chiru have been killed throughout their range on the Tibetan Plateau? In December 1998, the State Forestry Administration released this statement: "An official analysis according to confiscated pelts and wool, and discarded carcasses, has estimated that about 20,000 antelopes are poached each year. . . . An incomplete statistic shows that, since 1990, there have been over 100 cases [of poaching]. . . . 17,000 pelts and 1,100 kg of wool confiscated, 300 guns and 153 vehicles seized, nearly 3,000 people arrested and 3 poachers shot dead."

If the estimated average of 20,000 slaughtered chiru a year represents the correct order of magnitude, then 180,000 died between 1990 and 1998. The 1,100 kg of confiscated wool translates to about 11,000 chiru, based on about ten chiru hides per kilogram of wool. This figure, added to the 17,000 confiscated hides, totals 28,000 chiru. It is unlikely that more than 10–15 percent of the hides and wool in the trade are intercepted by police, making the official kill estimate very conservative. Looking at the annual shawl production in Kashmir during these years, one estimate is 5,000 to 11,000 shawls. There are roughly three chiru per shawl, so a total of 15,000 to 33,000 chiru died each year to support the deadly fashion. These crude calculations indicate, then, that at least 250,000–300,000 chiru died during the 1990s.

The hides would have been sold to traders who in 1995 paid the equivalent of thirty-five to fifty dollars per hide in Golmud, the town closest to Kekexili; by 1999 the price had risen to seventy dollars. Next, guard hairs (that is, the coarse outer hairs of an animal's coat) and the soft inner wool had to be plucked from the hides. This was done casually and in the open, as we had witnessed in Gerze in 1990, but with more rigorous enforcement it was hidden away in back rooms in Lhasa and elsewhere. Then the wool, still mixed with guard hairs, had to be smuggled to India, to the city of Srinagar in the state of Jammu and Kashmir, to be manufactured into shawls. There are several main smuggling routes. A favored one is by truck over the highway from Lhasa to Kathmandu in Nepal. Sacks of chiru wool can be hidden in trucks loaded with sheep wool, stored in a false ceiling of a truck, sewn into mattresses and sleeping bags, and stuffed into empty gasoline barrels.

In February 1999, I watched trucks pass through the Chinese border post of Zhangmu and the Nepal post of Kadari. Few trucks were checked, especially not those whose driver slipped money into the hand of the border guard. At other places it is easy for small caravans to sneak over a remote mountain pass into Nepal, a country infamous for its laxity in interdicting the illegal wildlife trade. Once in Kathmandu, traders can travel by plane, bus, or train to Delhi and on to Srinagar. Other routes go directly from Tibet into India. For example, south of holy Mount Kailas is the border town of Burang, from which wool can be carried over the high Lipulekh Pass into India. And there is the ancient trade route west to Leh in Ladakh. The border was officially closed when the India-China war erupted in 1962. As border control became more assertive, new smuggling routes had to be found. One long detour takes smugglers to far western Xinjiang and by road to Pakistan, where, it is said, profits from smuggling assist the activities of militants, and on to Kashmir. Wool is now even smuggled by air via Singapore.

China made an increasing effort during the 1990s to control poaching, but the Tibetan Plateau is vast, patrols were few, the poachers determined, and the borders porous. Although there was some interdiction of wool at borders, much of this contraband filtered through. Between 1993 and 1999, for example, Nepal officially confiscated 659 kg, and just from 1992 to 1994 India confiscated 708 kg. However, it is not possible to estimate how many kilograms of such wool actually remain confiscated. Nepal custom officials have been accused of reselling to India seized chiru wool labeled as "rabbit fur," a tactic somewhat reminiscent of Australia in 1924 when two million koala pelts were exported disguised as "wombat" to elude public protest. Customs officials in China do not necessarily inform the Forestry and Wildlife Departments of chiru wool seizures. The wool may be turned over to the Animal By-Product Department, which has been rumored to resell it illegally. On occasion, traders from China may also barter chiru wool for other wildlife products, such as musk deer musk and tiger bones, which are used in traditional medicines. Thus, tigers are slaughtered in India to provide medicine of dubious value in China, while chiru are slaughtered in China to provide a fashion fix elsewhere.

When, in the early 1990s, I had made the Tibet Forestry Department aware that chiru poaching was not just a local issue, and that trade in the wool had become an international problem, officials encouraged me to publicize this worldwide. This I did in the years that followed. The Wildlife Conservation Society alerted the conservation community, and prepared a "Facts about Shahtoosh" sheet after noting that the Bergdorf Goodman department store in New York still sold the shawls in 1995. Many of the prominent fashion houses and other outlets to whom the fact sheet was sent, Bergdorf Goodman included, took the shawls off their shelves. The World Wildlife Fund (WWF) and International Union for the Conservation of Nature (IUCN) alerted its international members and the public as well.

In India, I was fortunate to be brought into contact with Ashok Kumar, the director of TRAFFIC–India, who was responsible for wildlife trade matters. Later he joined conservation activist Belinda Wright at the Wildlife Protection Society of India, an organization she founded in 1994. Together, they had a tremendous impact on chiru conservation by monitoring the shahtoosh trade in the country, working with police to apprehend dealers in these illegal shawls, and trying to force Kashmir to adhere to the country's international agreements in the trade of endangered species. In 1997, they published an influential report on the chiru trade entitled "Fashioned for Extinction."

Much was soon known about how the wool passed from the chiru killers to the traders and on to the smugglers, but relatively little attention had focused on the manufacturers of the shawls in the city of Srinagar in Kashmir and those who distribute them worldwide. How the manufacture of a shahtoosh shawl begins is a process described well in *Wrap Up the Trade*, a 2001 report published by the International Fund for Animal Welfare and the Wildlife Trust of India. It takes from one to one and a half months to produce a shawl. As a first step, the guard hairs have to be separated from the fleece or underwool, a delicate task done only by women, each of whom may produce merely fifty grams in a day's work. The belly of a chiru has the highest proportion of fleece to guard hairs. White fleece from the belly of chiru and from males in their courting pelage is more valuable ($750/kg) than the typical soft brown ($500/kg). Next the wool goes to the spinners, again women exclusively, who spin the wool into threads. Only Kashmiri women have learned to handle the short, fine fleece, one reason the wool has for centuries gone to them. The threads now have to be soaked in a special starch and resin solution to make them stronger, after which they are inserted into the loom for weaving. Only men weave the actual shawl. Afterward washers clean the shawl of starch and resin. A clipper removes protruding threads, a dyer adds color, and a darner closes any holes and removes imperfections. Finally a designer creates special and distinctive designs which an embroiderer then adds to the shawl with silk thread. During the late 1990s, an estimated 14,300 Kashmiris were involved in this eleven-step production process, three-quarters of them women.

William Moorcroft noted in the early 1820s that at the time only two of the many looms in Srinagar wove shahtoosh shawls. Even around 1950, a mere 20–30 kg of chiru wool was estimated to have reached Kashmir annually. By 1997, the amount had risen a thousandfold to around 3,000 kg or the product of 30,000 chiru, according to *Wrap Up the Trade*. By the turn of the new century there were seventy shahtoosh manufacturers at work in Kashmir.

Many shahtoosh shawls are blended with 50 percent or more pashmina wool to make them wear better and retain their elegance longer. The fibers of chiru fleece are so short that they tend to escape the weave and make a shawl look ragged, "like an old dish cloth," as one article phrased it. An average woman's shawl is about 2 m by 1 m (6.5 feet by 3.3 feet) in size, and a man's is 3 m by 1.5 m. One kilogram of wool (guard hairs and fleece) separates into about 350 g of fleece, enough to make about three shawls. Shawls of pure shahtoosh may require the fleece from three to five chiru. Even if blended with pashmina, any woman who wears shahtoosh has the bodies of three chiru draped over her shoulders—a shroud, not a shawl.

Prices of shawls depend on the size, the color, and the extent of embroidery. A manufacturer in the 1990s might sell a simple beige or white shawl to a trader in India for perhaps $800. The retail price on the international market would have been at least double or triple that figure. And a particularly beautiful embroidered shawl might have a price tag of $15,000 or more.

Shahtoosh shawls have for centuries been a prized adornment on the Indian subcontinent. Shawls became fashionable in Europe, especially in France, in the late 1700s, most of them no doubt of cashmere, made from goat wool. However, Napoleon is said to have given his wife Josephine a genuine shahtoosh shawl. Shawls were then items of male attire, and at first Parisian women did not know what to do with them. Josephine and her friends apparently had the idea of draping shawls over their shoulders, initiating a fashion craze for cashmere which Napoleon tried to curtail by banning imports in 1806.

I have little idea how the craze for shahtoosh started in developed countries. In Italy the couturiers promoted the dyeing of shawls into different colors and embroidering them with beautiful designs, making them more attractive than the natural beige and white. And in 1964, Stanley Marcus of the Neiman Marcus department store found shahtoosh shawls in India and imported them into the United States. But it was not until the late 1980s that the trade so exploded that it became a crisis for the species.

By the late 1990s it was still legal to sell shahtoosh in only two places: Switzerland and Kashmir. Switzerland finally acceded in 1998 to the international CITES convention, which regulates trade in wildlife. Kashmir is of course officially a part of India, but in its accession agreement with India in 1947, Kashmir was allowed to decide some of its own internal regulations even if these were contrary to the laws of the central government in Delhi. India had signed CITES, joining 141 other countries at that time, whereas Kashmir remained vigorously recalcitrant when confronted both by Delhi and the international community. As Kashmir's chief minister at the time, Farooq Abdullah, said: "Shahtoosh will be banned in Kashmir over my dead body." (He survived the later ban.)

Starting in 1994, enforcement agencies in various countries began to raid and seize shawls in high-end boutiques, from traders in expensive hotels, and in other locations visited by the wealthy. Between 1994 and 1999, for example, the number of confiscated shawls in Hong Kong was 538, United Kingdom 172, France 617, Italy 355, Nepal 559, and India 800, for a total of 3,041. Seizures continued with 537 in Switzerland between 2000 and 2007, 90 in Dubai in 2004, and 230 in India between 2002 and 2007, to give an idea. The confiscated shawls from just these samples represent conservatively around 11,700 chiru.

The illegal trade continues as greed triumphs over morality. In a letter dated August 21, 2009, Ashok Kumar wrote me: "There have been a number of seizures at Delhi airport in recent months, all going to the Middle East." When I passed through Dubai in 2007, I visited a couple of Kashmiri shops. I fingered the cashmere shawls on the shelves and then asked for something finer. Shahtoosh shawls readily appeared from beneath the counter.

To hold, indeed to fondle, shahtoosh, to feel its softness and lightness, is truly a luxurious experience. I can understand why the shawls so readily entered the wardrobes of the wealthy. A human hair is about 100 microns in diameter (1 micron equals 1/1,000 mm). The fleece of an ibex is 14–17 microns, no different than fine cashmere or pashmina. The vicuña, a South American relative of the camel which was once considered to yield the ultimate in fine wool, has fleece of 12.5 microns. But chiru wool averages 10–12 microns. Human touch can detect a difference of a mere 1 micron. No wonder the chiru has become such a fashion attraction.

Anyone who has sold or bought shahtoosh shawls from the late 1990s onward is well aware that it is illegal, that they are buying not just a shawl but the lives of chiru. Police and customs officials of various countries had by 2000 made a major effort to control the trade. London's Metropolitan Police, with its small but dedicated Wildlife Unit under the leadership of Andy Fisher, initiated Operation Charm to inform the public about wildlife trade. In 1997 his operation seized 138 shawls worth $565,000 from a boutique named "Kashmir" in London's exclusive Mayfair district. The shop was owned by the Renaissance Corporation, whose parent company, the Indian Cottage Industries Exposition, advertised shahtoosh as coming "from the chin of the Ibex goat."

In October 1998 two dedicated members of the Wildlife Conservation Society, Catherine Cahill and Alison Stern, hosted a luncheon for some of their acquaintances and friends. I was asked to show photographs of the Tibetan Plateau, of the beautiful spacious terrain, of wild yak, cranes, and other wildlife, including chiru females suckling their young. And then, casually, I showed slides of chiru carcasses and severed heads. "It was hysterical," recalls Catherine Cahill to Bob Colacello as quoted in a November 1999 *Vanity Fair* article. At first "everyone was oohing and aahing. And then there was this nomad with a leghold trap, and there was an audible gasp and all over the room you could see shahtooshes sliding surreptitiously under the tables. . . ." But the sight of bloody hides is not enough to deter everyone from buying shawls. As Bob Colacello further notes, "several women reportedly left the luncheon and went straight to the nearby apartment of an art-book publisher, where the former model from Paris was on hand to sell them more shahtooshes."

Four years earlier, in November 1994, a charity event had been held at New York's Mayfair Hotel to benefit an anonymous group, the Dream Team, which helps terminally ill patients at Memorial Sloan-Kettering Hospital. Hosted by well-known socialites, the event drew a large crowd concerned with doing good—and interested in buying shahtoosh shawls, which had been provided by Cocoon America, a company based in Hong Kong. No one suspected that special agents Tara Dunn, Nancy Hillary, and others of the U.S. Fish and Wildlife Service's Division of Law Enforcement were investigating the illegal importation and sale of shahtoosh. One outcome was that those who bought shawls at the event were issued with subpoenas nearly five years later, in July 1999, to appear at the United States District Court in, of all places, Newark, New Jersey. No buyers were actually prosecuted because few seemed to be aware of the illegal nature of their purchase of an animal product whose import into the United States had been illegal since 1975. Some buyers even gave up their shawls to the Fish and Wildlife Service. However, that sentiment was not shared by all, as Colacello discovered when interviewing a number of ladies for his article:

> "And let me tell you, once you own one shahtoosh, you want more and more and more."

"What do you mean, people have to turn in their shahtooshes? I haven't heard anything so ridiculous in a long time."

"The shahtoosh thing is all a fiction of the animal-rights fanatics."

Awareness about the massacre of chiru seeped into public consciousness slowly at first. As early as 1993, *National Geographic* published an article by me that discusses the shahtoosh issue; in 1995 the *International Herald Tribune* did a piece, and other articles began to appear as well. But it was not until the late 1990s that the media focused on the problem, partly as a result of the Newark court case involving high-society figures. There were articles in the *Wall Street Journal* and the *New York Post*, in *Time*, *Newsweek*, *U.S. News & World Report*, and *People* magazines, and also in more specialized magazines such as *BBC Wildlife* and *International Game Warden*. *Paris Vogue* published a piece entitled "Alerte, shahtoosh interdit." Yet some fashion magazines still didn't get it. In June 1998 *Harper's Bazaar* carried an advertisement, placed by the Malo boutique, offering shahtoosh shawls for $2,950 each, while the following June *British Vogue* promoted shawls as a "survival tactic" for dull parties.

The 1994 benefit at the Sloan-Kettering Memorial Hospital had repercussions, too, for the company that provided the shahtoosh shawls. Two officials of Cocoon America were each fined $32,000 and the company itself was fined $10,000. Navarang Exports of Bombay, which supplied 308 shawls to Cocoon, was fined $5,000 (the price of one shawl). These were the first such U.S. prosecutions. The following year Mansfield Enterprises, a retailer in Beverly Hills, California, was fined $175,000 for importing shahtoosh in the mid-1990s. As part of the court settlement, it was also required to take out a public service advertisement in fashion magazines expressing regret for its actions.

How do you distinguish shahtoosh from pashmina and other wool? This is a critical question when bringing retailers and others to court. The problem becomes even more complex because many shawls contain a mixture of chiru and goat wool. Early court cases had collapsed because there was no proof of identification. Forensic laboratories in the United Kingdom, France, and Italy, as well as the

U.S. National Fish and Wildlife Service Forensic Laboratory analyzed guard hairs and fleece of chiru, domestic goat, and ibex, among
others. The hairs of each species have a distinctive scale pattern on
the surface. This pattern is easy to discern in guard hairs, but not in
fleece. However, some guard hairs, or kemp fibers as they are sometimes called, inevitably can be found in shawls. These fibers are crin-
kly and brittle in chiru if compared to those of the domestic goat. In
chiru these hairs are oval in cross section, whereas they are kidney-
shaped in goats. These and other forensic features became admissible
evidence for the first time in a court case in Hong Kong. In 1997,
Hong Kong authorities raided a private venture in the Furama Hotel and seized many shawls. On April 13, 1999, Bharati Assomull, the
owner of the enterprise, received a three-month suspended sentence
and a fine of $40,000, the conviction obtained with the help of
the U.S. Fish and Wildlife's Service Forensic Laboratory. These days,
DNA as well as fiber characteristics are widely used for identifying
shahtoosh in court cases.

The court cases and media attention markedly changed perceptions. There was increasing disgust against the shahtoosh trade,
against a beautiful species becoming a fashion victim and a walking
graveyard. By the close of the twentieth century, celebrity models in
the fashion industry even took a stand against wearing shahtoosh.
Women who continued to wear the shawls were sometimes openly
criticized by peers who now considered the shawls "dead chic."
Stores selling shahtoosh were occasionally boycotted. For wearing
shahtoosh, socialites and celebrities, such as Donna Karan and Prin-
cess Marie-Chantal of Greece, made public "worst-dressed" lists.

In spite of such actions, the attitudes of shahtoosh wearers with
more money than morals did not change. *Harper's Bazaar*, in a February 2000 article entitled "Crimes of Fashion," elicited these responses:

> "A law doesn't make a bit of difference on cold Park Avenue."
> "It's such a boring subject."
> "A Himalayan goat? It's so far removed."

Wear it and be damned, seemed to be the attitude. Private sales
were probably the largest source of shawls in the late 1990s and

they still continue. Buyers fly to Delhi for private showings, and return with a suitcase full of shawls. It's so easy for most passengers to pass through customs. On the custom declaration one simply lists "shawls"; even the word "cashmere" does not point to a particular species. "Every single divorcee who needs some extra cash that I know in London sells them," an informant told Bob Colacello in 1999.

When I gave talks in the 1990s about my Tibetan work at such places as the Asia Society in New York, I naturally showed photographs of the chiru slaughter and Tibetan poaching camps. Rather naively I did not anticipate an occasional outraged reaction from some members of the audience. I was treading on romantic preconceptions of Tibetan nomads living in harmony with all living beings, people who thus would never kill chiru and if they did, certainly not for profit. I was also inadvertently muddling the political agenda of Tibetan organizations in the United States that placed all blame for poaching on the Han Chinese. I was accused of being a voice of the Chinese government, once of dressing up Han Chinese to look like Tibetans for my photographs, and other misdeeds. My policy has always been to work on behalf of conservation with any government, no matter its politics and policies, with everyone from Afghanistan and Russia to Iran and Myanmar, and from Mongolia to the United States. After all, the people of every country depend on a healthy environment for their future. So I simply continued my work in China, observing, writing, and cooperating with the government and local scientists to promote conservation.

In an attempt to curtail the trade in chiru wool, the Secretariat of CITES and China held a workshop October 12–14, 1999, entitled "On the Conservation and Control of Trade in the Tibetan Antelope." The workshop was held in Xining, the capital of Qinghai, a province that had seen a great deal of chiru slaughter. Officials from customs, environmental ministries, wildlife and forestry departments, conservation organizations, and others from China, Italy, France, the United Kingdom, Nepal, India, and the United States attended. Out of the meeting came, among other things, the Xining Declaration, which urged all countries to ban the internal trade of shahtoosh, strengthen law enforcement, and share information within and between countries.

The century and millennium thus ended with shahtoosh finally on the international agenda. But there was still one major problem: Kashmir continued to manufacture the shawls. The demand for shawls seemed insatiable, and, as with any illicit high-priced goods such as drugs, someone is always ready to supply them. After all, as one dealer said, selling shahtoosh is like "minting money."

In April 1998, the Wildlife Protection Society of India (WPSI) petitioned the Kashmir High Court to ban the trade of shahtoosh in the state and to adhere to the country's Wildlife Protection Act of 1972, which includes the chiru as a fully protected species. Four years later, after various delaying tactics, the Kashmir government finally gave the chiru full protection—and took no action to implement its decision whatsoever. Not deterred, WPSI went to India's Supreme Court, which in April 2006 ruled that anyone who had not obtained a certificate of possession for any shahtoosh shawl, scarf, or blanket within two months was likely to have it confiscated. Yet again nothing much changed. The illegal trade continued. As one newspaper noted in August 2007, the Kashmir "government is turning a blind eye to this flourishing business." At least India's media was showing concern over the chiru's plight. When it became known that Jacqueline Sundquist, the wife of the U.S. ambassador to India, had purchased a shahtoosh, there was a furor over this "shawl of shame."

It was finally admitted by those involved in the trade that the chiru is the source of the wool—but not that the animal was killed to obtain it. The Kashmir State Handicraft Department, for example, still denied in 1998 that chiru were actually being slaughtered. And Mohammad Nisin of the Kashmir Wool Board had gone before parliament the previous year and asserted against all evidence that the wool was plucked from bushes. The Kashmir Trader's Welfare Association asked rhetorically, "Do you think we would kill the goose that lays the golden eggs?" Of course they would: it's literally a cut-throat business. Traders wondered why, if the chiru was so rare, the wool supply had actually increased over the preceding five years, not realizing that the surge would be followed by a crash when the herds had been so decimated that hunting the scattered remnants would become arduous and unprofitable. Seemingly concerned about the status of chiru, India decided to survey the chiru population from the air in Ladakh. China, of course, was off limits to an Indian helicopter, and Ladakh was known to have at most a few hundred chiru in a remote corner, many of them visitors from China during summer. Omar Abdullah, the union minister of state for commerce, soon reported that "we have found no evidence of poaching on the Indian side. If there is poaching on the Chinese side, then why should our people be punished for it?"

In August 2000 the Shahtoosh Association still maintained that "shahtoosh is not obtained from slaughtered animals," and Kamal Nath, India's union minister for forests and environment, asserted that "there is no evidence of slaughter of chiru." Yet a senior official from Minister Nath's own department had attended the 1999 chiru conference in China, where all such matters were presented in detail. Still, in 2001 a dealer was quoted as saying: "There is no proof that the animal is killed for its wool."

When facts are conveniently ignored, perceptions congealed, and income threatened, and when politics intervenes, then it becomes necessary to find conspiracy theories. An Indian newspaper, *The Hindu*, reported on January 11, 1998, that "the traders believe that it is an influential American lobby which is behind the crisis. The aim, they say, is to edge the Kashmiri shawl out of global competition." No, it's really a Chinese conspiracy, other Kashmiris say, according to the *Hindustan Times* of December 26, 1999:

> According to the shahtoosh trade, Kashmir is suffering because of a Chinese plot to control the world pashmina trade. . . . The only threat to the Chinese stranglehold on the world pashmina trade is shahtoosh, which is far smoother than the Chinese silk pashmina. The Chinese do not have the expertise to weave it by hand. . . . Conceding that this sounds paranoid, Kashmir government officials point out that with the exception of Schaller's original report, much of the information about chiru poaching comes from the Chinese government. Why, they ask, should we believe the Chinese when it is clear they have a commercial interest?

When the producers of shawls realized in the late 1990s that production might be banned, they petitioned the Kashmiri government for compensation if jobs were lost. Weavers and others were naturally concerned. As shahtoosh shawl production declined some manufacturers left the business. More and more weavers of cashmere had shifted to shahtoosh. A woman weaving cashmere earned one dollar per day, whereas one weaving shahtoosh earned up to four dollars. By 2001, however, according to *Beyond the Ban* (2003), published by the Wildlife Trust of India and the International Fund for Animal Welfare, about 55 percent of the workers had shifted completely from shahtoosh back to cashmere, 16 percent wove both kinds of wool, 11 percent were unemployed, and the remaining few still did shahtoosh.

The Kashmir shawl trade has many problems. Some Kashmiri weavers are said to have moved to Kathmandu in Nepal. Once, the name "pashmina" signified a cashmere-wool product of highest quality. Soon almost all shawls, whether made in China, India, or elsewhere, were called "pashmina," regardless of quality, thus depriving real pashmina shawls of their exclusive luxury cachet. Weavers of goat wool in Punjab state also manufactured what they called "Kashmir" shawls. And, finally, basic cashmere shawls are now machine-made, except for washing, clipping, and embroidery, at a great loss of jobs. Shahtoosh, however, remains entirely handmade. With the word *pashmina* reduced to meaning no more than "cashmere," there is now an effort to produce a high-quality handmade product under the name of "Kashmina" or "Shahmina." To add to the confusion of names, a company in Italy, Iltex S.r.l., now markets shawls of goat wool under the name of "ecotoosh" and "ecoshahtoosh."

When confronted with the decline of an endangered species, officials search for a quick and easy solution, and the idea that all too often comes to mind is: "Let's build a captive breeding facility." It may not be known how to capture and maintain the animals properly, and there may be no plan of how and where those bred can safely be returned to the wild, but the appearance of action is what counts.

Besides, the money a government provides to build the facility is attractive to local officials. No wonder defunct breeding centers litter the globe. The Jammu and Kashmir state government promptly promoted captive breeding of chiru in the early 1990s, less to save the species than to earn money from the wool. It even erected a sign in Ladakh: "Chiru Breeding Centre." Since India barely has any chiru of its own, it would have to obtain them from China, a vague dream. With one shawl requiring the wool of three chiru, how many captives would be needed to produce more than a token amount of wool? And how do you remove the wool? You cannot yank the fleece and guard hairs from a live animal by the handful. If a chiru were sheared like a vicuna, the fleece would be too short to weave. Fortunately, the breeding center does not so far exist beyond a sign proclaiming it.

Qinghai offers a useful lesson in managing a breeding center. In the 1990s it fenced off 200 hectares (500 acres) of the Chang Tang in the chiru's natural habitat adjacent to the Golmud-Lhasa highway. This pen was stocked with young chiru captured in the wild, but so many died that the idea of a breeding center was abandoned. The program actually made no sense, economically or otherwise, because the region still harbors thousands of chiru which need only protection from poachers. The breeding center became a chiru orphanage. Once a youngster is grown, it is given its freedom.

With the dawn of the new century there was a perceptible change for the better, partly because of rigorous antipoaching measures, including the confiscation of most guns from households, and also because of increased media attention. (In a gustatory note, the *Bangkok Post* reported in 2002 that chiru "have started to appear on Shanghai restaurant menus.") Newspapers and magazines throughout China published chiru stories and China Central Television ran documentaries. A feature film based on the exploits of the Wild Yak Brigade titled "Mountain Patrol–Kekexili" gained worldwide distribution. Several Chinese nongovernmental organizations, such as Friends of Nature, Green River, and the Snowland Great Rivers Environmental Protection Association, promoted chiru conservation both in the field and among the public. And the chiru became a mascot of the 2008 Olympic Games held in Beijing.

Not that poaching ceased, but it was much reduced. Motorized gangs found it more difficult to operate with impunity, though individuals continued to kill. The motorcycle is now ubiquitous on the Tibetan Plateau and it has become a principal weapon of the hunt. Dawa Tsering, then of World Wildlife Fund–Lhasa, told me that hunters bounce cross-country at 60 km per hour and chase chiru until they collapse, wholly exhausted, and are then killed. Or the hunter drives up beside the frantically fleeing animal and clubs it to death. By these and other means chiru wool is still obtained to fuel the shahtoosh shawl trade, particularly in western Tibet, as described by Joseph Fox and his two colleagues in a 2009 issue of the journal *Oryx*:

> Antelopes are still hunted for their wool and, although traditional trapping is still involved, modern rifles are available, sometimes supplied by illicit traders or local officials. . . . It is well known in this area that itinerant traders from eastern Tibet now bring guns and motorcycles to Gertse County to trade for antelope skins and sometimes also participate in the hunting.

In February 2009, news reports surfaced that customs at the Delhi airport had seized two shipments, one with 455 shahtoosh shawls and the other with 1,290 shawls consigned for export to Dubai, Oman, Qatar, and other Gulf countries, though Europe also continues to be a market. In June 2010 Farooq Ahmad Shah, chairman of the Traders and Manufacturers Federation of Kashmir, said without apparent concern, "The sale and export of shahtoosh shawls in the Kashmir art and handloom showrooms situated in various five-star hotels has been good in the past few years." Why are such shops not raided by police? Much remains to be done in India and elsewhere.

But, on the whole, the situation has improved, particularly in China, to which our frequent surveys on the Tibetan Plateau can attest. Many local officials now protect the chiru with support of their communities. As a result, most chiru living in pastoral areas are noticeably tamer than they were a decade ago, often just watching passing vehicles or walking slowly away. Indeed, along the

Golmud-Lhasa highway and adjoining railroad they may even ignore trucks roaring past. In some areas the chiru are definitely increasing in number, according to local people and also judging by our counts.

Constant vigilance of the populations in China and of the international trade in shahtoosh will have to be maintained to assure the chiru its survival. But after the dispiriting mass slaughter of the 1990s, the increase in chiru numbers during the past decade is a sign that the species may have a reasonably secure future.

Chapter 5

A Gift to the Spirit

In the summer of 2007, I meet Abu as usual on my arrival in Lhasa. He has recently retired as head of the Tibet Forestry Department, a position from which he always greatly helped me. From a nomad family, with a liking for the Chang Tang, he is a person of forceful intuitive and impulsive actions. Recently returned from a horseback trip to the Tian Shui River, he excitedly tells me about the many pregnant chiru females and newborns he has seen there—very near where we had been in mid-July 1991 when we observed migrating females and young without realizing that we were so near the calving ground of the Central Chang Tang population. After the carnage of the shahtoosh trade, the news of many females and young at a calving ground excites me greatly, and I am immediately concerned that poachers might invade this area, as they have others, and that we must find out more about it.

With this information, Kang Aili and I definitely want to visit that calving ground. Two years pass, both of us busy with other projects. But in 2009 we are finally ready to begin our sixth trip together to chronicle wildlife on the Tibetan Plateau and the Pamir Mountains. On the staff of the Wildlife Conservation Society's China program, Aili has been its main field biologist. The European Union-China Biodiversity Programme gave the Wildlife Conservation Society and its partners, including the Tibet Forestry Department, the World Wildlife Fund, and the Tibet Academy of Agricultural and Animal Sciences, a grant to study the wildlife and pastoral communities of the Chang Tang with the goal of producing a conservation plan. Since the chiru is a classic landscape species, defining the Chang Tang with its wanderings across various habitats, it is a perfect subject for study in this program. But scientific and conservation issues aside, I simply look forward to visiting the site, this time early enough to find newborns.

On June 12 we leave the county town of Nyima in two Land Cruisers and a truck. Our route takes us north through a series of basins, some dry, some with lakes, but all of them wintering grounds of the Central Chang Tang chiru population. A few male chiru loaf around there but the females have gone. Kiang are abundant as usual in these fine grasslands—we count 475—before we reach the Rongma *xiang*, a regional administrative center by the lake Yibug Caka. A male kiang lies by the roadside, his groin bloody but his cause of death unknown. Someone has hacked off his sex organs to be used for traditional medicine, but at least the carcass has been opened for scavengers, and already two Himalayan griffon vultures and three ravens are feasting. A little farther on an old female kiang had a foreleg caught in the mesh of a livestock fence and died there.

From Rongma a dirt track climbs onto a high plateau where the huge glacial massif of Ma-i-kan (Meyer Kangri) fills the horizon. A few male chiru are here too. High on distant slopes are two herds of wild yak, one numbering 75, the other 179. But we are still in an area with pastoralists and their livestock. Wild bulls abscond at times with domestic females and hybridize, and, unless this is prevented, the wild yak as we know it could disappear from the Tibetan Plateau.

As the road winds off the plateau, we catch up with the female migration. The animals are scattered like confetti in a broad valley leading northwest. Aili and Liu Tong, a man in his early twenties with an upturned nose, scraggly goatee, and infectious enthusiasm, count those in sight and tally 2003. Herds flee from us in long waving lines, the evening sun glinting golden on their hides. At 16,000 feet in view of low rolling hills and a snow-covered range, the Seru Kangri, the rough vehicle track ends at a two-room cement Protection Station, empty at present. Phutsong, a local herdsman and wildlife guard, arrives on his motorcycle to join us as guide. The county government moved a dozen families into this valley a decade ago, right into the supposedly protected core area of the reserve, and, as we now discover, right into the main migratory path of the chiru. Having been given land rights, such new settlers cannot easily be moved out. I worry that livestock fences, heavily promoted by government, will disrupt the migration. There is, unfortunately, little cooperation between the Tibet Forestry Department, the Agriculture and Animal Husbandry Department, county administrations, and others, making integrated planning inside and outside of the reserve—good policies, good management—an elusive goal, yet one that is still nevertheless essential for maintaining the ecological integrity of the Chang Tang.

We remain two days at the Protection Station to become familiar with the area. Aili and Tong count chiru in the valley one day and obtain a figure of 6,824, to which in another part of the same valley Zhang Ming Wang, another coworker with the Wildlife Conservation Society, and I add 2,055. In this one valley there are on the order of 9,000 females, and we have no idea how many have already passed. Ming Wang and I also stroll over the pastures to collect fresh droppings of chiru and domestic sheep. Preserved in formalin, one tube for each animal, the droppings will later be analyzed by veterinarian Stephane Ostrowski of the Wildlife Conservation Society and his Chinese coworkers to see if they contain parasites such as the eggs of roundworm and tape worm, or any of various protozoans. This will determine which parasites are shared between wild and domestic animals and might affect health.

The chiru will soon give birth and we must hurry on to await them at the calving ground. The Tibetan truck driver and his assistant, who have also been hired to cook, refuse to go on, afraid for themselves and their erratic truck. Awang Ren Qing of the Forest Police, a small, hunched Tibetan permanently engulfed in the smoke of his cigarettes, responds with his usual decisive inaction. The dynamics of some field teams are good, whereas in others there is a divide between those who want to go home or contribute a minimum to the collective effort, and those dedicated to the work. We already have such a split. The Tibetan driver Lun Zhun, the three Han Chinese, and I are keen to learn, whereas the others play cards and sleep late, even the cooks staying in bed while we scavenge for breakfast. Not all of us acquired a taste for the Chang Tang. Phut-song, a charming, quiet man with shoulder-length hair and a cow-boy hat, does not readily fit into either group. When I write notes, he sometimes sits on the tent floor beside me and reads aloud from a booklet of pika fables which I wrote to convey how ecologically useful pikas are to the grasslands. Since the fables have been ren-dered into Tibetan, I do not understand what he says though we commune nonverbally.

Because the truck drivers refuse to budge, we now follow the chiru with a peculiar caravan consisting of two Land Cruisers, a small tractor-pulled wagon, and three loaded motorcycles, the new transport hired from local households. On the other side of several low ridges is Garkund Lake, and here we watch about a thousand females in several herds move toward the northwest and then many more appear. The tractor's engine quits. We camp nearby while the Land Cruisers return for the marooned baggage. I argue that we need to take cans of gasoline, not crates of cabbage, and that we must have the truck. The next day a hefty increase in the salary of the truck drivers infuses them with willpower and the truck with horsepower. While waiting for the transport to be organized, Tong and I climb high into a valley of the Seru Kangri and there we meet a lynx. The sky is clear but the wind roars and pounds us without respite. I happily hike over plains and into mountains all day, feeling fit and content to be on foot. Occasionally a team member com-ments that I'm doing well for my age. What a depressing thought; I am but seventy-six years old and in good health, and my body and mind feel young.

The chiru follow a valley that slices north through the Seru Kangi to the Tian Shui River. On one hillside are sixty-five well-beaten trails, made by the hooves of centuries. The valley, however, is so boggy that the truck cannot advance. Again we must leave it behind and use the Land Cruisers to ferry food and equipment to a base camp by a small lake above the river. Chiru females move past single file onto the river flats. Our big kitchen tent is up, all our gear is under cover, and research can now begin.

We see many chiru cross the river to vanish northward into the hills. One of our cars follows them, but I prefer to spend that day,

June 21, on foot, strolling and counting the herds which are moving rapidly, twenty and thirty females together. One female stands alone and suckles a baby one or two days old. When the other team members return they report seeing thousands of chiru and twenty-two newborns. We have arrived here just in time.

Lying in the cocoon of my sleeping bag during the long hours of night waiting for dawn, my thoughts distill life past and present. In over half a century of fieldwork I still sleep in cold tents, frost crystals around my face in the morning, just as I did during the 1950s in Alaska, during the 1970s in the Himalaya and Karakoram of Nepal and Pakistan, and from the 1980s onward on the Tibetan Plateau of China and other parts of Central Asia. What am I accomplishing? Why am I doing the same kind of work decade after decade, though in different places? At my age it's come time for a mental summing up.

I strive to do solid science and promote conservation, but, at the same time, I seek a life outdoors, in part a self-indulgent escape from a daily routine. When searching for a personal philosophy, I recall the words of the German poet Johann Friedrich von Schiller: "What the inner voice says will not disappoint the hoping soul." But that inner voice nags at my being a scientific fossil with a narrow focus, unchanging, while others do "hard" science with acronyms like GIS and DNA. I console myself that natural history remains the cornerstone of conservation, that it must be learned on the ground, asking questions, observing, listening, taking notes, getting the boots muddy. Technology helps to open the world but technology can also close it unless one learns directly from nature.

Still, my inner voice points to failures. I have not built anything, no conservation organization, no university department with students, and I have not written a synthesis of my field. Nor, I feel, have I had a basic and original insight, or thought of something that my peers admire and use to create new concepts and ideas. I tend to avoid conferences, seldom give lectures, and shun the spotlight. In sum,

I have not lived up to my potential. I am neither leader nor follower, and instead inadvertently subscribe to the dictum of Ralph Waldo Emerson:"Do not go where the path may lead; go where there is no path and leave a trail." It affords me great pleasure to observe the rich and complex life of another species and to write its biography. After all, the mountain gorilla, tiger, giant panda, and chiru are among the most beautiful expressions of life on Earth. I have published interesting and useful scientific information. But all scientific work, unless there is the grand, everlasting insight of a Darwin, Einstein, or Newton, is soon superseded, forgotten, or rated at most a historical reference as others build upon your research. That is how science must proceed. I have received accolades for my work, such as conservation prizes from organizations in China, India, Japan, Germany, the Netherlands, and the United States, and these I treasure.

In the darkness of my soul, I nevertheless look for something upon which my heart can rest, some accomplishment of lasting value, something beyond myself. I promoted the establishment of nature reserves in China, Pakistan, Brazil, and other countries. But a reserve is stationary, and no matter how well protected and supported by local communities, it may well be subject to climate change, shifting habitat and species, or even elimination because of politics. A reserve may not persist in its present form, if at all, unless it becomes part of a carefully managed landscape.

My wildlife articles and books have inspired some students to seek a life as naturalist. Young local biologists accompany me on most journeys, as on this one to the Chang Tang. I believe that my greatest gift to a country is to leave behind trained nationals who will continue the fight to protect nature's beauty. In this way my legacy of knowledge and spirit will flow onward long after I have ceased to be even a memory.

It is a comforting thought.

The river flats and hills are bleak and the soil stony. Vegetation often covers no more than 1 percent of the ground—just a few cushion plants, tiny tufts of grass cowering in the cracked soil, and patches of coarse *Carex*. What attracts chiru to these desolate hills? Climbing up a slope, we suddenly come upon an oasis, a small drainage with three valleys strikingly green with grasses, the legume *Oxytropis*, its leaves closely cropped by chiru, cushions of silver-leafed Edelweiss, and others. And everywhere are chiru, feeding, resting, ambling, at ease in this secret haven after their long, hard journey. We are entranced by the beauty of the scene. Wonderful. Wonderful. To see all these animals leading their ancient and traditional lives, seemingly unaffected by humankind, is truly a gift to the spirit.

Rapture must give way to hardheaded science in the form of a population count to give to the Tibet Forestry Department. Although, as we discovered, the calving ground extends over 150 square miles, this small, green oasis alone has 9,076 females—by far the most I have ever seen together—the river flats 6,032, and the hills south of the river 1,086, for a minimum total of 16,194 females—and one lone adult male who has blundered into this gathering of expectant mothers. Our figure is a minimum because we no doubt have overlooked animals, and small herds are still arriving, the tail end of the migration. The total includes both adult females and yearling females, although the latter will not give birth until the following year. Yearlings comprise about 13.5 percent of the total. Thus, I calculate that at least 12,500 young will be born.

"I think this may be the largest chiru calving ground in the Chang Tang," Aili comments.

"If you include the males," I reply, thinking of the males our surveys had shown that were mostly to the east and west of here, "this population could have 30,000 animals."

Seeing this great gathering of chiru reminds me of the Mongolian gazelles on the eastern steppes of Mongolia, which I studied during the 1990s, work that is still continued by Kirk Olson. Over one million gazelles persist there, the largest such surviving population of a wild ungulate in Asia. One day in July 1993, I had watched as Mongolian gazelles poured over a ridge and hurried northward. They first came in hundreds and then thousands in a tawny flood, many females accompanied by small young. The air vibrated to the code of yips and bleats by which mothers and their offspring kept contact in the turmoil of the moving throng. My colleague, Jeffrey Griffin, and I set up our tents. Still the gazelle came. We guessed that at least 25,000 passed us while it was still light enough to see. Later, lying in the darkness of my tent, I could still hear the patter of tiny hooves and birdlike cries as more and more Mongolian gazelles passed by until sleep overtook me.

Since the slaughter in the 1990s, at the height of the shahtoosh trade, I have not expected to see so many chiru. It is a great relief that we find no sign of poaching or of any human presence except our lone camp. Humans, however, have hunted here for millennia, and whenever we walk slowly, eyes focused on the ground along the banks of streams and elsewhere, we often find stone tools made by ancient hunters. Tong in particular is an adept spotter of stone tools. He brings me fragment of chert blades, serrated hide scrapers, and inch-long cores from which sharp micro-blades have been struck.

Stone tools of two kinds, of two technologies of different ages, have been found in many places of the eastern Chang Tang, as described by Jeffrey Brantingham, John Olsen, and myself in a report in the journal *Antiquity*. The stone tool sites have not been adequately dated, but, based on what is known from other sites, most were probably made from 13,000 to 15,000 years ago. One example of "large blade and bladelet" technology we identified could be up to 25,000 years old. It pleases me to think that these ancient hunters and I might be witness to the same wildlife spectacle.

Near where we are camped is evidence of another and more recent hunting method. There are long irregular lines of stone mounds, many no more than a foot high, along hillsides and low passes where chiru migrate. I realize that these are what the Tibetans call *dzaekha*: two stone lines, some 500 feet long and wide apart at the mouth, are built to converge and create a funnel. Chiru wander down the funnel and for unknown reasons hesitate to veer aside even though the small widely spaced mounds present no real barrier. At the end of the funnel are anywhere from three to twenty or more traditional foot traps. In interviews with nomads, anthropologist Toni Huber found no moral restraint in hunting pregnant females on their way to the calving ground. In fact the nomads have a saying: "If you kill a female antelope, you will have food; if you don't kill a female antelope, there will be no food."

A calving ground is a place of new life and death. We come upon a female that has just given birth; her wet newborn is trying to struggle to its feet. "Shall we weigh it or leave it in peace?" I ask Aili. "Leave it in peace," she replies, and we go on. Another newborn lies along our route. I put on surgical gloves to hide my odor and place the youngster, a female, into a bag. Tong weighs her at 5.9 pounds. He replaces her gently under the watchful eyes of the nearby mother. Three wolves trot among chiru and one of the wolves then chases a herd. When a youngster veers away from the herd the wolf grabs it and eats it alone. We find the frail body of a newborn partially eaten. What is the cause of death? I dissect the remains and find the tiny tooth punctures of a Tibetan fox on the throat. One female, we discover, died while attempting a breached birth. But another female is just then giving birth, as I record in my field notes:

It is 1203 at noon and a female lies on her side. She restlessly stands up, sometimes turns and lies back down again, a total of nine times in 23 minutes. At 1231 she lies with forequarters raised and kicks dust up with her hind legs. The newborn slides out wet and black, and sand sticks to its body. Its mother still lies but she licks her offspring vigorously. At 1246 she stands and the newborn struggles twice to its feet briefly and tumbles over each time. Both lie a few minutes and then stand up. At 1300 when only half an hour old, the newborn suckles and then circles its mother once. Both lie. At 1330 they walk off, the youngster quite steady on its feet. The scene transcends science and reaches the emotions, touching the heart. It strengthens my covenant to help the chiru endure.

Aili, Tong, Ming Wang, and I like to stand on a ridge overlooking the green oasis to observe such triumphs and tragedies in the lives of the chiru. The weather has been unusually good all month, pleasant for us and lifesaving for the newborns. Only the furious daily wind makes us envy the thick, woolly coat of a chiru. A black speck appears on a distant ridge. A Tibetan brown bear lumbers in our direction, nose to ground as if looking for a newborn or a carcass.

I have not seen bear diggings or old droppings here and surmise the bear has come from the nearby Seru Kangri, attracted by the sudden surfeit of meat. Coming from the other direction is a second bear, a large one, lumbering along with determination. There is no way to escape a curious or unruly bear in this place where the tallest plant is a foot high, and I lead the others into the valley.

The previous night, before seeing the bears, we had slept in the valley, simply stretched out in our sleeping bags, to be near the chiru early in the morning. I lay on my back looking at the stars. At this elevation there is no pollution and the air is strikingly clear. The stars are intensely bright, not twinkling but shining hard and steady like crystals frozen in time. In such a jeweled night, in such absolute silence, I floated through the immensity of the cosmos. Knowing now that a bear or two might investigate us, we do not sleep casually in the open again and instead seek the refuge of camp.

Our food and gasoline are low, and we must leave, although only about a third of the females have given birth so far. I would like to stay to continue observing the lives of the chiru in their secret haven, but on June 27 we start to retrace our route. Along the way, we pass a few small herds of females still hurrying to the calving ground.

The great gathering of chiru on the calving ground in 2009 was for me the most wondrous vision in a quarter century of following the species. Knowing the mating and calving sites and the route between these for each population will lead to better plans for their protection. But our knowledge of these migrations remains fragmentary. For example, only in 2006 did we learn of a population in Qinghai that travels east and west rather than north and south. Are there others still unknown to us?

I enjoyed following the migrations and exploring uninhabited terrain. But in doing so I neglected the chiru with a different lifestyle, those who remain within a certain area all year. Whereas the migrants typically stay wholly within reserves of the Chang Tang, most resident populations are found outside or partially outside reserve borders to the south, where they share the good grasslands with nomads and their livestock. I had joined Aili and her coworkers in surveying the size and distribution of several of these resident populations two years earlier, in November 2007. Winter is the best time to count animals because males and females have gathered at certain sites for the rut.

We found one such resident population in the general vicinity of Seling Co, into which the Zagya Tsangpo flows from the east. North of the river, in Balin (Baling) *xiang* (administrative area) is a huge plain and nearby is another lake, Qixiang Co. At this season hundreds of people, mostly Hui Muslims from the city of Golmud, have gathered at the lake to harvest the eggs of brine shrimp, which are so abundant that the water is streaked red. The chiru, we are told, are here for both the rut and birth seasons but they disperse widely at other times. We count 2,443 animals, but there may well be about 3,000. Fifty miles to the north is the Yachu *xiang* near the border of the Chang Tang Reserve. There we tally by coincidence about the same number of animals as at the previous site, 2,437 chiru. The following November, further surveys showed 1,980 chiru just west of Seling Co, and 1,412 chiru around two lakes south of the county town of Xianza (Shenzha). These are just a small sample of the resident populations we encountered, many of them typically on the flats of a lake basin. We still don't know how many such populations and number of animals there are—an indication that several years of work lie ahead of us.

I am delighted to find so many resident chiru. Except for one exceedingly shy population in the Balin *xiang*, where animals bolt into headlong flight as soon as they perceive a vehicle (a sign that they have been much hunted), resident chiru are remarkably tolerant of vehicles passing nearby. Local officials and herders assure us that they now protect the chiru, that killing of animals for the wool has almost stopped in this area, and that numbers are increasing. Better protection, greater awareness of conservation, and a resurgence of Buddhist religious principles, have all probably contributed to the change. This, together with our visit to the great calving ground of the Central Chang Tang population in 2009, which could lead to its greater protection, is an extraordinary conservation success story.

Our surveys, as well as information from pastoralists and local officials, indicated that wildlife in many areas was on the increase. Although the chiru was our focus, we included other species in our
counts as well, particularly kiang or Tibetan wild ass, Tibetan gazelle,
and wild yak. Over the years we made counts of wildlife during
mid- or late winter in the same large area in the eastern Chang
Tang Nature Reserve, not far from the community of Shuanghu, as
described in our 2005 scientific paper "Wildlife and Nomads in the
Eastern Chang Tang Reserve, Tibet." Below are the results of our
counts, clearly showing changes in wildlife numbers. I participated
in the 1991, 1993, and 2003 counts, and the Institute of Zoology of
the Chinese Academy of Sciences did the 2007 count.

There will always be some uncertainty in such counts, with animals inevitably overlooked in the hilly terrain. The size of the area
censused—6,500 square miles or a bit more—also varied from year
to year. Nonetheless, it is clear that twice as many chiru were seen
in 2007 than in 1991, that Tibetan gazelle populations had increased
steadily, and that kiang had also shown a growth in numbers—results that reflected the situation in some other parts of the Chang
Tang as well. Wild yak may not have increased much and instead
may have just moved back into old haunts from which they had fled
the poachers.

One basic problem in evaluating increase or decrease in number
of chiru and other species is that no one knows how many there
were in, say, 1950 or 1975, or even how many there are today. How
many chiru died during the carnage of the 1990s? No comprehen-
sive wildlife census has ever been done over the vast Chang Tang.
The description of travelers in the early 1900s leaves no doubt that
chiru, wild yak, and kiang were extraordinarily abundant wherever
grazing was good, but livestock has largely replaced wildlife on the
best pastures. About 4,000 nomad families lived within the Chang
Tang reserve in 1993. These had an estimated 1.4 million head of
livestock, two-thirds of which were sheep, at a density of 11 animals

Table 5.1

RESULTS OF WILDLIFE COUNTS IN AN AREA OF THE EASTERN
CHANG TANG NATURE RESERVE, TIBET

	December 1991	October 1993	April 2003	November 2007
Chiru	3,900	3,066	6,285	8,141
Tibetan gazelle	352	404	621	931
Kiang	1,224	1,229	2,266	2,314
Wild yak	13	2	240	204

per square mile. Wild hoofed animals were at a density of only about 0.8 animals per square mile. The livestock figures give an indication of the minimum wildlife numbers that the region could and probably did support before pastoralists moved in. There may well have been a million chiru. In the mid-1990s, during the high tide of the shahtoosh slaughter, I estimated that "perhaps fewer than 75,000" chiru survived. That guess was probably a little low, but with continued heavy poaching it may well have reflected numbers accurately by the end of the decade. Startled by this estimate, one publication predicted the imminent demise of the chiru, that it "will be extinct within five years."

Then the downward trend was reversed through better protection. Aili and her coworkers traveled widely through the southern part of Tibet's Chang Tang during November and December 2009, when both migratory and resident chiru had congregated for the rut. They counted 65,837 chiru. Not included in this minimum number were chiru in the northern Chang Tang of Tibet and in Qinghai and Xinjiang. Aili estimated that numbers "can reach 90,000–100,000." Liu Wulin assumed a total population of 150,000 in his Chinese-language book *Tibetan Antelope* (2008), a figure that may be of the correct order of magnitude at that time.

The antipoaching campaign naturally affected those Tibetan households that hunted for subsistence and a small number that lost income from the illegal sale of hides and wool, just as shahtoosh weavers in Kashmir were affected by the ban. Can chiru and other species benefit pastoral communities through tourism and possibly trophy hunting? Will it be possible someday to harvest wildlife legally and efficiently for meat and hides under strict management in such a way that all families benefit, not just the poachers? These are potential long-term management issues that need to be considered when thinking about the future of the Chang Tang and its unique wildlife.

The chiru and other species face many threats to their habitat, from intrusion into their realm by roads, damage from mining and oil exploration, fencing of pastures, and deterioration of grasslands through overgrazing and climate change. To achieve a measure of ecological harmony, we have to learn to manage the great herds under such ever-changing conditions. But for the present I find satisfaction in knowing that the chiru, kiang, and other wild species are once again on the increase. That so many individuals and organizations are fighting specifically for the survival of the chiru, a wild hoofed animal of modest size, one which almost no one outside of the region had ever heard of before, is surely a reflection of the changing moral values of humankind.

※ CHAPTER 6 ※

The Good Pika

PIKAS AND I HAVE SEEN MUCH of each other. We are both di-
urnal and acute observers of behavior, the pika to monitor
whether or not I am dangerous and I to delve into its life. Those
who enjoy nature can only marvel at the constant activity in a pika
colony. These plains-dwelling relatives of rabbits are extremely abundant at their favored sites. They are a distinct species, the Plateau pikas, called *abra* by Tibetans and *Ochotona curzoniae* by scientists. The
species name *curzoniae* was given in honor of Lord Curzon, viceroy
of India, who instigated the invasion of Tibet in 1904 by the Younghusband expeditionary force. In spite of the unfortunate burden
of its name, a pika is utterly charming in appearance, its silky fur
light brown with whitish undersides, its ears small and rounded, its
eyes shining, and its chunky, tailless body weighs about four to six
ounces. Though small in body, the pika has an outsized influence in
maintaining the ecological integrity of the rangelands on the Tibetan Plateau.

Pikas are most active in the morning and late afternoon, and that
is the best time for a visit. When I first enter a colony, pikas scam-
per into their burrows, but soon heads pop up again and sparkling
eyes judge my intentions. If I remain quiet, they resume their hectic
routine. Some nibble on grass, others munch on flower stalks, and
a few sit and groom themselves. Intensely social, youngsters chase
each other and tumble in play, and adults meet on runways between
burrows and touch noses in greeting. When a minor dispute erupts

between two animals, each rears up and boxes with furry paws. A few pikas just sit and watch, alert guardians who give a shrill, sharp call to warn the colony if a hawk sails nearby. If a geyser of dirt erupts from the ground, it is a pika clearing out or enlarging its underground home. Pikas may collect grass, leaves, and flowers and store them in little piles near their burrow where they dry into hay, or underground where they provide food when the weather is bad. Since pikas do not hibernate, they have to find food even in winter when snow may cover the ground.

In the eastern part of the Tibetan Plateau, the alpine meadow habitat has a thick turf layer. There a pika family lives in a long, complex system of tunnels with three to six entrances. I once had a fit of energy while doing wildlife surveys in Qinghai and decided to excavate one such system to learn about the pika's underground life in the dark. There were twenty-seven feet of tunnel dug just under the one-foot-thick turf layer. In the tunnels were fourteen latrines, small niches in the tunnel wall where pikas deposit their feces.

Life in a pika colony seems chaotic, with animals dashing here and there, coming and going along their tiny runways like commuters rushing to and from work. I had no idea how this society was organized until I read papers by Andrew Smith and Marc Foggin. They discovered that pikas live in families consisting usually of one adult male, one adult female, and up to a dozen youngsters from two litters, both born during the same summer. The father watches out for the safety of his offspring, and older siblings keep an eye on younger ones. Each family occupies about 1,200 to 1,800 square feet. With its rapid reproductive rate, the pika can achieve high population densities, as many as 40 to 180 per acre. Such numbers are possible only if food is abundant, as it is on the great expanses of alpine meadow where the Smith and Foggin study was conducted in Qinghai.

So far no intensive research comparable to that on alpine meadow has been done on the alpine or desert steppe of central and western Chang Tang, where vegetation is often sparse. In the early 1990s I excavated seven tunnels on desert steppe in the northwestern Chang Tang. Each tunnel consisted of only a single entrance with one underground passage twenty-seven to ninety-one inches long, angling downward for twelve to twenty-three inches to end abruptly, except one that enlarged to a chamber with a grass nest. These pikas may have a somewhat different society than those living on lush alpine meadows. I once watched a pika in desert steppe for four hours. It seemed to subsist on the low *Ceratoides* shrubs, visiting thirty-seven different ones during my time with it, and it used three separate burrows.

During my first trip to Qinghai in 1984, I became aware that all was not well in pika land. I described my perceptions at the time in a 1985 article in *Defenders* magazine:

> One noon I climbed upward toward a limestone massif. Rumpled hills extended to the horizon except to the south, where they broke against snow mountains. A bearded vulture rode the updrafts along shimmering cliffs, and from far below, where the Gongtsa Monastery is barely visible in the folds of the hills, rise the sonorous tones of two horns. I should have felt exhilarated climbing into space with music of an ancient culture suspended around me to give human measure to this vastness, yet I was troubled; something seemed amiss.
>
> Then I realized there were no pikas. The many burrows I had passed lacked fresh earth at the entrances. The droppings in the outdoor latrines were dry, without luster, and the hay piles were sodden, uncared for. I was in a city of the dead, a Pompeii where a catastrophe had terminated the flow of life.

On returning to camp, I related the discovery to my Chinese coworkers. Was the absence of pikas due to disease, a mass exodus, or what?

"They have been poisoned," the Forestry Department official traveling with us informed me. Later I learned that Qinghai had started a widespread pika poisoning program in 1962, at first using zinc phosphide and sodium monofluoroacetate (also known as compound 1080), a deadly poison used in the United States for killing wolves, coyotes, and other predators. These poisons were replaced in the mid-1980s by the toxin botulinum type C. Between the early 1960s and 1990, about 80,080 square miles of Qinghai rangeland were saturated with poison.

But why? "Pikas are bad," asserted one of my scientific coworkers, who is based at a research institute in Xian. "They eat the grass
needed by sheep and yaks." "They cause erosion by digging burrows," added another scientist, "and they may cause a horse to break
its leg in a pika hole." I am startled. Tibetan nomads have given me
precisely the same reasons for killing pikas as these two. Even with
my limited experience, I know that faulty observations here have
led to faulty perceptions. People are often ecologically blind, imagining what they cannot see. I had already noted that pikas eat various poisonous plants such as an iris and a yellow-flowered poppy
which livestock does not touch, something that surely benefits the
latter. And I also have the advantage of knowing about a comparable
case, that of the U.S. government and ranchers with precisely the
same negative opinion for the same questionable reasons about prairie dogs, five closely related species occupying the same ecological
niche as the Plateau pika.

The prairie dog is a two-pound, sand-colored rodent which
was once abundant on the short- and mixed-grass prairies of western North America. There the animals typically live in colonies of
1,000 or more animals, with densities of up to twenty per acre. Like
the pikas, they excavate burrows, and their tunnels run up to fifty
feet long. However, unlike pikas, a prairie dog family consists of
one or two males with a harem of several females and their young.
Family members live within a territory no more than two acres in
size, which they defend against intrusion by neighbors, as John L.
Hoogland has described in *The Black-Tailed Prairie Dog*. The species
was shot and poisoned to such an extent that by the 1970s it was on
the verge of extinction, its distribution reduced by 98 percent.

The reason for this eradication pogrom: prairie dogs and livestock were thought to compete for grass. But research has shown
that these rodents colonize areas that livestock has overgrazed, probably in part because they prefer burrows with a view, with grass
no higher than four inches tall. Plant biomass and the number of
plant species are greater in a prairie dog colony than elsewhere, and,
in addition, the plants are more nutritious with a higher percent
of crude protein content. No wonder that livestock, bison, prong-
horn antelope, and other herbivores prefer to forage in prairie dog

colonies. Instead of being "pests" that "infest" pastures, prairie dogs have a highly positive effect on grasslands by increasing plant diversity and supporting many animal species that prey on them, from prairie falcons and eagles to badgers and bobcats. They preserve the function of the ecosystem in a way that benefits both native species and livestock. It is clear that the antagonism of government and ranchers toward prairie dogs was in part based on purposeful ignorance, even when accurate knowledge was available, and on vested interests in continuing a well-funded killing pogrom no matter how outdated and harmful. The story of the pika has been remarkably similar.

After that first journey through pika land in 1984, I spent most of my time farther west with Tibetan antelope in alpine steppe habitat where pikas are only locally common. But my interest in the species continued. I knew that Qinghai continued its pika vendetta—as it still does in 2011. Meanwhile, good research was pointing to the further value of pikas. Li Weijing and Zhang Yanming of the Hebei Alpine Meadow Research Station in Qinghai found that the top 10 cm of soil had both more organic matter and moisture in areas with pikas than without, and that even 50 cm underground it was moister. This benefits plant growth, as do the minerals brought to the surface by the excavations of pikas and the feces deposited in the burrows. The digging of pikas also loosens the soil and enables it to hold water like a sponge, thus preventing runoff and erosion and flooding downstream, something particularly important now with glaciers melting and a water shortage looming for the people in the lowlands, as we'll see in Chapter 7.

On the Indian side of the Tibetan Plateau, Sumanta Bagchi and his coworkers, in a 2003 article in *Biological Conservation,* noted that there are more plant species in places that pikas inhabit than elsewhere, yet the vegetation cover remains almost the same. It has been calculated that pikas eat 2.2–2.7 ounces of herbage a day. Fifty pikas would eat as much as one sheep. However, pikas prefer herbaceous plants whereas sheep, horses, and yaks concentrate on grasses and sedges. In one Qinghai area I collected forty-eight pika food plants, of which thirty-seven were herbaceous. As researchers from the Chinese Academy of Sciences have shown, pikas are usually not in

competition with livestock—except when pastures have been heavily degraded by too many domestic animals grazing without respite
for weeks and months, never giving the plants time to recover.

Pikas reach their greatest abundance in broken, fragmented, and
eroded areas where the turf layer has slumped to expose barren
soil. Anything that breaks the smooth expanse of turf, such as frost
heaves, road construction, sharp hooves of livestock cutting a trail,
and yak wallows, may cause a whole slope to break up. When a section of turf slides downhill, it creates a terrace of soil up to a foot
high overlain by turf. Erosion by wind, water, and excavations by
pikas create a hollow in the soil that is roofed over by turf. With the
roots of sedges and other plants suspended in air, the vegetation dies,
the turf turns black and breaks off in chunks. The terraces of soil
make it easy for pikas to dig tunnels. But, as with prairie dogs, pikas do not initiate the degradation and erosion, though livestock all
too often does. To emphasize: pikas are *indicators* of overgrazed and
degraded pastures, not the *cause*. Unfortunately, scientific evidence
tends to be ignored, disregarded, or not readily available to officials
and the general public.

The pika is a perfect food for many predators, moderate in size,
locally abundant, and easily caught. A pair of saker falcons which
I observed at the nest fed their two youngsters with 90 percent
pikas and 10 percent birds. Upland hawks sit motionless near pika
burrows, patiently waiting. Tibetan foxes prowl pika colonies and
pounce on the unwary. Wolves prey heavily on pikas when larger
prey is scarce. Tibetan brown bears dig up pikas; in the late 1800s
the Russian explorer Pyotr Kozlov found twenty-five pikas in the
stomach of one bear.

One day I came upon a dead polecat, a type of weasel with
a black mask similar to that of the American black-footed ferret.
The ferret was poisoned almost to extinction along with the prairie
dogs on which it preys and in whose colonies it lives. This polecat,
its fur wet and matted, had died in a poisoned pika colony. I prefer
to remember another polecat in the same area of Qinghai which
I met one morning at seven o'clock. I spot a lithe, dark creature
emerging from a burrow in hot pursuit of a pika. Both vanish into
another burrow, but the polecat emerges without its intended prey,

the chase a failure. The polecat glides underground again and almost immediately reappears at the heels of a frantic pika. Grabbing it by the scruff, the polecat takes the body to yet another burrow, leaves it there, and continues to hunt. Ignoring me, the polecat searches two other burrows without success and then comes from a third carrying a pika by its back. She takes that victim to a previous burrow, emerges within thirty seconds, and slips into another burrow. When she reappears with a pika, a lurking dog rushes up. The polecat drops the pika, which the dog swallows with one gulp, and retreats into a tunnel. I marvel at the efficiency with which the polecat has caught three pikas in just twelve minutes. I wait. At ten o'clock two black-masked young peer from a burrow.

Pika burrows provide shelter and homes to many animals. Spiders live in them, catching flies and other insects which seek cover during wind-, rain-, and snowstorms. A small lizard, *Phrynocephalus*, lives at these high, cold altitudes and may find warmth and safety in burrows. Several species of snow finch and the perky groundpecker, a small light-brown bird with a curved bill, select abandoned burrows as nest sites. It is always strange to see a small bird simply vanish underground or appear as if from nowhere. As Andrew Smith and Marc Foggin have shown, these birds decline drastically in number when pikas are poisoned, because the unused burrows collapse with time and seed eaters such as snow finches die from eating poisoned grain.

As I write this, I feel like a lawyer making a case in defense of an innocent victim. However, not until 2006 was I actually witness to the crime being committed. Up to that time the pika's travails were of concern, but my emotions were not deeply involved. That changed when we came into contact with a mass-poisoning campaign in the winter of 2006 after we had crossed the Chang Tang in a traverse west to east. Gama, the village leader of Cuochi, told us of the immense pressure on his village to use poison, but he had refused to comply because he thought killing pikas was unnecessary.

Households throughout the region had been ordered by government to spread poison or be fined. Does the Buddha urge love, respect, and compassion toward all living beings—except pikas? Some households, we were told, buried the sacks of poison instead of scattering them. When I asked a nomad about the poison program, he replied: "Only the Han nationality do that sort of thing. Outsiders come to this land and I cannot stop that." Around Madoi, where we were at the time, it was true that Han Chinese were being paid to spread poison, but in many places local Tibetan communities did so as well.

At the first poison-distribution camp we came to, I saw sacks of grain and glass bottles filled with highly toxic botulinum type C raticide. The clear fluid is mixed with the grain, either wheat, barley, or oats, and distributed in small bags to individuals. The poison is made from the bacterium *Clostridium botulinum*, which occurs usually in trace amounts in soils and organic matter. When in concentrated form, the poison affects the body by paralyzing the motor nerves. A lively pika becomes weak less than a day after eating the poisoned grain, falls down when dashing around, and has difficulty swallowing, squeaking, and focusing its eyes. Toward the end it lies gasping for breath in its burrow and dies.

On December 14, near the county town of Madoi, a line of about twenty people walks across the rangeland on a broad front. Each person carries a small white bag of poison and a trowel or long-handled spoon with which to put the poisoned grain into pika burrow openings. There is an icy wind and a snow flurry, and the extermination team finds it easier just to scatter the grain rather than placing it into the holes, making the poison easily accessible to domestic yaks and other animals. One official tells me that he has seen small birds dead in poisoned pika colonies but not larger animals. I told him my tale of the dead polecat.

The following day, on the shore of Ngoring Hu, we come upon a poison-distribution camp with green-colored grain sacks piled high in front of tents. "Third County Station, Mouse Prevention Station" announces a sign in Chinese characters. We stop and talk to the team leader, a pleasant and thoughtful man. The team, he tells us, has been here forty days. All of Madoi county will be poisoned, pikas killed now in winter and then mice in spring. Only the plains are being poisoned, not the hills, he says, so that some pikas are left in the "food chain." The government wants a 90 percent kill. Livestock is not affected by the poison, the team leader asserts.

That the poison pogrom occurs in the Sanjiangyuan National Nature Reserve is particularly distressing. This huge reserve, established with a national mandate in 2003, has as its explicit purpose the preservation of the full ecosystem with all its plants and animals in order to help maintain the livelihood of Tibetan communities. With the reserve including the headwaters of three great rivers, the Yellow, Yangtze, and Mekong, habitat preservation is essential if the millions of people living in the lowlands downstream are to be assured an adequate water supply. Yet the poisoning mindlessly degrades rangelands and reduces biological diversity.

In 2006, I wondered for how long the large-scale expensive poisoning pogrom will continue, and still do so today, six years later. It has been in progress for half a century, yet rangelands still deteriorate even in areas with few or no pikas. "There was no apparent increase in forage production in areas where plateau pikas were controlled," wrote Roger Pech and others in a 2007 article in the *Journal of Applied Ecology*, based on their detailed pika study in alpine meadow habitat east of Nagqu in 2004 and 2005. "It was not evident that control programmes are warranted or that they will improve the livelihoods of Tibetan herders." In brief: bad policy, bad rangeland.

My concern obviously extends beyond pikas to the chiru, snow finch, blue poppy, and all other animals and plants on these uplands, to retaining the overall harmonious pattern of life and sublime ecological wholeness. And the hapless pika is a key member of this ecosystem. The pika is considered a "keystone species," one that has a uniquely important ecological role, as emphasized by Smith and Foggin on a 1999 article in the journal *Oryx*. The loss of pikas would have a disproportionately large effect on other species. Sea otters, for example, were exterminated along much of North America's western coast. Their principal predator gone, sea urchins exploded in number and devoured the kelp forests upon which many fish and invertebrate species depended for survival. When wolves were annihilated in the Yellowstone National Park region, elk became so abundant and concentrated to such an extent in their favored riverine habitat, especially in willow thickets, that vegetation was browsed almost into oblivion, a loss which affected songbirds and other species. In both situations there was a cascading disruption in the rich web of life, leading to ecological impoverishment. I can readily think of a dozen critical contributions that the "keystone" pika makes to the Tibetan rangelands. They bring minerals to the surface with their digging, fertilize soil with their feces, eat plants poisonous to livestock, offer shelter or serve as food to many species, and retain soil moisture, to mention just a few benefits. A small creature like the pika can indeed have a large influence on many plants and animals with which it shares its world.

I returned home for Christmas in 2006 after completing our traverse of the Chang Tang, and spent some time checking on the effect of botulinum type C (there are seven other strains) on wildlife. Humans are susceptible to the toxin. From a 2005 article by Iveraldo Durta and others in a Brazilian veterinary journal, I learn that naturally occurring botulism outbreaks among cattle are common in Brazil. In one case about 9,000 cattle became partially to wholly paralyzed, about 20 percent of them fatally, probably from drinking water contaminated with decomposed animal carcasses and vegetal matter. In California several botulism strains affect cattle, with type C being particularly virulent. In one case, reported in a 2003 veterinary journal by Robert Moeller and coauthors, 427 of 444 Holstein dairy cattle died after eating feed containing a dead cat infected with type C toxin. I wonder why no deaths in sheep and yaks wandering over poisoned pastures have been reported from Qinghai and Tibet. I have had these articles translated into Chinese and passed them along to relevant authorities. But I may merely be a lone voice crying for the wilderness.

My colleagues and I sometimes wondered what one could do to change the strong and unwarranted antipathy of many Tibetans toward pikas. Zhaduo and Lu Zhi noted that we must reach young minds with new and accurate information and teach old minds to see with new eyes. I should write something about the benefits that pikas bring to rangeland and the pastoral households, they suggested, and that this could be translated into Tibetan. Instead of writing a straightforward account, I decided to send our message in the form of fables. I wrote a dozen fables and the Tibetan versions were published as booklets entitled in Qinghai "Tales of the Pika" and in Tibet "Tales of Pika Tsering." Below are three of these fables as I wrote them originally in English.

PIKA WELCOMES TWO FLIES

Pika is at the entrance to his burrow. Only his head peers out. His wife and children are deep in the burrow, cozy and warm in their grass nest. A cold wind blows and snowflakes fill the sky even though it is already summer.

As Pika looks out at the bad weather, thinking it too cold to look for some lunch, two large flies land before him. They have hairy abdomens but still they are shivering.

"Please let us into your burrow," says one fly. "It is so windy that we can't fly well and we are cold."

"Then why don't you go home?" asks Pika. "Why come to my burrow?"

"We have no home," says the second fly, stamping its six feet because they are wet with snow. "Usually we seek shelter in an empty pika or marmot burrow. But in this weather we could not find a place quickly."

Pika grumbles, "Why should I give hospitality to flies in my home?"

"Oh, let them in. Be kind to strangers," calls Pika's wife from deep within the burrow. Pika obeys his wife, as usual.

Pika squeezes to one side and lets the flies walk in. Once out of the wind the flies shake their wings and wipe themselves dry with their forelegs.

"What are you doing out in such weather?" asks Pika.

"We were pollinating flowers when the storm surprised us," answers the first fly. He explains that they fly from flower to flower seeking sweet nectar. At the same time they inadvertently carry pollen on their legs and hairy abdomen from one plant to another. In this way they help to fertilize the gentians, poppies, primroses and many other flowers. The plants can then produce seeds that later grow into new flowers.

Pika ponders this. Finally he says, "You mean you help flowers bloom?" And he ponders some more about what this might mean.

But Pika's wife has a quick mind. Her voice comes once more from within the nest. "Don't you realize, Pika, that our two visitors help us grow our food? Without them we would not have so many delicious plants to eat. Nor would the yaks, sheep, and marmots. We must always offer shelter to flies."

Pika sits motionless, his head now inside the burrow. It helps him to think more clearly. He realizes that he often meets flies near his burrow but has paid them little attention.

"It is good to give hospitality and show kindness to strangers," he muses. "One never knows how they might repay you."

WOLF LOOKS FOR A NEW HOME

Wolf squeezes through a gap in the pasture gate and looks left and right. He sees several pikas, all of them busy running along their tiny winding pika roads, ducking in and out of burrows, and looking for food. One pika hums a little song:

> This is a mouthful of grass,
> This is a wild pea,
> This is a flower and this a tender leaf,
> A lunch for you and me.

Nearby, Pika watches Wolf, only his nose and bright eyes visible at the burrow entrance.

"What brings you here? We rarely see your kind on this pasture," queries Pika. Wolf looks around and spots Pika.

"Well," says Wolf, "I'm here to catch pikas. But you're safe for now."

"You haven't answered my question," responds Pika.

Wolf decides to be civil and tells Pika, "I hunted for months across pastures to the north. They were my home. I mainly had pikas for breakfast, lunch, and dinner and for snacks in between. Only rarely did I kill a sheep. One day many people came and spread poisoned grain all over the pastures to kill pikas. Nearly all the pikas died. Have you heard of that before?"

Pika does not like this conversation. He does not like to think of being eaten by Wolf. And he cannot begin to understand why humans would want to kill all the pikas. So Pika merely shakes his head in response to the question.

"Anyway," continues Wolf, "with most pikas dead there was little for me to eat. So naturally I killed sheep. The herders had mostly ignored me until then. But suddenly they were determined to kill me, too. See, the tip of my left ear is gone. Someone had a gun, and a bullet almost got me. So I left. Maybe I'll stay here awhile. There seem to be a lot of pikas."

Just then Wolf spots two gazelle, a mother and her baby. Few gazelle have survived in this area. The many pasture fences greatly hinder them when they try to escape a dog or wolf. Most fences are too high for gazelle to leap over.

"Watch me," says Wolf. "I have developed a special technique for catching gazelle. The fences really help me." With that, Wolf approaches the gazelles slowly in a crouch.

Suddenly Wolf sprints toward the gazelles. Startled, they flee. Wolf is soon at their heels. Ahead is a fence. The mother gazelle zigzags and turns sharply away from the fence. Her less experienced baby dashes at full speed into the wire fence. Half stunned, it bounces back, its thin legs flailing. And Wolf is there ready.

Pika watches and ponders and considers the effects of poisoning pikas and building fences. People, he concludes, don't think ahead. They do not consider the consequences of their actions.

PIKA AND THE DANCING HARE

Pika sits by his burrow when Hare hops up. "Where are you going?" asks Pika.

"I come from behind me and I'm going ahead," replies Hare. Hare looks down at little Pika and chuckles, *pfft-pfft*. Hare's cleft lip quivers when he makes that sound.

Pika does not know why Hare chuckles. Before he can ask, a gust of wind blows sand in their faces. Pika backs into his burrow, but Hare says, "Wait, wait," as he wipes the sand from his face with his forepaws. "The sand reminds me of a story. You want to hear the latest? Well, maybe it's not so new. Another hare told me, and he got the story from someone else, who. . . ." Hare leans over and whispers: "The whole village danced—on pikas."

That got Pika's attention.

Hare laughs and wiggles his long ears. Then he twirls around and wiggles his white, fluffy tail and stamps his furry feet, THUMP THUMP, in a hare dance. Then Hare continues, "A Production Team from the village was building a fence. Pika holes everywhere. Wind blew sand into people's faces. Shoes sank into soil made soft by all the pika burrows. Gajia, the leader, had an insight: pikas cause sandstorms and erosion by digging and they eat all the grass. You know how people jump to conclusions."

Pika nods in agreement.

"Anyway," says Hare. "Gajia gave an order: 'The soil is too soft. We must pack it down. We must fill the pika holes.' The next day the villagers all came. You know how Tibetans love a picnic. They came with thermoses of butter tea, bread, and chunks of boiled mutton. They ate, and laughed, and were in a good mood. Then they went to work. At first they just stamped their feet." THUMP THUMP goes Hare. "After that they danced, stomping the ground and singing, and holding their arms aloft."

Hare thumps his feet, rises up, and spins around singing though his voice sounds like a squeak. THUMP-SQUEAK-THUMP. "After that they shoveled sand into the holes. It did pack the soil down."

"What happened to the pikas?" asks Pika.

Hare chuckles and his lip quivers again. "We hares don't dig much. A scrape here and there. But you pikas are fanatics, always digging. Nothing happened to the pikas: they simply fixed up their homes. But Gajia was angry. He wanted hard ground and he lost face. So he got poison from the government. End of pikas."

Pika is unhappy with that story. He lowers his head and his whiskers droop. Hare notices and says, "Wait! An interesting ending. You should be able to guess it. But you dig so much you don't take time to think like us hares. Action is easy, thought is hard. With the pikas gone, the soil packed down. When it rained, the water ran off, causing erosion. Soft soil absorbs and holds water. Grass grows well when it has moisture and is tender and nutritious. Grass grows poorly on hard soil and is tough to eat. Your digging helps all those who eat grass. Gajia had thought you pikas are harmful pests."

Pika says smugly, "A little knowledge is a dangerous thing."

Hare wiggles ears, nose, and tail, and laughs. "Let's dance." He hops in a tight circle and bounds away singing and thumping. THUMP THUMP. Here is his song:

> Soft soil
> Moist soil
> Green grass
> Good grass
> Cheers for Pika

The pika fables were distributed to schools and to villages in Qinghai and Tibet by such nongovernmental organizations as the Shan Shui Conservation Center and the Wildlife Conservation Society. I hope they aroused interest, changed perceptions, and above all warmed the hearts of children and adults alike. After all, in many respects the pika's family life resembles that of the Tibetans with whom it shares the land, a good basis for empathy. Pikas, people, livestock, and rangelands have existed together for several thousand years, their lives connected without acrimony. Almost everyone from government official to herdsman now recognizes that vast tracts of rangelands have been degraded by too much livestock. Yet the pika is still being made a scapegoat. Ignored is the fact that if we treasure nature it will repay us, whereas if we hurt nature we will only hurt ourselves. The pika stories are reminders of this basic truth. But when I casually meet pikas scurrying around their burrows, my mind usually does not focus on conservation issues. Instead, it relaxes with the pleasure of observing these delightful creatures.

CHAPTER 7

Chang Tang Traverse

TWO BRITISH MILITARY MEN, Captain Montagu Sinclair Wellby and Lieutenant Neill Malcolm, passed Lungmu Co, also known as Tsagger Co, a small lake in the far western Chang Tang of Tibet, in early June 1896. They had started in India in the town of Leh with thirty-nine mules and ponies and a staff of eleven Ladakhis, determined to be the first expedition to cross the highest and most desolate part of the Tibetan Plateau. Traveling mostly eastward, they crossed the Lanak La, a pass of around 18,000 feet, at that time the border between Ladakh and Tibet. There, near Lungmu Co, as Wellby wrote in his book *Through Unknown Tibet* (1898), "we decided to give up all searching for routes and to find a way for ourselves, marching due east as much as possible."

One hundred and ten years later, on October 31, 2006, our expedition team of fourteen—ten Tibetans, three Han Chinese, and myself—riding in two trucks and two Land Cruisers, leaves the highway at Lungmu Co and also heads east, following roughly the same route Wellby and Malcolm had taken. We started in Lhasa, driving west past the headwaters of the Yarlung Tsangpo, where we counted 956 kiang (Tibetan wild ass) in scattered herds, and on past holy Mount Kailas with its snow-capped summit gleaming like white jade on a bank of cloud. Then heading north to the town of Rutog and on to Pangong Co, the long, narrow lake that extends into Ladakh, we continued until finally, after five days and 1,134 miles of travel, we are now ready to begin our traverse of the Chang Tang. Unlike

Wellby's expedition, we have ample food and fairly good maps and we know more or less where we are going. But it is winter and temperatures may drop to −40°F. Our elevation will be at least 15,000 feet and as much as 17,500 feet, which, with the cold, guarantees memorable misery. Nevertheless, travel in winter is easier than in summer because both ground and streams are frozen hard.

Like Wellby, we are exploring but with a more definite purpose than traversing the landscape. We want to know how much wildlife remains in these desolate uplands in winter, in contrast with my summer visits to parts of the region, and to learn something about the availability of grazing grounds. I have read Wellby's book and became intrigued by his trip. It could be fun to do a bit of old-fashioned exploring, even if by vehicle, over a route that has not been taken for over a century. I had no definite plans for such a trip until David Breashears, a mountain climber and filmmaker, contacted me and suggested that we team up and follow Wellby's route. He offered most of the required funds as well as such equipment as tents and sleeping bags.

To make plans is stimulating, to turn these plans into reality often less so. The straight-line distance of our proposed route on a map will be about 1,100 miles through Tibet and Qinghai, and this required permits and cooperation from both provinces. Karma Khampa and his Lhasa trekking company fortunately agreed to organize the vehicles, food, gasoline, drivers, and camp staff for the projected two-month trip. The Tibet Forestry Department agreed to provide the necessary permit to enter the Chang Tang Reserve, but it had no strong desire to participate further, except for a large fee. So I went instead to the Tibet Plateau Institute of Biology and asked if they would sponsor our trip. I had cooperated with the Institute on several previous projects, and was especially delighted when Cang Jue Drolma, the research director, not only agreed to the project but also offered to join the expedition. The National Geographic Society also provided some funds and planned to send a photographer, but Qinghai refused to give him permission to enter restricted areas through which we had to pass. Yet after a year all the different aspects of our plan were coming together. Then suddenly Breashears decided not to go—leaving a huge gap in our budget. But with the help of the Wildlife Conservation Society and a generous donor from the National Geographic Society, we were finally able to leave Lhasa.

After we head east from Lungmu Co, we traverse undulating land that unrolls silent and snow-covered with horizon giving way to horizon. To the north rises the luminous rampart of the Kunlun Mountains. This wild emptiness is alluring and appeals to a sense of the unknown, a veil of hidden enchantment just beyond the next ridge. We are at last penetrating the wildest and most remote parts of the Chang Tang, and dependent only on ourselves, severed from the chains of society, free to roam.

Our car is in the lead with Tador driving. Being ahead of the others enables us to record wildlife before it flees too far. With us is Danda, a lean man in a cowboy hat who is head of the forest police in western Tibet and has a reputation for strenuous efforts to control poaching. And there is Kang Aili again on a field trip with me, an ideal companion with her quiet efficiency, self-reliance, and congenial temperament. In the other car is Tashi Dorjie Hashi—or Zhaduo as he is generally known—with a broad kindly face partly hidden by a short scraggly beard. He is a Tibetan from Qinghai, the founder of the Snowland Great Rivers Environmental Protection Association, and a former member of the Wild Yak Brigade, the antipoaching team so active in efforts to save the chiru. Here too is Wang Hao, lecturer at Peking University, who has been in the Chang Tang with me before, as has Cang Jue, whose cheerful presence has always been welcome on a trip.

We continue across plains and over ridges into the spacious desolation. A Tibetan gazelle watches us alertly as we pass by, and a little farther on a gray wolf bounds away over a rise. A Himalayan griffon vulture floats in a sky intensely blue. Steam rises into the icy air above a gentle slope and we stop to investigate. It is a hot spring, an isolated pool no more than three feet across with a rivulet draining from it. Li Zhen Chun, who has accompanied Cang Jue as assistant, dips his hand into the pool and catches a black pulsating creature half an inch long. A leech! How did it get to this tiny, isolated pool? We add it to our wildlife observations.

Ahead is a black tent made of yak hair, squat like a giant tarantula, the home of a nomad family. We have traveled only ten miles

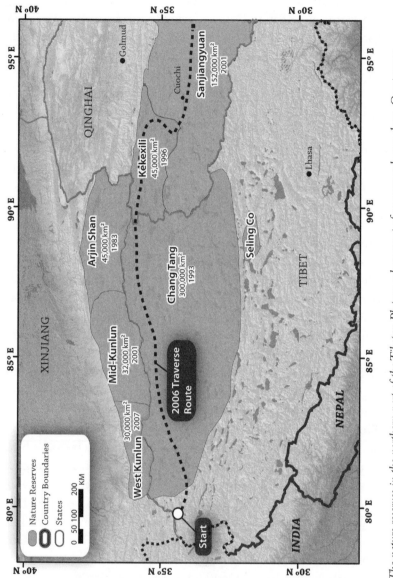

The nature reserves in the northern part of the Tibetan Plateau where most of our research was done. Our traverse route through the Chang Tang Reserve of Tibet and into western Qinghai is shown.

from the highway but it is late afternoon and we decide to camp here at 17,000 feet. Karma's staff is highly efficient in erecting the tents. The cook tent, fifteen by fifteen feet in size, is the domain of Tsering (meaning "long life" in Tibetan) and Nyima ("sun"); another tent is for the drivers Sakya, Tador, Kalden, and Ngawang. The rest of us each erect our own small tents. Tonight, as every night, we camp near a frozen stream. Karma, large and powerful, uses an axe to chop chunks of ice to melt for drinking and cooking. Nyima lights a stove, fueled from a gas cylinder, and Tsering, helpful as always, prepares tea. I huddle near the stove for warmth. Aili, Danda, and Zhaduo soon return from a visit to the nomad family, which consists of Zhaxi Tsireng, his wife, and seven children. Zhaxi has told them that there are no other families east of us because grazing is so poor. These are the last people, it turns out, that we will see until we reach the Golmud-Lhasa highway after twenty-three days and 1,049 miles of cross-country driving.

Karma Tsering chops meat off a frozen sheep carcass with a cleaver. We have brought fourteen dead sheep and half a yak for the trip. Stir-fried mutton with cabbage and boiled rice is our dinner. We eat hurriedly and retreat to our sleeping bags for warmth. I try to write notes but my ballpoint pen freezes. The thermometer by the tent door reads −12°F. Several times at night the drivers start the truck engines, fearing that they will freeze.

At dawn, frost crystals glisten on my sleeping bag and the inside wall of the tent. A note from my journal:

The usual misery of getting up, into cold clothes, tying bootlaces with numb fingers. Toothpaste frozen, skin cream frozen, even urine in the night bottle frozen. Go to cook tent. I'm usually the first one. Karma asleep in a corner, but Tsering and Nyima are already preparing breakfast. I get hot cup of cocoa. At 0800 hours, a pink and yellow streak on horizon. Sunup at 0900. A pied wagtail by camp. What does it eat?

Breakfast presents a choice of rice porridge or *tsampa* mixed with tea and a spoonful of sugar. A century earlier, Wellby and Malcolm set out "having breakfasted off our antelope meat and some good tea." We clean the campsite carefully before leaving and carry litter away in sacks on one of the trucks.

Faulty wiring in one of the trucks delays our departure until ten o'clock. We drive up a valley under a pale sun. The north-facing slopes are deep in snow, but the south-facing ones are covered with a yellow grass stubble. Danda spots several tan dots in the distance. Chiru! Aili rests her scope on the half-open window and reports: "Four females, one young. At about 300 meters." Then: "Five animals at about 1,000 m, too far to classify." "Seven adult males, 400 m." I take a GPS reading: 34°37' N, 80°40' E.

We drive slowly to count chiru within sight of our route. Grazing is good here with feather grass (*Stipa*), a favored winter food of chiru, abundant on the slopes. Nearly half the female chiru have a calf at heel, signifying good survival. There are also many adult males. The rut will soon begin and the herds will probably remain here, much farther north than I expected. When the Swedish explorer Sven Hedin passed through this area in October 1906 he observed "flocks of antelopes," indicating that our sightings may not be unusual. By late afternoon we have driven forty-two miles and counted 467 chiru.

Our camp is comfortable, the food good, the cook tent warm, and our team chats happily in Tibetan, Chinese, and English. Just north of us, Wellby and Malcolm were in a quite different situation in June 1896. Wellby at this point had trouble with staff, which he found "careless and untrustworthy," and which he tried to prevent from "forming any scheme for desertion." A snowstorm had killed several of their pack animals; they were down from thirty-nine to twenty-eight and soon it would be only twenty-one. They had to lighten their loads, discarding much equipment by a large lake which they named in honor of the occasion: "Lake Lighten." It was just one of many geographical features which Western explorers of that era named unsuitably after obscure events and obscure persons, but most of these names have fortunately vanished from maps. Today the lake has a Tibetan name, Gozha Co.

I can imagine these two military men, Wellby and Malcolm, sitting dirty and bearded in their tent by a smoking fire of what they called *boortsa*, a dwarf shrub (genus *Ceratoides*) whose tiny gray-green leaves are eaten by pika, hare, chiru, kiang, and others. The image is quite different from the photographs in Wellby's book. Of Captain Wellby of the Eighteenth Hussars only the head and shoulders are pictured. He wears a pillbox cap tipped to one side, a mustache twirled up at the tips, and a jaunty expression. His first name is Montagu, but that never appears in the book. Lieutenant Malcolm of the Ninety-Third Argyll and Sutherland Highlanders stands erect dressed smartly in a tartan kilt and knee-high socks, his left hand resting on a sword, with a cape over his shoulders. His first name is not mentioned. Indeed, I wonder if they ever referred to each other by their first names during their many months together.

It is −29°F at dawn. The Land Cruisers are dead, but, unlike Wellby's pack animals, each can be resurrected by pulling it with a truck until the engine comes to life. Along the snow-streaked hills we count 455 more chiru and a number of wild yaks, including a group of seven hulking bulls which flee in a massive trot, their long hair skirts swinging. All chiru are shy, fleeing fast and far, vehicles to them being messengers of death. The following day we come to a basin almost free of snow where many chiru graze, a total of 1,410. There are also nine kiangs, the first we have seen on the traverse. Grazing must be good here or they would not have selected this place. Wang Hao and Cang Jue set out temporary plots one square meter in size within which they count the plant species and measure the density of each, something they do at intervals to determine composition and abundance. They also clip all the vegetation in the plot and weigh each species to determine the biomass available to grazers. Soil samples are collected for later analyses of mineral content.

Next we come to a huge plain. To the south is a "magnificent snow range," to use Wellby's words, a massif more than 21,000 feet high known as Toze Kangri. Near its base is a lake, Puerh Co. I am now in familiar terrain, one also visited by various explorers. Captain Henry Deasy was here in July 1896, and, seeing thousands of chiru, had named it Antelope Plain. Like most British intruders into Tibet in that era, he was a military officer, in part an explorer, in part a vacationer, and probably in part a spy. Seven years later Captain Cecil Godfrey Rawling came to the same plain at the same season and wrote in his book *The Great Plateau* (1905):

Almost from my feet away to the north and east, as far as the eye could reach, were thousands upon thousands of doe antelope with their young. Everyone in camp turned out to see this beautiful sight, and tried, with varying results, to estimate the number of animals in view. This was found very difficult however, more particularly as we could see in the distance a continuous stream of fresh herds steadily approaching; there could not have been less than 15,000 or 20,000 visible at one time.

I first came here in June 1992, intent on following the chiru migration of the West Chang Tang population, as we had named it, to its mysterious calving ground, but the herds continued out of Tibet into Xinjiang to the north. Later that year, we had also tracked the chiru with their newborns on their return migration southward in late July and early August to the Aru Basin. Given our knowledge of the migratory route, I expected these plains to be empty in November. Yet here were several thousand chiru seemingly settled in for the rut. Do some chiru now stay here because of all the poaching in the south? Are we dealing with a separate population that migrates westward for the summer? I have no answer.

We spot a wolf, a handsome tan and gray animal with luxurious fur. It has just killed a female chiru. We examine her body. She has been choked and not a drop of blood is visible. She weighs sixty-two pounds; her internal organs and bone marrow are devoid of fat, indicating that she would have had difficulties surviving the long, hard winter. Meanwhile the wolf waits patiently nearby to reclaim its meal.

Today, November 5, we decide on a day of rest. Karma and I go for a walk. I need to move, to feel the terrain underfoot, not roar across it imprisoned in a metal cocoon and immersed in engine noise rather than wind. We trudge for six hours, chatting with each other—Karma speaks excellent English—counting a few chiru, and watching a Tibetan hare bolt from its shallow scrape beneath a shrub. Our notes are scanty but my body is rejuvenated, my senses heightened by the hard grandeur and huge emptiness of the land. Later, as I sit writing notes in my tent, Wang Hao comes and says, "George, wolf!" About thirty feet from camp stands a cream-colored wolf inspecting us. We all gather to inspect it, too. When it walks off,

I follow walking parallel and about twenty feet away, neither one of us apprehensive or hurried. I stay behind when the wolf angles up a slope. Danda later comments, "When you see a wolf near where you travel it is good luck."

We continue eastward into a vast snow-covered space becalmed in time. A few chiru forage where sun and wind have exposed *Carex moorcrofti*, a coarse, sharp-tipped sedge which ungulates usually ignore. The landscape turns into low corrugated hills, peeled to bedrock by the elements, its valleys furrowed by dry watercourses. Tibetan Buddhism distinguishes eighteen kinds of "void," and this landscape, a place of desolation and emptiness yet possessing a raw, haunting beauty, is another such void. When we stop for a rest, I stride ahead through a land of light, the snow glistening and the air vibrating with the sun's energy. Not even a bird calls in the dense silence. My boots kick up lunar dust. As the explorer Fernand Grenard wrote in 1893, it is a land "where nothing passes but the wind, where nothing happens but geological phenomena." I absorb the landscape into my being.

Ahead is a pyramid-shaped mountain which Wellby had named Helmet Hill. His expedition had difficulty finding fresh water in this arid region, even having to dig for it in likely places. We carry ice in containers. Wellby's group lived by hunting, with "one great continuous anxiety" always lurking—"finding enough game to shoot." One day "while enjoying a midday halt a couple of antelopes and sand grouse came to drink and fell victims to our guns for their greediness." Just before reaching Helmet Hill two of their camp staff tussled over a shotgun and one blew the jaw off the other by accident. The wounded man rode along for several days before he and another headed south and vanished. Only fourteen pack animals were now left.

Plains and hills sweep out on all sides. Barren, utterly barren, ground alternates with expanses of grassland, sometimes hidden by snow. Even where there is grass, the cover is often less than 10 percent, the remainder just sand, silt, and stone. We come to another chiru concentration, this one in an area where black volcanic boulders litter the ground. To the north, on the border with Xinjiang, is the huge Muztagh massif, 21,500 feet high. There is a chiru calving ground just north of Muztagh, one which Aili had surveyed earlier this year, and we wonder if these animals came from there. To count and classify the chiru now takes willpower when outside a vehicle, calm days having given way to snow and fierce wind. Around noon the wind barrels out of the west unimpeded over hundreds of empty miles. It scours the bald peaks and blasts across lake flats, howling with a wolf's voice and throwing up curtains of dust; it rips at the clothes, pounds the body, and abrades the face. Yet Aili stoically peers through the scope, a red wool cap pulled low on her head, steadying the tripod with one hand, as she counts the animals and gives her tally to Zhaduo or Danda to write down, while I scan the horizon for more wildlife.

Several teams have crossed the Chang Tang in recent years, not in vehicles but on bicycles. One such team consisting of Janne Corax, Nadine Saulnier, and Steffan Johansson, two Swedes and a Canadian, bicycled across the Chang Tang north to south. They started their journey in the autumn of 2003 by crossing the Arjin Shan Reserve into Tibet and continuing past the eastern shore of Dogai Coring and the west side of Purog Kangri, as they later described their trip in a 2007 issue of *Japanese Alpine News*. For about three-quarters of the 650-mile route they had to walk, pushing their bicycles. Hunger tortured them so much they considered eating a dead and rotten wolf on the steppe but resisted the temptation. After a month and a half they reached the road north of Shuanghu.

At night we try to find a spot for our tents that is sheltered from wind, such as the lee of a ridge or a cutbank. Tsering serves yak stew with turnips and potatoes. Afterward I copy notes that others have taken to combine with mine, and pass along my own. We chat about many things, from the size of wildlife populations and the possibility of tourism to the future of nomads. Tibetans from different parts of the Tibetan Plateau speak different dialects and may have trouble understanding each other—as, for example, do Zhaduo and Cang Jue. I am taught Tibetan animal words: dog—*chi*, sheep—*luk*, brown bear—*dom*, fly—*bhanbu*, vulture—*shaghe*. Five of our team members belong to the Communist Party, and one evening they suggest that I too should join. I point out that I do not belong to any party anywhere. It is finally decided that a foreigner would not be allowed to join anyway.

November 12, a memorable day. We drive in our car over the ice near the shore of Xuejing Hu, a lake hemmed in by steep hills, but soon realize that the others are not following. Backtracking we see one truck submerged seventy-five feet from shore up to its headlights in water. The two trucks had followed each other closely and their combined weight was more than the nine inches of ice could hold. Luckily one truck reached shore. We have six hours before darkness descends and the water will freeze. The whole team works frantically to unload the truck and hack with axes and iron poles a channel through the ice toward shore but to no avail. The truck sinks deeper into mud. We try to pull it out with the other truck, but the engine lacks power and the mud clutches its victim tightly. Kalden the driver is dejected that night in camp. It is his private truck, needed to earn a living. When I ask Karma if the truck is insured he replies, "Tibetans don't know about these things." (Later, Karma and I give Kalden enough to purchase another truck.) By morning the truck is frozen solidly in the ice and we abandon it, unfortunately adding litter to the landscape. Not far from here, Wellby found the first sign of human presence in weeks when "one of the men picked up the entire leg bone of some baggage animal . . . for still adhering to the leg was a shoe."

Assuming that the remains of a "baggage animal" implied that nomads lived nearby, most in Wellby's team rebelled. When asked to continue, "they sullenly replied that they would go no further, and hurriedly taking up their belongings amongst a heap of baggage, they moved off in a body." They soon changed their minds but Wellby allowed only one of them to rejoin. Soon eight more pack animals died; their bloated stomachs suggested that they had eaten a poisonous plant, most likely a kind of legume. The expedition continued on foot, Wellby, Malcolm, and four Ladakhis, using the last few pack animals to carry baggage.

The amount of snow and wildlife changes daily. On the morning of November 15 the thermometer outside my tent reads −31° F, the sky is azure, and the plain ahead is almost free of snow. We count 1,137 chiru, surprisingly many, and as usual we have no idea where they spend the summer—perhaps in Xinjiang's Arjin Shan Reserve to the north. Or perhaps many stay here. When the inveterate traveler Sven Hedin passed through in July 1901 on one of his futile quests for Lhasa, he noted "abundant droppings of khulans [kiang] and antelopes." Our tally of wild yak that day is eighty-five, the highest total so far on the trip. The following days are warmer, but still only −15°F, with a wan sun behind a thin veil of cloud. The terrain is deep in snow, drifts to two feet high, and wildlife is scarce. The wind, however, is a constant presence, "furious, merciless, fiercely roaring," as Fernand Grenard phrased it in his 1903 book *Tibet: The Country and Its Inhabitants*.

On November 17, after nearly three weeks and 675 miles of travel, we stop on a ridge approximately marking the border between Tibet and Qinghai. I have brought a string of prayer flags, red, blue, white, green, and yellow. Danda and Zhaduo each hold one end of the string, and then shake hands, the first passing team leadership to the second in a gesture of goodwill and cooperation. Here we pass from Tibet's Chang Tang Reserve into Qinghai's Kekexili Reserve, an area that Zhaduo knows well from his antipoaching patrols over a decade earlier.

Before beginning my work here I had read all the old accounts of the Western travelers who crossed the Chang Tang, and now, as we crossed their routes, they joined me as I tried to see the uplands through their eyes. Most of the travelers provided only incidental observations on wildlife, often in the context of shooting a meal, while pursuing their real goal, that of reaching the holy city of Lhasa. Many entered Tibet heavily armed and with imperial arrogance tried to gate-crash Lhasa but were stopped by the Tibetan military. Coming from the north, two Frenchmen, Gabriel Bonvalot and Prince Henry of Orleans, crossed the Chang Tang in mid-winter 1889 when temperatures dropped to −54°F. Two men on the expedition died and only two pack animals survived when the Tibetan soldiers stopped them ninety-five miles from Lhasa. Four years later, Fernand Grenard, along with another Frenchman, Jules-Léon Dutreuil de Rhins, left Xinjiang in September and with eleven men and sixty-one pack animals tried to force their way to Lhasa. Many of their animals died and many of their staff deserted, and then the Tibetans forced them eastward. Near Yushu, de Rhins was murdered in a dispute over stolen horses. We also crossed the route of Clement St. George Littledale, a wealthy British landowner who left Xinjiang on April 12, 1895, with 250 pack animals, his wife Teresa, a terrier, and a nephew named William Fletcher. (Teresa Littledale was the first Western woman known to have crossed the Chang Tang before Nadine Saulnier did on her 2003 bicycle trip.) They encountered their first Tibetans on June 26, and, after various disputes with local officials, were sent westward only forty-nine miles from Lhasa. The door to Lhasa was finally forced open in 1904 by the British military expedition led by Colonel Francis Younghusband. The invasion was prompted by a combination of faulty information—in this instance, concerning supposed Russian influence in Tibet—and hidden political agendas, a pretext for attacking another country not unknown a century later when the United States invaded Iraq.

An occasional foreigner did reach Lhasa unobtrusively before that 1904 invasion. There was the British eccentric Thomas Manning, who joined a caravan and marched to Lhasa in 1811. A Japanese Zen monk, Kawagushi Ekai, wandered into Lhasa in 1901 after roaming around Tibet for nine months, and stayed quietly in the Sera monastery there for an entire year. Ironically, Sven Hedin failed in his frontal assault on Lhasa the same year.

In fact, Tibet does not have a long history of repelling foreigners. Its doors were open until the seventeenth and eighteenth centuries. Early Jesuit missionaries were welcome. To name just two, the Portuguese Antonio de Andrade laid the cornerstone for a Christian church at Tsaparang in southwest Tibet on April 12, 1626, and Ippolito Desideri established a mission in Lhasa on March 18, 1716. When a quarrel over the succession of the Dalai Lama erupted in 1717 between Tibet's two most powerful Buddhist sects, the Yellow Hats and Red Hats, they asked the Mongolians for help in settling the dispute. A Mongolian force arrived and promptly pillaged Lhasa. China was in turn asked for assistance in evicting the Mongolians. A Chinese army came in 1720, trounced the Mongolians, and stationed a permanent garrison in Lhasa headed by an official, the *amban*. Nepal attacked Tibet in 1788, and China was now asked to repulse this invader, too. China preferred to exclude the rest of the world at that time, and under Chinese influence Tibet barricaded itself behind the mountains, discouraging outside contact.

For some explorers the quest for Lhasa was all-consuming, almost an obsession, and the Chang Tang was to them a purgatory through which their path would lead to fulfillment. Gabriel Bonvalot found the solitude of the Chang Tang "weighing heavier than ever," and Fernand Gerard was "terrified at this endless mountain desert" and "had an ardent longing to escape from it." Yet the desolation and boundless emptiness is to me what makes this wilderness so exceptional, and its perils have left it beautiful, largely devoid of development. I find my emotional center and am comfortable in a place like this. Certainly it suits my inner landscape, reflecting a certain self-contained spirit.

My father, a member of the German diplomatic service, was posted as consul in Chicago, where he married my American mother in 1932. We lived in Germany and other European countries before World War II, and in Denmark and again in Germany during that war, although my father was relieved from his post before the war ended because he had an American wife. I remember vividly that Danish children were not allowed to play with me because of my nationality, and the same then happened in Germany during the war because of my mother, though I had to go to school in both countries. My mother returned to America in 1947 with my brother Chris and me, and there we were generously taken into the home of my grandmother's brother and his wife, Talcott and Paula Barnes, in Webster Groves, a suburb of St. Louis. I was fourteen years old. With only rudimentary English, I was immediately sent to high school where, as someone from a country that had inflicted unspeakable horrors on the world, I was not cordially received by everyone. This history of being repeatedly a stranger in a strange land may have helped to infuse my character with its social restraint and continual longing for a sense of my own place. That said, not being gregarious, or being unwilling to seek just any companionship, does not imply being asocial. I seek a feeling of community, with my family, my expedition members, and congenial persons of similar interests.

We leave Tibet on our continuing expedition across the Chang Tang and descend into Qinghai over a rocky tract to the shore of Lixi-oidian Co. On the bank of a stream flowing into the lake we find stone tools, among them two obsidian cores from which microliths have been struck, perhaps to haft these sharp slivers onto a wooden handle to make knives. The stone tools are a reminder that hunters have camped here as many as 10,000 years ago, that ancient eyes have roamed a similar primitive scene of glaciers tumbling from the Kunlun Mountains, often with herds of wild yak grazing on lush pastures. The desert steppe and alpine steppe through which we have been driving for days are now grading into alpine meadow, a vegetation formation that thrives where annual precipitation is twelve inches or more. Now we also find marmot holes and spot four Tibetan gazelle, two species which like succulent vegetation.

We camp that afternoon near Taiyan Hu. On a high beach line by the lake is a tablet inscribed with the word "hero" in Chinese characters, marking the spot where the protector of chiru, Suonan Dajie, was killed by poachers, as I related in Chapter 4 on the shahtoosh trade. Tador, usually a loud presence, quietly ties a *kata*, a white ceremonial scarf, around the tablet to show his respect, and Tsering and Nyima fasten a string of prayer flags in tribute. Dark snow clouds rest on the glaciers across the lake.

We drive over an outwash plain of gravel between hills and lake and then come to a well-worn vehicle track. Suddenly we see before us a valley churned into a rubble of fresh mine tailings by heavy machinery, a scene of lifeless desolation. It is a major commercial gold mine in what is supposed to be a national reserve, probably an illegal venture that received a permit from some corrupt official. No one is there in winter when all water is frozen, but litter shows that the mine must have been in operation the previous summer. Will this be a memory of the future? To extract gold, gravel is shoveled into sluices and washed with water pumped from streams and temporary ponds. Once the gold-bearing silt has been separated from the gravel, it is treated with mercury, which combines with and concentrates the gold. The mercury contaminates streams, groundwater, and soil; it may also react with certain soil bacteria to form methylmercury, a nerve toxin that accumulates in tissues of animals and plants.

From now on we follow a deeply rutted track made by heavy trucks. The following day, November 20, we come to Zonag Co, a lake which I had tried to reach in 1997. Wellby, I knew, had passed just south of the lake and seen "immense herds of antelope, all females and young ones." I had been intrigued by that statement and had wanted that summer to discover the calving ground. But, as described in Chapter 2, our vehicles had bogged down again and again in sodden, sandy soil and we had to abandon our quest. Even Wellby's pack animals "sank deep at almost every step." Now we easily trace the shore of Zonag Co over frozen ground, but we see only four chiru.

Sedge-covered meadows cover whole hillsides, ideal yak habitat. With their black bulk they take up the entire visual field. We can spot them from miles away, making them easy to count; we tally 713 in just two days. One slope has a herd of 201 and another of 215. Until recently Chinese expeditions, market hunters, gold seekers, and others had shot yak for meat, and I am immensely pleased that the animals seem to be doing well here at present. I could project myself both into the future and back a century and imagine the wildlife as Wellby described it when "in whatever direction I chanced to look numbers of wild yak and kyang [sic] could be seen grazing," and "on one green hill we could see hundreds upon hundreds of yak grazing." Could that vision be revived with continuing protection of the region?

Wellby also saw "sitting below me, huge marmots. They were of enormous size, as large as men." This observation is as puzzling as one made earlier by Garbriel Bonavalot on January 18, 1889, near Shuanghu in the southeastern Chang Tang: "We see monkeys crossing the frozen river and playing upon the rocks . . . with red hair and almost imperceptible tail and small head." Probably these visions cannot be revived.

I think we may reach the Golmud-Lhasa highway tomorrow. Most members of our team pull out a cell phone to check if there is reception. This unsettles me. The daily routine and our compatible group will be disrupted. Danda, Cang Jue, and Li Zhen Chun from the Tibet Plateau Institute, and Kalden, whose truck remains in the lake, will return to Lhasa, and Wang Hao will leave for Beijing. One of our Land Cruisers suddenly stalls. Sakya, a former monk, is an adept mechanic and he and Tador work on the engine, but to little avail. The vehicle is disinclined to move except in brief spasms. We camp. A light snow falls, but at 0°F the night seems warm.

That evening talk turns to the future of the Kekexili Reserve and its thousands of square miles. I worry that herder families will populate the whole area with domestic yaks and that hybridization with the wild ones will follow, in effect eliminating this iconic species. The Kekexili is probably the best final home of wild yak. Perhaps only about 15,000 to 20,000 are left in the world, all on the Tibetan Plateau and all in China except for a few stragglers across the border in the Ladakh part of India. Zhaduo notes that the rangeland here is poor for domestic sheep and yaks in many places, whereas Danda points out that where he comes from in western Tibet these pastures would be considered excellent. Certainly with increasing human population pressure there will be demands for opening the reserve to livestock, as well as to mining and other development. Before the highway was finished in 1954, this whole region was devoid of people, except for an occasional passing caravan, but now herder families have settled most parts.

We reach the highway the following day, November 23, at 2:30 p.m., after a cross-country drive of 1,000 miles. I shake everyone's hand and express my gratitude for their hard work, patience, and companionship. Five of our team members will return home, but the rest of us will continue eastward over hundreds of more miles of rangeland, though, unlike our route so far, it is all inhabited by pastoralists.

As Wellby and his remaining small team moved east they first came upon a stone mound and then "on one of the adjacent hills I had noticed, through my glasses actually, a man with a little dog." They had not seen another person for four months. A few days later they came upon tents of Tibetan merchants traveling from Lhasa to Xining in a huge caravan with 1,500 yaks. Merchants usually banded together to protect themselves from robbers, particularly from marauding Golok Tibetans to the east. A caravan such as this carried dried dates, sugar, and other items imported from India and would return with tea, tobacco, and cloth.

This ancient caravan route has also been used by foreign intruders into Tibet. Two French Lazarist priests, for example, Evariste Huc and Joseph Gabet, quietly reached Lhasa on January 20, 1846, and remained there for two months before being asked to leave. More typical was the Russian scientist-explorer Nikolai Przewalski, discoverer of the Mongolian wild horse and black-necked crane, who came with a band of armed Cossacks to fulfill his dream of reaching Lhasa but was turned back by the Tibetan army in Nagqu.

Wellby was in approximately the same place as we are now. Of their thirty-nine pack animals only five remained. Of our four vehicles one has not survived and two are sick. The lurching Land Cruiser reaches the highway with a final short spurt and collapses, its engine refusing to start again, and the remaining truck barely limps along. We have only one functional vehicle left. The Chang Tang is a merciless place for beast and vehicle alike. Wellby and Malcolm joined the caravan for several days, and, after buying provisions from the merchants, headed northeast over the Kunlun Mountains and on to Beijing, leaving for India after a journey of seven months.

Compared to Wellby's expedition of many months with pack animals and on foot, our twenty-three days by vehicles have been effete. However, we have achieved the purpose of our journey so far, that of counting wildlife and studying its habitat. Our tally shows the following number: 6,909 chiru, 977 wild yak, 515 kiang, 146 Tibetan gazelle, 2 Tibetan argali sheep, 20 wolves, and 12 Tibetan foxes.

Of course, we have no idea how many of each species are in the region because we could count only those within sight of the vehicle, but chiru and wild yak are certainly more abundant in these places than I expected. Our count at least provides useful information to any future survey. Brown bear and marmot are in hibernation at this season and only occasional diggings have revealed their presence. We have also recorded eighteen species of birds, including all the usual winter residents such as upland hawk, golden eagle, saker falcon, horned lark, Hume's groundpecker, and three kinds of snow finch.

I am deeply satisfied with the trip so far. We have become a true team, without the disputes and personal agendas that can so easily disrupt an expedition. Our route has covered a cross-country distance that equals New York to Chicago or Paris to Warsaw or Delhi to Calcutta, and the whole is uninhabited except for the chiru and other wildlife. Where else in the world can one still do this? Where else can one stand on a hill, eyes sweeping across plains to distant snow ranges in all directions, and know that no other humans are there for mile after mile? Such solitude touches the soul. China has a treasure in these uplands, one measured not in gold or oil, but in a unique landscape and natural community of animals and plants that enthrall all those who enter with an open heart. Never must anyone dig up these remote parts of the Chang Tang, develop them, settle them, "improve" them. They must be treated with restraint, respect, and compassion.

Our traverse of the Chang Tang now begins its second phase. We have lived in the past and now we are abruptly propelled into the present and future with all its concerns and problems. When Wellby and Malcolm continued toward the Kunlun Mountains they were still traveling through uninhabited terrain. Today, however, Tibetan households with domestic yaks, black-faced sheep, and goats are scattered throughout the region east of the highway. At 15,000 feet, the elevation to the east is somewhat lower and grazing is generally good. But before continuing farther, we first must drive north to

Golmud to pick up more supplies and meet the new members of our team. Our truck pulls the disabled Land Cruiser slowly over the Kunlun Mountains and the long descent into town, a drive of over four hours. I luxuriate in a warm hotel room and a hot bath. Aili and I meet Xi Zhinong, China's premier wildlife photographer, who had worked in the Pamir Mountains with us studying Marco Polo sheep and who will now be joining our expedition. He has brought a coworker, Wu Lixin, and a newspaper reporter, Qin Qing. Cai Ping of the Qinghai Forestry Department will also come with us, as will two staff members of the Kekexili Reserve protection staff.

While in Golmud we inquire about the two major and several minor gold-mining operations we know about in the Kekexili Reserve. We are told informally that mines have been operating for three years and that some pieces of heavy equipment, such as bulldozers, are brought in through the backdoor from Xinjiang through the Arjin Shan Reserve, indicating collusion by officials from two provinces.

Our truck and one Land Cruiser are unable to continue cross-country and we must obtain replacements from Lhasa, a process that will take several days. Instead of remaining in Golmud, we move to the Suonam Dorjie Protection Station, where an antipoaching team of the Kekexili Reserve is based. The rust-red buildings beside the highway are of metal. Moisture condenses on the inside walls during the day and drips on us and then freezes at night, turning the rooms into refrigerators. The station has a large bunkroom for our use, and the staff is most hospitable. From here we can check on the wildlife in an area which I first surveyed in 1985.

Beside the Protection Station is a large fenced area that serves as an orphanage for chiru. The fluffy, charming youngsters are bottle-fed with goat milk by two keepers, Guo Xue Hu and Jiang Yong, who obviously are fond of their charges. There are also two adult males, strikingly handsome, strutting around with raised muzzles in display, or pointing their rapier horns in threat at each other. Suddenly one of the males charges me, though Aili is closer to him; I dash to the seven-foot fence of the enclosure and pull myself up as far as I can, the male below with his menacing horns near my drooping bottom. Qin Qing snaps a photo. That evening when she flips through the photographs on her digital camera, the one of me clinging to the fence causes great hilarity.

The new railway line between Golmud and Lhasa passes parallel to the highway for much of its route, and we drive alongside it. Started in 2003, the 706-mile rail link was completed in 2006, just months before our visit. It is a great engineering feat. Damage to the environment is minimal and limited, and much care has obviously been taken in construction, and even replacing damaged turf. There are many underpasses in the Chang Tang section, 143 of them 300 feet or more wide and many smaller ones, enabling wildlife to pass easily back and forth through them. Most underpasses were built primarily to keep the railroad bed level in the undulating terrain or to bridge streambeds. A guide from the protection station shows us the underpasses which chiru herds prefer to use in their east-west migration to and from their calving grounds. This migration is new to me. It also goes to Zonag Co, I am told, to the same region as a route that crosses from Tibet into Qinghai and another that moves north within Qinghai. With three chiru populations calving around Zonag Co, that region is obviously critical to the species. The Kekexili has immense value as a protected area, an area where the structure and function of a high-altitude ecosystem can be studied and monitored and compared with changes elsewhere.

At migration times, the Kekexili Protection staff and Green River, a Chinese conservation organization, may halt traffic on the highway to permit the chiru herds to pass safely. We observe kiang, Tibetan gazelle, and a few chiru near the highway, seemingly indifferent to the traffic, a dramatic change from the 1980s when all wildlife fled at the approach of a vehicle. Even a wolf ambled past the protection station.

On November 30, our caravan now made up of one truck and three Land Cruisers leaves southward on the highway at first light. We pass Wudaoliang, a roadside community of restaurants, shops, and gas stations, much grown in the past two decades. We note that Tibetan gazelle are unusually common near the road; maybe their favored food plants grow better in disturbed soil, we speculate, or perhaps they feel safer from predators if near people. After about one hundred miles we leave the highway to head east on a dirt track into the Sanjiangyuan Reserve, its name meaning the "Source of Three Rivers Reserve," an area of about 58,000 square miles extending east and south across Qinghai. China's laws inside and outside of reserves are similar, with hunting and tree-cutting prohibited, and consequently management is much the same.

Our track winds through eroded hills. The turf layer is cracked and broken into blocks which have slid downslope to expose barren silt and rock. After fifty miles we reach the village of Cuochi, one of our objectives. The word *village* conjures a vision of a cluster of households and shops, but here there is only an administrative office, community hall, medical dispensary, and temple (*gompa*). The village families with their livestock are scattered over an area of about 770 square miles. Our interest in Cuochi had been aroused by Zhaduo, who started a community conservation program here, supported in part by Conservation International and the Center for Nature and Society at Peking University. Two months before our arrival, Cuochi and the Sanjiangyuan Reserve administration had signed a pathbreaking agreement permitting the community to manage its own conservation initiatives. Vice Party Secretary Gama, a robust and quietly forceful man, invites us into his home for butter tea and the warmth of a stove. I had met him the previous year at a workshop in Kanding, Sichuan, at which officials, community leaders, monks, businessmen, biologists, and others discussed local conservation issues.

We learned from Gama that rangelands here have greatly deteriorated, so much so that many families are no longer able to subsist on the land. Of 235 families and 1,046 persons in his village last year, 59 families have moved to Golmud and 16 elsewhere, leaving only 160 families with 710 persons at present. At least one-third of the grasslands are considered seriously degraded. I ask, "Why have pastures deteriorated so greatly?" It's a simple question but it becomes the focus of discussion with Gama and various households for several days. Gama tells us that there were no settled pastoralists here before 1966, only seasonal ones from the east. The region had the heaviest snowfall on record in 1985 and temperatures hovered around −40° F for days. Much livestock starved. I tell Gama that I was in the area then and saw many dead domestic sheep and much dead wildlife, chiru and Tibetan gazelle especially, as related in Chapter 1. After the storm the quality of rangelands declined, Gama noted; a three-year drought in the early 1990s made the situation worse, and the grass never recovered. After the storm, the families had little livestock and many were hungry. The men had to hunt wildlife to survive. But if you kill wild animals, it was said, the deities of the nearby mountain Morwadan Zha and other holy sites will punish you; if you protect wild animals you will be rewarded. In any case, the village banned hunting in 1988. The government gave families some sheep and yak, but livestock has not increased to former levels.

The disintegration of the turf layer on the alpine meadows is a stark reminder to the pastoralists that their livelihood is threatened. Alpine meadow covers about half of the grazing lands, mostly in the eastern half of the Tibetan Plateau and sporadically in a swath across the south. A dense mat of the sedge *Kobresia pygmaea* grows on a turf layer of roots and other organic matter from a few inches to over a foot thick. The sedge mat is so closely cropped by livestock that it has the appearance of a well-manicured golf course. Yaks in particular thrive on these pastures. However, the alpine meadows are deteriorating so rapidly that this vegetation formation may not exist in the future. Whole hillsides of turf have broken into clumps that are sliding down the slope to expose barren ground, as is so evident around Cuochi. What is the cause? I once pointed out such a desolate slope to a forestry department official, and he blithely said, "The damage is done by pikas." Some Tibetans hold a similar opinion, as we saw in Chapter 6, though there are few or no pikas in many eroded places. Looking more closely at the damaged terrain, I realized that the cause of the problem was more complex.

Anything that cuts through the turf layer may set a slope in motion, cracking and sliding and breaking. Road construction is one such cause, and so too are deeply worn livestock trails, and the cutting of turf blocks to build corral walls. Water from rain and melting snow seeps beneath the turf and the expansion and contraction of alternate seasonal freezing and thawing lubricates the hillside, causing the turf to slump into terraces and break into isolated clumps which dry out and die. Pikas find such broken terrain congenial, and their digging may in some places contribute to the degradation. Wind and water erode the exposed soil, and soon a hillside is bare except, perhaps, for a few turf blocks as remembrance of the past. A sparse cover of grasses and forbs may colonize such bare areas, but nothing will grow on exposed rock.

Sometimes a turf layer breaks into a network of cracks for no obvious reason. A close examination may reveal that up to half of the *Kobresia* plants are dead, which leaves the surface dark-gray in color, splotched at times with white lichens. This may be due to days and months of heavy trampling and grazing by livestock. If a plant is grazed repeatedly without being given a rest during the growing season, it will use up any energy it has stored in its base, its roots and leaves will have no chance to grow and store nutrients, and it will soon wither and die. Without a moist leaf cover the turf dries and cracks, the first step toward disintegration. Whatever the details, government policy promoted an increase in livestock numbers and these populations doubled and tripled in size within a decade or two on the same limited pastures, without giving these lands a rest until the 1980s when overgrazing led to a drastic degradation of the rangelands. Further policy changes, such as the privatization and fencing of rangelands, hastened the destruction, and the results are now starkly visible.

The views of the Tibetan pastoralists about rangeland conditions and other matters were quoted at length in an excellent set of articles on the Sanjiangyuan Reserve published by the Chinese Committee for Man and Biosphere in a special 2010 issue of its magazine. In "Entering the Black Tents," Mola, a former party secretary of Cuochi, describes the transformation of the land to author Lin Lan:

> From 1972 to 1984, the number of livestock just kept growing. . . . The Township (Commune) had some 270,000 animals. All of us followed a nomadic life and lived in tents. There were no houses. It wasn't until 1987 that some families started building

houses. . . . In 1985 a snowstorm almost wiped out our entire herd in a single week. . . . Since that year, the grassland has been bad. The Household Contract Responsibility System (privatization) had just been adopted with livestock distributed among individual families. . . . After the grasslands were divided and distributed among the households, people started building houses and settling down in one place and stopped their nomadic way of life. . . . In the past, we would move to various pastures according to the month and stay there for about three months at most. Now we use the same plot of land all year round, day in and day out. This never happened in the past. The grass is eaten as soon as it comes out of the ground.

Jigme Ri, also of Cuochi, makes similar points: "In the old days we would move our animals from place to place and it was good. . . . Because people are staying in one place all year round, the grassland has turned dark. With people moving less and less, the grassland is getting worse and worse."

Government policies which serve to intensify grazing pressure in such ways are futile, making rangelands ever more vulnerable to further deterioration. With more and more people in need of land, household allocations become smaller. When Jigme Ri's son got married he received 500 acres, far too little to subsist by raising livestock. As the nomads clearly realize, pastures require rest. Without several months of recovery, degradation can become irreversible, to which the eroded hills we're seeing, once covered with lush meadow, give ample testimony. Indeed, for some areas toward the eastern Chang Tang the degradation started 2,000 or more years ago, as research has shown, with forests cut and burned to produce more pastures.

Degraded pastures have fewer plant species than healthy ones, more bare ground, lower nutrient content of the plants, less organic matter in the soil, and more unpalatable plants, to name just a few differences. Consequently, livestock weighs less and matures more slowly, and females raise fewer offspring. The solution seems obvious: more freedom by communities to manage their rangelands in ways beneficial to land and inhabitants alike. Communities can, for instance, encourage households to graze pastures communally as they did in the past (a few have done so, and in Tibet rangelands are often allocated to groups), regulate livestock numbers to suit pastures and weather conditions, and, more generally, combine traditional and scientific knowledge to create an optimal and sustainable system.

Cuochi has become known for its conservation initiatives, and I ask about those. A small mountain range with wild yak, the last ones in the area, has been the focus of one initiative. The village resettled a dozen households to preserve the pastures for the wild yak. This was not wholly altruistic. The community feels that it needs a wild yak population because households like to hybridize the wild and domestic yak to generate offspring that are larger and bring a better price. To the north of us is a plain known in Tibetan as a *lechi*— the home of the chiru, and the focus of another initiative. Together with a neighboring village, Cuochi has reserved part of this plain for chiru during winter. In addition, the village carries out a conservation monitoring program. Four times a year, each of the village's three production units counts the wildlife within its area, keeps track of lake levels and snow depth, and makes general observations. Difficult times here have inspired people to examine their values. Cuochi is concerned about its environment and its future, based not on government edicts but on ecological and Buddhist religious conviction that their livelihood depends on being good guardians.

As we drive among the hills to visit scattered households and learn more about the area, Zhaduo one day points to slopes near several craggy peaks and casually notes, "When I was a child that was our rangeland." After his parents died he was raised elsewhere by relatives, but promoting conservation in his homeland draws him back again and again. The lives of pastoralists are changing rapidly and conservation is a critical issue. Households have at least one summer and one winter range for their livestock. Sometimes the two ranges are as little as an hour's walk apart, but sometimes

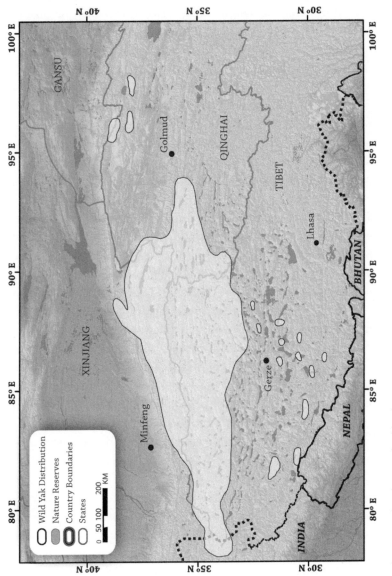

The current distribution of wild yak.

twenty-five miles or more may separate them. The government's division of most rangelands into family plots, leased for thirty to seventy years depending on area, has created a new set of problems for the households and the wildlife. If a heavy snowstorm or drought deprives the livestock of grazing, a family can perhaps rent pasture from a neighbor or, in sparsely inhabited parts, try to find some open communal land. In recent years the government has promoted the fencing of pastures by providing salaries to those who construct fences, subsidies of 80 percent or more to households which buy fencing material, and other incentives. Fenced pastures, however, deprive wildlife of forage and hinder its movement. What are local feelings about fencing? What are attitudes toward sharing pastures with wildlife? To obtain answers to such questions we conduct household interviews.

Large black Tibetan mastiffs bark and lunge to the limits of their chains as we approach Wujin's house. Zhaduo knows the family, and Wujin and his wife Drolma invite us in. We settle by the stove, Zhaduo, Aili, Cai Ping, and I, and are each served milk tea and a small bowl of rich, creamy yak yogurt. Wujin is forty-two years old and has a family of six, including two children and a grandmother who sits quietly spinning a prayer wheel. He has never gone to school but learned to read Tibetan from his parents. The family has 200 sheep, 40 to 50 yak, and 2 horses—a modest amount of livestock—and they also keep 500 sheep for other families, receiving in payment a certain number of lambs each year. In addition, Wujin keeps six yaks for a neighbor in return for 6 kg of butter and 6 kg of other milk products annually. His own rangeland is not productive enough to support all this livestock and he rents additional pasture from others. The family kills two yaks and twenty sheep per year to eat. Some livestock, sheep wool, and butter are bartered to local traders for *tsampa* flour and other needs. But the price of *tsampa*, a staple food, is increasing. And there are other problems. Wolves killed most of the family's sixteen horses and they sometimes lose seven to eight sheep in a month. Once about sixty sheep died in a single year due to a disease. However, conditions in general improved when they invited a monk to pray for his family. Rangelands this year and last are fairly good, he says, because of ample rain.

Wujin remembers when, thirty years ago, pastures such as his could support 2,000 sheep, whereas today he cannot maintain 200 of them. He believes the climate is changing. Rainfall is more erratic, the winters are warmer, and wind- and sandstorms are stronger. Springs have dried up. Pikas have increased in number, creating more bare patches. Drolma interjects as she puts more yak dung into the stove that the turf layer on slopes is breaking up more rapidly. This year the family has built more fences, as required by the government. Wujin does not mind fences because they prevent conflict over pastures with neighbors, and livestock does not need to be herded as closely. But sometimes a kiang breaks a fence by running into it. "No, killing wildlife does not resolve conflict," responds Wujin to one of our questions, and Drolma says that she feels good when she sees wild animals near their home, except wolves. With our discussion concluded, we thank our host and hostess for giving us this two-hour insight into their life.

We conduct a total of sixteen household interviews of this sort. All primary respondents, except one, are males ranging in age from twenty-two to seventy-two, and all are or were pastoralists who were born in the area or moved here when young. Three are village leaders who earn a government salary, and the rest depend on livestock. Nine of the persons have never attended school, four went for just one to two years, and one reached the equivalent of junior high school level. Most can read, but only one man can communicate in Mandarin Chinese.

Thirteen households provide information on their livestock. They have a total of 3,275 sheep and goats and 77 yaks. Two households lack livestock and receive a government subsistence allowance of about 125 yuan ($20) a month; to supplement their incomes, they work for other households herding livestock, butchering, and so forth. One household sold all its livestock in 2005 because there was no one to herd it and the children were in school, but the father has a government salary of 900 yuan per year and he opened a shop from the profits of selling his 100 yaks at about 1850 yuan ($260) each. Household annual incomes ranged from that of one person with over 125,000 yuan ($17,600) down to bare subsistence at 1,500 yuan ($215) per year. Most households have only a modest income gained mainly from selling or bartering livestock or its products to obtain clothing, *tsampa*, cooking oil, and other essential items. In addition, a family needs meat, milk products, droppings of sheep and yak for fuel, yak for transport, and yak hair for making ropes and tents. Motorcycles have largely replaced horses, and gasoline is now the costliest household expense after food.

If the livestock of the richest owner is excluded, the average household has only 173 sheep and goats and 63 yaks, barely enough to subsist. Angqu, for example, like Wujin, can barely subsist on his 150 sheep and 30 yaks. This year he killed fifteen sheep for family use, but wolves killed forty-five sheep and four yaks. A few years ago he lost ninety-six yaks to disease, probably anthrax, and in the spring of 2004 a severe winter killed twenty sheep and four yaks. Such losses cause great hardship at a time when livestock is increasingly sold to buy gasoline, motorcycles, solar panels, TV sets, and other items new to traditional lives. Wujin, Angqu, and others like them have little hope of maintaining themselves, of remaining economically independent, especially when pitted against the certainty of drought, deep snow, livestock diseases, and degraded pastures. Many households have already left or been resettled by government in towns like Golmud. There they are given housing and an inadequate monthly government subsidy, and this makes some feel like "empty sacks that can't stand up by themselves." To make ends meet, a household will often keep at least one family member on its land, retain some livestock, and rent pastures to others. In other words, moving families to town does not necessarily give a rangeland the opportunity to recover from its earlier degradation.

For wildlife, the fences themselves can be harmful. Most fences are four to five feet high and may have a strand of barbed wire on top, too high for animals to leap over. Gazelle, chiru, blue sheep, and others instead become entangled and die when they try to struggle through or under a fence. Long fences obstruct movements and migrations of chiru, kiang, and others. We try to persuade households at least to remove the strand of barbed wire that may hook a leaping animal and leave it to dangle on the fence as it slowly dies.

I note with some surprise that in all our interviews here in the Cuochi area not one person blamed rangeland degradation on too much livestock or on related aspects of poor management. Yang Yongping, in an article in the magazine *Man and the Biosphere*, provides an insight: "The nomads are reluctant to accept that overgrazing exists but they do confess that in the past they did rear too many animals and sold them for slaughter, and thus as a consequence they have committed sins and the grassland is suffering. . . . They see it as punishment for killing too many animals and committing too many sins and this is their way of accepting the overgrazing accusation."

With night temperatures at Cuochi often at −15°F or lower, global warming may seem like a problem far from this part of China but in fact it has arrived in force. The Tibetan Plateau is said to have 46,298 glaciers and the Himalaya 18,000, covering a total of 73,000 square miles, the largest expanse of ice outside of the northern and southern polar regions; sometimes this part of Asia is called The Third Pole. Half of these glaciers were in retreat on the Tibetan plateau in the mid-1900s, but now 95 percent of them are, according to Chinese scientists who are monitoring 680 glaciers. Forty percent of these glaciers could disappear by 2050, and glaciologist Yao Tandong predicts that 70 percent of the glaciers will have disappeared by the end of the century, leading to "an ecological catastrophe."

Climate change will have a huge biological, economical, and cultural impact on the Tibetan Plateau. Temperatures on the plateau have been increasing at 0.3°C per decade since the 1970s, twice the global average. As more rock from melting ice is exposed and heated by the sun, the rate of glacial retreat will increase. In addition, pollution from soot and dust also contributes to the rate of glacial melting. The dark soot particles absorb sunlight and this again warms the surroundings. At first there will be floods in the lowlands downstream from the plateau and then acute water shortages. China considers the eastern half of the Tibetan Plateau its "water tower," its lifeline, the source of the Yellow, Yangtze, Mekong, and Salween Rivers draining from the plateau. About 75 percent of the arable land in northern China depends on irrigation water from rivers originating on the Tibetan Plateau, and countries of Southeast Asia, from Myanmar to Vietnam, depend on some of these rivers, too. China must plan for its own food security; no other country can afford to feed its 1.3 billion or more people. Without water from these rivers there will be food and electricity shortages, migration of millions of people, and political unrest. In addition, the Indus and Brahmaputra, to name just two more rivers, have their source on the Tibetan Plateau and these nurture the civilizations of South Asia.

A concern for water is nothing new in China, though past ecological wisdom there, as elsewhere, has usually been ignored. The Chinese emperor Tao Tu Yu noted 3,600 years ago, "To protect your rivers, first protect your mountains." One passage of the *Tao Te Ching*, written about 2,300 years ago, states: "When you drink water remember its source." This message to take nothing for granted, not even a cup of water, has special resonance today.

With increasing temperatures on the Tibetan Plateau, other changes have been occurring as well. Winters have become warmer, the length of time with a snow cover has decreased, and there are on average seventeen more frost-free days than there were a few decades ago. In the eastern part, precipitation has increased in winter and decreased somewhat in summer. Warmer temperatures and more frost-free days can increase plant productivity. However, nutrition of plants declines with warmer temperatures, and less soil moisture in summer inhibits plant growth.

Zhu Liping and his coworkers give a useful overview of the large ecological effects in *Impacts of Climate Change on the Yangtze Source Region and Adjacent Areas*, a 2009 publication of WWF–China:

> Studies of temperature, precipitation, lake levels, and lake sediments on the Qinghai-Tibet Plateau have revealed a distinct trend of increasing temperatures, a less distinct trend towards decreasing precipitation, and an overall increase in the rate of evaporation of surface water on the plateau over the past century. . . . These impacts have included not only increased evaporation and decreased precipitation, but also the rapid melt-off of glaciers that provide the source waters for many plateau wetlands as well as the widespread degradation of permafrost that underlies many

plateau wetlands and prevents deep infiltration of surface waters. . . . As a result of these four factors, many seepage fields, streams, wetlands, ponds, and small lakes have already dried up, and many more are threatened with a mass drying up. The widespread disappearance of surface water resources on the plateau will have severe consequences for both humans and wildlife inhabiting the Qinghai-Tibet Plateau, as well as for the economic development of the entire region.

About half of the Tibetan Plateau has permafrost, permanently frozen ground, about three to six feet below the surface. But permafrost, despite its name, may not be permanent: it is now melting. Permafrost retains water near the surface of the ground because it cannot seep downward—as we discovered all too often by getting stuck in mud during summer. As the water seeps more deeply into the ground when the permafrost melts, all vegetation will be or is already being affected by the lowering of the water table and the loss of soil moisture. The alpine meadow habitat will more rapidly dry out, crack, and slump, and the exposed soil will be eroded by wind and precipitation, until it may ultimately disappear. The *Stipa* grass on the alpine steppe, a favored food of wild and domestic ungulates, is short-rooted and may die out in most places. The sedge *Carex moorcroftii*, which has deep roots and grows well on sandy soils but is not liked much by ungulates, may replace it, a process hastened in grasslands degraded by livestock. The whole region could become a wind-blown desert if present trends continue.

The turf of alpine meadow has accumulated and stored a great deal of carbon in its organic matter. Microbes in the soil use oxygen to convert the carbon into carbon dioxide. As the turf is destroyed a huge amount of carbon dioxide is released into the atmosphere. So too is methane gas, which has twenty times the heat-trapping capacity of carbon dioxide. The destruction of alpine meadow habitat may by itself contribute considerably to climate change.

Whatever the details, climate change coupled with the other forces of rangeland degradation will have serious consequences for all plant and animal species and the livelihood of the people at Cuochi and elsewhere. Will the chiru be able to persist? By listening

to officials and heads of households we realize that the region has
no practical land-use policy based on ecological understanding—on
the kind of information that would enable pastoralists, livestock, and
wildlife to coexist. Instead, policy is based on impulse and intuition, which inevitably leads to unintended consequences, usually
bad ones. Talking to households about the price of *tsampa* may seem
somewhat dull, even remote from ecological concerns, yet conservation depends on the goodwill and participation of communities,
and this in turn depends on mutual understanding.

Gama organizes a meeting in the community center to discuss
and share ideas on various topics, from monitoring wildlife and
tourism to climate change and range management. The walls of the
community center are draped with red-and-gold banners, all of them
awards to production teams for reaching quotas and other achievements. About fifty pastoralists attend, as do three novices, about ten
years old, dressed in the robes of monks from the local *gompa*. Some
of the pastoralists wear traditional hats of red fox fur and sheepskin
chubas, whereas others sport fashionable jackets with logos of Honda
and other international companies. Village director Losang presides,
Zhaduo is moderator, an expert one, alternately spellbinding and
amusing. He conveys his knowledge not in the language of science
but of the community. My remarks in English consist of a sentence
or two which Aili translates into Chinese and Zhaduo then converts
into Tibetan, often talking for five minutes or more. I wonder what
I have said. This is followed by a long, vigorous discussion by the audience, often all talking at once. We all participate, commenting and
learning. The meeting lasts all day. Afterward I present Gama with a
gift of 3,000 yuan (about $425) to help the monitoring team record
the arrival of the first bird migrants in spring, the first blooming of
flowers, and other events. After the traditional group photograph,
Losang drapes us with *katas*.

From Cuochi we drive farther east and then north toward the village
of Duo Xu. A red fox lies curled in a depression out of the icy wind

and watches us sleepy-eyed, its coat a lustrous brick-red. I hope it will not become a Tibetan hat. Here the red fox shares the landscape with the smaller Tibetan fox, which has a pale russet coat, a grey rump, and a fluffy face that give it the appearance of a stuffed toy.

In Duo Xu, Vice Director Cai Ren Zhan Do, a tall, lean, and friendly Tibetan, provides us with two rooms. The following day he takes us on a tour. In one valley we spot several Tibetan argali sheep high on a slope, two of them rams with massive curled horns. We are excited about spotting a total of twenty-six argalis in the valley, a rare sight. Cai Ren tells us that with protection from his community these animals are increasing after having been almost wiped out by hunters.

Later that day we stop on the crest of a ridge to scan a plain. Four wolves trot out of sight in single file. Below us is a concentration of chiru. They, like the argalis, are also entering the rut. I wish we had time to tarry, to continue observing the chiru as males prance with a high-stepping gait around females or chase each other in glorious bursts of speed, tails raised, heads held low, and roaring. The sight of rutting chiru takes me back to 1991, when I spent days with them at this season; one occasion was particularly memorable, as described in *Tibet's Hidden Wilderness*:

Once I walked among the chiru and sat down immobile, an inanimate hump. The animals soon ignored me. A wolf strolled along a distant cutbank. Even a nomad's tent huddled by a far ridge was part of this landscape. All around me the chiru males bellowed their challenges and pursued each other into the blinding light of the horizon, all around me chiru danced on the tawny grass in their annual ritual of renewal. I sat at the center of this consecrated space, quietly celebrating the harmonious balance of a fleeting moment.

Cai Ren detours past an encampment of twenty white canvas tents, seven jeeps, and many motorcycles. A truck is filled with white sacks, each marked with skull and crossbones, which, I am told, are filled with grain—to which poison will be added. Men stand around in clusters. I learn to my consternation that this is a communal gathering to poison pikas. This senseless poisoning campaign infuriates me (as I related in Chapter 6). But my morose feelings are lifted by a festive evening. It's Aili's thirtieth birthday. Tsering and Nyima have somehow baked a lovely chocolate cake inscribed in English with "Happy Birthday." Aili blows out the single candle. The Tibetans sing traditional songs and Tsering dances while we clap to his rhythm. Karma produces a beer for each one of us, the first we have seen in over a month. Aili stands beaming, dressed in her usual red wool cap and draped with *katas* from us all.

We continue east over a rough track. There are many gazelle—we count 809 today. A red-brown wolf trots past eight gazelle at about 500 feet. They watch the wolf with rump hairs erect and fanned outward, white heliographs signaling danger to gazelle farther away. The wolf is not hunting and continues casually, yet its mere presence has added tension to the landscape. Late afternoon brings us to the *xiang*, or administrative center, of Qumarhe, a one-street town of government offices and shops. Zhaduo's older brother lives here. After surviving half a dozen lunging mastiffs chained in his courtyard, we are given the hospitality of the guestroom. In a community such as this, one walks carefully, not cutting closely around corners and not going near anyplace from which a snarling mastiff might erupt. The others conduct household interviews the following day, while I nurture my back, which is throbbing from endless days of bouncing cross-country and over even worse tracks.

We leave the Qumarhe *xiang* to the sound of monks chanting on loudspeakers. Our route is northward now over flats and hills through a snowy landscape brittle with cold and wind that shakes the vehicles. The region has few nomads and no fences. We stop at a house to ask for directions. Four dour women barely answer our questions, unusual in a highly hospitable culture, and several mastiffs roar and run around the posts that chain them, an almost sinister encounter, though I realize that the women are simply apprehensive of strangers.

The route brings us to a valley— miles of a gray, undulating mass of sterile gravel, mine tailings, the gold extracted, a place of beauty ruined for centuries. It is one of several here in the foothills of the Kunlun Mountains. Tibetan pastoralists generally do not approve of this mining but they lack a political voice. They believe that if one destroys a river he or she will be reborn as a hungry ghost, naked and ugly. Nyima Gyaltsen wrote in an article in *Man and the Biosphere* magazine:

> The dragon that brings good weather, rain, and winds has left the grasslands and moved off to a distant place. Machines are all over the plateau cutting into the ground. The place is bloated with greed. The nomads have lost their grasslands and the animals have been swept away.
>
> The children of the dragon, who have lost their blood, will live in pain and face endless calamities.
>
> If the earth falls sick who can we turn to for help?

Mining disrupts the water regime of a whole drainage and deprives pastures of essential moisture during the short summer growing season. These are all private mines, some funded by foreign capital, I'm told, and all are in a national reserve where they are officially prohibited.

At dawn the thermometer by my tent registers −9°F. Unsure of our route we meander through the hills eastward on obscure tracks that seem to lead nowhere and vanish under snow. A gorge blocks us and we backtrack. We spot small, round, black bumps on the snow that suddenly vanish at our approach. They are heads of pikas popping in and out of their burrows. The heater in our Land Cruiser is poor and the windows are frozen shut, but the sun will ultimately warm us. Later we come upon two figures on a snow-free plain, a herder and his wife, guarding a large flock of sheep. They are so swaddled in clothes against the frightful wind that only their eyes are visible. We ask for directions to the Madoi *xiang* but they have no idea where the track might be and only point vaguely southward. Backtracking yet again we come to a lake with a tent on the shore. We set up camp nearby after saying hello to Gongda, his wife, and two daughters, seven and ten years old. When we return later for a household interview, Gongda appears in his finest clothes, the ones usually reserved for festivals and other public occasions. His *chuba* is trimmed with leopard and otter skin. I ask how much it cost and he replies 6,000 yuan (around $850). For a poor family to spend so much to make a fashion statement . . . !

We are finally on the right track. Wind whips dust into dense clouds that engulf us as they race past. Off and on the route traverses broken turf for jaw-rattling hours. After a long day we arrive in Madoi *xiang*, a desolate cluster of building with refuse and feces everywhere, so depressing that even the dogs bark with little conviction. However, Vice Director Luo Song Zhasi greets us cordially and offers a room with a stove in government quarters.

Luo Song is concerned about conservation and has founded the Yellow River Environment Protection Association. A festival was held here this year to promote environmental awareness. I ask about the valleys destroyed by gold mining. Yes, he answers, there is much mining and mercury is used, and the Tibetan foxes act strangely. Driving toward Madoi, we have noticed that gazelles and kiang are remarkably shy, bolting in great panic from our vehicles. Yes, Luo Song agrees, this is because market hunters come from Golmud on a track through the mountains to shoot wildlife. We are distressed to learn from Luo Song that we cannot continue eastward along our planned route because the bridge over the Yellow River has collapsed. The Land Cruisers might be able to cross on the ice but perhaps not the truck. We have learned our lesson about trucks on ice. Instead, suggests Party Secretary Song Bu, head eastward as far as the source of the Yellow River, a distance of only thirty miles, and then go south. We take his advice.

At the village of Guoyang we meet Party Secretary Zimi, aged sixty-one, who resembles a sunburned version of the actor Peter O'Toole in a *chuba*. Zimi agrees to guide us to the headwaters of the Yellow River, and then we interview him about this region. He is voluble and expansive, a good subject for Xi Zhinong to film. When he moved here at the age of seven in the 1950s, Zimi tells us, the combined Qumarhe and Madoi *xiang* had 120,000 head of livestock and no rangeland conflict. Now there are 50,000 head and people fight each other for pasture. Much good turf is now just sand and stone. "Will there be no livestock in a hundred years?" We have no answer to his question. Chiru used to be common. The last time he saw any was in the 1990s.

A trickle of water on a marshy hillside marks the ultimate head-water of the mighty Yellow River. In the valley it becomes a creek, now frozen. Prayer flags mark the site, as do two stone tablets, one inscribed "Source of the Yellow River" in calligraphy by China's former general secretary of the Communist Party, Hu Yaobang, and the other, a larger one, by former president Zhang Zemin. Zimi reminds us that this is the homeland of the mythical King Gesar, who designated thirteen holy mountains in the vicinity. Just to the north, rising out of the plain, is the holy mountain Yao Ra Da Ze. The Yellow River is a dragon and the two small streams of its source are its horns. Zimi goes on to note that we are in the "Capital of Wild Yak." Herds of a thousand yaks roamed here in the past, and even in the 1990s herds of up to two hundred could still be seen, but the remnants continued to be heavily hunted. They are gone now, all of them gone.

A quote from William Woodville Rockhill, who traveled through here in 1889 and wrote about the journey in *Land of the Lamas*, confirms what Zimi tells us. "The hills around this plain, and also Karma-t'ang, were literally black with yak; they could be seen by thousands, and so little molested by man have they been that we rode up to within two hundred yards of them without causing them any fear."

We want to complete our traverse of the Chang Tang at the large twin lakes of Gyaring and Ngoring, which lie near the eastern edge of the great rangelands. But because of the broken bridge over the Yellow River we must detour far southeast to the county town of Qumarleb, and then loop east and north, an extra 350 miles of driving. The vehicle vibrates as blasts of wind and snow whip in sheets across the road to form drifts. A broken-down jeep blocks the road, but together we bodily lift it to the side and continue. In Qumarleb, Xi Zhinong and his crew leave us to head back westward to film chiru. The town is at 14,100 feet, our lowest elevation in over a month, except for the brief visit to Golmud. The Chang Tang now far behind us, we continue all the next day down a valley, flanked by buckthorn brush along the river and gnarled juniper trees on the slopes, to the county town of Zhidoi, where Zhaduo has a home. I was here in 1984, but the town has grown so much in the intervening years that nothing looks familiar. As we continue, irrigated fields appear and poplar trees line the road. Yushu, altitude 12,100 feet, a prefecture town, is large, crowded with noisy traffic, and polluted. (The town would be destroyed by an earthquake on April 14, 2010.) Zhaduo and members of his conservation office in Yushu lecture widely on the environment in schools throughout the region; when we visit the office they are rightly proud of their accomplishments.

In a snowstorm, beneath scudding gray clouds, we drive northward for six hours to the county town of Madoi. The next day, December 15, we close the missing link of our traverse as far west as Ngoring Hu, a sheet of ice at this season. Back in Madoi, I summarize how much wildlife we have seen since leaving the Golmud-Lhasa highway on November 30. In 1,231 miles of driving through suitable habitat, not including the main roads in the past few days, my count is 719 chiru, 1,090 kiang, 2,675 Tibetan gazelle, and 46 argali sheep, as well as 17 wolves, 48 red and Tibetan foxes, and one manul cat. The bird list includes one vagrant red crossbill high on the plains, far from its usual conifer forest. A good reservoir of wildlife remains, except that the few remaining wild yak in the Cuochi region have a precarious future. Chiru have been exterminated in the eastern 150 miles of their range since the 1990s, but they could recolonize this area if afforded good protection.

As our traverse comes to an end, I can only reflect with sadness on the extent to which the high rangelands of the Tibetan Plateau have deteriorated in the past half century through bad livestock management, unsupervised gold mining, and unrestricted hunting. The relatively intact Kekexili area gave me a glimpse into the past, whereas trends here offer a gloomy peek into the future. We have to find ways to better protect and manage the landscape. Of course, no ecosystem remains static and local cultures adapt and change. There is an urgent need to develop new ideas, approaches, and policies appropriate to changing ecological conditions and therefore social and economic conditions. The basic goal should be to conserve the function of the ecosystem for the pastoralists who have no alternative livelihood and for the plants and animals which have no alternative whatsoever.

The reality is, roughly, that environmental management is people management. Local concerns must be addressed if wildlife and pastoralists are to coexist with a measure of ecological harmony. Solutions are always complex and require an integrated approach, not a simplistic one like poisoning pikas. It has become axiomatic that conservation can be successful only if local communities are fully involved in planning and implementing management efforts. Indeed, rangelands lend themselves well to long-term conservation as long as the approach is adaptive and flexible, and pastoralists can remain mobile. Other countries, such as the United States, Australia, and many African countries, have degraded their rangelands extensively through indifference, negligence, greed, imperfect scientific information, and lack of suitable policies. We can learn from their mistakes and should apply any relevant knowledge here, an initiative largely the responsibility of Chinese scientists in cooperation with provincial and local officials and with community leaders.

As Sangjie told us during a household interview, "The largest problem we face is changes in ourselves."

Hundreds of prayer flags on poles flutter and rustle on a hillside near Madoi. Nearby is a small *gompa*. I have brought prayer flags from Lhasa. We climb onto a knoll and stand side by side, each holding the string of prayer flags, a symbol of our continuing bond. Seven of us have made the whole traverse—Karma, Tsering, Nyima, Sakya, Zhaduo, Aili, and myself. As we shake hands, hug, and pat shoulders, we are all happy that we arrived safely and in good health. It has been one of my most enjoyable journeys in China.

CHAPTER 8

Feral Naturalist

WHAT IS IT ABOUT the huge emptiness of the Tibetan Plateau, a wild and raw terrain where lakes are the color of molten turquoise, that has so ensnared me, that has drawn me back again and again over decades of fieldwork? I am still uncertain. I don't know why the trajectory of my efforts on behalf of nature has been "up"—up in Alaska, Africa, and Asia, up where mountains vanish into cloud, up with wind song and intense, pure light. I have been a cloudwalker up among mountains, hiking, dreaming. This has little to do with being a naturalist. But neither is it aberrant professionally, because a feeling of unity with a landscape and its creatures can be sought anywhere. My childhood did not predispose me to a special love of mountains or to any other particular terrain, and neither environment nor heredity bear direct responsibility for how I was assembled. Maybe I simply prefer the beauty of a hermetic world suffused with stillness.

"I was born a naturalist," Charles Darwin wrote in his autobiography. This blunt statement stimulated me to reflect on my evolution as naturalist and what had brought me here. I have none of Darwin's self-assurance when it comes to the origin of my own interest in nature. To tease apart motives, to pinpoint the complex reasons for any quest, is difficult if not impossible. Feelings, desires, and cool reason are inextricably linked to any goal, and there may be subtle changes with time. As the Taoist master Laozi said:

Many words cannot fathom it,
But look, it is in your heart!

As a child in Europe I moved from country to country, and later as a naturalist my research took me to many more. Being forever itinerant, and burdened with the melancholy of an outsider, I became perhaps an internal exile with a detached and reticent character. Fieldwork demands stoicism, a tolerance for pounding winds and lashing snows as well as balky porters and vehicles, and, most difficult, often renouncing time with those you love. Passions are selfish, and it is Kay who bore the burden of mine. My aversion to city life, crowds, noise, and the public eye, combined with an austere childhood in Europe, has perhaps predisposed me to travel in remote places where rigors may be such that one settles at times for mere survival. Whatever the explanation, I like to ramble over wild topography or sit quietly to watch an animal in its universe so different from mine. A naturalist basically wanders and observes. That is what I have loved to do as far back as memories take me. Such a desire does not foretell a scientific career, however. I never hunted a future. But I was offered choices that, once taken for whatever reason at the time, pointed me toward what in retrospect seems an inevitable life as a naturalist.

The study of animals over the decades has defined me and, in a way, superseded me as a person. I am judged by what I have published and by my other professional activities. But when it comes to wildlife and their habitat it has become a necessity, indeed a moral obligation, to preserve what one studies. Consequently I have become less of a conventional practicing scientist, less devoted to publishing academic papers and monographs with all their statistics, tables, and graphs, no matter how important, and more focused on promoting the need for conservation. I now ask the question, "What facts do I need to help protect and manage a species and its habitat? So I continue to adapt, ready for new insights, actions, and memories. Unlike Darwin, I do not consider myself a born naturalist; instead I seem to have haphazardly evolved into one—and continue to evolve.

I officially became a naturalist with my first field project in 1952—a study of Arctic birds in northern Alaska—after my freshman year at the University of Alaska. Until then my life had been without discernible direction. In searching through the web of my past, I find it difficult to retrieve shadowed childhood memories about nature, though at times they intrude unexpectedly. Once, walking across Tibet's uplands, I had a vision of myself running through a German meadow full of yellow primroses in bloom. Now at my feet were primroses whose sweetly distinctive scent triggered the memory which repossessed my childhood. The European cuckoo is widespread in eastern Tibet where patches of forest grow interspersed with alpine meadow. When I hear the cuckoo's resonant and repeated call, I see myself walking through a German forest, holding my father's hand, as he sings in a monotone "*Kuku-kuku ruft durch den Wald*" ("Cuckoo-cuckoo rings through the forest").

Between 1933, the year of my birth in Berlin, and 1939, we lived first in Prague, now the Czech Republic, and then in Kattowitz, a city in Poland, where my father was a diplomat in the German legations. After that, war disrupted life. I started school in 1939 in Radebeul near Dresden while we lived with my father's parents in a pleasant house surrounded by a garden and fruit trees. Later that year my father was posted to Copenhagen in Denmark, where we stayed for three years, I went to school, and my brother Chris was born. On returning to Germany in 1942, I again went to school near Radebeul, but in 1944, at the age of eleven, I was sent to boarding school. The Hermann Lietz Schulen consisted of a network of schools, usually housed in old castles (*Schlösser*) in the countryside, and of these I attended four different ones.

The first school was Schloss Ettersburg, but my stay there was brief. One day military officers of the Waffen SS came and handed out chocolate bars, a wartime rarity. This was followed by an order to vacate the school, which was located not far from the concentration camp Buchenwald, a place we knew merely as a prisoner-of-war camp. The military provided a train to evacuate us to another school, Schloss Bieberstein. On the way, while we were on a siding in Halle, an Allied air raid demolished part of the city as we crowded into a railway underpass. A bomb hit one entrance and a hurricane of debris blasted over the moaning crowd. The train survived, battered and tattered but functional, and we continued.

From Schloss Bieberstein some of us were soon transferred to another school, a former farm called Grovesmühle near the Harz Mountains. There we worked in the fields more than in class, hoeing rows of sugar beets and digging potatoes on various farms, a labor for which the school was paid in produce. As the American army swept eastward across Germany, we were also ordered to dig trenches, retreats of safety. One night the ground shook and distant explosions thundered. From the trenches we observed flares arcing across the sky and a flaming horizon: the retreating German army had blown up an ammunition dump. Within days two American half-track vehicles filled with combat troops pulled into the school courtyard. Our principal ordered all students to lie in their beds. Soldiers, dusty and unshaven, walked from bed to bed, automatic weapon aimed at us as they scrutinized each face to check for any German soldier hiding among us. A few days later, the school was invaded by a swarm of Serbs and other East Europeans who had been released from a German labor camp. Again we took to our beds while the school was looted of food, clothing, and even the cats. Loaded with as much as each man could carry, the swarm moved on.

I had not heard from my family in months and had no idea what happened to them. One day I saw a stocky man walking alone down a lane toward the school, a rucksack on his back. It was my father in search of me.

To escape the Soviet advance from the east, many Germans moved westward, including ultimately my family. While my father was away on assignment and I was still in boarding school, my mother and Chris visited a friend in Dresden. The date was February 13, 1945. That day two British air raids and the following day an American one annihilated the beautiful city and killed an estimated

135,000 people in the bombings and resulting firestorms (more people than were killed at Hiroshima). Mother and three-year-old Chris had taken refuge in a cellar when the air raid sirens howled. Shortly after 10:00 p.m., as my mother would later record on tape,

> we were shaken by a tremendous thud. The walls swayed and soot blew out of the chimney base. Detonations were loud and close. The building seemed to heave back and forth, and there was a loud cracking sound. The air was filled with dust, and breathing became difficult. . . . The cellar door had blown off its hinges. . . . What a sight greeted us! Our five-story building was just not there anymore. . . . Most of the buildings were now gutted. Live wires were down everywhere. We could hear muffled cries for help coming from some basements.

Mother and Chris escaped to another friend's house in the suburbs by walking all night through the devastation.

My family then moved to Bad Orb, a resort town in the American zone near Frankfurt, where we rented a room. War's end brought severe food shortages in the cities, and my American grandfather, Frank Beals, a former Chicago school superintendent, sent CARE packages to us. From these we extracted luxury items such as soap and cigarettes, which my father and I traded for bread at farmhouses when I was home from boarding school. American troops, or "Amis" as we called them, were billeted in a nearby hotel. I waited at the back entrance by the garbage bins, a large tin can in hand. When a soldier came to dump uneaten food from his mess kit, I snagged pieces of pancake, slices of bread, fragments of omelet, and other bits which then became our family meal.

My father wanted to visit his parents near Dresden, now under Soviet occupation, to pick up some belongings which he could sell or barter for food. He asked me to join him. Going east was no problem, but heading back from the Soviet-occupied zone on November 13, 1945, became a memorable journey. Four years later, when I was a high school student in the United States, our teacher asked us to write an autobiographical sketch. I remembered that journey vividly and described it for my assignment:

In Dresden, we boarded a train with missing windows and a shattered roof and headed west toward the city of Leipzig. Near the city limits of Dresden, we rode through the most wrecked and bombed-out part of town where now only a few people lived in old basements and one-room huts made of wooden crates and boxes. We needed to continue from Leipzig to Erfurt, but it seemed impossible to get on the waiting train. People were lying on the roof, sitting on the engine, and standing on the running boards. But I knew of a small, windowless cubby, usually in the last coach, for dogs. My father closed the tiny door after me and I was in pitch darkness. [No dogs were in residence.] As the train rattled on for hours with occasional stops, I began to wonder what had happened to my father, if he was even on the train. Finally someone opened the door. My father had lain on the roof the whole trip whole trip, wrapped in a blanket with the temperature at about 40 degrees Fahrenheit.

Two local men agreed to take us to the border over a high ridge and across a three-mile strip of neutral land to the American-occupied zone, and they were even willing to carry some of our heavy baggage. It poured rain. The mud was deep and water streamed down the hill. When we reached the top of the ridge, we crouched behind low bushes and waited for the next patrol to pass by. The border guards were German ex-soldiers, paid by the Soviets, and notorious for robbing the possessions of anyone they catch. Finally a three-man patrol passed, and we hurried on into the three miles of neutral zone. About halfway across, our helpers decided to leave us. Ahead were the lights of Sondershausen in the American zone. Step by step my father and I pushed and pulled our suitcases across a plowed field to a road. Twice we jumped into a ditch to hide from a Soviet patrol wagon. Our final obstacle was a river with a bridge guarded by Soviet soldiers.

My father went into the water first, carrying a suitcase over his head. I followed, the water reaching just under my arms until I stepped in a mud hole. With the water now up to my nose and my feet sinking deeper into mud, I nearly dropped my suitcase.

I called my father with a muffled cry, hoping the guards wouldn't hear. . . .

War experiences such as these may have little relevance to shaping my later life as a naturalist but they probably did influence my willingness to adapt and endure difficulties in the field.

I was sent from Bad Orb soon thereafter to another boarding school, Schloss Buchenau. Living in a castle may sound romantic, but among my most vivid memories are frost on the inside stone walls of our unheated rooms in winter and outdoor latrines consisting of a mere horizontal bar across an open pit. As at Grovesmühle we worked in fields, especially fields of rutabaga, which we then received as mush for breakfast, fried for lunch, and soup for dinner. I have avoided that root vegetable ever since. Our teachers were often of poor quality, survivors of the war: a shell-shocked air force officer; a mathematics professor ancient and abstruse; a local Catholic priest who taught history and gave grades on the basis of church attendance, something against which I rebelled; and an athletic director with part of his skull missing who insisted on playing soccer with us even though an errant kick could have penetrated his throbbing brain.

But here at Schloss Buchenau, now at the age of thirteen, I discovered for the first time nature for its own sake and the feelings of joy and contentment that come with it. One of my friends was a forester's son, and we searched the nearby woods for nests of crows and buzzards and tried to spot long-eared owls perching motionless high up on a branch. I began to collect bird eggs, carefully taking one fresh egg from a nest, pricking each end with a needle, and blowing out the contents. Soon the eggs of greenfinch, blackbird, mistle thrush, collared dove, starling, and others nestled in a box protected by cotton wool.

With another friend, I went trout fishing in a clear, fast-flowing creek near the school. Wading slowly, our hands searched the hollows under cutbanks until we felt the smooth skin of a hidden trout. Ever so slowly and gently our fingers glided up the trout's belly, barely touching it, until we could grab the fish at the gills. We impaled the trout on a stick and roasted it over a fire, savoring our success as hunters.

My mother wanted to return to the United States with Chris and me, whereas my father intended to come later. After some days in an internment camp for displaced persons, we boarded a troop transport, the *Ernie Pyle,* on September 10, 1947, and on September 21 reached New York, where we were interned on Ellis Island. My Grandfather Beals came and released us. Chris and I went ashore as enemy aliens. Grandfather gave me twenty-five cents, with which I bought a can of pineapple.

Mother, Chris, and I moved to Webster Groves, a suburb of St. Louis, into the home of my Uncle Talcott and Aunt Paula, his wife. For my uncle and aunt, both in their fifties, to offer shelter to a teenager, a five-year-old, and my mother is something for which I have been forever grateful. Mother, a good artist, soon moved with Chris to New York to be with her mother, and she became a designer of fabrics. (My father stayed in Germany, my parents eventually divorced, and each remarried; Chris became a lawyer in California.)

I remained with my aunt and uncle, having started high school immediately after arrival in Webster Groves. Judging by Aunt Paula's accounts, I was a disagreeable teenager. In 1950, for example, she wrote to my mother of my treatment of the unusually tolerant Mrs. Julia Haley, a devoted housekeeper who took wonderful care of everything, including me: "He is still young for his age and at times still difficult with Mrs. Haley. He enjoys teasing and tormenting her as well as sometimes talking very cross to her. . . . One cannot just get any job for George as he is no good if he has to do work he is not interested in." But a little later Aunt Paula expressed some reason for hope: "He seems to be growing up some. He is learning to live with other people in a more peaceful manner." But Mrs. Haley always claimed, "He's a good boy." The upsetting experiences of the war years and their aftermath, the complete disruption of our family, and the stress of being displaced from one culture into another may have destabilized me. However, my mother could claim that I had showed an irascible character even early in life. She wrote a friend after seeing me for the first time shortly after my birth, "there was the furious face of George Beals Schaller. . . . The boy is strong physically [8.5 pounds, 21 inches long] and has a beastly difficult disposition."

In high school, I was a mediocre student mainly because I lacked interest in most of the courses. The results of an aptitude test produced the verdict that I was not college material but that I might make a good mechanic. I retained, however, the casual enjoyment in the outdoors that I had developed in Germany, and now joined my school friend Jim Reuter in scouring the woods for skinks, milk snakes, ringneck snakes, and other reptiles which each of us kept in a terrarium. Uncle Talcott and Aunt Paula had two sons, Bill and Ed. Ed, the older of the two, had a decisive influence on my future by exposing me to wilderness during my high school years. He had studied mining engineering at the University of Alaska and owned a small island covered with tall pines on Rainy Lake, Ontario, not far from the U.S. border at International Falls. There, assisted by Jack Kehoe, a lumberjack friend of the family, he built a cabin in 1949, felling trees, peeling them, and notching the logs. I was invited to participate, but, more important, I also went canoeing there, photographed a porcupine and great blue heron with my box camera, and at night heard the howl of wolves.

The following summer, before starting my last year in high school, Ed drove his father, Jack Kehoe, Old Man Lindsey (an acquaintance), and me in his truck up the Alaska Highway to Whitehorse in Yukon Territory. Old Man Lindsey had prospected for gold on the Big Salmon River, and claimed to know the precise location of the "white band"—the mother lode. For us it was a simple outdoor adventure, but for Old Man Lindsey, then in his eighties and nearly blind, it was a return to his youth. In Whitehorse, Ed bought an outsized rowboat, attached an outboard motor, and we set off down the Yukon River, along Lake Laberge, and then churned up the Big Salmon River, the current so strong we could make no headway even with the outboard at full throttle. Ed, Jack, and I pulled and pushed the boat upstream, walking in the icy water.

We camped on gravel bars to escape the mosquito hordes and to dry our clothes on driftwood fires. Old Man Lindsey looked vaguely at the hills through cloudy eyes, unable to recognize anything. I relished the freedom of our daily existence. All too soon we drifted back downstream to the Yukon, where we hailed a sternwheeler, the *Aksala*, which hauled supplies to isolated outposts; we loaded on our boat and gear, and returned to Whitehorse.

We then continued up the Alaska Highway to Fairbanks. At the outskirts of the city is the University of Alaska, then a small cluster of buildings on a hill with a wide view across flats toward Denali, the highest mountain in North America. Forests of spruce, aspen, and birch extended in all directions, and this spaciousness greatly appealed to me. After returning to Webster Groves, I took Ed's advice and applied for admission to the University of Alaska. With high school graduation coming up, and my being of an age to be drafted, enrollment in a university would have a further advantage: draft deferment. Aunt Paula had rightly noted in a letter to my mother, "I think the thought of [the] draft sends chills up and down his spine." Indeed, having witnessed war, I found the thought of guns and bombs abhorrent—and still do.

After completing my senior year, I took a summer job with one of Ed's friends, Jack Gosen, as rodman with a U.S. Geological Survey team in the Badlands of South Dakota. The government soon fired me because I was still an enemy alien. (I became a U.S. citizen in 1957.) I then went to a local employment office and became a temporary farmhand, helping to bring in the wheat harvest.

Although I had not heard back about my application from the University of Alaska, I packed all my belongings into one duffel bag and in September flew to Fairbanks anyway. The university had no record of my application. However, in those more relaxed times, the university simply permitted me to pay the $60 out-of-state registration fee and accepted me as a freshman. Making a seemingly unconscious decision, I chose several zoology and anthropology courses as my electives.

The University of Alaska opened a new world for me, a new stage of life in which I discovered what became my destiny as a naturalist. My mind was suddenly aflame. I enjoyed classes and for the first time ever received good grades, which earned me a small scholarship. Brina Kessel, an enthusiastic young biology professor and ornithologist, became my mentor. I discovered scientific journals. An article by the Swiss zoologist Rudolf Schenkel on the behavior of wolves particularly stimulated my imagination, perhaps because I had once heard their mournful howls near my cousin Ed's island. At what was called the Cooperative Wildlife Research Unit, located in the main administrative building, graduate students—David Klein, Cal Lensink, and others—gathered to discuss their projects on mountain goat, marten, and grayling fish, to name just three. From them I learned what hands-on research really entails, information that cannot be gleaned from textbooks. I volunteered to assist with such tasks as cleaning muskrat skulls and skinning wolves that had been victims of predator control, their tongues still greenish-yellow from the cyanide used to kill them. And I listened intently as the graduate students debated the need for such a wolf pogrom. The odor of boiling skulls and decaying wolf viscera wafted through the administrative building and drew attention to wildlife research.

Brina Kessel obtained a grant to study birds on Alaska's Arctic slope during the summer of 1952. Unable to go, she designated Tom Cade, an expert in hawks and falcons, to do the fieldwork, and he would need an assistant. Two older potential candidates declined to go before Brina asked me; I accepted without hesitation. In early June a floatplane dropped Tom and me off on a small lake near the headwaters of the Colville River, which flows 340 miles north to the Arctic Ocean. Each in a collapsible canoe, we began the descent of the river, stopping mainly to record birds, some of them, such as the red-spotted bluethroat, summer visitors from Asia. Rough-legged hawks, gyrfalcons, and peregrine falcons, together with ravens and, to my surprise, Canada geese, nested on the river bluffs. We made bird lists, recorded number of eggs or young in nests, and shot a few specimens for the University of Alaska museum. Late each day we made camp where we skinned the dead birds and stuffed them with cotton. Tom took a young gyrfalcon and two peregrines from the nest, intending to train them to hunt, and I selected a raven as companion. We continued downstream each with our birds perched on the canoe. Occasionally we found fragments of mammoth tusk washed out of a silt bank, saw bands of caribou, and discovered grizzly tracks tracing the river's edge. My heart spoke to this unpeopled vastness where white-crowned sparrows and Lapland longspur sang under the midnight sun.

We passed the oil exploration camp of Umiat, little realizing that this modest development would within a quarter century lead to an industrial sprawl nearby that would ruin the ecological integrity of much of the Arctic Slope forever. As we approached the Colville River delta, we added whistling swan, Arctic loon, ruddy turnstone, and other birds to our list to give us a total of sixty-two species for the journey. The land became so flat that it was impossible to judge distance, and light refraction made small objects appear huge. We saw a tower ahead.

"What's that?" I asked Tom.

"Beats me," Tom replied. "I didn't know there was a tower around here."

Ten minutes later we approached the tower—a mere oil barrel. Sea fog rolled over the delta and, unable to see ahead, we camped on a sandbar in the river. When we awoke, a wall of sea ice gleamed just ahead: we had stopped on the last spit of land, and beyond was only the Arctic Ocean.

Eager for more such Alaskan wilderness experiences, I worked the following summer for the U.S. Fish and Wildlife Service on a study of the Nelchina caribou herd north of Anchorage. I tracked caribou on foot over the hills to record their food habits and wanderings. The summer of 1954 found me in Katmai National Monument on the Alaska Peninsula as assistant to park service biologist Victor Cahalane. We encountered many huge brown bears during our wildlife survey, and studied the new vegetation that was colonizing the Valley of Ten Thousand Smokes, created by the cataclysmic eruption of Mount Katmai in 1912.

With only about 350 students, classes at the University of Alaska in those days were small and the same students took many of them with you. With the 1952 fall semester, a new woman attended several of my classes. She had golden hair, a trim figure, vibrant personality, and stylish clothes. Kay Suzanne Morgan was from Anchorage, a transfer student from "Outside," as the rest of the United States was known (Alaska at that time being still a territory, not a state). Kay was an anthropology student a year ahead of me. We occasionally shared a meal in the cafeteria or played a game of ping-pong or horseshoes, and I took her to the wildlife laboratory to induce her to clean skulls. She had first become aware of me when she saw me waving my arm and shouting at the sky until a raven, my free-living pet from the Colville River, hurtled down to land with a whoosh and accept some food. I found her most attractive.

Brina encouraged me to attend graduate school. She had obtained her PhD degree under John Emlen, an ornithologist in the zoology department at the University of Wisconsin, and suggested I apply there. Accepted, I moved to Madison in mid-1955 and became fully immersed in course work.

The summer after my first year of graduate school saw me back in Alaska, however. Olaus Murie, president of the Wilderness Society and a well-known naturalist, and his wife Margaret (Mardy) planned a biological survey of northeastern Alaska, a wilderness extending from the Brooks Range to the Arctic Ocean, and I volunteered as field assistant. Also included in the team were Brina Kessel and graduate student Bob Krear. The New York Zoological Society (now the Wildlife Conservation Society) sponsored the expedition, my first contact with the institution that was to become my scientific home for over five decades. Olaus selected the Sheenjek Valley on the southern slope of the Brooks Range as the base from which to study the natural history of the region. We tallied 85 bird species, collected 138 kinds of flowering plants as well as many spiders and insects, and excitedly shared our experiences around the evening campfire about meeting migrating caribou and grizzly bears. Olaus examined wolf scats, showing me the hair of ground squirrel and caribou. "Gee, this is wonderful," he said, and I admired his enduring enthusiasm for looking deeply into the details of nature at an age of nearly seventy.

Our goal in and around the Sheenjek Valley was to gather the kind of information that would ultimately lead to protection of the area, America's last great wilderness. Conservation depends on science, Olaus and Mardy stressed, but we must also recognize preservation of the natural world as a moral issue. We must consider the "precious intangible values" of a region, the feeling that comes with being in mountains that stretch to the horizon, where the only roads are made by wild sheep, caribou, and grizzlies. The Muries' wisdom has guided me ever since.

After we left the Sheenjek Valley, Olaus and others began a campaign to safeguard this wilderness. On December 6, 1960, it was established as the Arctic National Wildlife Range, 14,000 square miles in size. In 1980, President Carter more than doubled the reserve to 31,000 square miles and it was renamed the Arctic National Wildlife Refuge. This initial victory made us jubilant. I was still naïve, assuming that once a reserve was established it would be safe from exploitation. Little did I realize that the tranquil, remote Arctic Refuge would become the focus of a great conservation battle to prevent oil companies from drilling in the biological heart of the refuge, a battle that still rages after a half century. It taught me that the forces of pillaging and plunder will always seize any opportunity to destroy, and that never-ending vigilance and commitment are needed to protect a country's natural treasures and save fragments of wilderness for future generations.

Back at the University of Wisconsin in the fall, John Emlen, or "Doc" as he was known to his students, had received a grant to study the development of fear in birds. He gave me the task of investigating this in a rigorous scientific manner, one that would lead to a PhD degree. I raised chicks and ducklings from the time of hatching alone in boxes provided with light, food, and water, and noted their flight responses during the first week or two of life to slowly approaching objects such as a cardboard rectangle or a rubber owl. Avoidance appeared by the age of ten hours and increased to the age of about one hundred hours. I also tested nestling bronzed grackles to see at what age they crouched in response to a strange object; this happened at the age of about nine days, three days after their eyes opened. I soon had a surfeit of animals to care for, a room full of chickens, ducklings, two squawking great blue herons, and a chirping great horned owl. Although the work was fascinating and taught me good quantitative science, I soon realized that laboratory work was not for me.

I had convinced Kay Morgan, my friend from the University of Alaska, to stop in Madison on her way to Copenhagen, where she hoped for a museum job in anthropology. She agreed to tarry in Madison; on August 26, 1957, we were married at Cousin Ed's home in Minnesota and then went canoeing on Rainy Lake. My emotional center was now Kay, and later our two sons Eric and Mark. For the first time, I had someone of similar interests to share feelings and concerns, and a devoted companion with whom to build a future.

When I entered Doc's office one day to ask a question, he leaned back in his chair and in somewhat joking tone asked, "Would you like to study gorillas?"

"Sure," I replied impulsively. Then, and later, I grasped opportunities without much concern for detail. Desire and impulse were good enough reasons; I could always find justification later. My project of scaring chickens (as I thought of it) came to an abrupt end in favor of observing gorillas. I already knew that this was the beginning of a new stage in my existence.

On February 1, 1959, Doc and I and our wives left for Africa to observe mountain gorillas, animals of such reputed belligerence that several scientists had warned that we had little hope of success. The New York Zoological Society sponsored our project, as it had the project in Alaska three years earlier. At first we visited all parts of the gorilla's range in what is now Rwanda, Uganda, and the Congo (then the Belgian Congo) to obtain information on the distribution and ecology of this remarkable animal which ranged from the hot equatorial forest at about 1,500 feet above sea level up into cold mountains at 13,000 feet. The Emlens returned to Madison in July, but Kay and I stayed on to study mountain gorillas intensively. We had selected the Virunga Volcanoes in the Congo's Albert National Park, now the Virunga National Park, as our base. Fifty-five porters carried a five-month supply of food and equipment into the saddle between two inactive volcanoes, Mount Mikeno and Mount Karisimbi. There at the edge of a small meadow surrounded by gorilla forest at 10,000 feet was a cabin of rough-hewn boards. It became our home for a year.

At first I tried to creep silently close enough to gorillas to observe them without the animals becoming aware of me. As described in *The Year of the Gorilla* (1964), I did obtain glimpses: "A female gorilla emerged from the vegetation and slowly ascended a stump, a stalk of wild celery casually hanging from the corner of her mouth like a cigar. She sat down and holding the stem in both hands bit off the tough outer bark, leaving only the juicy center which she ate. . . ."

Even observations as mundane as this were new and exciting, recording peaceful activities as no one had done before. But I wanted more intimate contact—I wanted rapport. Instead of hiding, I decided to settle myself in full view of the gorillas on a low branch of a tree. The gorillas were more curious than afraid: "They congregated behind some bushes, and three females carrying infants and two juveniles ascended a tree and tried to obtain a better view of me. . . . Junior, the only black-backed male in the group, stepped out from behind the shrubbery and advanced to within ten feet of the base of my tree."

I identified ten gorilla groups around our cabin, ranging in size from eight to twenty-seven members and totaling 169 animals. Each group was led by an adult or "silverback" male. The faces of gorillas are so distinctive that I recognized them all and knew them by name. The gorillas now were our neighbors, our kin, beautiful in their shiny blue-black pelage and kindly, brown eyes. Kay and I gossiped about them: "Mrs. Patch had a quarrel with Mrs. Blacktop; Calamity Jane let her baby ride on her back for the first time; the injured eye of Mrs. Bad-eye looks worse."

After many days in close contact, so tolerant were some groups that I could spend day and night with them. One night, I decided

Plate 1. George Schaller on the Tibetan Plateau.

Plate 2. Two male chiru in striking nuptial pelage pose during the December mating season.

Plate 3. Pastoralists have traditionally hunted for subsistence, here using a cradle made of the hide of kiang or Tibetan wild ass.

Plate 4. The kiang, a species of wild ass unique to the Tibetan Plateau, has increased in number with better protection in recent years.

Plate 5. My wife Kay clips vegetation on a plot to determine biomass, species composition, and diversity.

Plate 6. We wear rubber gloves to pick up and weigh a newborn chiru to prevent our scent from possibly causing its mother to reject it.

Plate 7. A chiru female with a month-old calf is migrating south from the calving ground to better pastures.

Plate 8. Liu Yanlin (right) and Kang Aili track a radio-collared chiru young with antenna and receiver on the calving ground.

Plate 9. Tibetan hunters have killed 22 chiru. The carcasses will be eaten, the horns sold for medicine, and the wool from the hides, stored in the tent, will be smuggled to India to be woven into shahtoosh shawls.

Plate 10. A Tibetan colleague holds handfuls of chiru hair and wool; the long guard hairs will be separated from the short wool fibers which are used in weaving.

Plate 11. A herdman's family in its tent during a bitter cold winter. The horns of a wild yak hang on the tent post and are used as milk pails.

Plate 12. Most pastoral households have moved out of tents into mud-brick houses at least for the winter, and many have solar panels, TV antennas and satellite dishes.

Plate 13. The plateau pika is a key species in maintaining biological diversity in the Chang Tang yet is considered a pest and poisoned.

Plate 14. This wolf by its chiru kill had no fear of us in the northern Chang Tang, probably because it had never seen a human before.

Plate 15. Our night camp in the spacious northern Chang Tang. In our west to east traverse, we did not encounter any people in 1000 miles of cross-country driving.

Plate 16. Zhaduo is moderator in a discussion of environmental problems at a community meeting in Cuochi, a village which on its own initiative established a conservation program.

Plate 17. Near the village of Zhachu in southeastern Tibet, the Yarlung Tsangpo roars through the deepest gorge in the world

Plate 18. Porters climb toward a pass, the Doxiong La, across which lies the 'hidden land' of Pemako in southeastern Tibet.

Plate 19. Interviewing a villager about wildlife in the 'hidden land' of Pemako in southeastern Tibet are, from right to left, Zhang Endi, Zhang Hong, a villager, and our guide Dawa.

Plate 20. Hamid Sardar, a trekking colleague, watches a herd of tame Himalayan tahr goats at a small monastery in Nepal, located within a sacred 'hidden land' or *beyul*.

Plate 21. Kirghiz women in the Afghan Pamirs wear their finery, including necklaces of silver coins, at a wedding.

Plate 22. Marco Polo sheep rams in the Pamirs of Tajikistan. Photo by Beth Wald

Plate 23. Our guide in Tajikistan scans the terrain for Marco Polo sheep. The Mustagh Ata massif across the border in China is in the background.

Plate 24. Wu Lan crawls out of the winter den of a Tibetan brown bear, pleased to have found a bear scat.

Plate 25. A male Tibetan brown bear (left), with the snare that caught him still on the right forepaw, looks out the window of a house into which he had retreated before we radio collared him. (Photo by Bu Hongliang) A female Tibetan brown bear (right) wears a satellite radio collar. (Photo by Wu Lan)

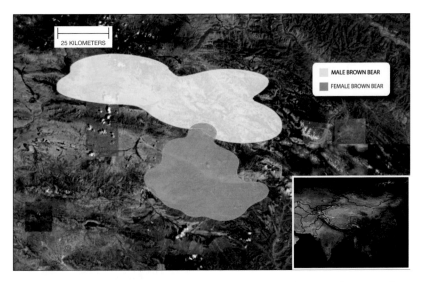

Plate 26. The ranges of the female Tibetan brown bear with two cubs and of the male between late June and mid–September 2011. Map prepared by Lisa Petracca.

Plate 27. At dawn the wife and daughter of our host Ouzhu in the bear study area are already milking their yaks.

Plate 28. A phantom of the peaks, the snow leopard is difficult to spot even when in full view.

Plate 29. The blue sheep, here a young male, is a principal prey of snow leopard on the Tibetan Plateau.

Plate 30. The monk Zhaxi displays his painting of a Kozlov's or Tibetan bunting, an endemic bird in eastern Qinghai where he lives.

Plate 31. At a village festival in Qinghai that is devoted to conservation a lama blesses participants.

Plate 32. Monks at the Xia Ri monastery feed trusting Himalayan griffin vultures—an ideal vision of nature and humankind as one.

to sleep near Big Daddy and his family. Toward dusk, I settled myself quietly near Big Daddy and watched as he reached out to bend the branch of a shrub and push it under a foot. He pulled in all other branches within reach, rotating slowly, until he had constructed a crude nest around his body. After that he reclined, legs and arms tucked under, his silver back toward the sky. At half past five, Big Daddy slept and so did all twenty-three other members of his group. Quietly I placed a tarp on the ground and unrolled my sleeping bag on it. I could hear the rumble of gorilla stomachs as I fell asleep, not the least concerned about being so close to these apes. I had spent nights with gorillas before, and had always been treated as an innocuous creature at the periphery of the group. Not until seven o'clock, after the morning sun had climbed over the distant ridge, did two females rise and wander slowly around, but Big Daddy rested awhile longer.

No one had ever before delved into the private life of gorillas, one of our closest relatives, as I was doing now. I was interested in everything about their daily routine, their food habits, their social interactions within and between groups, the extent of their travels—all basic aspects of their existence in these cloud-shrouded mountain forests. Naturally, I was also intrigued by how their society compared with that of humans. But beyond that, I knew that information about the needs of this rare and beautiful ape was essential for protecting it and its habitat. Our months with the gorillas were idyllic, as well as contributing something new to science and conservation.

And then the idyll was shattered. Belgium announced that on June 30, 1960, the Congo would receive its independence, *uhuru*, freedom. I expected turmoil and took Kay to Uganda. The Congo erupted soon thereafter when the Congolese army mutinied and the Belgians fled. I returned to my gorilla friends briefly and also helped the Belgian park biologist Jacques Verschuren calm the Congolese park staff. But I knew that my project was finished.

Kay and I returned to Madison after a brief interlude in Sarawak to observe orangutans. I wrote the gorilla's biography, *The Mountain Gorilla* (1963). Some scientists criticized me for giving names to gorillas, of being anthropomorphic, but today the practice is common.

My work had revealed a much-maligned ape as a gentle giant. I now also realized that if a naturalist studies a large iconic species, one that stirs strong emotions and is considered in some way charismatic (a lovely word meaning "gift of grace" in the original Greek), both scientific and popular attention may follow. This not only confers a certain status on the research but can also help promote conservation by bringing alive for others the nature of an animal's life. I realized, too, that studies of large enigmatic species in remote places attracted me, that I wanted to strive for something new, to dispel the mystery of life about little-known creatures. Everyone has two futures, it has been said the future of desire and the future of fate. In the gorilla project the two came together in that the project defined my desire and determined my future. Perhaps this is the end of the story of my becoming a naturalist. But not of *being* a naturalist. Every project offered new challenges for studying a species and for protecting it. I have continually had to adapt and evolve.

After the gorilla project, I never wanted to do anything except study animals in the wild—no teaching, no administration, no laboratory work. What began as pleasure and passion became an essential part of my being. I was extremely fortunate in the decades ahead that exciting projects continued to come my way, so much so that I never broadened my horizon into other fields of endeavor. I was content with small achievements such as gaining new insights into a species, promoting the establishment of reserves, and stimulating young biologists to focus on conservation. Besides, I am not a creative thinker.

I felt guilty at leaving the mountain gorillas to their fate when the Congo erupted into chaos. But soon other researchers, among them Dian Fossey, devoted themselves to these apes, and they have continued to do so for over half a century, adding immeasurably to our knowledge and providing protection for the area in spite of local uprisings, wars, and other turmoil. Once an animal has entered my heart, I find it difficult to ignore it. I read the latest news about it, and, when possible, return to check on its well-being. I knew that gorilla tourism had in recent years boomed in the Virunga Volcanoes, thanks to the efforts of Amy Vedder and Bill Weber of the Wildlife Conservation Society, who initiated the program. Kay and I returned to Rwanda in 1991 to climb once again on mud trails into these mountains; I also returned in 2001 and in 2009, the fiftieth anniversary of our study. I was greatly impressed with Rwanda's dedication to the gorillas. In spite of crushing social needs, the country has established a model program of gorilla protection and monitoring. Tourists are strictly managed and revenues from tourism are used to provide schools and health services for the local population. The guides are impressive, knowing every gorilla by name, and dedicated antipoaching teams risk their lives to protect the gorillas. Poachers had reduced gorilla numbers by half after we left but now the population is back to its former level of about 450 to 500. It is a model program which needs to be emulated for tigers, Tibetan antelope, and other species.

Kay and I decided to have children before beginning another overseas project. Eric was born in July 1961 and Mark in November 1962, and in September 1963 we all moved to India. The Johns Hopkins Center for Medical Research and Training, based in Baltimore and Calcutta, asked me to join their ecological unit specifically to study the ecology of ungulate species as possible hosts for diseases such as anthrax, brucellosis, and tick-borne diseases that may affect wildlife, livestock, and humans. After searching widely for a suitable study site, I found it in remote Kanha National Park of central India. Not only were there ten species of various deer, blackbuck antelope, and gaur (a kind of wild cattle)—but also the tiger.

With formidable claws and teeth, the tiger was considered so fearsome that studies up to that time had been conducted only along the sights of a rifle. As George Bernard Shaw noted, "When a man wants to murder a tiger he calls it sport; when the tiger wants to murder him he calls it ferocity." I wanted to learn about the tiger's true nature as it lived in its jungle realm, preying on the ungulates which in turn have an impact on the plants they eat. I sought to do a broad ecological study, one that also included the impact of the livestock grazing in the park and the villagers living within the park. This approach went beyond the more narrow focus of my gorilla study, enriching my ability as a naturalist to discern natural patterns. Besides, with its flaming beauty, lithe grace, and great power, the tiger is one of the most wonderful expressions of life on earth. A tiger, I realized later, needs much space and much prey—a medium-sized deer a week. By providing this large predator with the space it needs, thousands of plants and other animal species in the same area also are protected.

We moved into a small bungalow nearly fifty miles from town, with a village of Baiga tribal people and a park warden our nearest neighbors. Life was not easy with two small boys. Food was scarce, and the bungalow lacked electricity and water. During the hot season, April to June, the daily temperatures exceeded 100°F. But at that season, herds of chital deer, elegant in their spotted coats, and gaur filed in from the forest to drink at waterholes in a large meadow by our home. And tigers came, too. Sometimes we all rode on an elephant to look at wildlife, but more often we cruised in our Land Rover along the dirt tracks in search of a tiger. As with gorillas, I wanted to know the tigers as individuals. I soon noted that their stripe pattern on the face, particularly just above the eyes, was distinctive. Before long I recognized the resident tigers around us, a huge male, a tigress with four cubs, and two other females, as well as half a dozen other tigers which occasionally wandered through the area.

Only a week after our arrival, I was told by a local Baiga that a tiger had killed a cow and had dragged the body into a thicket. When I cautiously followed the drag mark in the leaf litter, a low, continuous growl conveyed that my intrusion was not welcome. I then waited for hours by a nearby pool until the raucous calls of peacocks announced the coming of dusk. Suddenly a tigress appeared a hundred feet away and crouched by the pool to lap water. She stared at me once, bared her teeth briefly in warning, drank, and then casually ambled back to her kill. Shiki, a nineteenth-century Japanese poet, wrote:

> The speech of insects
> And the speech of man
> Are heard
> With different ears.

I realized that in spite of our different ears, I could interpret the tiger's signals and that, as I'd done with gorillas, I could study the cat at my leisure.

Nighttime is tiger time. Cut-ear, a tigress with a tattered ear, had killed a gaur in a ravine. She was a lovely animal—I should have named her Sundari, meaning "Beautiful" in Hindi—and she had four large cubs. I settled myself on the low branch of a nearby tree. Several vultures were around me, ruffling their feathers, also waiting by the gaur but for a different purpose. Already gorged, the tigress and cubs slept the hours away until it was dark and then they fed under a sliver of moon. Cut-ear roared once, a mellow *aaouuu*, and from far away she received an answer, *aaouuu*, *aaouuu*—"here I am." I sat uncomfortably on the branch all night. At 8:00 a.m., the male tiger appeared and mingled peacefully with the family, the cubs rubbing against him in greeting. Without eating he soon left to patrol his domain, again solitary but certainly not asocial. The tigers in the area all knew each other and kept in contact, to me a memorable insight. I never would have discovered this if I had not learned to recognize the tigers as individuals and spent nights with them.

Of course, I also collected the kind of detail expected of a scientific study. To fulfill my obligation to the medical aspect of the study, I checked tiger kills for external and internal parasites and collected blood samples for later analyses. I teased apart 335 scats to find out about the tiger's food habits—52 percent chital deer, 10 percent sambar deer, and also gaur, langur monkey, and others. After fourteen months in Kanha, I had at least gained some insights about tigers and their impact on the prey populations, the first such ecological study of the tiger.

After we returned to the United States, I became immersed in other projects, ranging from jaguars in Brazil to wildlife on the Tibetan Plateau, but the tiger in India has continued to be one of my particular concerns. As with the mountain gorilla, others have continued tiger research. When I revisited Kanha in 1991 I was accompanied by Ullas Karanth, whose research on India's tigers had set a new standard of excellence. And on my return in 2009, Joseph Vattakaven had just completed an intensive four-year study there. The Kanha tigers have fared reasonably well, with the park enlarged and some villages resettled outside of the park's core. But massive management problems remain. Kanha now consists of a 362-square-mile core zone and a buffer zone of similar size occupied by 100,000 people in 168 villages and 80,000 cattle and buffalo. Kanha and other tiger reserves have become a huge attraction for Indian and other tourists. During 2007–2008 tourist season there were about 132,000 visitors to Kanha, in contrast to our stay in the early 1960s when it was rare to encounter any tourists at all. Private tourist facilities now crowd the edge of the park; from these the local people benefit far too little.

I had barely finished writing my project report, published as *The Deer and the Tiger* (1967), when John Owen, the director of Tanzania's national parks, asked me to come to the Serengeti to answer the question, "What effect does lion predation have on the prey populations?" Kay and I had visited the Serengeti National Park briefly in 1960, and we accepted the invitation with alacrity. The Wildlife Conservation Society gave me a position as research biologist in 1966, an ideal solution which enabled me to continue leading a life I had come to love.

In June 1966 we moved to Seronera, the park headquarters, and remained there for three and a half years, the happiest of our lives. We lived in a wooden bungalow shaded by flat-topped acacia trees upon which giraffe browsed and beneath which lions occasionally spent indolent hours. Food was delivered from the town of Arusha, two hundred miles away. We had stimulating contact with park warden Myles Turner, research director Hugh Lamprey, hyena biologist Hans Kruuk, and buffalo biologist Tony Sinclair, and their wives, to mention just four couples. Our son Eric was five years old and Mark three and a half when we arrived, old enough to enjoy watching migrating wildebeest, elephants in the shade of yellow-barked fever trees, and cheetah on a gazelle kill. Kay taught school to the boys, who many years later became university professors (Eric a molecular biologist at Dartmouth and Mark a social psychologist at the

University of British Columbia). I felt that we needed a pet, and at one time or another a sand boa, a banded mongoose, a baby warthog, and a lion cub found starving and abandoned all joined our family.

The Serengeti Park consists of 10,000 square miles of wild beauty with the largest concentration of wildlife in the world, at that time over half a million migrating wildebeest and zebra, uncounted Thomson's gazelles, and many others. It was a river of life, a grunting and braying flood of animals always on the move, which with the onset of rains flowed onto the great plain in November and December to feast on the tender new grass and then in May retreated northward and westward into the woodlands. Other species, too, thronged the Serengeti—buffalo, eland, impala, and topi. My observations, though, revolved around lions and their competitors, the spotted hyena, cheetah, leopard, and African hunting dog. Each of these predators has an impact on the prey species, and it was my task to find out if their combined influence was beneficial, by, for example, removing sick animals, or harmful by reducing the size of populations too much.

My approach to this lion study was similar to that of my tiger study, except here I was inundated, almost intimidated, by the sheer number of animals. Therefore, I concentrated my research on one general area, that around Seronera and on the nearby plains. The lion is unique among cats in the depth of its social life. In time I could individually recognize all thirty-eight lions in three prides around Seronera. This revealed that females are the permanent core of the pride and that males have tenure of only a few years before being evicted by new males which take over the pride territory. Some lions are nomadic. To find out what I could about the nomads among lions, I tranquilized some and clipped a colored and numbered tag into an ear. Male No. 57, as I knew him, roamed over at least 1,800 square miles until he was shot by a trophy hunter outside of the park. I followed two other nomads, male No. 134 and his female companion No. 60, day and night for nine consecutive days. In that time they meandered 67.5 miles around a cluster of rock outcrops or kopjes. They did not bother to hunt but merely scavenged by listening for the whoop of excited hyenas and then appropriating their kill.

I tried to capture my feelings about such days and nights in a passage in *Golden Shadows, Flying Hooves* (1973):

Watching animals alone, without fear of interruption, for hour after hour, one feels the senses take on a new dimension—they become more acute in discerning small nuances of behavior. Such intimacy adds immeasurably to an understanding of animals. These animals become individuals, and with that awareness a study moves to its most satisfying and sensitive pitch. For having become acquaintances, the animals evolve into discrete memories on which I can draw long after I have moved on to other tasks. Solitude provokes reflection and a study becomes a quest for meaning, not just of the animals but also of myself.

I watched the prides around Seronera intensively, too, especially when at a kill. The members competed with snapping jaws and flashing claws with the result that the big males may get the lion's share and the cubs little or nothing. Black Mane, a male of the Masai pride, once ate seventy-three pounds of meat in one meal. Of the seventy-nine cubs born in my prides, 67 percent died, fifteen of starvation, eleven killed by other lions, one each killed by leopard and hyena, and the rest simply vanished—a sad tally, but such statistics help reveal the life of a species. My calculations showed that all predators combined killed roughly 22.5 million pounds of prey in a year, or 7–10 percent of what was available, too little to have in itself any long-term impact on the prey populations. Such were the statistics which I compiled after months of intensive work. However, imprisoned in my vehicle much of the time while watching lions, I never felt any intimacy with them. There was no rapport and little dialogue. But as the philosopher Ludwig Wittgenstein noted, "If a lion could talk, we could not understand him."

A study should ideally last at least for the life span of an animal, perhaps fifteen to twenty years for lions. After nearly four years there, I grew restless. Many biologists were by that time also studying wildlife in the Serengeti, including lions. I had obtained a preliminary answer to the question that had brought me there, and now I sought new horizons. Kay was very reluctant to leave, and we both knew that never again would we live in a place of such special enchantment. But we departed, knowing that the tawny lions of the Serengeti would continue to prowl our memory ever after. I couldn't know it at the time, but my research in the spacious Serengeti would later help me adapt to the vastness of the Tibetan Plateau.

Studies of the Serengeti predators, prey species, and habitats have continued without interruption since the 1960s to provide the most detailed information about a functioning ecosystem anywhere in the world. Lions in the park declined drastically in the 1990s, due to canine distemper introduced by village dogs, but then rebounded in number. The human population along the western park border has tripled in recent decades, with the result that rangelands have become fields, trees are turned into charcoal, wildlife is poached both for local consumption and the market, and the migrating herds have lost much habitat when they venture outside of the park. In 2010, Tanzanian president Jakaya Kikwete proposed a major highway across the northern part of the park. This would hamper and ultimately perhaps destroy the great wildebeest migration, Africa's greatest wildlife spectacle. The government predicted that thousands of vehicles would use the highway every day. Donor organizations offered to build a southern route instead, bypassing the park. Even with this offer, and despite the international outcry against the desecration of this UN World Heritage Site, Kikwete in an interview with Tanzania's *Daily News* of February 9, 2011, affirmed his plan of ecological vandalism by saying the road will go ahead, that "there is neither justification nor explanation for not building this important road." Condemned worldwide, the Tanzanian government tried to placate its critics and released misleading and conflicting statements. Yes, the road will be built but not paved; no, it will not be built; yes, it will be built but the plan is being "revised." I bristle with anger. Like the Arctic National Wildlife Refuge, another natural treasure, the Serengeti will now face the constant threat of a major highway. And on December 23, 2011, Tanzania's Minister of Transport Omar Nundu announced that a Chinese company, the Civil Engineering Construction Corporation, will conduct a feasibility study for a railroad from the town of Arusha in Tanzania westward to Uganda. The shortest route for this railroad would follow the proposed major highway across the Serengeti National Park. In early January 2012, Mr. Nundu was quoted as saying that the railroad would not cross the Serengeti. We'll see. Outside of reserves, the lion's fate is uncertain, due primarily to illegal killing. Perhaps fewer than 30,000 lions remain in all of Africa, almost half of them in Tanzania.

My projects in the 1960s on gorillas, tigers, and lions had been conducted in national parks, which in spite of various problems had a measure of security, but they had, I felt, contributed little to conservation or to protecting "precious intangible values," to use Olaus Murie's phrase from the Alaska expedition. During the next decade, I would do something beyond myself by selecting projects on new species in new areas which had so far been ignored or neglected, to give voice to animals which have had no one to speak on their behalf. I initiated, for example, a study of the jaguar and its prey in the great swamps of the Pantanal in western Brazil, a project similar in concept and execution to the one on the Indian tiger. After three and a half decades, I still collaborate with my Brazilian colleague Peter Crawshaw on issues of jaguar conservation. But no place attracted me more than the Himalaya, the rampart of gleaming snow peaks which I had first glimpsed in northern India, and beyond which, I knew, was the mysterious Tibetan Plateau. I was intrigued by various Himalayan species of wild sheep and goats, such as the markhor goat with its spiraling horns, the argali sheep with its great curling horns, and especially the blue sheep, whose looks and behavior make it unclear whether it is a sheep or goat.

December 1970 found me in the Hindu Kush Mountains of northern Pakistan to observe markhor. One day, as I climbed up a steep scree slope broken by boulders, everything was motionless and silent around me as if devoid of life. My book *Stones of Silence* (1980) describes what happened next:

> Then I saw the snow leopard, a hundred and fifty feet away, peering at me from the spur, her body so well molded into the

contours of the boulders that she seemed a part of them. Her smoky-grey coat sprinkled with black rosettes perfectly complemented the rocks and snowy wastes, and her pale eyes conveyed the image of immense solitude. As we watched each other the clouds descended once more, entombing us and bringing more snow. . . . The snow fell more thickly, and, dreamlike, the cat slipped away as if she had never been.

It was a fleeting moment of transcendence. To see this phantom of the snows again and again and again became a quest, and it continues still, as I describe in Chapter 14.

From 1972 to 1974, we lived in the city of Lahore, Pakistan, where Eric and Mark, now almost teenagers, went to school. While Kay remained with them, I roamed the mountains to study goats and sheep. I traversed tribal areas near the Afghanistan border (today under Taliban control), observed the rare Punjab urial sheep in the private reserve of the Nawab of Kalibagh, and searched for ibex and Marco Polo sheep in the mighty Karakoram Range. Amanullah Khan, a former army major, and Pervez Khan, an avid trekker, were my frequent companions. One area in the Karakoram would, I felt, make a good national park. A newly built highway there over the Khunjerab Pass connected Pakistan and China. I suggested potential borders for such a park to the Pakistani government. The Khunjerab National Park was established by the order of Prime Minister Zulfikar Ali Bhutto in April 1975 for the protection of snow leopard, Marco Polo sheep, and other species.

To learn about blue sheep, I trekked twice through the Himalaya of northern Nepal to the Tibet border. One of the trips was with writer Peter Matthiessen, as well as Phu Tsering and other Sherpas, to the Dolpo district, where our base was the Shey monastery in the shadow of holy Crystal Mountain. Peter wrote his brilliant book *The Snow Leopard* (1978) about our journey. The blue sheep, I noted, were goats but with some sheeplike behavioral traits, a mix that was later confirmed through DNA analysis. My information about the area helped to stimulate the Nepalese government to declare this region as the Shey-Phoksumdo National Park, 1,370 square miles in size.

There were so many more animals to study in the Himalaya and other ranges, and so many more valleys and plateaus to explore, that I hesitated to end this particular project in 1975. I had collected valuable information on the distribution, status, and behavior of several species about which little had been known, and I had promoted the establishment of two protected areas. As always, I hesitated to end a project, having known even at the start that it would always be only a passing phase, a dual existence between life in the field and life at home. I yearn to retain both, to find a balance between contentment and longing. Whether I'm home in the United States or in Tanzania or in India or any other place, I'm briefly *in* it but don't feel *of* it. I feel rootless, unconnected, always traveling in my mind on and on as if with a hunger that is never quite satisfied.

And then my China years began.

In late 1979, the World Wildlife Fund (WWF) and China had signed an agreement for a joint study of the giant panda, and WWF asked if I would assist with the fieldwork. After having spent years with some of the planet's most charismatic animals, it seemed almost routine, even preordained, for me to delve into the mystery of this iconic creature, a precious and rare national treasure of China and symbol of WWF. I wondered at first if I had become a parody of myself. But it was a unique challenge and I accepted it with great anticipation. On May 15, 1980, Sir Peter Scott, chairman of WWF, his wife Lady Philippa Scott, Nancy Nash, a journalist whose initiative had made the project a reality, and I, together with a large delegation of Chinese, entered panda habitat in Sichuan's Wolong Nature Reserve, located at the eastern edge of the Tibetan Plateau, where pandas have a restricted distribution along six mountain ranges. We were, it was emphasized, the first Westerners actually invited by China into the panda's realm. The entrance fee for WWF: one million dollars for the construction of a panda breeding center and research laboratory. That day we reverently crowded around two panda droppings composed of bits of bamboo stem, my first evidence of a panda's presence.

Later that same year, in December, we began fieldwork at Wuyi-peng, the field station in Wolong. Here at 8,200 feet our camp of three tents and one hut hidden in snowbound forest made little concession to comfort. Two excellent Chinese coworkers were with me, Hu Jinchu, who had established this camp in 1978, and Pan Wenshi, a professor at Peking University. In addition, eight staff members from the reserve and elsewhere were assigned to various tasks. Kay arrived two months later with Howard Quigley, who would help to trap and radio-collar the first pandas. Pandas were adept at hiding in the dense bamboo, and I was there two months before actually seeing one, or rather observing two of them squabbling. In early March we collared a young male named Long-Long ("Dragon") and a female named Zhen-Zhen ("Precious"). From these and others—there were about fifteen pandas in the study area—we discovered that pandas were intermittently active day and night for some fourteen hours, and that their overlapping ranges were small, averaging about two square miles each. Pandas ate up to thirty pounds of bamboo a day, and as many as eighty pounds when juicy shoots were in season. Food habits, activity cycles, glimpses of social life—the research was little different from other projects. Except for the politics.

The enthusiasm for the project by some sponsoring Chinese organizations was highly lukewarm, and WWF ineptly caused consternation and misunderstandings. We sometimes did not know if the project would continue. Fortunately Wang Menghu of the Ministry of Forestry, whose name evocatively means "Dreaming of Tigers," smoothed over many contentious issues. Once he told me, "You will now work with us in China for the next forty years." I thought it an expression of politeness. But now over three decades later . . . !

To me the most wonderful encounters with pandas, as with gorillas and tigers, were quiet ones, though these were all too rare in the dense vegetation. But at times I heard a panda in a thicket crunching on bamboo, and I would sit down, waiting, hoping, for the panda to move in my direction. On one occasion, I glimpsed the collared female, Zhen-Zhen. Although I remained motionless, she sensed my presence, raising her nose as if testing the air. In *The Last Panda* (1993), I describe our encounter:

With a rolling motion she rises and moves from behind the bamboo into a bower from which a path leads to my clearing. She steps forward with a combination of shyness and audacity. Her black legs dissolve into the shadows to create an illusion of a shining lantern gliding toward me. She advances to within thirty-five feet. There she stops, her head bobbing up and down as she snorts to herself in wary alertness, her apprehension and mine a bond of shared feeling. . . . I look for some intimation of coming actions in her face, but it remains inert. . . . Not being a creature of self-expression, Zhen conveys none of her inner feelings. I wonder what she will do now. Certainly she does something unexpected. . . . Hunched in repose, forepaws on rounded abdomen as if meditating, she has the aura of Buddha. . . . The slow rhythmic heaving of her body reveals that imperturbably she has fallen asleep. . . . What intuition, what reason is there in that broad hard skull? A panda has its vision of the world and I have mine. . . . Zhen and I are together yet hopelessly separated by an immense space. . . . The panda is the answer. But what is the question?

Our research base was in Zhen-Zhen's home range, and, after some months, attracted by the smell of food, she began to enter our hut and tents. Coming home cold and wet after searching in vain for a panda, I was rather disconcerted one afternoon to find Zhen-Zhen peer out at me from my tent's window.

Pandas are found now in only about twenty-five populations, some of them in such small fragmented habitat that they are threatened with extinction. We made far-ranging surveys to evaluate threats to the animal. Forest destruction, including the conversion of even steep slopes to fields, was one major problem. In 1983, several species of bamboo suddenly mass-flowered and died, as they do every few decades. That pandas might be faced with starvation received worldwide publicity, though enough bamboo remained in most areas to assure the panda's survival. However, a few pandas did die, with the result that many were needlessly "rescued" throughout their range and taken into captivity. Two of our radio-collared pandas at Wolong were killed by poachers. I found one, a lovely female named Han-Han (meaning "Lovely"), strangled in a snare, mute testimony to what was probably happening to pandas throughout their range. Protection, even in reserves, was obviously inadequate.

In 1984, we established a second research base in the Tangjiahe Nature Reserve in northern Sichuan, where we not only studied pandas but also Asiatic black bears and a bulbous-nosed mountain ungulate, the takin. We particularly wanted to find out how panda and bear, so similar in size, differed in lifestyle. Bears, we discovered, ate mainly forbs, nuts, and fruits, and they ranged very widely for their scattered food sources.

By early 1985, having spent four years with pandas, I felt that we had collected much useful information about its natural history and defined what protective measures the government needed to take. Antipoaching efforts were most urgent. Forest destruction had to be reduced or halted and isolated panda populations linked by establishing forest corridors. Such corridors would prevent inbreeding in pandas by enabling individuals to travel from one population to another. And local communities needed to be involved in reaching these goals. After I left, research on pandas at Wolong would continue under the guidance of Hu Jinchu. In addition, Pan Wenshi established a new panda research base in the Qinling Mountains of Shaanxi province, where for the next thirteen years he not only conducted the best panda research to date but also trained many students, among them Lu Zhi, Wang Dajun, and Wang Hao, who now mentor a new generation of field biologists.

Immersed with wildlife surveys on the high Tibetan Plateau, I distanced myself from direct involvement with pandas after the mid-1980s. For a few years, the world's zoos and other institutions competed to exhibit pandas and China scrambled to provide them for hefty fees, a rent-a-panda business of little benefit to the species until a percentage of the funds was designated for panda conservation. On the whole, the panda situation has improved greatly since the 1990s, especially after commercial killing was greatly reduced. Captive breeding has become increasingly successful. About sixty reserves covering half of the panda's range have now been established. A logging ban since 1998 protects watersheds and preserves habitat. A "grain for green" program pays farmers not to plant crops but to plant trees instead. A census conducted between 1998 and 2001 estimated about 1,600 pandas excluding young, indicating a total population of about 2,000. A major earthquake on May 12, 2006, had its epicenter near Wolong, killing thousands of people and destroying the panda breeding center. Only one of the captives died, and the wild population appeared to have been little affected.

In recent years, China has obviously made a major commitment to offer the panda a secure future. In a foreword to a 2004 panda book edited by Donald Lindberg and Karen Baragona, I wrote:

> In the 1980s, I was filled with creeping despair as the panda seemed increasingly shadowed by fear of extinction. But now, in this new millennium, *Giant Pandas: Biology and Conservation* rightly projects hope, optimism, and opportunity. The panda cannot compromise its needs, whereas humanity can use its knowledge, self-restraint, and compassion to offer the species a secure wilderness home. . . . [If we do this] the panda will surely endure as a living symbol of conservation and luminous wonder of evolution.

Wang Menghu suggested that I next make a countrywide snow leopard survey. An irresistible proposal. I would be able to travel to all mountain ranges in western China, I realized, including the high Tibetan Plateau with its wild yak, chiru, and other species about which I had read for years. But I did not have even a vague notion that this project would occupy me for the next quarter century.

Year after year the highlands of China have drawn me back. I cannot stop. While others concentrated on chiru, I switched more to snow leopards, brown bears, and Marco Polo sheep. Not that I spent all my time in China. Between 1989 and 2007 I also made many trips to Mongolia, where I observed wild Bactrian camels, tracked Gobi brown bears, established a snow leopard project, and followed the great nomadic herds of Mongolian gazelles across the eastern steppes. I went to Iran in 2000 to cooperate with the government to help save the last Asiatic cheetah. I did brief fieldwork in Bhutan, Russia, Myanmar, and other countries. But I have always returned to China, as if Wang Menghu has somehow riveted my mental GPS, my global positioning satellite, to that country. Chance and fate brought me to China and time has now sealed the pact to continue our collaboration on behalf of the country's natural heritage.

CHAPTER 9

Two Mountains and a River

WHENEVER I FLY FROM CHENGDU in Sichuan westward to Lhasa, I take a seat on the port side of the plane. Below is an endless series of valleys bordered by forested slopes and sharp ridges broken by cliffs. Suddenly a huge ice massif, a glowing sentinel at the eastern edge of the Himalaya, comes into view. On some flights only the summit of Namche Barwa pierces a solid layer of cloud; on others billows of cloud roil around the massif, leaving gaps in which I glimpse a chaos of canyons. A second high peak, Gyali Peri, projects skyward just to the west, about 250 miles short of Lhasa. The Yarlung Tsangpo flows between the two in a canyon so deep that the river is invisible from the plane.

After descending west to east along the Tibetan foothills of the Himalaya and passing just south of Lhasa, the Yarlung Tsangpo enters a gorge and makes a large loop north around Namche Barwa before flowing south into India, where its name changes to the Dihang (Siang), one of the tributaries to the Brahmaputra River. The Yarlung Tsangpo is accessible along its upper reaches, but when its channel cuts through the Himalaya it enters one of the wildest corners of the earth. The plant collector Frank Kingdon-Ward explored part of this area in 1924 under great hardship. I had read his 1926 book *The Riddle of the Tsangpo Gorges*, and his descriptions of mythic waterfalls and sheer terrain aroused my curiosity. What wildlife is hidden there and elsewhere in eastern Tibet? The high mountains would have blue sheep and snow leopard, as in the Chang Tang, and the conifer and temperate forests would have wild herbivores with exotic names like takin, serow, goral, and muntjak or barking deer. But hidden behind snow ranges in lowland rain forests might well be new or forgotten species awaiting discovery. The Namche Barwa region was so enticing that I decided to investigate it, making several journeys to eastern Tibet between 1995 and 2000, as described in this and the following chapter.

At the edge of Lhasa is the Norbulinka, the former summer home of the Dalai Lama. On its grounds is a dismal small zoo which in the early 1990s held Tibetan brown bear, wolf, lynx, and other creatures behind bars, as well as assorted blue sheep, domestic goats, and also four large deer in small outdoor enclosures. These deer were stags whose antlers had been sawed off for use in traditional medicines. They stood about four feet high at the shoulder and were gray-brown in color, their pelage much lighter than that of the Sichuan red deer with which I was familiar. I assumed that these were Tibet red deer, also known as Sikkim stag, a unique subspecies of red deer once found in southern Tibet and parts of Bhutan. Indeed, in 1973 I had seen the distinctive antlers of this deer around monasteries in Nepal's Dolpo district near the Tibet border and was told that they had been brought from the Yarlung Tsangpo Valley. In accounts of endangered wildlife this deer, known locally as *shou*, was listed as "probably extinct." The four stags in front of me refuted this. To rediscover this deer in the wild, if there still were any, could make a useful and fascinating quest. Such old-fashioned exploration appeals to me. One either succeeds or fails. Besides, a search would take me in the direction of Namche Barwa and its wild canyon country.

I had already experienced the thrill of participating in the redis-covery of a missing species, the Javan rhinoceros, in Vietnam in 1989. Once widespread in Southeast Asia, this rhinoceros was known to survive now only in a small sanctuary on the western tip of Java. With Nguyen Xuan Dang and other Vietnamese coworkers, we searched the mountain forests northwest of Hoh Chi Minh City (Saigon), our team protected by armed guards in a country that had not long before concluded a devastating war with the United States. In the mud of a riverbank we found the distinctive large track of this rhinoceros. From these tracks, interviews with local people, and the remains of a recently killed animal we guessed that no more than ten to fifteen survived in this remnant population, their future prospects dismal. But at least conservation efforts on their behalf could now begin. (Those efforts failed: the last wild rhinoceros was probably gone from Vietnam by 2010.)

A grant from the John D. and Catherine T. MacArthur Foundation makes our wildlife explorations in the Namche Barwa region and other parts of eastern Tibet possible. It is October 1995 and the Tibet red deer is first on our agenda. Our team consists of Liu Wulin of the Tibet Forestry Department and Wang Xiaoming of the East China Normal University in Shanghai, a coworker of mine on the panda project. An energetic and dedicated field biologist, Wang Xiaoming went to France for an advanced degree with the result that his English now has a French accent. We plan to search for the Tibet red deer and to survey other wildlife for a month in the watershed of the Yarlung Tsangpo in the direction of Namche Barwa, but we will save the great gorge for a later visit.

Southeast of Lhasa, toward the disputed border with India, are the headwaters of several rivers, and old accounts mention the existence of Tibet red deer in that region. For example, Frederick Bailey, a British military officer, wrote an article for the 1914 issue of *Geographical Journal* in which he described shooting a stag near the town of Tsari, an area "considered sacred, and no crops may be grown and no animals killed." People in several communities there tell us that the deer were common until the 1960s and 1970s, when they were hunted almost to extinction. The deer are rare now, but their favored haunts of forests and rhododendron thickets remain. After much searching, we do find the fresh tracks and droppings of two deer at timberline.

In Zedong, a small town on the Yarlung Tsangpo, the Forestry Department shows us the fresh skin of a Tibet red deer, its color the same as the Lhasa animals. Head north to the village of Zhengqi, we

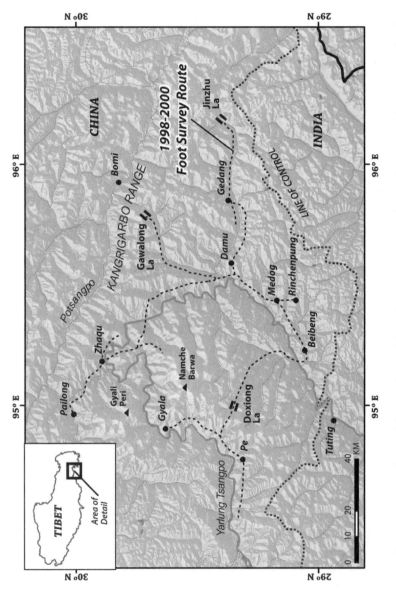

Our foot surveys in and around the great bend of the Yarlung Tsangpo in southeast Tibet, an area that is now within the Yarlung Tsangpo Great Canyon National Reserve.

are told, and you will find the deer. And there, in high rolling hills covered with a mosaic of alpine meadow and patches of willow and dwarf birch, we spot our first animals. A herd of ten females with their offspring feeds leisurely along the slope. Searching the hills, we find several more herds, a few accompanied by stags with large antlers, their tips characteristically bent inward. We estimate a population of 100 to 150, but villagers tell us more will descend from the high meadows with the coming of winter. We hear a rifle shot near camp. Police from the nearby town of Sangre, cruising in a jeep, have just shot a hare. I ask Dawa, a county leader accompanying us, if they would have shot a deer, too; "Probably," Dawa responds. When I ask why he can't put a stop to this, Dawa replies that he does not have the power to do so. When I ask who does, Dawa responds simply, "It is difficult to say."

These deer have survived only because of the tolerance and goodwill of the Zhengqi villagers. We hold discussions with them, and they agree that the establishment of a reserve would be a good idea as long as it will not affect their traditional lives, such as seasonal livestock grazing in the hills. Guards will try to prevent outsiders from hunting. The government officials with us recommend a local reserve to higher authorities. (Established in 1993, the reserve became a national reserve in 2005.) I am greatly pleased with our survey—but Namche Barwa, with its potential of finding interesting new species and promoting conservation, continues to beckon.

In 1812 the French naturalist Georges Cuvier noted that "there is little hope of discovering new species of large quadrupeds," yet the twentieth century had revealed the okapi and giant forest hog in Africa and a new species of wild cattle, the kouprey, in Indochina, as well as resurrecting supposedly extinct species and subspecies such as the Tibet red deer. My own quest to rediscover missing large mammals and even discover species new to science had taken me to Laos as well as Vietnam. One day, just a few months before we began the search for the Tibet red deer, I was in the Annamite Range, which straddles the border between Laos and Vietnam. A family of Hmong tribal people invited us for a meal in their hut. The remains of a pig bubbled in a big pot over an open fire and other parts hung from a smoke-blackened rafter. The pig was a *bote lin*, a yellow-colored pig with a long snout, I was informed, readily distinguishable from the *bote lud*, black and squat-faced. Two kinds of wild pig? I knew of only one, the common black one. After I had pried bits of boiled meat from the pig cranium for my dinner, I was fortunately able to save that part of the skull and also a small sample of fresh meat.

George Amato, now at the American Museum of Natural History in New York, analyzed the DNA and found it distinctively different from the DNA of both the wild and domestic black pig in Laos. Was this yellow pig a new species, we wondered? Colin Groves, an expert ungulate taxonomist at the Australian National University, compared our Laotian cranium with that of various pig species including the so-called warty pigs from Indonesia. Ours was indeed a warty pig but a unique one. Further investigation revealed that a French Jesuit priest, Pierre-Marie Heude, had, in 1892, bought the skulls of two pigs in a town near Saigon, recognized them as different from any known species, and gave them the scientific name *Sus bucculentus*. Heude sent the skulls to a museum in Shanghai. The species then vanished until I ate it for dinner a century later. Colin Groves diligently traced the missing skulls until he unearthed them in Beijing's Institute of Zoology. The Indochinese warty pig had now been rediscovered. I reminded myself to save the remains of any unusual delicacy that we might be served for dinner as we explored the forests of eastern Tibet.

When visiting Laotian villages in the Annamites, sometimes accompanied by colleagues Alan Rabinowitz and William Robichaud, I occasionally noticed unusually imposing barking deer antlers up to ten inches long in some huts. When later I saw a captive male with such antlers in a menagerie, the animal's large size, broad tail, and other characteristics showed that it was a wholly new species. Vietnamese biologists had found the same species in their country that year, and it is now known as the giant or large-antlered barking deer, *Muntiacus vuquangensis*. It was yet another instance in which Cuvier should not have given in to despair so easily.

Although the Namche Barwa region is only a hundred miles down the Yarlung Tsangpo from where we found the Tibet red deer in 1995, three years passed before I was finally able to explore the great gorge and its forests. But in the meantime, I learned as much as possible about the area by talking to people who had been there and by reading the accounts of travelers.

The Yarlung Tsango roars down a canyon between the two peaks that I had seen from the air, 25,446-foot Namche Barwa and 23,461-foot Gyali Peri (Gyala Balei), only thirteen miles apart. To the east of Namche Barwa are forested hills which in the north are guarded by the high Kangrigarbo Range and in the south by a disputed, closed border, the Line of Control separating China and India. Here, subtropical rain forest at 3,000 feet and perpetual snow and ice at 14,000 feet are only a few miles apart.

One of the fascinating chapters of Asian history is the exploration of this region, mainly by the British during the first half of the twentieth century. It was known in the early 1900s that the Yarlung Tsangpo flowed some 700 miles from west to east in Tibet. But then where did it go? Some geographers hypothesized that it continued east to join the Mekong or another great river, whereas others speculated that it turned south into India's Northeast Frontier Agency, as it was then called, to become the Dihang, which joins the Brahmaputra River in the plains. Yet if the Yarlung Tsangpo was the Dihang, the river must have dropped from over 10,000 feet above sea level to less than 1,000 feet in only 150 miles. Surely that meant major waterfalls along its precipitous descent. Indeed, there were already rumors of huge waterfalls and a monstrous gorge.

In 1911, the British sent an expedition of exploration up the Dihang via India's Northeast Frontier Agency toward Tibet. In the densely forested mountains the explorers were annihilated by the fiercely aggressive Arbor tribe, now called the Adi. Farther north, across the border in Tibet, the Lopa and Monpa tribes were known to be equally displeased by intruders. Because Tibet was forbidden territory, the British colonial administration trained Tibetan-speaking Indians to survey and to spy on the region. Disguised as pilgrims or traders, these spies, or pundits (as they were called), mapped their routes by pacing distances and recording these with prayer beads whose sacred number of 108 had been reduced to 100 for ease in calculation.

Kinthup, an illiterate tailor from Sikkim, became famous as a pundit after he twice penetrated the mysterious great gorge of the Yarlung Tsangpo at the behest of the British. In 1878, he went downstream as far as Gyala, the last village and the entrance to the gorge. Two years later, at age thirty-two, he set off again, this time accompanied by a Mongolian monk. They made their way through the gorge for four days to a small *gompa*, or monastery, called Pema-kochung. Later the monk gambled away their money and sold Kinthup into slavery. Kinthup had been told by the British to place 500 marked logs in the river. If the logs reached the Brahmaputra after it was joined by the Dihang, the link with the Yarlung Tsangpo would be confirmed. Remarkably dedicated to his task, Kinthup did place the logs in the river after gaining his freedom. He finished his four-year odyssey in 1884, but by then no one was awaiting the marked logs.

A large gap in the great gorge still remained unexplored, and speculation about a giant waterfall there persisted. In 1913, Colonel Frederick Bailey and Captain Henry Morshead left a military expedition in the Northeast Frontier and penetrated the gorge farther downstream than Kinthup had reached until they were stopped by sheer cliffs. They saw turbulent rapids but no major waterfall.

Kingdon-Ward set out to traverse that unexplored fifty-mile gap in 1924. He was accompanied by the Earl of Cawdor, although on most of his many expeditions he preferred to travel only with local people. He asked in *Riddle of the Tsangpo Gorges*, "Was it possible that hidden away in the depth of this unknown gorge there was a waterfall?" His expedition penetrated beyond Bailey's farthest point to where the canyon walls pinched ever more closely together. "Every day the scene grew more savage, the mountains higher and steeper; the river more fast and furious," he wrote. They pushed through leech-infested, sodden thickets and traversed precarious cliff faces covered with mosses and ferns. The mountains were in cloud, the gullies in mist. Finally they saw billows of spray that revealed a modest falls, which they estimated to be thirty to forty feet in height and named Rainbow Falls. The route ahead seemed impossible. They crossed a ridge to the village of Payu on the other side of the big bend of the Yarlung Tsangpo. Not far upriver from Payu, the Po Tsangpo joined the Yarlung Tsangpo. Bailey and Morshead had walked down the Po Tsangpo to the confluence some years earlier. Kingdon-Ward went to the confluence and searched for the falls a few miles upstream along the Yarlung Tsangpo, but everywhere the river was a "bouncing, bellowing flood." And without any great falls. An unexplored gap of a mere five to ten miles remained. The falls seemed to be a myth, a fantasy. The lost falls of the Yarlung Tsangpo, the great gorge, and the names associated with them retreated into obscurity in the Western world for several decades thereafter.

Immersed in the Chang Tang and various other projects, I had not realized in the 1990s that permits to visit remote Tibetan areas were suddenly more easily obtained than they had been, and that there was a scramble to claim various "firsts" there: to climb Namche Barwa, then the highest unclimbed mountain in the world; to discover the mythic waterfall; or to run the full length of this most dangerous of rivers.

A Chinese-Japanese mountaineering team made a reconnaissance of Namche Barwa in 1990. The following year the climbers failed in their attempt, but in 1992 they reached the summit. In 1913, Bailey had commented on the great depth of the Yarlung Tsangpo gorge by writing that the river is "16,000 feet below Namche Barwa." In fact, according to the Chinese Academy of Sciences the greatest depth of the canyon is 17,758 feet, three times the depth of America's Grand Canyon. Starting in 1990, Richard Fisher made four trips to the gorge, taking paying clients at times and heavily promoting the fact that the canyon is the deepest in the world.

Even more competitive was the search for the great falls. David Breashears and *National Geographic* photographer Gordon Wiltsie clambered through much of the canyon in 1993. At one point they saw far below two falls veiled in spray where the whole river squeezed between cliffs no more than about fifty feet apart. They photographed the falls but did not think with their eyes. One was the Rainbow Falls, discovered by Kingdon-Ward decades before, but the other was the great lost falls. "I certainly didn't consider it the fabled Lost Falls. I called it Kinthup Falls," Breashears told Todd Balf, author of *The Last River* (2000). The Monpa and Lopa tribesmen who hunted wildlife in the region were, of course, familiar with the falls. However, discovery by explorers from afar implies recognition and dissemination to a wider world. By these criteria the falls remained "lost."

A hundred years after the Sikkimese pundit Kinthup had placed 500 logs in the Yarlung Tsangpo to trace its course, Breashears added a generous footnote to this endeavor. In late April, 1993, he wrote the following message, stuffed it into a one-liter Nalgene-plastic water bottle, and threw it into the Po Tsangpo: "In memory of Kinthup (K. P.). Whose stout-hearted unflagging dedication to service in his exploration of the Tsangpo, epitomized the spirit and tradition of the pundit and 'native' explorers employed by the Survey of India. No. 501. If found please mail to David Breashears, 65 Gray Cliff Rd. Newton, MA 02159 USA. For a Rs 200 reward." On October 22, 1998, the note was returned to Breashears by a Dhundup Tsering, P.O. Tibetan Colony 581411, Karnataka, South India. How did it get there? Delighted, Breashears wrote Dhundup wanting to know when and where the bottle had been found. He got no reply. On receiving the information from Breashears, I too tried to contact Dhundup, enclosing a 300-rupee award with my letter. Again there was no response.

In August 1997, another group of explorers arrived at the great canyon: Ian Baker and his friend Hamid Sardar, the brothers Gil and Troy Gillenwater, real-estate developers from Arizona, and Kenneth Storm, a bookseller from Minnesota. All had been here previously. After entering the canyon country the group split, Baker and Sardar to explore around Namche Barwa and the others to penetrate the gorge farther downstream. A Monpa named Jyang guided the latter on hidden trails into the innermost gorge. "At our feet was Rainbow Falls, clouds of mist wrapping the trees overhanging the river on the left bank," wrote Storm in a chapter in Frank Kingdon-Ward's

Riddle of the Tsangpo Gorges (2001), edited by Kenneth Cox. "Just below, hidden beyond a hairpin bend, the river pooled, then darted to the left and exploded over another great drop—a 'new' waterfall." Michael McRae in *The Siege of Shangri-La* (2002) quotes a much more exuberant Storm. "We found them!" Storm cried out. "We found the Falls of the Brahmaputra!" "I was trembling," says Storm. "What had been such a vital force in the Western imagination had been lost, because explorers had lost faith in the falls. They'd lost their vision." More concisely, Gil Gillenwater wrote in his journal, "AMAZING! THE MISSING LINK."

The discovery by the Gillenwaters and Storm should have led to their acclaim. Instead it resulted in a bitter 1998 wrangle between some of the individuals involved, the National Geographic Society, and the Chinese Academy of Sciences. It was that year when I first visited the area.

When our team reaches the Namche Barwa area in April 1998, I am not much interested in the falls of the Yarlung Tsangpo, "a wild display of hydrolics" as Hamid Sardar calls them, but in the wildlife and in conservation. Monpa hunters accompanying foreign and Chinese expeditions into the gorge routinely kill the cattle-sized takin and the small red goral for food, even though both species are fully protected by law. Neither species is as yet endangered there, but each would benefit from more information about its status. In the hills to the east are the last tigers in Tibet. Qiu Mingjiang, formerly of the Kumning Institute of Zoology and a coworker of mine on the panda project in the early 1980s, spent several months in 1995 to record tiger predation on livestock in that area. Only three small isolated reserves are shown on maps of this region. Yet the diversity of plants and animals is unrivaled in Tibet. The Chinese Academy of Sciences had so far recorded 3,768 species of vascular plants, among them 218 species of orchid, 154 of rhododendron, and 52 of primrose. Some 2,300 species of insects and 232 of birds had been catalogued. Are there mammals like the Tibet red deer and giant muntjak awaiting discovery? My major aim of investigating the area, however, is to promote its greater protection.

As a first step, I have planned a reconnaissance in order to become familiar with the area and then decide where best to concentrate our work. I arrive in Lhasa on April 16 accompanied by Lu Zhi, who had worked with me in the Chang Tang the previous year. She will conduct household interviews of the Monpa, Lopa, and Tibetans in the area to learn about their lives and their impact on the wildlife. Liu Wulin of the Tibet Forestry Department had the responsibility of arranging our joint work before our arrival and then accompanying us. But nothing has been done—no permits for me, no vehicles, no supplies, and no equipment. The MacArthur Foundation had donated a vehicle for our project. "The car is gone," says Liu Wulin. "It has been transferred to another department during reorganization." For several days we have restrained discussions about funds, time in the field, and other matters. Finally seven of us, including Xu Binrong, a short, muscular official, two drivers, and a cook, leave in two vehicles.

It is a two-day drive from Lhasa on a road under construction up over a pass and down a valley of the Niyang River to the prefecture town of Bayi (Linzhi). We check with the Forestry Department and the police for my required permits and with the local Ecological Institute for a botanist to accompany us. All are surprised by our appearance; no one has heard of us or been notified about our proposed work. Well, I think, the aim of a Buddhist pilgrimage is to be awakened rather than to reach a destination. As a naturalist on a reconnaissance I'm here to absorb the landscape rather than to achieve a goal.

We cross the Yarlung Tsangpo over a bridge at its confluence with the Niyang and then head downriver. Here the river is slow and wide, and wind whips billows of dust from sandbars. Willows are in fresh leaf, peach trees are in bloom, and fields are green with winter wheat. Brown-headed laughing thrushes scuttle in small flocks through roadside shrubs. Namche Barwa offers an occasional glimpse between roiling clouds. Just past the village of Pe we stop at a small army post where we are allowed to settle for the night in a couple of bare rooms.

Here, not far from the gorge entrance, the river narrows and turns into a series of rapids. After we drive around a mountain spur the next morning, Namche Barwa fills the horizon. The wall of rock and ice rises in a series of sharp peaks to culminate in a summit pyramid. We stop at homes to inquire about wildlife. Each family offers us a drink of *chang*, a murky, sour barley beer. Men here often wear vests made of red goral skin. We are shown the knobby horns of takin, and the spreading horns of blue sheep, as well as the skins of Assamese macaque monkeys, black bear, and yellow-throated marten. We also see the feathers of blue eared pheasant and the remains of a cinereous vulture.

The road ends at the village of Chibei, elevation 9,850 feet, where a valley leads toward Namche Barwa. Here we will rent horses to carry baggage closer to the mouth of the great canyon. After setting up our tents, Lu Zhi and I amble near the village to add birds to our list: turtledove, Daurian redstart, gray-backed shrike, rock bunting, green-backed tit, red-billed chough. All are common species, but to be able to name something is deeply satisfying. It connects me to the landscape. I also hear the insistent call of the large hawk cuckoo, known as the brainfever bird in India, and it brings back memories of tiger jungles.

The trail is narrow and winds high above the river through patches of oak and pine. The horses have to be unloaded and led carefully on rickety log paths across the face of cliffs. Ahead, on the other side of the river, is the stupendous face of Gyali Peri mediating between earth and sky. At five o'clock we reach Gyala, the last village in the canyon, a cluster of stone huts with wood-shingled roofs surrounded by walnut trees. Putsoa, the headman, is tall and lean. Sherun, our guide from the previous village, translates for us. We learn that seven families totaling forty-two persons reside here. Putsoa has five children of whom one is in school at Pe; he wants all his children to leave because they have no future here. As always, we ask about wildlife. Two kinds of muskdeer occur here, a black one in the forest and a more light-colored one higher up. A few snow leopards survive, he says, and small packs of rust-colored wild dogs occasionally pass through.

We want to investigate the other approach to the great gorge where the Po Tsangpo (also known as the Pailong), flowing from the east turns south and joins the Yarlung Tsangpo. To get there, the next day we follow the road as it swings north through spruce and larch forests, some heavily logged, across a plateau at 13,700 feet, and down to Pailong, the administrative center of the area. Around the cement buildings crowded by the road is a flourishing illegal trade in wildlife products, something obviously condoned by the local administration. One villager tries to sell us the fresh hide of a rust-colored barking deer and another several dried goral skins. An elderly man pulls a couple of musk deer pods, used in high-priced traditional medicines, from his pocket. A woman carries a basket with several long-haired macaque skins in it. We talk to someone from the Forestry Department. He is indifferent when we mention the wildlife trade. Today there is a festival, and villagers use the occasion to make a little money. We also learn that the forest may not be cut within 200 meters of the road or on ridges. Nevertheless, typically a third more forest than the official quota is felled illegally and sold to timber companies.

To escape the crowded community, Lu Zhi and I walk down the road to where a bridge crosses the Po Tsangpo. Our plan tomorrow is to follow a river trail down to the Yarlung Tsangpo, a two-day walk. Camped near the bridge is a team of kayakers, among them Scott Lindgren and Charles Munsey, who plan to descend the white-water river. Nearby are three more tents also belonging to foreigners. And I had been told that it is extremely difficult to get permits to come here.

We introduce ourselves to the occupants of the tents. One is a tall, curly-haired American, Ian Baker, who says on hearing my name, "I wondered when you would show up here." Not that he seems especially psychic, just that he learned of my roaming around the region, just as I had heard of his wanderings around Namche Barwa. Another is his companion on these treks, Hamid Sardar, whose family left Iran at the time of the revolution in 1979 and settled in France. Sardar is now working for his PhD in Tibetan and Sanskrit studies at Harvard. Analyzing the meaning of esoteric phrases in ancient texts does not satisfy his active mind, so he moved to Nepal where he met Baker, who is also deeply involved with Tibetan Buddhism past and present. The two have already made several long journeys through the region to explore the gorge and to investigate how both pilgrims and residents have shaped the landscape—the spiritual geography, in their minds, as opposed merely to the visible parts. The third member of the team is Ned Johnston, a photographer. The meeting is most fortuitous for me. Baker and Sardar describe in some detail the cultural dimensions of the sacred and secret land here, which has a great influence on my perceptions.

In the eighth century, they tell me, the Indian sage Padmasam-bhava, also known as Guru Rinpoche ("Precious Teacher"), estab-lished Buddhism in Tibet by converting powerful and belligerent deities and demons into protectors of the new faith. During his wan-derings in the Himalaya, Padmasambhava created eight remote sanc-tuaries—hidden lands or *beyul*—each a place of inner peace and outer tranquility, an earthy paradise so beautiful and filled with power that no one ever wants to leave. They are refuges in times of strife. Pad-masambhava wrote visionary guidebooks to the *beyul* in the form of scrolls and secreted them in caves. At critical times only those of faith would find them and decipher them. The whole Namche Barwa re-gion, including the Medog (Motuo) area east of the mountain and on across the Line of Control into India, is a hidden land, first identified as such in the seventeenth century when the Mongols invaded Tibet.

This landscape has meaning beyond its reality, Baker and Sardar emphasized. I look at the visible portion, the mountains, the fir trees, the hoopoe flapping by like a giant butterfly. I may even embrace the wilderness in its mythic concepts, and in fact do the science in part because of these. But still, I may be unaware of the intangible forces recognized by local people who see the land with different eyes and hear it with different ears. The writer Herman Melville expressed this concept when he wrote, "It is not down on any map: true places never are." With my heart and mind awakened, I will not merely descend the path down the Po Tsangpo but enter the *beyul* of this region, Dechen Pemako, the Hidden Land of the Lotus, gen-erally referred to as Pemako.

A female deity, Dorjie Pagmo ("Diamond Sow"), reclines across this Hidden Land. The deity wears a small pig head as an ornament, representing the transformation of ignorance, symbolized by the pig, into awareness. The peak Gyali Peri is Dorjie Pagmo's head, Namche Barwa and Kanglagarbo her breasts, and Rinchenpung, a small marsh near the town of Medog, her navel, the Center of Bliss. The Yarlung Tsangpo is her main energy channel. The lower part of her body lies south of the Line of Control and still has to be identified.

A person from the Linzhi Forestry Department, Sang Xiling, has now joined our expedition, rigid and dour. He wears army camouflage, carries on his hip a pistol and on a shoulder strap an automatic weapon with which he constantly fiddles. His aggressive presence aggravates me because it changes the tranquil aura of our trek. Besides, I have an aversion to unnecessary display of weapons. Occasionally I have been assigned armed guards in unsettled countries such as Myanmar, Afghanistan, Vietnam, and Pakistan. There is logic in that. But there is no safer country than China for traveling in remote places. An occasional awkward encounter in the past has also shaped my attitude toward weapons, such as being held up by drunken Congolese soldiers in 1960, or mistakenly rounded up as a terrorist by Argentine soldiers in 1975, and placed face-down in a pickup truck with guns at my back as we roared off into the night.

A good foot trail lined with white-flowered viburnum, larkspur, and patches of virulent nettles follows the Po Tsangpo. We traverse either canyon walls or steep brush-covered slopes, former sites of shifting cultivation. The tumultuous river beside us is without quiet nooks or calm bays. Six porters, villagers going home from Pailong, carry our loads. In late afternoon we reach a shady beach with a rivulet of warm water from a hot spring. The amount of trash indicates a major campsite. Here at only 6,000 feet, cicadas screech and large horseflies search for a blood meal. Baker and his team with fifteen porters arrive soon after us. The kayakers come too, on foot, having after a brief attempt given up on running this section of the Po Tsangpo. "We want to return alive," says one. The campsite is crowded and noisy and cooking fires burn, far from a quiet wilderness experience.

After breakfast of *tsampa* porridge, we cross a swaying cable bridge, the river foaming below. Wild white strawberries grow along the trail and we browse on them. A yellow-blue *Agama* lizard, a foot long, basks on a rock, and a yellow-billed blue magpie flashes by. Standing broadside on the trail ahead is a huge mithan bull black with white stockings. Mithan are domesticated gaur, a species of wild cattle found in forests from India to Malaysia. Uncertain of his temperament, I wait until he withdraws into a thicket. The trail then angles steeply up to a sloping plateau and the village of Zhachu. There are about a dozen houses here surrounded by plots of barley, potato, onion, and rape, as well as poppies and cannabis. Cattle are used for milking and plowing, the mithan mainly for status, and the many black pigs for eating. Below us the Po Tsangpo bends around a peak before joining the Yarlung Tsangpo. Looking up and down the huge canyon with its dark forests beneath a brooding layer of cloud and with the river in either direction vanishing into a maze of sharp ridges, I am intimidated by this seemingly hostile terrain.

We visit the village leader, Sonam Nima. The village has seventy-three people, he tells us, four of them retarded. (Gyala has five out of forty-two people.) Few children are around because most are away at school at Pailong or Bayi. Families want children educated so that they can escape the "useless life" here. Takin, red goral, and black bear are becoming scarce, the village leader tells us. Once they could be hunted near the village, whereas now it requires a trip of several days. We have already heard similar comments elsewhere, and I worry increasingly about the future of wildlife here.

Next we go to the home of Lama Topgye. He is of the Nyingma sect, the oldest in Tibet, introduced by Padmasambhava. Monks of this sect may marry and Topgye has an expansive, voluble wife. The Lopas, the aboriginal tribe in the region, had a village here, he relates, but a 1950 earthquake destroyed it. Now Lopas and Monpas live together in this village. Monpas had emigrated from Bhutan in the sixteenth century during political turmoil there. Tibetans are latecomers, according to Topgye. His wife brings out a dried barking-deer hide. It is dark-brown, different in color from what I expect. I'm uncertain of the species, and so for later DNA analysis I snip off a skin fragment, a sample that will have an interesting repercussion.

Liu Wulin has called a village meeting to exchange views about wildlife conservation and to listen to local concern. Lu Zhi is moderator and Sang Xiling translator. His armed, stiff presence intimidates the village crowd in the room, and, unlike our meeting in Gyala, the people are unresponsive. Obviously our questions are modified in translation. When we asked if village life has been improving, the supposed answer was that it has been very good since 1949, which happens to be the year the Party assumed power in China. Lu Zhi closes her notebook, the meeting over. We are not learning anything of value. Sang Xiling, in keeping with his disposition, will report us to officials in Bayi, claiming that we asked inappropriate questions.

It rains for much of the night, perfect weather for leeches. As we begin our return up the trail toward Pailong, leeches by the thousands, black leeches and yellow-brown ones up to two inches long, wait on leaves a foot or more above ground. Holding on by their large sucker, they point their small suckers rigidly like sticks toward the trail, alert for warm blood. I marvel at the evolutionary perfection of a leech. While abrading the skin to make a wound it injects an anesthetic so that its presence will not be detected. Then it uses an anticoagulant to keep the blood flowing. No doubt leeches have an important function of some sort in their habitat, but I find it difficult to love them. I nervously check myself so often for intruders that I do little more than glance at the large white rhododendron blossoms that have unfolded in the past few days.

We had said goodbye to Baker, Sardar, and Johnston at Zhachu. They planned to cross the Yarlung Tsangpo to photograph Monpas hunting the sacred takin. According to Buddhist principles, all life is sacred, especially in the Hidden Land of Pemako. The Monpas, however, rationalizing away a religious dictum, claim that takin were created specifically for them to eat. Takin resemble a stocky moose in size, though with a peculiarly bloated muzzle, and offer a great deal of meat. No adverse consequences will follow the killing of a takin, Monpas believe, as long as you perform a rite to liberate the animal's life force. On this trip, we later learned, the takin were not ready to sacrifice themselves and left only their dung behind as they vanished high into the hills. The team then penetrated the gorge far enough to obtain a grand view of the great waterfall which the Gillenwaters and Storm had seen the previous year and could claim as their discovery by Westerners.

Baker, Sardar, and Storm returned yet again in 1998, in the autumn, this time funded by the National Geographic Society and accompanied by video photographer Bryan Harvey. When Sardar noticed that the storyline for the film would be focused on the "great white explorer" Baker, he separated himself from the expedition. Taking four porters, he continued into the gorge, exploring the remaining gap that had never been crossed by a foreigner. Meanwhile, Baker, Storm, and Harvey, guided by a Monpa named Buluk, reached a spot just above the "lost" falls on November 8. There the photographer "had Baker and Storm stop to narrate the moment of discovery," to quote McRae's book *The Siege of Shangri-La.* "We're not sure what we'll find," said Baker awkwardly. "Let's go," Storm broke in. "We have a waterfall to find." Storm and Baker each rappelled down to just above the falls, their rope tied to a pine, to measure its height. They calculated the falls at 105–115 feet, and named them the Hidden Falls of Dorjie Pagmo in honor of Pemako's deity.

On January 7, 1999, the National Geographic Society issued a two-page press release entitled "Lost Waterfall Discovered in Remote Tibetan Gorge." "'It's very exciting to find the waterfall of myth to be real,' said Baker . . . who led seven previous expeditions in the Tsangpo Gorge region. . . . Team member Ken Storm, on his fifth expedition to the region, had been a doubter. 'I didn't believe in the waterfall; I thought reports from the past were right—that it probably didn't exist,' he said." Nowhere in the release was there a hint that Baker, Sardar, and Johnston had seen the falls earlier the same year, and that the Gillenwaters and Storm had actually recognized and photographed the falls in 1997. Baker and Storm had documented the height of the falls—not discovered it.

When the Chinese Academy of Sciences became aware that teams of foreigners might "discover" new falls on the Yarlung Tsangpo and perhaps something else of note, they mounted a massive expedition to the region. The previous April, an Academy scouting party of six Land Cruisers had passed us, driving fast, on the road to Pe. The Academy arrived with three large teams that autumn, one in the Medog area, one on the Po Tsangpo, and one down the Yarlung Tsangpo gorge. Baker and Storm finished their task of measuring Hidden Falls and departed while the Chinese team was still bogged down with supply problems at Pemakochung.

The jubilant news release by the National Geographic Society naturally irritated the Chinese Academy of Sciences, which had billed its own effort as "one of the most important expeditions of the century." The newspaper *China Daily* of January 29, 1999, tried to counteract the worldwide coverage by the *National Geographic* by headlining "Chinese explorers got to the falls first." It noted that a helicopter pilot of the People's Liberation Army named Che Fu had taken photographs of Rainbow and Hidden Falls in late 1986 and that these had then been named No. 1 and No. 2 Zangbo Balong Falls.

I hope Dorjie Pagmo will forgive this turmoil over her sacred waterfall.

According to rumor, the Chinese Academy of Sciences was interested in more than geography and natural history. During its 1998 expedition, it may have been making a survey for a huge hydroelectric project on the Yarlung Tsangpo. As noted by the *South China Morning Post* of July 9, 2010, quoting another source, a dam would "transform the landscape, economy, and ecology of the region and will have far-reaching impacts all the way down to the river delta, harming agriculture, flooding homes, and degrading landscapes and local cultures." Officials claim it "would benefit the world." This proposed dam is still being actively considered. A tunnel would be blasted through the gneiss and other metamorphic rocks of Namche Barwa. The region is on the collision zone of the South Asian and Eurasian tectonic plates, and earthquakes are frequent and sometimes catastrophic. Build a tunnel through Namche Barwa? On August 15, 1950, Kingdon-Ward and his wife were camped about 150 miles east of Namche Barwa when "suddenly a most extraordinary rumbling noise broke out, and the earth began to shudder violently," Ward wrote of this earthquake, one that registered 8.6 on the Richter scale, in a 1952 *National Geographic* article. "As the ground shook, avalanches of rocks rolled and rumbled down the mountainsides. . . . A later view revealed that the mountains up to 15,000 feet . . . had been ripped to pieces and scraped clean, and that millions of tons of rock had been hurled into the narrow valleys." Tectonic considerations aside, China would, by damming the Yarlung Tsangpo, destroy a magnificent natural treasure, much as the United States did on a smaller scale in the 1960s with the Glen Canyon Dam that drowned the spectacular gorge of the Colorado River. Other dams on the upper Yarlung Tsangpo are also being planned or are already under construction, and India is damming rivers on its side of the border.

The Yarlung Tsangpo also became the last great first of river running. A rivalry, similar to the race for the Hidden Falls, began in 1998 between Chinese, Germans, and Americans. The National Geographic Society funded a team of American river runners at the same time as it did Baker's group to "find" the "lost" falls. But that year the river was unusually high after torrential monsoon rains. A German expedition, after looking at the Yarlung Tsangpo, decided that it was not possible to run. The American team, perhaps pressured by ambition and a sense of obligation to their sponsor, decided to challenge the fearsome power of the water. One of the main river runners, Douglas Gordon, had on April 21 (before he had seen the river) commented on the *National Geographic Explorer* television show "it's not particularly dangerous." When the attempt was made that autumn, the river was so violent and the waves so huge that the kayakers could paddle only short distances along the margin before having to portage boats and equipment around places where the surging water slammed into cliffs. It was not river running but boat-assisted climbing. On October 16, not far downstream from Gyala, Gordon's boat was dragged sideways over an eight-foot falls and pulled under a cascade of foaming water. Unable to roll himself upright in his kayak, Gordon was swept away; his body was never recovered. Shortly afterward a Chinese rafting team reached Pe and wisely decided against continuing.

As we hike back up along the banks of the Po Tsangpo, our reconnaissance completed, I decide that the terrain in and around the great gorge is too rugged and wildlife too scarce to justify a further trip at this time. Instead I am eager to survey the forests to the east, the last haven of tigers in Tibet.

Later in 1998 the National Geographic Society asks if I am interested in visiting the area east of Namche Barwa in 1999 with Ian Baker and Hamid Sardar to survey wildlife while they focus on the local people. It will be a simple expedition, organized by a Lhasa trekking company, to start next January. I naïvely say yes. A trip with Baker and Sardar appeals to me because I like them personally and I admire their respect for the spiritual life of local peoples. Like Kingdon-Ward, Sven Hedin, and occasional other explorers, I prefer to travel only with local companions, but, like them, I sometimes make exceptions. I notify the Tibet Forestry Department about our proposed journey and ask them to send a staff member. Now matters get complicated. The National Geographic Society designates David Breashears as trip leader, but a month before our departure he drops out, saying he has "no time." Then, to my consternation, two more members are added to the team, the photographer Maria Stenzel and mountaineer Michael Weis, who will be in charge of "safety." A mob of five foreigners makes a trip unwieldy, dilutes interactions with local people, and draws unnecessary attention.

We arrive in Lhasa on February 9. On that day the Tourism Bureau announces that all Chinese and foreign expeditions to the Namche Barwa region are now prohibited. Our permit has been cancelled, as have the permits of several river expeditions. This is the Year of Ecotourism in China. Along with two Tibetan representatives of the trekking company, I have an informal meeting with Abu, head of the Tibet Forestry Department and a person who has always supported our joint work. Abu is ill at ease as he frequently smiles sprawls back in his chair, and raises hands palms up: he can do nothing, we can't go. Why am I associating with the other two foreigners, Baker and Sardar? They caused China to lose face over the discovery of the waterfall. The area has been shut down on order of Beijing. Abu turns to the two Tibetans and says, "Don't push this or you will be shut down."

One person from the trekking company tells me that Public Security came to his office several times and asked questions about Baker, Sardar, and me. I have been accused of discovering a new wildlife species last year and smuggling it out of the country. For a moment I am wholly puzzled by this, but then I reply: "This is completely untrue. I identified a black barking deer. This was the first one recorded in Tibet. It is not a new species, but found in several Chinese provinces. Liu Wulin of the Forestry Department was with me on last year's trip. He gave me permission to take out a small piece of skin, perhaps two square centimeters in size, for DNA analysis. This test determined that this barking deer is also found in Tibet. It's all in my report to Forestry." Who is trying to make trouble for me with Public Security?

Only later do I learn that the grandstanding, or loud beating of gongs and drums, as the Chinese might say, by the National Geographic Society so incensed the Chinese Academy of Sciences that it instigated the closure of the Namche Barwa region. I had greatly underestimated the potential response of the Academy to last year's debacle. The canyon is, of course, a natural treasure of China and it has to determine how best to manage it. But we are a glum team as we discuss our next move.

My spirits lift, however, when the Forestry Department tells me that the whole Pemako region, including Namche Barwa, would, as we had recommended, later this year be established as the Yarlung Tsangpo Great Canyon Reserve.

Hamid Sardar suggests that the two of us fly to Kathmandu. There in Nepal, he knows of another Hidden Land, another *beyul* established by Padmasambhava deep in the mountains. To entice me further, he mentions that many Himalayan tahr, a wild goat species unique to parts of the Himalaya in Nepal, India, and China, are quite tame around the monastery there. Having studied tahr a quarter century earlier in a part of Nepal where they were shy, I am easily persuaded to join Hamid to learn more about the ecology and behavior of this species.

In central Nepal, we follow a dozen porters carrying enough food and equipment for a month up a gorge in the shadow of 26,800-foot Mount Dhaulagiri. Huge cliffs flank us on one side and a torrent on the other. Here and there on more gentle terrain are huts and fields and, high above, stands of forest. It is March, not yet spring. The air is hazy from fires that consume tussock grass, and fanned by wind, roar through conifer forests; the casual vandalism by these Tibetan villagers is destroying the last forests upon which they depend for timber and fuel. When Hamid, who speaks Tibetan, asks a man why they set fires, he replies with the desolate words, "We have always burned." We raise the same issue with a Hindu official from the lowlands who is posted here against his will. He responds, "What to do?" as he waggles his hands.

We enter a side valley, the entrance to the Hidden Land of Kyimolung, the Valley of Bliss. Hamid and I are *nedrog*, pilgrimage friends, each of us on a quest of discovery. Hamid, self-contained and focused, is both a realist and spiritual seeker. A strong hiker, he is usually ahead of me as if eager to return to a place of solace. I look forward to a new awareness in a sacred land at the edge of geography. After two days, the narrow valley opens to spacious villages and fields. Along our route are *mani* walls, mounds of stones incised with prayers, and various *chortens* large and small, symbolizing the one Buddha. We stop at a *gompa*, a small place of meditation. A monk chants, beats a drum, and burns incense of juniper twigs to assure us a good trip. Villagers, we are informed, hunt muskdeer for the prized musk gland and Himalayan tahr and blue sheep for meat. As in Pemako, there is discordance between the Buddhist principle of compassion toward life and a seeming lack of ecological concern for the wild inhabitants of forest and alpine meadow.

Soon we will reach the small monastery in the secret heart of Kyimolung, where all negative thought will vanish. This monastery has been in the lama's family for ten generations, and Hamid tells me that the current lama wants to keep its location secret to protect its tranquility from outsiders. Therefore, I will call the monastery Sertang—Tibetan for "Gold Mandala." Our trail is arduous along cliffs and through forests where wind hums through the fir trees. Finally Sertang lies ahead, tucked beneath a snow-streaked precipice. Wind drags clouds over nearby summits. Young nuns dig a new potato field. As we draw nearer, we note monks dancing in the courtyard of the three-tiered temple. A flock of silver snow pigeons banks in winged unity over fluttering prayer flags.

Here the human and divine can merge, here one can absorb the power of Kyimolung. But we have a shock, one keenly felt by Hamid. The old temple is hemmed in by ugly new barracks, another temple is under construction, and much of the ancient forest nearby has been cut for its timber. We set up our tents in a meadow. Monks come to watch and chat. Fifty monks and thirty-six nuns are already at the monastery, we are informed, and more will come. A tranquil place of meditation is turning into a community out of harmony with its surroundings, both spiritually and ecologically.

When we meet the lama, a lithe, intense man perhaps in his late forties, we ask him about all the discordant development. He explains that foreign donors make the construction possible. His goal is to expand the *dharma*, the ideal truth leading to salvation, by training many monks and nuns and educating many children. His vision is growth. We point out that the *dharma* is threatened if the land is degraded, that Sertang is too small for such a large community. Many hemlock and fir, two hundred years old, have already been felled, with most of the wood left to rot after only a little of it has been used for roof shingles. Why are the tahr protected but not ancient trees? The lama replies, "Trees don't meditate." They have no nervous system like animals and because of that are not sentient beings. I explain that research has shown that plants can communicate with each other. Does that not make them sentient? I have noted in both monks and laymen that religious conviction about living beings, about nature, seldom includes ecological awareness and understanding. Sertang, we realize, represents in a microcosm the worldwide conflict between development and the moral values of conservation.

Fortunately, Himalayan tahr offer daily pleasure. They arrive in herds of ten to twenty to graze on the spring grass around the temple. Most are females and youngsters; the adult males are still high on the slopes. With their short, curved horns and scraggly brown coats, the tahr could be confused with domestic goats as they forage peacefully, oblivious to the monks strolling around and the construction workers banging and sawing. I linger near the tahr and adapt to their schedule of morning and afternoon activity and midday rest. At night, unlike me, they seek safety in precipitous terrain. The tahr are a reminder, just as are the wolves in the remote Chang Tang, that wildlife will live companionably near us if we would just permit it.

One monk looking at all the construction activity tells us, "The *beyul* is finished." Certainly Hamid's tranquil retreat is finished. Yet this hidden paradise is not quite lost. Instead it must be rediscovered, not just with merit but also with ecological knowledge and a commitment to protect the beautiful landscape and all its wild inhabitants. Perhaps my optimism transcends experience. But the day we leave Sertang we see the track of a leopard heading toward the heart of Kyimolung, no doubt to hunt tahr. A symbol of wildness, the leopard conveys that this hidden land still remains basically intact, that the Valley of Bliss can survive in splendor and peace.

CHAPTER 10

Into the Hidden Land

IN MAY 2000, THIS TIME WITH PERMITS in hand, we enter the Hidden Land of Pemako after assembling early in the month at Bayi (Linzhe). There are five of us. Lu Zhi has joined the expedition again, as in 1998. Also with us is Zhang Endi, then the director of the Wildlife Conservation Society's China program and a fine biologist, who joined me on a wildlife survey farther east in Tibet the previous year. Zhang Hong from the Tibet Forestry Department, young, strong, and pleasant, had demonstrated his ability to withstand hardship on our Chang Tang expedition in 1997. Finally, the Linzhe Agriculture and Husbandry College appointed Duo Qiong to accompany us as botanist. With three previous coworkers whom I admire and enjoy, our new venture should be a congenial one. We will trek from the Yarlung Tsangpo eastward across the mountains, wander around the Pemako lowlands, and then head northward via a pass of the Kangrigarbo Range and on to the town of Bomi.

The Tibet Autonomous Region's designation in 1999 of the Yarlung Tsangpo Great Canyon as a state reserve has been followed this year by its elevation to a national reserve, 3,700 square miles in size. The reserve includes all of Medog County in the heart of Pemako, and parts of Mainling, Nyingchi, and Bomi Counties. Padmasambhava's vision of an earthly paradise, the Hidden Land of Pemako, has seemingly reached a new level of compassion and concern in the form of official protection. The old name of Pemako is Bemakang, meaning "lotus," a metaphor in Buddhism for an awakening mind—precisely what is shown by a concern for the environment.

However, two matters, one deferred and one immediate, cause me a measure of apprehension. In October 1999, the Tibetan Forestry Reconnaissance and Design Institute published a master plan for the new reserve. The emphasis of the plan is on economic development, especially tourism. By 2003, the plan envisions a new administrative bureau and education center in Bayi, a road into the reserve, four tourist reception centers, "family hotels with the scale of 200 beds," management stations, libraries in each county, and four steles "with the name written by state leaders." There is also to be a captive breeding center, one for plants and another for animals, a botanical garden, and handicraft centers. Management staff will be trained, and so will residents who engage in tourist business. By 2005 the reserve is expected to "become a famous ecotourism region" catering to 5,000 Chinese and other tourists, and by 2010 the number is predicted to reach 100,000. Tourism does have considerable potential, especially along the main highway, on the major trails leading to the gorge, and in Medog itself if a road is built. But this plan seems rather grandiose. One of the tasks for this trip in 2000 is to appraise for the Tibet Forestry Department the actual potential for tourism and the effects of such intrusion.

My second and more immediate concern is that an official in Bayi tells us that since April 9 the Yigong River has been blocked by two huge landslides that have formed a high, wide dam. The Yigong joins the Po Tsangpo just upriver from the Pailong *xiang*, the administrative center. I had driven up the Yigong in 1998 to look for black-necked cranes which stop over on the wide river flats during migration. That a landslide has dammed the river does not surprise me. In my journal that year I noted "many places of recent landslips. The mountains here are very unstable, the vegetation in constant renewal." When Bailey and Morshead traveled through this valley in 1913, they were told of a landslide that had blocked the river in 1901, and scars on the hillsides made by the turbulent flood after the dam broke were still evident to them a dozen years later. Now the official in Bayi warns us not to leave Pemako by the Po Tsangpo Valley because of fears that the dam will burst.

We reach the village of Pe the evening of May 7. Here porters will be hired to carry our baggage over the Doxiong La, at 13,000 feet a principal pass into Pemako. A rented truck takes our team and porters up a logging road to the base of a steep slope. The porters argue that we have too much gear and the loads are too heavy for them. Since each porter already has his own basket stuffed with *tsampa* and other private goods to sell for red peppers and rice in Pemako, there is indeed no room for our food and equipment. Negotiations lead nowhere. At the instigation of the truculent village head, the porters abandon us and head back down the road. After we load our baggage back on the truck, the porters return and want not only a day's pay but a ride back to the village. No way. We pay nothing and let them walk back. As we learned in 1998, local officials have made no attempt to regulate porters in this region, with the result that they are undisciplined, often stopping to strike for higher pay, adopting a slow-down policy to add days to a trip for extra pay, and pilfering from the baggage and hiding the loot by the trail to be picked up on return.

The following day our team divides into two, some going to the next village to find new porters, and the rest sorting baggage into precise loads of twenty kilograms each. Afterward, with the gleaming crystal wall of Namche Barwa filling the sky, I amble along fields and thickets by the village to add more bird species to my list: Tibetan partridge, beautiful rosefinch, great tit, long-tailed shrike, and Godlewski's bunting—a new species for the area. Porters arrive early the next morning, and without problems they toil upward in single file, bent under their loads. At 12,000 feet we leave the last fir behind and then the rhododendron thickets; now there is only hard-packed snow. In the early afternoon, just past a corniced cliff, we reach the pass. As we wait for the porters, I stand at this convergence of snow and sky, my face lifted up toward the mountains, afloat in space. Several dragonflies are at my feet, embedded in the snow, translucent wings still extended as if in flight.

We descend a south-facing valley, hemmed in by cliffs, the snow soft in the sun. With each step we sink in, sometimes to the thighs. Villagers came from the town of Medog two days before, and avalanches have already obliterated their tracks in places. I glance nervously at the slopes; no team member has ever been injured on any of my expeditions. With safety a main concern, I urge everyone to hurry past the avalanche danger. Descent from the high valleys is slow as we cross ravines of hard-packed snow, but finally we find purple primroses in bloom. Two monal pheasants glide downhill, singing. The trail leads to a cave and a patch of dry pasture where we stop for the evening. Dehydrated from the day in sun and snow, I beg a cup of hot tea from the porters while my companions cook dinner. Later, as I gaze at the luminous silver peaks, I'm saddened that we are just passing by, of no more consequence than the droppings of migratory birds.

We soon leave all snow behind. We pass rhododendrons with large red blossoms and campsites marked by piles of trash, mostly cans from military rations and liquor bottles. *Baijiu*, a rotgut that tastes of dirty socks, seems to be the drink of choice around here. With weird logic someone has built a sheet-metal hut on an avalanche path, with predictable results. At about 8,000 feet, the forest of conifers gives way to oak, maple, magnolia, and other broad-leaved trees, their trunks sheathed in moss. Tree ferns provide an archaic aura. Eventually we reach a military post of two huts surrounded by refuse. A smiling Tibetan has a hotel here, a shed with a plastic sheet for roofing. He serves us tea and rice with tinned army meat. The soldiers next door dine, I note, on freshly killed takin.

The porters do not arrive by nightfall. Only now does the botanist Duo Qiong tell us that they won't come until tomorrow, having successfully added an extra day to the journey. Duo can identify only a few plant species and these only by their Chinese names. As a translator he has a similar story: he does not know any of the local languages and cannot even speak the Tibetan dialect here. When we deal with porters, he stays silent with hanging head. Such a superfluous person, must, we half-jokingly conjecture, have been delegated to spy and report on us.

From the mountain coolness we descend into a humid heat of wild bananas and leeches, and along a narrow cliff trail through a gorge with a river rumbling below. Where the gorge suddenly ends, bare fields cling to slopes, denuded by slash-and-burn agriculture. I carelessly trip over a rock and smash one of my knees on the trail. It's only the third time in decades of fieldwork that I've even slightly injured myself. We reach the Yarlung Tsangpo miles downstream from the great gorge, its pale-brown water soon flowing past the nearby Line of Control into India. The swaying Liberation Bridge takes us over the river to a military guard post. Beyond, on a small plateau at only 3,000 feet in elevation, is the Beibeng *xiang*. Painfully I drag myself along, supported by a stick. The *xiang* has rooms for rent. Buddhist belief reminds you to recognize the precious nature of each day. That for me is a challenge, but at least tomorrow we will rest here.

It rains much of the night and into the next day, a prelude of things to come. The *xiang* leader tells us that the government is so fearful that the Yigong dam upstream will burst that the school near the river has already been closed and all the slats from the Liberation Bridge and other bridges will be removed by May 25. Fortunately, we can leave Pemako by one of two passes across the Kangrigarbo Range to the north.

All valleys and hills within sight of Beibeng are devoid of forest. According to the *xiang* leader, the nearest forest is a two-hour walk away. Monpa and Lopa are slash-and-burn cultivators. After the forest has been cut and burned, the soil can be planted for only a year or two and then must lie fallow for at least five years to replenish its nutrients. Ancient forest is preferred for new fields because the soil is richer. The shifting cultivation here is mainly to grow maize—and the maize is used mainly to make an alcoholic drink. Tibetans have permanent fields in the valleys where they primarily grow rice. Although there is a surplus of rice, it is too expensive to carry out of the area to sell. A road is needed—a refrain I hear again and again. One tiger was killed near Beibeng three years ago and another last year; I wonder if any survive now in the area.

It rains as we leave upriver along the Yarlung Tsangpo toward the county town of Medog twenty-two miles away. I cannot bend my swollen knee. A horse is brought for me to ride, its wooden saddle lacking stirrups: horses here are for baggage, not persons. A Monpa leads the horse while I duck under vines and branches overhanging the trail. Leeches attach themselves to the ankle of my injured leg. Unable to bend over enough to pluck them off, I soon feel the sticky wetness of blood in my boot. We are utterly weary after several hours in the muggy heat. As we near Medog, two men from the Forestry Department meet us, bringing cold cans of Coca-Cola and Sprite in an insulated box. What a wonderful gesture! After a twelve-hour walk (or, in my own case, ride), we reach Medog in the heart of Pemako, a cluster of metal-roofed government barracks, shops, a restaurant, two new three-story buildings, and a military post surrounded by vegetable gardens growing green peppers, squash, and beans. All of us share a room with Chagul, a Tibetan deputy director of the Bayi Disease Prevention Station who plans to visit all of Medog's sixty-one villages to give anti-polio vaccines. Malaria is a problem here and so is tuberculosis, he informs us.

Tattered clouds rest in valleys and ravines as if exhausted by the night's rain. A man from the Forestry Department takes us to a mourning party in a nearby Monpa village. We enter a soot-blackened room with clay pots and ladles lining the walls. A man, seventy-seven years old, sits cross-legged by an open fire. His wife died yesterday. He mumbles drunkenly to himself except for one loud, clear sentence: "I want to express my gratitude to Chairman Mao." We talk to Beijia, a former village headman, seventy-eight years old, with tufts of white whiskers. There is not much wildlife here now, he says, except a few wild pigs and barking deer. "I am happy with life," he proclaims and urges us to drink. The choice is a weak, cloudy drink made from maize and buckwheat, or a potent rice wine mixed with butter and egg. An offered drink is often preceded by the words, "It's all right," a reference to a former (?) Monpa habit of poisoning unwelcome visitors.

Laoji, the vice governor of Medog County, invites us to dinner. Officials are preoccupied with the potential Yigong dam break. All villagers living near the river are being moved to higher ground. I converse mainly with Han Yuan, an administrative assistant, talkative, cheerful, and very well informed. He has seen me on a television program about Tibetan antelope. A tiger was killed near Medog town this year, he tells me, and small packs of wild dog occasionally attack cattle and horses. I ask about the highway from Medog to Bomi eighty-seven miles away and outside of Pemako. It was built in 1994, Han Yuan tells me, but most of it has been destroyed by landslides and washed away by rains. Snow blocks the Gawalong

Pass leading in and out of Pemako in winter. In some years part of the road is repaired so that trucks can at least cross the pass for a short period in summer. About 15,000 people in 2,400 families live in the newly created reserve, 50 percent of them Monpa, 10 percent Lopa, and the rest Tibetan, not counting the military, administrative personnel, construction workers, and others. Han Chinese may be here only by special permit. Fueled by drink, our conversation continues haphazardly on various topics for three hours. Villagers no doubt collect edible mushrooms and medicinal plants. Are these sold commercially to provide both an income and an incentive to protect forest, I ask? No, Han Yuan replies, only a little rattan is sold. There are large wild lemons, walnuts, and cultivated oranges in the area but no way to get them to market.

At first I do not realize how tense the officials are about my presence. Someone has been sent to the village to inquire about what questions I am asking. Zhang Hong, I find out later, has been interrogated, and I notice that he acts subdued, especially in the presence of officials. I am even uncertain whether Zhang Endi and Lu Zhi have fully conveyed the true situation to me. Medog seems to be in a time warp of the Cultural Revolution. I stop bird watching with binoculars, afraid of being taken for a spy.

Rinchenpung, the sacred navel of the deity Dorjie Pagmo, is a four-hour walk southeast and 3,000 feet up in the hills. I want to visit this part of the region's spiritual topography. Pemako, like all *beyul*, consists of three parts, as Ian Baker describes in *Heart of the World* (2004). The first is the landscape as I perceive it. I have admired the sublime snow peaks, roaring rivers, orchid-laden trees, and variety of birds. I am also acutely aware of the incessant downpours, slippery trails across unstable landslides, and intrusive invertebrates such as gnats, mosquitoes, fleas, and leeches. Ian Baker quotes a lama, "When leeches infest your legs, think of them as drawing out all Karmic impurities." The second part is the inner symbolic region of deities and demons, known to pilgrims and residents but beyond my power to discern. However, I try at least to probe this inner realm and raise awareness of mind and spirit. Finally there is the third part, the door to paradise, toward enlightenment, which has to be discovered through hardship and merit.

A trail goes straight up toward Rinchenpung, surmounts a crest, and dips into a basin with forested slopes and a marsh at the bottom. There on a knoll is the Rinchenpung temple, three-tiered and surrounded by prayer flags tied to upright poles. Seven families live along the basin's rim growing barley and millet. A rugged Tibetan invites us into his home for rice wine and tea. He moved to Pemako in 1959 at the age of sixteen and is now waiting to die in this paradise on earth. Traveling with us now is a stocky, middle-aged Monpa named Dawa who was for eleven years the party secretary of Gedang, the place we plan to visit next. We already find him a great asset. His presence gives us credibility and he is greeted cordially everywhere. He loves to share gossip and news, and he provides us with insight into various issues. Away from town, the atmosphere among our group is relaxed.

Norbu, Rinchenpung's caretaker, meets us at the temple door. He is seventy years old, lean, five feet tall, and missing his left hand. Norbu was a monk, he tells us, then became "red" during the Cultural Revolution, and is now a monk again. The temple was wholly destroyed during the 1950 earthquake, as were most buildings in Medog. It was rebuilt only to be destroyed again in the late 1960s during the Cultural Revolution and then rebuilt by the government in 1985. In the main hall, stacks of religious texts wrapped in cloth line one wall. On other walls are shelves with small statues of deities, rows of demonic masks, and a photo of the deceased Panchen Lama. A tabletop is covered with the litter of statues smashed during the earthquake and later events. Above rows of burning butter lamps glows the golden figure of a wrathful Padmasambhava, four-armed and draped with *katas* (ceremonial scarves), his eyes glaring and white canines flashing. Passionate pilgrims, local and from afar, come here braving adversity to purify their perceptions. Although the temple is new, it has an aura of neglect, not a place where I would expect sky spirits to dance.

Behind the temple is a shack with several bare rooms. A pilgrim is in one, and we hear him chanting the mantra *OM MANI PADME HUM*, "the jewel is in the lotus." One night of meditation at Rinchenpung is said to equal one year elsewhere. We move into another of the rooms. In the soft light of a fire we chat among ourselves of leeches and tigers, safe subjects. The last tiger at Rinchenpung was shot in 1968. To Dawa and the rest of the team I relate impressions gleaned from a month I spent earlier in the year just south of here across the Line of Control in the part of Arunachal Pradesh that is still in dispute between India and China. With habitats so similar on both sides of the border, I had gone there in March to compare the status of tiger, takin, and other species with conditions here.

The border dispute over this area is long-standing. An Anglo–Chinese treaty in 1906 and an Anglo–Russian treaty the following year confirmed Chinese suzerainty over Tibet. Later, in 1913 and 1914, there were other meetings attended by representatives from China, Tibet, and Great Britain in Simla, a hill station in the Indian foothills of the Himalaya, to negotiate their spheres of influence and to agree on borders. Henry MacMahon, head of the British delegation, proposed that the frontier should follow the crest of the Himalaya, a suggestion still known as the MacMahon Line. This new frontier would be highly advantageous to the British; they would gain a great swath of land in the west, in the Kashmir region, and almost all terrain north of the Brahmaputra River in what was then known as the Northeast Frontier Agency. Under British pressure, Tibet signed the proposed agreement, whereas China merely initialed it and soon afterward repudiated it, leaving the border still in dispute a century later.

In the 1950s, the Indian government under Prime Minister Jawaharlal Nehru initiated a reckless "forward policy" by which it established small military outposts and made other forays north of the *de facto* border, the MacMahon Line, with the result that tensions between India and China grew until on September 20, 1962, shots were exchanged, as related in Neville Maxwell's excellent 1970 book *India's China War.* At the time, China had reached border agreements with Pakistan, Nepal, and Bhutan, but when on several occasions Chinese premier Chou Enlai approached Nehru about its border issue with India, he was rebuffed. The Indian military in the Northeast Frontier Agency was then led by antiquated generals, who, together with Nehru, had deluded themselves into thinking that China would retreat if attacked.

Indian troops gathered north of the town of Tawang near the Bhutan border, and on October 10 they made an attempt to over-run a Chinese outpost. Ten days later the People's Liberation Army moved south. It captured the town of Tawang within three days, and, battling resisting troops, advanced rapidly southward, taking Walong, Bomdila, and other places, and sweeping the Indian troops out of the hills. On November 20, at the village of Chuka just short of the Brahmaputra plains, the People's Liberation Army halted its advance. A day later it declared a unilateral ceasefire, and promised to with-draw to the MacMahon Line by December 1. This it did.

I first arrived in India the following year, 1963, with Kay and our two small sons to begin a study of tigers and their prey. The clash between India and China was still on everyone's mind. Now, thirty-seven years later, I would finally have a chance to survey wildlife in this area, one still restricted.

I reached Guwahati, the capital of Assam state, on February 27, 2000. The following day, the headline of the local newspaper, *The Sentinel*, read: "Nagen Sarma killed in Blast." Sarma was the for-estry minister, and his vehicle with five persons inside was blown up by rebels, an indication of the unsettled political conditions in the region. An army helicopter used for commercial flights took me to Arunachal Pradesh after we had been thoroughly frisked. At an airstrip near Itanagar, the capital, Jon Miceler met me. Tall and lean, Jon ran a trekking business but he also liked to explore new terrain. With him was his local partner Komkar Riba, a member of the Adi tribe. Together we would wander through remote hill for-ests of Arunachal Pradesh to gain an impression of this little-known habitat. The Adi were once known for resenting any intrusion into their forest, but Komkar is of a new generation. His soft round face was amiable, and used to town life, he seemed disconcerted when he realized that we plan to hike cross-country through uninhabited forests. However, he was invaluable as interpreter and as interlocutor with local officials.

We drove eastward along the edge of the Brahmaputra plain. There were five of us now including Hakim the driver and Sharma, a young Nepalese cook. The road was crumpled, potholed, and jammed with Tata trucks belching noxious black exhaust. White cattle egrets stood motionless along the edges of rice paddies. After seven bruising hours we reached the town of Pasighat sprawling by the Dihang (Siang) River, as the lower reaches of the Yarlung Tsangpo are called, before it reaches the Brahmaputra.

The road north toward the Line of Control was paved, but it traced every contour of each hill high above the river. Ferns, *Pandanus* palms, bananas, and an occasional patch of forest flanked us. Adi wandered the road's edge, their spindly legs showing beneath loincloths and jackets made of homespun. Some had short swords, sheathed in monkey skin, strapped across their chests. Nearly all carried rifles. One Adi had a dead brush-tailed porcupine in a basket on the back of his motorcycle. Wildlife was widely hunted and sold, the only cash income for many households. Mithan, those domestic forms of the gaur, lounged by the roadside; Komkar said they were mainly used for bride price.

Dense fog hugged the valley and the air was utterly still as we continued northward the next morning. Slash-and-burn agriculture, mostly for upland rice, has converted hill forests to scrub and scars of bare soil. The headman of Janbo, an Adi village, invited us into the thatched community hut constructed of bamboo and raised on stilts. Baskets and clothes hung on the walls. One wall had a display of about a hundred skulls, dating back to our host's grandfather, mostly of wild pig and also takin, serow, barking deer, and monkey. Takin occur now only a four-day walk to the northwest, our host informed us, and tigers do not come here anymore. We sat around the open fire as various neighbors crowded in to observe and listen to us as we ate dinner of rice and *dal*, a kind of lentil.

Early the next morning, we continued to Miging, an Indian army post and administrative center from where a forest trail went west, ideal for a short walk on our return. An Adi we saw at a nearby village wore a cloth belt diagonally across his chest, and attached to it was the upper jaw of a clouded leopard, teeth jutting outward. Another such belt displayed half a dozen big-cat jaws to show the hunter's prowess as a slayer of dangerous beasts. The Adi, and also the Mishmi farther east, hunted at times across the border in Pemako because tigers and other big cats had become so scarce here, and access over the low hills was easy.

Jon, Komkar, and I next headed for Tuting at the end of the road and only fifteen miles from the Line of Control. Government buildings were scattered over a series of low hills, with a dense community of Adi, Monpa, and Tibetans crowded onto the river flats. The Indian military was nervous about our presence, and we backtracked to Miging, where we hired several porters for a trek across the forest there. Two hunters returned to the village carrying shotguns, bow and arrow, and a woven bag with something bulky in it. When asked about the contents, the hunter pulled out a langur monkey with untidy gray hair on the back, a whitish underside, and a charcoal cap. Its black face was sad and human-like, eyelids half closed. This was a capped langur, which is also found across the border in Pemako within the large loop of the Yarlung Tsangpo. A villager also showed us the skin of a clouded leopard, killed the previous week, and that of a golden cat. Too many of my wildlife observations consisted of sad mementoes of once-vibrant animals.

We left with six porters, our route following a ridge of old-growth forest. A small white orchid was in bloom. All along the trail there were ingenious traps to catch rats, a desirable source of food: a bamboo pole extends across the trail about eight feet above ground to serve as a rat highway, and a snare with a trigger is fastened to the pole. When a rat moves the trigger, a bent bamboo pole snaps taut. The next day, after a Spartan camp, I left at dawn ahead of the others, hoping to encounter some animals in the morning silence. I examined a pig wallow and a scat, probably that of a clouded leopard, containing barking-deer hair. We camped that night by a stream. It poured all night, and the rain continued until midday. Every rock and stick on the trail was slippery as if glazed with ice. A small group of capped langur crashed away through the canopy. Now at least I had seen a living wild mammal. That afternoon, after crossing a river on a bridge made of a few strands of wire and several bamboo poles, the forest gave way to fields of maize and upland rice and then the village of Gaching. Wet and weary we settled into the local schoolhouse. My pants were stained with blood where leeches had feasted in cozy darkness.

As we left to head south, a toothless old man with long white hair raised his arm in a salute and shouted, "Hallelujah, praise the Lord." Along the trail we met a successful hunter in a shirt advertising Reebok. He had caught fifteen toads which were impaled through the belly and stacked on a sharpened stick, one on top of another. The toads were still alive, twitching. The males were bright sulfur-yellow, the females larger and gray-brown.

Our car was waiting at Mole, a three-hour walk from our night stop. We reached Along, a major administrative center, happy to move into a guesthouse where, after days of heavy rain, we could dry our sodden belongings. The district commissioner, a squat, phlegmatic bureaucrat, was nervous about our presence. What were we really doing here? We wanted a look at the mountains to the west, but, given the weather, we saw mostly the inside of clouds. We left Along on March 16, and within hours were on the warm, sunny, and polluted Brahmaputra plain. By evening we were again at Komkar's home.

I learned that India had established what it calls the Dibang-Dihang Biosphere Reserve, though it is not internationally recognized as such. About 2,000 square miles in size and extending 125 miles from west to east, we had actually traversed part of the reserve during our forest trek. The reserve was established the previous year to connect the Moulin National Park in the west with the Dibang Wildlife Sanctuary in the east. This network of protected areas would in effect be an important ecological extension of the Yarlung Tsangpo Great Canyon Reserve just north across the Line of Control—except that here too there is little effort made by the government to control hunting. The whole region is actually part of the same *beyul* and shares the same habitat and species, an ideal religious and ecological situation for protecting the whole landscape in a cooperative venture between China and India. I met Pekyom Ringo, the head of this new reserve. He was its only staff member and lived in Itanagar, far from the reserve about which his knowledge was meager. When I asked him about the intensive killing of wildlife by the Adi and Mishmi, he brushed the query off with "They have always hunted. Hunting is part of the local culture." I had hoped that the great forest of Arunachal Pradesh would be a reservoir from which tigers might replenish the few surviving ones in Pemako. But in the areas we had visited so far the forests were almost empty of wildlife, and we had not met anyone who confirmed the presence of tigers. They were always somewhere beyond.

We also wanted to visit the mountains in far western Arunachal. On the way, in the city of Tezpur, we stopped to ask for permission from D. Shakathar, the commanding general of the region. Jon Miceler discussed the advantages of tourism with him. Precise and straightforward, the general said, "God created this. Why not people enjoying it?" On the way north, near the foothills, we stopped briefly at the small Namgeri National Park. Established in 1878 as a reserved forest, it still has tigers, elephants, and perhaps the rare white-winged wood duck. This area adjoins a splendid tract of rain forest, the Pakui Wildlife Sanctuary in the foothills. Given a few decades of full protection, tigers could spread widely through the forests from here.

Continuing north over a good paved road, we ultimately crossed Sola Pass, 13,200 feet in elevation and flanked by a jagged range, and beyond it we finally reached the town of Tawang near the Line of Control and close to the Bhutan border in the west. A large monastery crowns a hilltop, and nearby is the birthplace of the sixth Dalai Lama, a whitewashed house high on a slope. Tsangyong Gyatso was born in 1683 and died under mysterious circumstances in 1706. His behavior as Dalai Lama was somewhat aberrant. He is still remembered for his songs and poems celebrating wine and love, as revealed by this stanza from one of his songs:

> I dwell apart in Potala;
> A god on earth am I.
> But in town the prince of rogues
> And boisterous revelry.

At Tawang, the superintendent of police, pleasant and interested in our endeavor to survey wildlife in the mountains to the east, designated Norbu to accompany us, and we also acquired Taka to arrange porters. The trail we took from here wound up through bamboo and pastures, and on past stands of oak and magnolia in bloom. At one village we found the hide of a goral stretched out to dry. It is a gray goral, a species different from the red one around Namche Barwa. I need to justify treks such as this one, and distribution records of little-known species give me a feeling of scientific validity. Stone buildings were crowded together in the village of Thimbu, and here at 10,000 feet there were still drifts of snow. The plant collector Kingdon-Ward had passed through here decades earlier, and the place probably looked much the same then. Some houses had a fertility symbol hanging outside from a rafter, a wooden penis or just a short stick.

Jon liked to forge ahead and he reached the village of Mago well before I did. When I finally arrived with the porters he told me that he had met a group of chanting men carrying a snow leopard tied to a pole. When they stopped, they raised their short swords in ritual. Now about twenty men sat in a courtyard drinking *chang*. Draped over bamboo poles was the skin of the snow leopard, a male. The skull was still within the skin, jaws gaping, tongue bloody—to judge by his teeth, a young adult. The men seemed morose as they drank.

Snow peaks shone in sterile splendor above dark fir forests as we hiked up a valley to timberline, saw a cackling flock of blood pheasant, spotted two herds of blue sheep high on a cliff, spent the night in a stone shelter that no doubt offered less comfort than a bear den, and then trekked back to Tawang, our brief survey in Arunachal Pradesh completed. The region has the finest forest tracts remaining in India, but wildlife was scarce, disappointingly scarce because of unrestricted hunting.

As we huddle around the evening fire in Rinchenpung, I relate details of that Indian trip earlier in the year. I feel guilty that I am unable to tell my companions uplifting stories about wildlife on the other side of the border. They convey by their subdued comments that the situation is equally bad around here. However, there are still tigers around Gedang, Dawa tells us, and we will go there the day after tomorrow.

The sun is already hot and the air enervating as we leave Medog for Gedang to the north. There are nine porters as well as Dawa and Tang, a pleasant and diligent construction worker who wants to be our cook on the trip all the way to Bomi on the north side of the Kangrigarbo Range, where we've planned for a car to meet us later. Fortunately, my injured knee is functional again. The old road is now just a foot and mule path littered with boulders and cut by ravines. Our route passes through overgrown or recently burned fields. On the other side of the Yarlung Tsangpo is forest, a small reserve established in 1975 and now part of this whole protected region. Loud booms indicate that someone is dynamiting fish in the river. We are tired when we reach a village of six abandoned huts and pile into one of them. People and livestock have been moved out because of the impending flood when the dam on the Yigong river bursts, as is expected. What we do not realize is that the fleas have not moved out and are all now voraciously hungry. Invertebrates especially favor Zhang Endi—I count sixty-three flea bites on one of his forearms the following morning.

It rains again the next day, as it does most days. The monsoon sweeps north until it hits the mountain barrier of the Kangrigarbo Range and Namche Barwa, with Medog town receiving about one hundred inches of rain a year. The following afternoon we reach the village of Damu at the confluence of the Yarlung Tsangpo and Chimdro Rivers. Here the great gorge opens into hills, and, after a final flourish of rapids, becomes relatively calm. This Lopa village is a center of wildlife trade. Although all hunting has been illegal since 1989, the Lopa readily show us what they have, secure in the knowledge that no one cares. One hunter has skins of both red and black barking deer, and says that the latter always lives at higher elevation, information of much interest to me. Another hunter has skins of red panda and clouded leopard. A goral skin sells for the equivalent of about $5, the various parts of a black bear—skin, gall bladder, paws—for a total of up to $150, and a muskdeer pod for as much as $300. In an area where the average annual income per person is $100 to $250, hunting contributes considerably to livelihood. The various skins here and elsewhere provide me with useful distribution records of species—but nowhere in Pemako do I discover any new or long-missing large mammals.

With five horses to carry baggage, we climb high above the Chimdro River into cloud, our steps muffled on a carpet of sodden dead leaves. The route crosses the Mahuang Shan, Leech Mountain, very aptly named, and descends into a valley with barley fields already ripening. At the village of Jaba, everyone greets Dawa and we settle on the porch of one of his friends. Homes here are of upright slats with roofs of wood shingles. Twenty families once lived here but only seven remain, the others having moved out of Pemako because children lack good schools, and, it is claimed, tigers kill too much livestock. Dawa invites three men in to chat so that we can collect information about tiger predation—number of cattle and horses owned, and number of livestock killed in the past twelve months, to name just two of our queries.

At noon we reach Gedang, a community consisting of government barracks, a small monastery, and twenty-nine households. Four of us occupy one room in a barracks, Lu Zhi another, and Tang the cook shed. When *xiang* leader Zhang Qiusheng, a Han from Sichuan, comes by, we explain the purpose of our visit. He is exceptionally hospitable, helpful, and interested. He has already summarized the local information on livestock killed by tigers in Gedang, and he generously gives it to us:

Table 10.1

LIVESTOCK KILLED BY TIGERS IN GEDANG VILLAGE, SOUTHEAST TIBET

Year	Livestock in *xiang*		Total livestock killed by tigers	
	Cattle	Horses/mules	Cattle	Horses/mules
1993	954	354	83	15
1994	899	307	113	29
1995	884	317	140	27
1996	829	341	49	5
1997	817	413	55	4
1998	843	424	60	4
1999–May 2000	879	437	67	8

We remark that predation was particularly heavy in 1994 and 1995. Zhang Qiusheng explains that one persistent livestock killer was shot in 1996; I wonder how many other tigers were secretly killed. The numbers of horses and mules increased during the decade, in contrast to cattle, which have remained relatively stable in number. Yes, that is because local people buy more animals elsewhere and bring them to Pemako. Using pack animals to transport supplies from Bomi across the Kangrigarbo Range, particularly for the military, is the most reliable way to make money here.

The night's rain has dissipated, and a soft golden light transforms the landscape into an idyll. Snow peaks glint, the river becomes a silver thread, dew glistens on walnut and peach leaves, and pale smoke rises through the roofs of houses. We pay our respects to Lama Baima Tamang at the monastery, and then we interview three households about tiger predation. Sitting on the porch, we sip butter tea while Dawa asks questions. One woman, aged sixty-six, tells us about the 1950 earthquake that destroyed all homes and the monastery and even, temporarily, dammed the Chimdro River, flooding her fields.

That evening, Zhang Qiusheng has a party for us. A three-year-old cow is shot (two bullets). About a dozen of us gather. Beef is the only item on the menu, that and much *chang* and *baijiu*. Zhang Hong, red in face, dozes off. Alcohol stimulates Zhang Endi's flea bites to itch mercilessly, and he scratches them furiously. Dawa relates anecdotes nonstop. It is a congenial evening.

We need more detail about tiger predation to find out if there is a way to mitigate it. The *xiang* has eleven villages with 126 households and 675 people scattered over 115 square miles. Obviously, we cannot interview all within a few days. Instead we sample twenty-one households in several villages. Zhang Endi, Lu Zhi, and I will later write a summary of our findings and publish these in a 2000 issue of *Cat News*, a conservation newsletter. Each household, we found,

had an average of 6.2 cattle, 4.4 horses, and 3.1 pigs. Of these a household lost, on average, 0.9 cattle and 0.2 horses during the previous twelve months; nine households had no losses. With a head of cattle selling for the equivalent of about US$370 and a horse for double that, the average loss of 1.0 head of large livestock has considerable economic impact. Average annual per capita income is $117, which, given mean household size of 6.9, indicate a total of $809. Even the loss of one animal reduces potential income by a third to a half, not counting the loss of future offspring, reduction in ability to transport loads for pay, and so forth.

The *xiang* as a whole lost about 7 percent of its cattle and 1 percent of its horses and mules in 1998, a typical recent year. In addition, some of its 571 pigs were also eaten by tigers and Asiatic wild dogs. One reason for livestock predation is, of course, the scarcity of wild pig, takin, barking deer, and other natural prey. Illegal hunting is intensive in this sacred Hidden Land, as we have well documented. Much of this hunting is commercial, with hides and other products sold openly in Pailong, Damu, and other places. Furthermore, a tiger seldom has the opportunity to consume the cow or horse it has killed because villagers scavenge the meat. What chance does the tiger have of surviving in Pemako under these conditions?

We follow mud trails on our way from village to village to conduct interviews, observe livestock herding practices, and (unsuccessfully) search for any tiger spoor. Only four or five tigers, including a female with large cub, are thought to frequent the Gedang area. Tigers are still being killed, as we found out in Beibeng, Medog, and here. We guess that perhaps only around fifteen tigers survive in all of Pemako.

Zhang Qiusheng calls a meeting of villagers to discuss tiger predation. About fifteen men and women assemble. The discussions mirror the ones we have had in household interviews. To our query about how predation can be reduced, we get comments such as "Nothing can be done" and "I can't think of a solution." But there is one suggestion: "Tigers should be killed; if possible, use dynamite." Cattle and horses, we have observed, are simply left unguarded in the forest. Why not guard them? Tigers here are shy—most villagers have never seen one—and are not known to attack people, we note. Most households have no extra members to spare for herding, we are told. Then why not organize a community herding program with households rotating guard duty? Tigers come close to villages because tall, dense bracken ferns on abandoned fields provide cover. Why not cut the ferns and turn the areas into pasture? Too much work. Why not stable livestock at night, when tigers are most active? Too inconvenient. In other words, let the government find a solution. I feel deflated by the local attitudes we encounter.

Dawa now rises to give a speech, quite tangential to our discussions, but it makes our team feel good. He will soon return to Medog. His presence has enabled us to obtain much useful information, and his fund of stories, related in a raspy voice, has lightened every meeting. "Today I will tell you the truth. I was a hunter. I have killed over 300 animals. For the past days we worked together and we were always thinking. You are right: the tiger needs wildlife or it will kill livestock. I promise not to hunt again."

In 1995 the Gedang *xiang* wrote to the Medog administration: "The people strongly urge economic compensation and hunting [of tigers]." Direct payment as compensation for livestock killed by predators has been tried in several parts of the world, and with rare exception it has proven inefficient as a conservation strategy. When we return to Lhasa we mention the issue of livestock predation to the Forestry Department. Its solution was to raise pigs in Pemako to feed tigers. Money was actually given to establish a government pig farm, but the project fortunately vanished when the money did. There are no easy short-term solutions to predation problems, as I discuss in Chapter 14. But at least the communities here can help themselves by implementing some of the suggestions we made at the meeting, and the government can enforce wildlife laws so that the number of takin, wild pigs, and other prey animals can increase.

Our guess that perhaps only fifteen tigers survive in Pemako would normally rate no more than a shrug. Except that this is probably China's largest remaining tiger population. China has complacently watched its tiger population dwindle since at least the Shang Dynasty more than 3,000 years ago, as ancient hunting records show.

At that time the cats were found throughout the eastern half of the country. Today, a few tigers have drifted from Russia into northeast China, where they live mostly on livestock, their natural prey having declined almost to the vanishing point due to poaching. An occasional straggler persists in the southeast, in Yunnan province, and there are the few in Pemako. During the late 1990s more tigers could be tallied as skins in a few Lhasa shops than exist in the wild in all of China.

With greater affluence, more and more Tibetans trimmed their traditional robes or *chubas* with leopard or tiger skin, something once reserved for the elite in society. Now it was a fashion statement and status symbol obtainable by anyone with the cash. From the 1990s until the past few years, wildlife protection had been unusually feeble in India, the source of most cat skins. Officials refused to acknowledge a problem even though a 2006 census revealed that perhaps no more than 1,400 tigers were left in all of India; a 2010 census reported 1,700 tigers, roughly half of the total world population in the wild. Meanwhile the illegal market in Tibet had boomed. In October 2003, a custom post on the Chinese side of Tibet's border intercepted a shipment of 31 tiger, 581 leopard, and 778 otter skins. Organized crime networks lead from poacher to dealer to smuggler who transports the skins to China, often via Nepal. One Delhi dealer alone, Sansar Chand, admitted in 2006 to selling 470 tiger and 2,130 leopard skins over the years. Poachers killed every tiger in some of India's best reserves, such as Sariska and Panna, while a large but unmotivated guard force sat idly by and the reserve directors claimed everything was just fine. (Tigers have now been translocated from other reserves back into Sariska and Panna.) Poachers can operate with little fear of prosecution if caught. Belinda Wright of the Wildlife Protection Society of India has done more than anyone to turn poachers and dealers over to the law. But, as she told me, among 882 persons accused of tiger crimes between 2001 and 2010 there were only eighteen convictions. (In spite of these problems, India retains extensive forest tracts and viable tiger populations; it only needs political will to save its most iconic species.)

During the 1990s and until 2005, years that included my visits to Pemako, I was aghast when I saw shops in Lhasa openly displaying illegal tiger and leopard skins. At village festivals in summer, with their horse racing and dancing, participants and spectators alike often wore such skins. Even monks occasionally had a tiger skin wrapped around the waist, despite the teachings of Buddhism. The Lhasa forestry police told me that they were afraid to do anything overt because it might cause a riot. Ruth Padel wrote in her evocative book *Tigers in Red Weather* (2006), "The roof of the world, water source, spiritual and cultural source for so much of Asia; you cast a new shadow now."

In January 2006, His Holiness the Dalai Lama held a Kalachakra, a traditional gathering signifying the Wheel of Time with a focus on peace and compassion, attended by thousands in south India. He used his moral authority on behalf of wildlife, saying that he was "ashamed" of the behavior of Tibetans who dressed in animal skins. He beseeched the pilgrims, "When you go back to your respective places, remember what I said earlier and never use, sell, or buy wild animals, their products or derivatives." Skins quickly vanished from Lhasa shops, and when I wandered around town in 2006 none were on display. In their enthusiasm to heed the Dalai Lama's words, Tibetans gathered in various towns, piled up their skins, and publicly burned them—much to the consternation of government, which viewed the gesture as political rather than religious. The skin market has now moved mostly eastward to the Han, where those of wealth derive prestige by paying $6,000–$10,000 or more for a tiger skin to show off in their home.

The body parts of tigers have long been used in traditional medicines, especially in China. Eating a tiger's eyeball is said to help epilepsy, eating a tiger's heart is said to give courage; tiger blood builds up the constitution, bile stops convulsions, whiskers are good for toothache. Bones are ground into powder, sold at around $1,500 a pound, said to cure headache, ulcers, typhoid, and rheumatism. Soak the body of a tiger in a vat of rice wine and you get a tonic—for sale at $750 a bottle.

Knowing that the supply of tigers in the dozen other Asian countries where the species still occurs is being rapidly depleted, in some cases to the vanishing point, China has established factory farms to breed the cats. It is estimated that these now house between 5,000 and 7,000 tigers. In a 2009 poll, 43 percent of Han Chinese admitted to having used a tiger product. The bones from factory-farm tigers would obviously have many customers, but their sale within China has been illegal since 1993. China wants to modify this law, but the international conservation community objects vociferously. The bones of a poached tiger from India, Nepal, Laos, Thailand, or any other country cannot be distinguished from a slaughtered captive. Poaching would no doubt increase in order to fulfill China's insatiable demand—driving tigers further toward extinction. (Cambodia recently lost its tigers and Vietnam may have done so, too.) But if bones are difficult to obtain, one can always visit a tiger farm near the town of Guilin to dine in a restaurant on strips of stir-fried tiger with ginger and vegetables.

Tigers cannot be saved in small isolated reserves where the few animals would have a precarious future because of inbreeding and other problems. A tiger population requires a whole landscape, a sustainable landscape including protected cores without people, where the cats can reproduce in tranquility, surrounded by carefully managed areas of human use including protected forests and other habitats through which tigers can travel from one place to another. This idea is behind my suggestion that China and India should cooperate in creating a tiger landscape across the border that includes Pemako and parts of Arunachal Pradesh. As stated in the Hindu epic *Mahabharata*, composed between 1,700 and 2,300 years ago:

> The tiger perishes without the forest,
> And the forest perishes without its tigers.
> Therefore the tiger should stand guard over the forest,
> And the forest should protect all its tigers.

Just before we leave Gedang, Lama Baima Tamang invites us to the monastery. We sit on cushions as half a dozen monks chant and play sonorous music on trumpets, cymbals, and a drum to wish us a good journey. The Kangrigarbo Range blocks our route to the north, to the town of Bomi and the highway, except for two passes. The heavy rains of the past two weeks have fallen as snow at high elevation, and no one knows if a crossing is possible. We leave in heavy rain, hunched under ponchos. Late afternoon brings us to the village of Kangzai, a quagmire of refuse, livestock feces, and ankle-deep muck. The headman Zhang is Dawa's friend, and we drink endless cups of lukewarm butter tea in his home. Zhang has fifty cattle near one pass, the Jinzhe La, but has no idea about snow conditions. Rather than sleep in that house and entertain its fleas, we entice the village teacher to let us stay in the one-room schoolhouse.

The next morning is sunny and we climb toward the pass with renewed energy. At 8,500 feet the leeches disappear, an event worth noting. Beyond, on our left, is a huge granite dome reminiscent of Yosemite; on our right are gray cliffs with a waterfall, formed, a porter says, by the 1950 earthquake. An abandoned cattle camp on a spongy meadow offers a campsite. Standing on a cliff face is a fox-red goral, its small curved horns reminiscent of the American mountain goat to which it is related. It is the only live mammal in the wild we have seen on this trip.

It rains again. The botanist Duo Qiong permits a complaining porter to reduce his load and suddenly all loads are deemed impossibly heavy. After an hour's argument we continue, up through a rhododendron forest sheathed in moss to an alpine meadow at 11,200 feet. Two men are in a hut guarding a herd of cattle-yak hybrids. A tiger occasionally ascends to this height to prey on livestock—the last time in 1998—and even crosses the pass into the forests of Bomi, we are told.

On June 1, the headman of Kangzai arrives to lead us to the pass. Seeing the deep snow above us, he wisely decides to examine the route first and to cut steps for the porters if necessary. Several of the men head up with him while the rest of us wait. There is a blood spot with musk-deer hair by one of the huts. No one hunts here, say the two herders innocently, then, responding to my skeptical look, they admit to having killed a female musk deer (females lack the musk gland) and eaten it. The men return exhausted in mid-afternoon. The snow is waist-deep and avalanche danger great. We have to retrace our steps for two days to Gedang and then move on to Damu and try to cross the Gawalong Pass.

When we reach Damu, we are told of a radio message stating that the bridge over the Po Tsangpo will be closed to all traffic as of tomorrow because of the anticipated flood when the Yigong dam breaks. Leaving Damu, our path ascends slowly up the former road, its surface covered with rock rubble and fallen trees. At dusk, after about twenty miles, we reach a place called 80K—eighty kilometers from Bomi. The site is a construction camp and supply depot with the road repaired each summer to this point. The next morning we continue, seemingly submerged in water, the rain torrential and path flooded. We have no choice except to camp on a fragment of road for the night. The porters erect a tarp and make a smoking fire. Finally toward noon the following day, after wading through slushy snow, we reach the pass. There is a steep and dangerous snow-covered slope on the north side of the pass, but once beyond that we descend past red-flowered rhododendron and stop at a small monastery. A jeep from the Forestry Department arrives, and we soon cover the remaining fifteen miles to Bomi. There we rent a truck to pick up Zhang Hong and the porters, who are waiting at the monastery. We receive permission to cross the Po Tsangpo bridge—but only today until 8:00 p.m. The truck has not returned by afternoon, and it is a three-hour drive to the bridge. Our only other alternative is to drive 200 miles to the Bangdo airport in eastern Tibet. We could take the weekly flight to Lhasa, but that flight left today. Or we can fly east to Chengdu and then back to Lhasa to report on this survey, and we take this option.

The effort to release the water slowly from the Yigong dam failed. The canals dug by the military widened rapidly in the soft soil until, at about midnight on June 10, the dam collapsed. A wall of water surged down the Yigong into the Po Tsangpo and on into the

Yarlung Tsangpo. Gary McCue, guiding a trekking group, followed the Po Tsangpo to Zhachu four months after the dam broke. He wrote me that the floodwaters had scoured the slopes at least 600 feet above river level, and, according to witnesses, the surge had lasted twelve hours. The vibrations from the tumultuous cascade triggered many landslides. The trail had mostly vanished. Because China had moved villages and dismantled bridges in ample time, the damage in Pemako was minor.

Not so in Arunachal Pradesh. Komkar Riba, my companion on the spring survey there, sent me accounts from the Itanagar newspaper. At 4:00 a.m. on June 11 the water rose 130 feet above flood level at Tuting. "All low-lying areas, airfield, craft centre, CPO Centre have been inundated." The flood roared downriver, tearing down bridges and smashing fifty-five villages. "Over twenty-five-thousand people were affected in the floods in all these three districts while about seven thousand families are taking shelter in relief camps . . . the death toll is estimated at 30. . . ." Even near the plain the river's water was still 65 feet above flood level. At Tapaun Taki, a villager told a reporter, "It was really a tragic scene when a dozen of mithans and cows were seen floating in the river to unknown destination, some of them seen murmuring *moo moo*." Much cultivated land in the Dihang Valley was covered with boulders and sand. At 11:00 a.m., twelve hours or so after the dam collapsed, the water reached the plains and the town of Pasighat, where I had been earlier that year. "Over 5,000 people in Pasighat were affected . . . 25 percent of the township area of Pasighat was converted into a sandbank. . . ."

It is quite clear that India had no intimation of the impending disaster on June 11. Emergency actions were already being taken by China in the Pemako region a month earlier, yet India was given no warning. "The landslide was not reported in the Chinese state media and apparently not explained to the Indian government," stated a later news release. I find such negligence utterly inexcusable. After all, the military from both countries holds monthly meetings at the Line of Control. I feel guilty that it did not occur to me to telephone a warning to Komkar Riba or the Indian embassy in Beijing.

Later that year we submitted an eighty-seven-page report on our two trips, in 1999 and 2000, to the Tibet Forestry Department and the Ministry of Forestry in Beijing. Our report merely gave the facts from a list of birds recorded to statistics about tiger predation on livestock. It also gave suggestions for protecting and managing the reserve, among them the urgent need to control hunting and to halt deforestation on steep slopes. A 1999 government report, as we've seen, visualized a huge development program for tourism. Skeptical about the glowing projections about the number of visitors and the benefits of the many construction projects, we looked around and listened.

For visitors, the highway between Bayi and Bomi offers lovely vistas, as noted earlier, and there are hiking trails at each end of the great gorge where trekkers can watch birds and butterflies and admire flowers. But Medog, the heart of Pemako, is another matter. Access is seasonal, and insects and leeches are intrusive. Monasteries are small and the people usually do not wear traditional clothing. Other parts of Tibet offer more attractions, though the remoteness and mysterious aura of Medog will induce visitors to come.

Road access to Medog is deemed essential by everyone we met. An all-season road would undeniably bring certain benefits. Trade would improve, and local people would be able to export rice, fruit, mushrooms, and other products. Some in Medog, however, would also be tempted to export timber to make money, further degrading the reserve. Households who make an income from their pack animals would lose their livelihood to trucks. Easy access would also bring an influx of poachers, traders, maintenance workers, and various businesses run by outsiders, from shops to restaurants. In brief, a road would change the local economy, not necessarily to the benefit of most Lopas, Monpas, and Tibetans, and it would make it more difficult to manage the area as a national reserve.

It is often assumed that revenue from tourism automatically benefits the local population. It does not—unless the government establishes strict policies. Outside tour operators bring in tourists and absorb most profits, and local facilities are usually owned by government or distant entrepreneurs. Tourism does, however, provide a few local jobs as guides, porters, and hotel labor.

In April 2000 the World Wildlife Fund–China program sponsored a trip for eleven Tibetan officials, including some from Bayi, to the Annapurna Conservation Area in Nepal. The trip was organized by Li Ning and Lu Zhi, then working with WWF. I had just finished the wildlife survey in Arunachal Pradesh with Jon Miceler and Komkar Riba and would soon head to Tibet for the work in Pemako described above. I met the group in Kathmandu and accompanied it. The purpose of that trip was to make the officials familiar with how Nepal manages a large protected area in all its aspects, from permit fees to refuse collection. Since its establishment in 1986 the Annapurna Conservation Area had become famous as an imaginative and successful example of implementing conservation through education, tourism, and community development.

For four days we trekked on tourist routes that were kept scrupulously clean by the reserve management. What I learned about the potential of tourism certainly influenced my perceptions in Pemako. The Annapurna Conservation Area resembles the Yarlung Tsangpo Great Canyon Reserve in that it has a major peak (Annapurna, 26,538 feet), is of similar size (2,940 square miles), and tourism is seasonal because of the monsoon. Over 67,000 tourists trekked into this easily accessible area in 1999. There are many small private hotels and shops along the trekking route around Annapurna, most owned by outsiders. Tour operators bring in most of their own porters instead of hiring locally. As a result, only 7 percent of the tourist money spent reaches the local people. After fifteen years of community development, a mere 10 percent of the resident population had benefited in some way from tourism. The rest continue to raise crops and livestock, often far from tourist routes. The arrival of so many seasonal outsiders has raised food prices for all households, a negative impact of tourism. The entrance fee to the Annapurna Conservation Area is the equivalent of $23 per tourist. This provides about 60 percent of the annual management budget—when funds are actually handed over by the government—and the rest depends on foreign donors. The cost of managing a major reserve for tourists while implementing effective community development obviously exceeds revenue.

Protection of native plant and animal communities is the major function of a reserve. Successful long-term conservation ultimately depends on community participation, something still lacking in Pemako. The roles and responsibilities of government and communities with respect to conservation have to be discussed, negotiated, and clearly defined, essential here in Pemako as well as in the Chang Tang and other protected areas. Communities need to understand why the reserve was established, why certain policies are necessary, how communities can best contribute to the management of natural resources, and how they might benefit from conservation measures.

The Yarlung Tsango Great Canyon Reserve is one of the most important protected areas in Asia, a landscape outstanding in its beauty and biological diversity. In our report, available in both Chinese and English, we proposed that the reserve be zoned into three categories. Core areas make up the first category—places where nature should be left alone, reservoirs of native plants and animals leading undisturbed lives. There should be no hunting, no agriculture, no logging, no livestock grazing, no human residents. We suggested five such core areas, the largest to include Namche Barwa and Gyali Peri, as well as the great gorge itself, an area virtually uninhabited. A second large area, wholly uninhabited, lies south of Gedang and east of Rinchenpung near the Line of Control.

Special management zones make up a second category. The principal zone of this type would be Gedang, where an effort must be made to protect tigers and strictly regulate human use of the land. Community development zones make up a third category. Villages and fields in this region are generally at altitudes below 8,000 feet and along rivers, and all development programs should be limited to these areas. However, the whole landscape must always be considered, with, for example, forest remnants preserved both to assist the dispersal of plants and animals and to provide resources for the communities.

We presented these and other ideas gained in Pemako and elsewhere in a lengthy report, dated September 2000, to the relevant government departments in Tibet and Beijing. Since then our team of Zhang Endi, Lu Zhi, Zhang Hong, and I have been busy elsewhere; none of us has returned to Pemako.

Have any of our suggestions been implemented in the past decade? Without actually revisiting Pemako and the forests across the border in Arunachal Pradesh, I cannot say much about what has actually happened there since my last visit over a decade earlier. Others have given tantalizing fragments of information and I have read brief accounts by visitors. In May 2010, for example, a reporter from *Newsweek* magazine wrote about his trip to Zhachu village at the big bend of the Yarlung Tsangpo. "The Namchabawa Visitor Center, offering an exhibition about the canyon's history and facilities for hikers—including a medical clinic for those struggling with altitude—is designed to blend in with the scenery." Medog officials "are now beginning to offer trekking tours and rafting trips."

Tourist development had obviously proceeded rapidly since the flood of 2000. To find out more, I talked with Wang Hao at Peking University, a coworker on two of my Chang Tang trips who conducted biological surveys in Medog during 2007 and 2008. He told me that many tourist hotels have been built in the city of Bayi. The road from Bomi to Medog is now open except when winter snows close the Gawalong Pass, and, in fact, it has been extended south to Beibeng. However, I heard that a tunnel is being built underneath Gawalong Pass through the mountain to bypass the winter snows. Simple huts for travelers have been constructed. The roads within Medog town are now paved. There is a large resort hotel and other tourist facilities. The place was crowded with Chinese tourists in 2007. A number of households from outlying areas have been resettled in a housing development at the edge of Medog, possibly to reduce cultivation of steep hillsides, with its destruction of forests and erosion, issues of concern to the government.

Hunting of wildlife continues unabated, according to Wang Hao. The control of poaching was one of our principal management suggestions, but it has obviously been ignored. Zoning of the Pemako landscape for different levels of human use has also lagged, assuming that the concept had even been considered. A few tigers are still said to survive. Parts of Pemako will be lost to development, but I hope that the Lopa, Monpa, and Tibetans will always be enlightened enough to revere the spirit of Dorjie Pagmo and treasure the natural beauty of this Land of the Lotus.

❈ CHAPTER 11 ❈

Tibetan Wild Sheep Scandal

HIGH ROLLING HILLS FLANK US as we drive up a remote valley in central Qinghai, heading generally eastward as part of our 2006 Tibetan Plateau traverse, described in Chapter 7. It is December 5 and here at over 15,500 feet it is bitter cold. On a ridge crest, we spot a Tibetan argali sheep, a large ram standing proudly erect, head raised and displaying his massive curled horns as if on guard duty. His size is impressive at about forty-five inches high at the shoulder and a weight of perhaps 300 pounds. He continues to pose while we admire his elegant nuptial pelage in this season of rut, designed to attract females, a dramatic change from the rather drab pelage during other months. A white ruff spreads over his neck and chest, contrasting sharply with the dark color of his shoulders. At his opposite end is a large white rump patch surrounding a tiny tail. A black line traces the front of each leg, and a dark flank stripe separates the gray-brown back from the marble-white undersides. Not far below him, almost invisible against the sere winter slope, are eleven ewes and lambs at rest. The ram ambles to a ewe and with a stiff foreleg kicks her in the side and at the same time twists his lowered head sideways. When she rises he follows her closely but she keeps walking, ignoring his repeated kicks toward her rump, not yet interested in his sexual overtures. Another ram crosses the valley ahead of us, walking with determination as if in search of a receptive ewe. Farther away, on the other side of the valley, we see two more small herds, ewes and lambs and a ram with a broken horn, for a total of

twenty-nine sheep in this encounter. I take a GPS reading—34°59'
N, 93°48' E—and we drive on.

I have traveled thousands of miles over the high plateau, often
through hills of the kind favored by argalis. Yet I seldom met these
animals, and, when I did, it was usually just a few small herds in an
isolated population. The reasons for their scarcity puzzled me. Hunting no doubt decimated them in areas occupied by pastoralists or
accessible by road. Local people have told me that argalis used to be
in an area but had been shot out. With their long, thin legs, argalis
are adapted to open terrain where they try to escape danger through
swiftness, whether outrunning a wolf or human hunter. (By contrast,
the stocky blue sheep seek the safety of cliffs and other precipitous
terrain where they are difficult to pursue.) However, argalis are rare
even in places far from human habitation. Occasional deep snow, as
in 1985, may have wiped out whole populations, and diseases transmitted by livestock could also have reduced their numbers.

The argalis—*arghali* means "ram" in Mongolian—are the largest of the world's seven species of sheep. They are confined to such
mountains of Central Asia as the Tibetan Plateau, the Tian Shan of
China and Kyrghystan, the Altai of Mongolia, and the Pamirs of
Tajikistan, Afghanistan, and China. Over this vast range, the argalis
show minor differences in horn shape, body size, and pelage color.
It is now agreed that all argalis belong to one species, *Ovis ammon*,
based on general physical similarities and the fact that all have the
same diploid number of fifty-six chromosomes, differing in this
from other sheep species, which have fifty-two, fifty-four, or fifty-
eight. Do the differences in argalis justify creating the new taxonomic category of subspecies or race? That is, are the differences
large enough to add a formal subspecific Latin name to the species name of *ammon*? Taxonomists have various opinions about how
large a difference there has to be before designation of a new subspecies is justified. The result has been utter confusion. Argalis have
been burdened with at least sixteen subspecific names, at times in
an embarrassingly sloppy manner. The Tibetan argali on the Tibetan
Plateau is now designated *Ovis ammon hodgsoni* for Brian Hodgson
who described a specimen, obtained in Nepal from a hunter, in
1841. This animal's name has had over fifteen synonyms during the

following years, but its taxonomic position seems now to have stabilized. However, identification of other subspecies remains in flux, with claims, some of them dubious, of seven to nine subspecies of the species *ammon*. The validity of a subspecies or species is no trivial matter: national and international conservation laws depend on taxonomic accuracy.

Science is presumed to be based on facts objectively observed, interpreted, and reported. Each person, though, brings his or her subjective bias to a scientific endeavor. Too often you look only for what's already in your mind. A trivial difference in skull measurement or pelage color to one investigator is perceived by another as indicative of a new subspecies or species and deserving of a new scientific name. And, of course, an expedition's ability to announce the discovery of something new confers validity and prestige to its quest and increases its profile, inducements that certainly affect perception.

All too often new argali species and subspecies were established on the flimsiest evidence. One museum scientist named species and subspecies based on complex measurements of horn angle in rams, ignoring all other criteria. Some investigators seemed unaware of the fact that argalis change their pelage color and length with age and season of year. There are also environmental factors with an impact on appearance. Animals on pastures with nutritious food have larger bodies and longer horns than those which live on a meager diet. Given these variables, is an observed difference due to genetic, environmental, or individual factors? Valerius Geist, author of *Mountain Sheep* (1971), noted that the only valid criteria for classifying argali subspecies are differences in the pattern and color of the nuptial pelage of adult rams.

My interest in these seemingly arcane matters was peripheral. During wildlife surveys to find out the status of species and to protect them, I was not concerned if a so-called subspecies of kiang, blue sheep, or argali was taxonomically valid. The classification of an animal may seem dull but I was, of course, aware of its importance to conservation: the amount of attention, and success in obtaining funds and legal protection, depend in part on rarity. The Convention on International Trade in Endangered Species (CITES) and the U.S. Endangered Species Act are two such laws which affect argalis.

CITES proposed listing the Tibetan subspecies *hodgsoni* (but not any of the others) as endangered in 1973, and three years later it was listed as endangered by the United States. This was done to prevent exploitation of a subspecies that was presumably rare, making it illegal to transport any part of the animal across international borders and to import it into the United States.

All this background is relevant to a wildlife case in which I became peripherally embroiled, a legal scandal which involved selective use of evidence, lack of candor, perversion of academic integrity, and other such devious behavior. What was little more than academic uncertainty about the subspecies *hodgsoni* initiated legal battles lasting several years, costing millions of dollars, and tarnishing the reputations of various individuals and organizations. But at least all this raised awareness of a basic conservation issue.

Responding to a tip, law enforcement agents of the U.S. Fish and Wildlife Service in April 1988 met four hunters returning from China at the San Francisco International Airport and confiscated the heads and hides of four argali sheep. The sheep were, the agents said, the endangered *Ovis ammon hodgsoni*. The Chinese export permit merely identified them as *Ovis ammon*. Little more would have been heard about this incident except that one of the hunters was oilman Clayton Williams, who at the time aspired (unsuccessfully) to become governor of Texas. He had traveled with his wife Modesta, Robert Chisholm of Kansas, and Malcolm White of Colorado to the Yema Nan Shan ("Wild Horse South Range"), a subrange of the Qilian Shan, which I knew fairly well from a visit in 1985 and which extends across the northeastern corner of the Tibetan Plateau along the border of the Qinghai and Gansu provinces. They were on an argali hunt for which each paid a $25,000 permit fee to China.

Accompanying the hunting group was Richard Mitchell, a burly, bearded zoologist who had once collected small mammals in Nepal and now aspired to bigger game. At the time of the hunt, he worked for the U.S. Fish and Wildlife Service's Office of Scientific Authority, which identifies species in need of protection. He also had a temporary appointment at the Smithsonian Institution, where his supervisor was Robert Hoffmann, the director of the National Museum of Natural History. Mitchell's aim on that trip was merely to collect tissue samples from the animals shot by the four hunters. It was a legitimate association between hunter and scientist—except that *hodgsoni* was listed as endangered, the only argali subspecies in that category—and the Smithsonian's policy prohibits its staff being associated with the killing of rare animals.

The situation wasn't quite as simple as this may sound. Mitchell had established a private tax-deductible organization which he called the American Ecological Union. He solicited funds for it from various sources including Safari Club International (SCI), which he approached saying he might be able to facilitate obtaining permits for trophy hunts in Pakistan and China. As Kim Masters wrote in the *Washington Post* on March 31, 1992, Mitchell "led wealthy hunters to remote parts of China and gave them a chance to stalk rare animals. . . . Mitchell's expenses—as well as those of at least two Smithsonian scientists who accompanied him on trips in 1987 and 1988—were paid by the hunters." For example, in August 1987, according to reports, Robert Hoffmann and Mitchell accompanied the hunter Donald Cox to China, where Cox shot a blue sheep, a Tibetan gazelle, and a rare Przewalski's gazelle, the latter found only around Qinghai Lake, where about 350 were thought to survive.

On July 30, 1988, I was in Ruoqiang, a small town at the southern rim of the Taklimakan Desert in China's Xinjiang province. My Uygur and Han Chinese companions and I had just completed a wildlife survey in the nearby Kunlun Mountains that trace the northern edge of the Tibetan Plateau. Staying in the same hotel was a team from the Xinjiang branch of the Chinese Academy of Sciences, but its members were reluctant to speak with us. Finally, one of them confided in me that they were awaiting the arrival of Mitchell and his party. After we departed, Mitchell, Smithsonian biologist Chris Wozencraft, and two hunters, Donald Cox and James Conklin, arrived. Each of the hunters, it was later revealed, had shot a Tibetan antelope, even though this species had been listed as endangered (Appendix I) in CITES in 1979, prohibiting all international trade.

I did not know then that Mitchell's American Ecological Union and the Chinese Academy of Sciences had previously, on April 12, signed an agreement for the "rational exploitation and utilization of natural resources"—in other words, trophy hunting. Nor had I heard of the argali hunt earlier that year in April which was creating such an international uproar.

After returning to the United States in late October, I was contacted by John Mendoza and Larry Keeney, special law enforcement agents of the U.S. Fish and Wildlife Service, about the Clayton Williams argali hunt. They gave me photographs of the huge dead rams, their noses and lustrous white ruffs smeared with blood, while hunter and guide posed behind the bodies and held up the heads by the horns. Later the two agents came to my office at the zoo in New York, bringing the hides for me to examine. They were *hodgsoni* in nuptial pelage, making them one of the easiest subspecies to recognize. Raul Valdez of New Mexico State University, whom I had met in Iran where he was studying wild sheep, came to the same conclusion independently. And Valerius Geist, in a March 23, 1989, letter to the director general of the International Union for the Conservation of Nature and Natural Resources (IUCN), stated in his straightforward manner that "the specimens in question fit only *hodgsoni* and nothing else."

India had proposed that *hodgsoni* be listed in Appendix I of CITES in 1973. Argalis were indeed rare in Ladakh and other Indian parts of the Tibetan Plateau. The argali range on the China side of the border was thought to be only in southern Tibet along the Himalaya, even though the old literature mentions *hodgsoni* from various other parts of the Tibetan Plateau as well. No one seemed to have bothered to check the published sources, and with disquieting scientific carelessness the mistake in distribution was copied and recopied until it achieved the aura of a settled fact. In the late 1880s, the Russian Pyotr Kozlov traveled widely in the northeastern part of the Tibetan Plateau, even in the Nan Shan near where the argalis were shot in 1988, and he described the wild sheep there as *hodgsoni*. Later the Swedish explorer Sven Hedin brought two argali rams back from the northern rim of the Tibetan Plateau, one of them shot near what is now the Arjin Shan Reserve, and these were described in 1904 as *hodgsoni*. Przewalski reported *hodgsoni* from the Burhan Buda Shan south of Qinghai Lake in the account of his 1876 expedition. Ernst Schaefer, a member of the Brooke Dolan expeditions of the 1930s, saw *hodgsoni* near the headwaters of the Yellow River in Qinghai. How could these and others have been overlooked or ignored?

Now a new level of confusion is added. During his fourth expedition in the winter of 1884–85, Nikolai Przewalski shot argalis close to where Sven Hedin later obtained his *hodgsoni*. Przewalski considered his specimens a new species, as he reported in 1888 to the Imperial Russian Geographic Society. "Considering the small differences between currently known species of argalis, this newly discovered argali may also represent a separate species. I propose to name it after the Tibetan national divinity—Dalai-lama argali (Ovis Dalai-lamae n. sp). . . . The argali is characterized by its small horns." The article, a translation of which was kindly made available to me by law enforcement agent John Mendoza, has a sketch labeled "a male (5–6 years old) in winter pelage." The horns are indeed small, but they are of a subadult male perhaps three or so years old. As Valerius Geist has rightly emphasized, based on pelage and horns, Przewalski shot a juvenile *hodgsoni*, not a new species or subspecies.

The validity of *dalai-lamae* as a separate subspecies has been questioned for over a hundred years, yet it continues to drift uncritically in and out of the scientific literature. Now, with the 1988 argali hunt, the obscure scientific wrangle entered the courts. How can a lawyer or judge decide on the validity of a subspecies when scientists have not bothered to resolve the issue? It mattered legally, of course, because *hodgsoni* is considered endangered and *dalai-lamae* is not.

The Chinese were approached for an opinion. Cui Guiquan of the Chinese Academy of Sciences had said in a 1985 article that *hodgsoni* occurs in the disputed area. The Ministry of Forestry did not like that conclusion and went to Guo Tenzhou of the Xian Institute of Biology. He said that *hodgsoni* and *dalai-lamae* are the same, but then asked in vain for permission to shoot some animals to verify his conclusion. Now the Ministry turned to Lanzhou University in Gansu province, where four professors, one a fish expert, spent two days, July 25–26, 1988, to conclude that *dalai-lamae* was in their view definitely valid as a separate subspecies but that another subspecies *darwini* occurs "in the same area" where the hunt took place. Scientific criteria for designating subspecies stipulate that they can be distinguished in some aspect, and that they be ecologically or geographically isolated from each other and not "in the same area." *Darwini* occurs north of the Tibetan Plateau toward Mongolia, on the other side of a broad, flat valley in Gansu province. How the researchers reached their quick conclusion is unclear.

Now everyone had a choice of three subspecies with which to label the shot animals—*hodgsoni*, *dalai-lamae*, and *darwini*.

Enter a new aspirant in the sweepstakes of names. In 1990, Thomas Bunch and Alma Maciulis of Utah State University, along with Richard Mitchell, published a paper in the *Journal of Heredity* in which they analyzed the chromosome number of one ram shot on the 1988 hunt, which they now called the Gansu argali. They gave the name *jubata* to the subspecies. *Jubata* occurs north and northeast of the Tibetan Plateau and is thought to be extremely rare. The name *dalai-lamae* is ignored in the paper, which the journal obviously had not sent to peers for adequate review.

Are you confused yet? Now there were four subspecies names for the participants in the court case to select from. What to do?

When first confronted with this scientific mess, the hunters selected *darwini* as the subspecies that they had shot (and thus not endangered), but then switched to *dalai-lamae*. One problem was that Klineburger Worldwide Travel of Seattle, the outfit that had arranged the hunting trip, in its Hunt Report of 1987–88 advertised "the first check-out trip for Tibetan Argali (*Ovis ammon hodgsoni*) in 1988." And Mitchell in an unpublished chapter for a book wrote, "I treat *O. a. dalailamae* as synonymous with *O. a. hodgsoni*."

To resolve the dispute, the U.S. Fish and Wildlife Service turned to the Nomenclature Committee of CITES. It used a 1982 scientific paper by the Russian V. Sopin as the standard for its conclusions because it was the most recent review of argali taxonomy. Sopin's criteria for selecting subspecies were not well defined and his descriptions were vague and misleading. At any rate, the Committee report was slipshod and was withdrawn when several scientists, including me, objected.

The Smithsonian tacitly continued to back Mitchell, as shown by its participation in a July 1988 hunt for the endangered Tibetan antelope after the argali scandal broke. When interviewed by a reporter, Robert Hoffmann was so astutely vague that neither he nor the Smithsonian could be held accountable. "There is so much individual variation," he said to an interviewer, "that it is not possible to say that an animal belongs to one subspecies or another." Commitment to candor was not much in evidence among most participants in the case.

When rich and powerful hunters were being inconvenienced by dedicated law enforcement agents, and when they were expected to show responsible behavior in their quest for trophies, it naturally aggravated them. In a letter dated July 25, 1988, G. Ray Arnett, a former Assistant Secretary of Interior, wrote to Chris Klineburger: "You and your expeditionary force of pioneering sportsmen are to be congratulated. . . . That such a good beginning attracted the arrogant harrassment [sic] you have received from Special Agents of our own U.S. Fish and Wildlife Service is deplorable but not altogether surprises [sic]."

That the hunters did not remain idle in their defense is shown by a letter from Chris Klineburger to Safari Club International, dated May 31, 1988. "For your information Clayton Williams met in Washington DC last Thursday with 4 senators and 3 officials from the US F & W, all together, and I understand that some very positive things will result from that meeting."

One of these "things" was that the government dropped the court case against the hunters, because, it was assumed, of political string-pulling. The trophies were returned to the hunters in November 1989. Another "thing" was that on November 24, 1989, the U.S. Fish and Wildlife Service officially recognized that *hodgsoni* was distributed over the whole Tibetan Plateau, in one stroke clearing the clutter of subspecies there. The issue became further moot on June 23, 1992, when under the Endangered Species Act the U.S. Fish and Wildlife Service classified the argali regardless of subspecies throughout its range as endangered except in Tajikistan, Kyrgyzstan, and Mongolia. The Safari Club promptly sued the Fish and Wildlife Service in an attempt to overturn the ruling, but a U.S. district court in Texas favored the argalis.

Argali trophies continued to enter the United States despite the ban. In 1996, the Public Employees for Environmental Responsibility issued a report castigating the Fish and Wildlife Service for violating its mandate. "The U.S. Fish & Wildlife Service is driving protected foreign game species to extinction by illegally issuing permits to politically connected hunters to import game trophies. . . ." It specifically mentioned Mitchell because he "offered his services as a big-game hunting guide."

In 1992, Mitchell was indicted by a federal grand jury on nine counts for conflict of interest, tax evasion, and smuggling endangered species. Robert Hoffmann, at the time, the Assistant Secretary for Science of the Smithsonian Institution, strongly defended Mitchell and his hunting companions. When the 1987 and 1988 trips with Donald Cox were discussed, Hoffmann labeled his companion "a dedicated conservationist." In a January 1991 *Audubon* article by Ted Williams, "Open Season on Endangered Species," Cox was also lauded—but with irony: "Cox's accomplishments are mind-boggling. He has hunted in 68 countries in all, and taken 208 different species, including 125 in Africa alone . . . Phew! Congratulations Donald Cox. . . . He sits with Samuels and Snider on SCI's Gold Circle for World Slam of Wild Sheep . . . Phew!"

After a five-year investigation followed by a five-day trial in May 1993, with six Smithsonian attorneys present, the jury convicted Mitchell on only one count, that of smuggling an urial sheep and a chinkara gazelle trophy from Pakistan into the United States. Paul Broun, a Safari Club member, testified that Mitchell had told him, with respect to the urial sheep, that "the inspectors wouldn't recognize one sheep from another and it would come in the country without any problem, . . ." Mitchell, as a staff member of the Office of Scientific Authority, was, according to Broun, "the person who cleared animals in anyway." Mitchell received two years of probation and a $1,000 fine. He appealed the conviction to the Court of Appeals of the Fourth District and then to the full District Court but lost both times. The Smithsonian had paid $650,000 in legal fees with federal funds, taxpayer money, for Mitchell's defense. Congress and the government's General Accounting Office objected to this handout and made the Smithsonian pay the government back

$284,000 from profits of souvenir sales. Mitchell was reinstated at the Fish and Wild Service as a liaison to the Endangered Species Office where he evaluated the status of species, among them those for which he had just been convicted. The credibility, integrity, and reputation of the Smithsonian had received a serious blow from fostering such a tangled relationship between science and trophy hunting, combined with political intrigue and economic expediency.

I thought that the corruption of information was now at an end. But it seemed to live on. A decade after his previous chromosome paper, Thomas Bunch appeared with another one in a 2000 issue of the French journal *Mammalia*. Coauthors of the paper were Robert Hoffmann (no surprise), Raul Valdez (his flip-flop on this issue a surprise), and four Chinese. The data were based on five argalis shot by the ubiquitous and peripatetic Donald Cox in 1996 and 1997. (Phew!) Of these, two argalis, a male and female *hodgsoni* from southern Tibet, were donated to a museum in Lhasa. In addition, "an 8-year-old Dalae-lamae [sic] male in nuptial pelage (*O.a.dalae-lamae*) was collected in Animaqing Shan (Anyemaqen Shan) approximately 300 km southeast of Xining, Qinghai Province. . . ." I had presumed that *dalai-lamae* had gone quietly extinct, given the U.S. federal ruling and other information, and that only *hodgsoni* had for several years been recognized on the Tibetan Plateau. Not only had these authors apparently resurrected this defunct subspecies, but they also had it migrating much farther south than it had formerly been recorded. Ignorance or misrepresentation? Not surprisingly, their paper concluded that *hodgsoni* and *dalai-lamae* were "phenotypically alike"—that is, they looked similar.

DNA might help to unravel subspecific problems, but it, like traditional taxonomy, depends to some extent on subjective interpretation of results. Jiu Feng analyzed mitochondrial DNA of various argali populations in China and Mongolia. She wrote in her PhD thesis at the State University of New York that "a subspecies should represent a genetically and evolutionary distinct lineage, and we consider molecular phylogeny to be the foundation of subspecies recognition." She confirmed the presence of *hodgsoni* in various parts of the Tibetan Plateau. However, in the northeast corner, the site of the dispute, she found evidence of two argali lineages "suggesting a secondary contact" with *darwini* to the north. A long, broad corridor separates the plateau here from hills north of the plateau, and it is crowded with human settlements and fields. Tracing the corridor for much of its length, the Great Wall was built two thousand years ago, during the Han Dynasty, and was renovated and strengthened during the Ming Dynasty five hundred years ago. It is unlikely that *darwini* was able to circumvent the Great Wall and gain access to the Tibetan Plateau within the past centuries, but the two lineages could certainly have mixed in the past with *hodgsoni*, retaining some *darwini* genes without affecting their appearance.

I have related only a part of this complicated and protracted episode but enough, I hope, to show that science is not always a noble endeavor. I was also disillusioned by the hunters, who, instead of supporting efforts to uphold wildlife laws and cooperating to resolve a contentious issue, responded mainly with a selfish attempt to evade accountability and, at all cost, maintain the indulgence of killing any animal anywhere—a "bestial amusement," as one writer phrased it in the sixteenth century.

For decades I have encountered trophy hunters in pursuit of what is called "big game" from Alaska and Uganda to Brazil and from Pakistan and Tajikistan to Mongolia, some responsible ones and others just armed vandals. This has led me to examine my attitude toward hunting wildlife. I don't mean a herdsman killing a Tibetan antelope for subsistence, a farmer shooting a white-tailed deer for the cook pot, or a naturalist collecting a few specimens for a museum. Years ago, for example, I trapped mice and other small mammals and shot a variety of birds—without hesitation—for the University of Alaska museum. But I have only once been on an actual hunt during which I shot a large mammal. In the 1950s, I joined my cousin Ed Barnes and his wife on a caribou hunt in Alaska. It was autumn and leaves had turned to yellow and red. Walking quietly through spruce forest, I came to the edge of a clearing. Two caribou bulls stood there sleeping, dreaming, their heads lowered under the weight of ebony antlers and white necks gleaming. They were a mere hundred feet away, an easy shot, but I was reluctant to interrupt this peaceful scene. I walked slowly into the open yet they still failed to notice me. Finally I fired. One bull collapsed and lay there, legs tucked under, puffs of breath visible in the cold air. Instead of fleeing, the other bull stood over his dying companion. Even though I later enjoyed steaks from that bull, I still feel guilty about a killing that was more execution than hunt.

Few people in the world hunt for recreation and even fewer have the money to seek an exotic trophy for their private mortuary. Some hunters find pleasure in killing an animal, and others perhaps see it as a virile endeavor that enhances their self-importance, or as simply exciting, exotic, and offering an escape from a mundane life. Certainly when the Safari Club glorifies someone who has shot a ram with horns half an inch longer than all previous rams, or enshrines someone into its Hall of Fame, it confers a certain status to a member of the brotherhood. (Few women hunt.) Much hunting, no doubt, is done for such social reasons, a pursuit of blood, beer, and brag. I can understand these rather straightforward desires, even if they inflict unspeakable pain on an animal and hide the violence they've done under a congenial mask. But some hunters justify their killing with a vague rationalization such as "keeping in touch with nature," a seeming euphemism for something dark lurking in the depths of the mind. Hunting is not a sport; animals don't just lose, they *die*. Why not photograph an animal, something far more difficult than killing an argali at 500 yards? The development of the rifle signaled the end of the truly skilled hunter. The trophy hunters I have encountered in the field had little interest in feeling themselves part of nature: they wanted a trophy as quickly and easily as possible, and then they left. Perhaps trophy hunters are so anxious and incoherent in justifying themselves because they know that more and more people have come to question the moral basis of killing for amusement.

That said, I believe that trophy hunting can have a positive impact by contributing to conservation—if certain guidelines are met before such killing is accepted. First, the species should not be listed as endangered in the country or by international agreement, and it should be abundant enough that the removal of a few animals has little impact on the population. Second, the species should be protected by wardens or guards, with animal numbers monitored carefully by a competent staff and managed in a sustainable manner.

Finally, a considerable portion of the funds derived from hunting permits or the leasing of a hunting concession must be distributed to local communities that survive at a subsistence level, not only to enhance their livelihood and well-being but also to involve them directly in the protection and management of the species and its habitat. The second and third points are seldom evident in a country, although this is slowly improving, with, for example, China and Nepal permitting trophy hunts for blue sheep from which communities benefit. I believe it's the moral responsibility of hunting organizations in the United States, France, Germany, Russia, and other nations to induce the cooperation of countries where they hunt and to hold those countries accountable for implementing and enforcing such guidelines—or face loss of income through sanctions against trophy hunts. Organizations such as the Safari Club also need to uphold a code of conduct among their members to assure that trophies have been obtained in a responsible manner—and not just purchased in some village, or killed by a guide because the effort is too strenuous for the hunter, or blasted from a vehicle, to name just three corrupt practices. Scientists, trophy hunters, and hunting organizations need to share a collective vision to prevent another incident like the Tibetan wild sheep scandal.

Unlike some subspecies of argali, such as the Marco Polo sheep, no attempt has been made to survey and count the Tibetan argali throughout its range on the Tibetan Plateau. Still widespread, though everywhere sparse in small local populations, a few thousand Tibetan argali may well still exist. Until we know more about the status of this magnificent sheep it should retain its full legal protection as a rare and unique member of Tibet's upland fauna.

❋ CHAPTER 12 ❋

Wild Jcon of the Pamirs

OVER FORTY PERSONS GATHER for a workshop in Urumqi, the capital of China's Xinjiang province, on September 28, 2006, to discuss the future of wildlife and local cultures in the Pamir Mountains, the so-called Bam-i-Duniuh—"the Roof of the World." Four countries—Pakistan, Afghanistan, Tajikistan, and China—share these uplands from which some of the world's highest ranges radiate: the Himalaya, Hindu Kush, Karakoram, and Kunlun. The icon of the Pamirs is the Marco Polo sheep, the "wild sheep of great size" that Marco Polo noted in 1273, and one still found today in these four countries. Marco Polo sheep, snow leopard, and other species such as wolf and ibex routinely cross political borders from one country to another. If this mountain landscape with its wild animals, rangelands, and local cultures is to be preserved, cooperation among these countries is critical. We are in Urumqi to discuss the establishment of a four-country Pamir International Peace Park, or Pamir Trans-Frontier Protected Area. Around the world, over a hundred such peace parks involving many countries have proven the value of managing joint resources for mutual benefit, but with each country determining its own program. One example is the Glacier National Park in the United States and Banff National Park across the border in Canada; another example is China's Qomolangma Nature Reserve on the north side of Mount Everest and Nepal's Sagarmatha National Park on the south side. These parks promote friendly

273

relations among neighbors through sharing information, collaborating on research, and discussing joint problems.

After two days of discussion, general agreement among delegates from the four countries has been reached on an action plan for the peace park, including goals in legislation and policy, community development, and collaborative management. And there is agreement on proposed borders for the park. As H. E. Mostapha Zaher, director general of Afghanistan's National Environment Agency, concludes: "The environment knows no borders. The environmental degradation of Afghanistan will threaten the security of its neighbors. The only solution is to consider and coordinate a regional approach. This project presents more than just a peace park for the protection of animals, but a great chance, as scientific and environmental protection can provide a way for other forms of cooperation in the future."

I am elated and have a feeling of accomplishment after spending so many years promoting conservation in this corner of the world. Since 1974 I have roamed around the edges of the Pamirs, first in Pakistan, and then in China, and finally during more recent years, in advance of this workshop, deep in the Pamirs of Tajikistan and Afghanistan. In 1987 I had suggested "the creation of one large reserve" encompassing all four countries to help protect the wildlife that moves back and forth across borders. After so many long journeys and consultations with officials, my dream of a Pamir International Peace Park of at least 20,000 square miles might become reality.

It may seem that I have strayed from my focus on the Tibetan Plateau westward to the Pamirs, but actually the two areas share the same mountain ranges, such as the Kunlun and Karakoram, except that they crowd together in the west to form a tumultuous chaos of peaks before spreading out again. This precipitous terrain between the Tibetan Plateau and the Pamirs has affected the distribution of some species. The Tibetan argali is confined to the Tibetan Plateau, and, adapted to rolling but not precipitous terrain, it has never penetrated west to the Pamirs, where instead a closely related argali subspecies, the Marco Polo sheep, established itself. By contrast, snow leopard and once-Tibetan people, both being more adaptable than argalis, spread throughout both areas. In the second half of the eighth century, the Tibetan empire extended across the Pamirs and northern Pakistan as far west as Uzbekistan, over much of Xinjiang, and south to the Ganges River in India. Tibetans also attacked China and in 773 captured its capital Chang'an (Xian). But by the tenth century the Tibetan empire had collapsed.

While doing wildlife surveys in northern Pakistan in 1974, I heard that the best place there to find Marco Polo sheep was in the upper Hunza Valley, which slashes for eighty miles through the Karakoram Range to the China border. An American trophy hunter had seen a herd of sixty-five rams in Hunza in 1959, and horns often adorn military posts and government offices in the region.

A Marco Polo ram stands about 45 inches high at the shoulder and may weigh 300 pounds or more, not markedly different from the Tibetan argali; however, the horns are the longest of any sheep, flaring widely and curling in long slender tips. The world record, measured along the outside curve, is 75.5 inches. John Wood brought the first set back to England, where the subspecies received its scientific name in 1841. By the end of the century the sheep had attained almost mythical status, with trophy hunters and museum collectors trekking to the remote Pamirs to kill animals, sometimes in considerably excessive numbers. In 1888 the British hunter St. George Littledale shot fifteen rams and two ewes, for example, and in 1926 James Clark and William Morden shot fifteen rams and ten ewes for the American Museum of Natural History, as shown in photographs of their "bags."

Naturally I wanted to observe this grandest of all argali sheep, its scientific as well as common name honoring Marco Polo, *Ovis ammon poli*, and I set off for the Hunza Valley. This valley alternated between dark crags and villages surrounded by terraced fields, and groves of apricot, walnut, and mulberry. The ice mass of Rakaposhi, 25,550 feet high, filled the sky. Our progress was slow, with hundreds of Chinese blasting and shoveling to widen the road which connects China and Pakistan. My Pakistani friend Pervez Khan had again joined me on the trip, and Ghulam Beg, quiet and efficient, was liaison officer. We left our Land Rover near the village of Sost to trek for several days up a valley, past the village of Misgar, the last one before the China border. The valley then forked, one branch

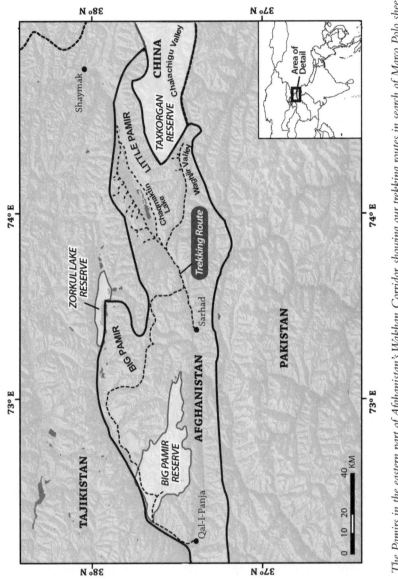

The Pamirs in the eastern part of Afghanistan's Wakhan Corridor, showing our trekking routes in search of Marco Polo sheep.

leading to Mintaka Pass, part of the ancient Silk Road, and the other to Kilik Pass. We stayed the night in an empty stone hut at a place called Haq, a smoldering yak dung fire barely warming us a little in the November cold. The next day, the sheer, gray slopes retreated and the mountains became rounded, indicating suitable Marco Polo sheep habitat. As we approached Kilik Pass two gray-brown wolves trotted along a slope, and the tracks of a snow leopard descended the valley toward us. Here at 15,600 feet, I stood with one foot in Pakistan and one in China. A ridge to the west belonged to Afghanistan, and beyond, across the valley, was the Soviet Union (now Tajikistan). The only sign of life was a fox track. Later we saw the tip of a Marco Polo sheep horn protruding from the snow. At least some of these animals come here seasonally.

We returned to the highway and drove toward Khunjerab Pass, 15,250 feet high, a well-known site for the sheep. From near the pass, I toiled alone up toward a high ridge, and two hours later reached the crest at 17,000 feet. After tracing the edge of a glacier, I could see the Chinese border post where the valley narrows and ultimately opens into the Taghdumbash Pamir. Slowly I scanned the slopes through my scope, but again there was no sign of Marco Polo sheep. I did find some horns, but was told later that almost all the sheep around here had been killed by Pakistani army engineers while working on the highway. Only a few animals now visit Pakistan from the Chinese side of the border.

A year after my visit, Pakistan established the 2,368-square-mile Khunjerab National Park, including the area of my futile search for Marco Polo sheep, and nine years later, in 1984, China created the adjoining 6,100-square-mile Taxkorgan Nature Reserve. In effect, then, there already was an international peace park, although the Pamirs cover only a fraction of that total area. (Both of these protected areas would later be incorporated into the proposed peace park.) Taxkorgan is large, extending from the border of Tajikistan eastward as far as K2, the earth's second highest peak. I had been in Taxkorgan in 1985, but for security reasons was not allowed to survey the Pamir area. Not easily deterred, I returned in June the following year with a permit to enter Taxkorgan's Chalachigu Valley, which protrudes west like a gnarled growth between Tajikistan and Pakistan to the Afghan border.

From the town of Kashi (Kashgar) in southwest Xinjiang, the Karakorum highway leads southward toward Khunjerab Pass, past Kongur and Muztagh Ata, both ice giants around 25,000 feet high, into the Taghdumbash Valley which marks the approximate eastern edge of the Pamirs. We stopped at the small town of Taxkorgan (*tash-korgan* means "stone fort"), a trading center for caravans along the Silk Road long before Marco Polo passed here. History is ever-present in this knot of mountains with its mix of Tajik, Afghan, Kazakh, Uygur, and Han, as well as with its conquering armies, spies, pilgrims, and expeditions. Today the town caters to highway traffic to and from Pakistan, and to tourists.

We drove south to the Chalachigu Valley, nine of us, including colleagues from the Xingjiang Forestry Department as well as Kay and me. At checkposts and herder huts we inquired about Marco Polo sheep. The usual answer was *hen xiao*, very few. Divided into teams, we explored side valleys. I found the remains of a dozen Marco Polo sheep at one place, all lambs and yearlings; they had apparently starved to death the previous winter when snow was unusually deep, and afterward many bones had been cracked by a brown bear. The horns of some fifty Marco Polo sheep were scattered around herder's huts, an indication of why the sheep were scarce.

The guide Tawang and I were near Kilik Pass, where I had been in 1974, when he said *"panyang yige"*—that is, "argali one." Then I saw it, trotting up a ridge: my first Marco Polo sheep in the wild. My field notes described him as "a young male, 3 years, his horns a sickle above his head, light brown with white rump patch, a spot of black on his chest." On another day, I scrambled up a scree slope and peered over the crest into the next valley. Thirteen ewes and young, including a newborn, foraged and rested below me. Our survey of the valley yielded a total of only eighty-nine sheep, none of them adult rams. Where were the rams? We surmised that they spent the summer in neighboring countries, yet they obviously returned here in winter, judging by the many large horns lying around the hills. We measured 129 horns of rams and counted age rings. The animals had a short life, most of them dead between the ages of four and nine years, and few surviving as long as ten years. The rams obviously wandered widely, probably crossing borders into Pakistan, Tajikistan, and Afghanistan. Cooperation between countries in protecting the animal was, I concluded, essential.

I longed to know how Marco Polo sheep were faring in Tajikistan and Afghanistan. But with wars and other turmoil in the countries during the late 1980s and 1990s, it was not the best time for wildlife surveys. Finally, at the turn of the new century, the Pamirs of the two countries opened up to me.

TAJIKISTAN, 2003

On June 18 we leave the capital of Tajikistan, Dushanbe, in two vehicles to begin our study of Marco Polo sheep, a project that will, I presume, continue for several years. Most of the Pamirs lie in Tajikistan, and the country is, therefore, critical to the conservation of this sheep. I had arranged this expedition the previous year with Tolibjon Khabilov, vice director of Khujand State University and a bat expert. A small, smiling man with flashing gold teeth, he has a hunger for equipment, judging even by our initial correspondence, and seems to relish the array of equipment I've purchased for the project, everything from a vehicle to binoculars, walkie-talkies, and camping gear. My main coworker is Abdusattor Saidov, soon to become director of the Institute of Zoology and Parasitology of Tajikistan's Academy of Sciences. He is in his forties, companionable, and able to speak English; we work well together. Having visited Abdusattor's institute, I can also understand Tolibjon's desire for equipment. The institute is open only two days a week, has no functioning telephones—the line was cut during the civil war—but it does have one computer. Its research budget for the year is $1,500. Also with our team are two old university friends of Tolibjon's, brought, I suspect, mostly to provide them with a stipend from me. One is a botanist who does collect plants, and the other is an expert on bird parasites who knows few birds and is then relegated to the position of camp cook.

Our route is eastward, passing through spring-green wheat fields and over grass hills. Skeletons of trucks, burned-out tanks with gun turrets askew, and other rusting remains of war litter the roadside. Once part of the Persian empire, Tajikistan was absorbed in the 1800s by Russia's great eastward expansion. In 1929 it became a separate Soviet republic, a mountainous region of a mere 55,000 square miles, a third of it Pamirs. When Tajikistan became independent in 1991, and could no longer count on the social benefits and other support the Soviet Union had provided, the economy collapsed. Failure by the communist and democratic political parties to agree on sharing power led to a civil war that lasted from 1992 to 1997. Small and with few natural resources, the country remains extremely poor.

On entering the Pamirs, we drive up along the turbulent Panj River, which farther down becomes the Amu Darya, once known as the Oxus. Afghanistan lies on the other side of this river but no parallel road exists there, only a treacherous trail tracing the foot of the mountains. After several military checkpoints, we reach Khorog, the capital of Tajikistan's Gorno-Badakhshan province. Located at the junction of two rivers, it consisted of a mere 133 huts when a traveler passed through in 1899, but today it is a pleasant town with about 25,000 people and a university. We have to visit various government offices to explain our intentions, though we have the requisite research permits for a Marco Polo sheep survey, and we also want to pay our respects to the biologists at the Pamir Biological Institute. The office of the Ministry of Nature Protection views us with suspicion and orders us to take Davlatyar Pervonobekov along to monitor us; he is a man of around fifty with the dynamic energy of a snail.

We need to make a plan of our proposed route. Surveys often provide a minimum of fact and a maximum of mileage. We have agreed on two months of fieldwork, enough time to become familiar with the Tajik Pamirs and its Marco Polo sheep. The western part of the Pamirs here is rugged, lying mostly within the vaguely administered Pamir National Park, not much of it suitable terrain for the sheep. But to the east the gorges and glaciers give way to wide valleys and gaunt, rolling hills seldom more than 17,000 feet in elevation. It is a high-altitude steppe with a sparse cover of vegetation, mainly of grasses and dwarf shrubs such as sage. Even in summer the land looks gray-brown, bleached, except in the upper valleys where melting snows provide moisture and where alpine meadows are green and speckled with flowers.

Tajik and Russian biologists agree that by the early 2000s the number of Marco Polo sheep had declined greatly since the 1960s, but they don't agree on current numbers. Some say 3,000, others 14,000. During this season, as we soon discover, the sheep are high up on the slopes where plants are succulent and nutritious. Daily we hike up and down valleys and over ridges in search of animals. Or rather Abdusattor, driver Alijon Alidodove, and I do, alone or together. Tolibjon reclines propped on a pillow in our communal tent and drinks tea; the others usually stay around camp, too. Not uncommonly, the appearance of having an expedition is more important to an institution than the results. I'm an idealist but without illusions; determined to continue with our project, I prod us on.

In the north, around the great Karakul Lake which lies inside the Pamir National Park, we see only three Marco Polo sheep. But near an official trophy-hunting camp within the park is a large cairn of horns. In another place outside the park, we count thirty-six sheep. Farther east, in the Rankul area, we establish a camp and survey several valleys. Visible from a high ridge is jagged Mustagh Ata across the border in China. Our Kyrgyz guide Manas is excellent at spotting the *gulja*, as Marco Polo sheep are known here. Our tally is 261 animals including a herd of 111. We also examine a fence built by the Russians in the late 1970s and early 1980s near the Chinese border. About 200 miles long, the fence is over six feet high with eighteen strands of barbed wire, as well as an overhang with six strands. No animal can get through except perhaps a marmot. However, in the southern part the local Kyrgyz have dismantled sections of the fence to use the poles for firewood, allowing free passage to wildlife.

On the way to another site, we stop in the district town of Murghab for a meal. Marco Polo sheep is on the menu of the restaurant, delicious without the strong flavor of mutton or the stringiness of yak. The meat is part of a favorite Tajik dish called *plog*, which consists of a greasy mix of rice and shredded carrot. We eat with intense pleasure after days of a meager diet consisting all too often of flat bread, tea, and condensed milk, the culinary skills of the ornithologist being as limited as his ability to identify birds. Illegal hunting of Marco Polo sheep and ibex is widespread and uncontrolled, we learn. In winter, when deep snow forces wildlife into valleys near roads, government officials, public security details, and the military—the only individuals with ready access to guns—spray animals with Kalashnikov automatics. This explains why Marco Polo sheep flee high up and over a ridge as soon as they see us or even just hear a motor.

Abdusattor and our two drivers interview households about their life and its relation to wildlife, an essential component of a conservation project. Such facts about local conditions are a starting point, not a conclusion. All too often conservation is approached with enthusiastic ignorance, focused on principles while ignoring the actual aspirations, desires, and needs of the people. Practical conservation usually can survive only by compromise.

After I hear the stories my colleagues have gathered in the twenty-four household interviews they completed, I am filled with empathy for the Kyrgyz herders. In Soviet times the region was divided into herding collectives on which every household was employed. The system provided health and veterinary services, schools, electricity to communities, and other benefits. It all disintegrated when the Soviets withdrew during the breakup of the Soviet Union and the emerging independence of Tajikistan, though schools continued to function. The educational level of the people we interview is extremely high, much higher than herder families on the Tibetan Plateau. Of adults seventeen years old and older, 86 percent have completed secondary school of ten or eleven years, and of these 12 percent have continued their education to become teachers, business people, or other professionals. Here the average household has only forty-six head of livestock, far too little to sustain it; by contrast, herders in northern Tibet usually have 250 to 500 head. Two-thirds of the households here say that their livestock has decreased during the past five years: they have had to sell or barter animals to buy essentials such as flour, salt, tea, matches, and clothes. Snow leopards and wolves have also killed livestock, and so has disease. Morkurov's family is typical, as related in our trip report: "He has a wife and 4 children aged 4 to 14. Five years ago he had 35 yaks. During the past year he sold 5 yaks and 150 kg of yak meat and bartered one yak for 8 bags of flour (45 kg each). He lost 2 young yaks to wolves and one to disease. He now owns 20 yaks and one horse."

Families seldom eat their livestock, subsisting instead on bread, tea, and milk products. Half the households say that they do not have enough to eat. Many men have left home to find jobs in Russia or have joined the army. Families are often dependent on food welfare, mainly flour and cooking oil, from the Aga Khan Foundation, the United Nations, and ACTED, a French relief organization. Lack of winter fuel is also a problem, partly the result of too few yaks to provide droppings, as well as cessation of the periodic coal deliveries of Soviet times. Consequently, low shrubs such as sage and a kind known locally as *teresken* (*Ceratoides*) are pulled up by the roots and dried for fuel. Large tracts are denuded, depriving both livestock and wildlife of forage.

Naturally, households hunt ibex and Marco Polo sheep of all ages and both sexes in order to provide themselves with meat and to sell for cash in town. On those few occasions when a family shares its hospitality by serving meat, that meat is Marco Polo sheep, and I feel guilty eating even a little of something so precious to them. Why should the community's hunters observe wildlife laws when they see officials kill wildlife with impunity and trophy hunters shoot animals on their land without their receiving any benefit from this?

Our surveys take us south to the Afghan border where guard posts are still manned by the Russian military. Along the border nearby is Zorkul (Sirikol) Lake, the 335-square-mile site a *zapoved-nik*—a strictly protected area. From there I look into the Wakhan Corridor of Afghanistan, that crooked finger of land pointing eastward between Tajikistan and Pakistan, which also has Marco Polo sheep and which is surely in need of a survey. I am now at an ancient crossroads. On February 19, 1838, John Wood reached Zorkul Lake, "a noble frozen sheet of water." Long before that, the Chinese Buddhist pilgrim Hiuen Tsang (Xuan Zang), returning home from India through this area in 645, noted that "in the midst of a mountain is a lake in which dwells a mischievous dragon." Which lake did he see, Zorkul or Chakmaktin in the Wakhan Corridor, or some other lake farther north?

The most famous account of the region is, of course, that of Marco Polo, who passed through here in 1273, though his precise route is still a subject of debate.

> And when you leave this little country [Wakhan] and ride three days northeast, always among mountains, you get to such a height that 'tis said to be the highest place in the world! And when you have got to this height you find a great lake between two mountains, and out of it a fine river running through a plain clothed with the finest pasture in the world; in so much that a lean beast there will fatten to your heart's content in ten days. There are great numbers of wild beasts; among others, wild sheep of great size, whose horns are good six palms in length [forty-two to sixty inches]. From these horns the shepherds make great bowls to eat from, and they use the horns also to enclose folds for their cattle at night. . . .
>
> The plain is called *Pamier*, and you will ride across it for twelve days together, finding nothing but a desert without habitations or any grown thing, so that travelers are obliged to carry with them whatever they have need of. . . .

Even when Marco Polo sheep are scarce, I enjoy my rambles over the hills. I examine wolf scats—their content is mostly Marco Polo sheep and marmot; I search for snow leopard tracks, take note of a hare crouched in a scrape by a boulder, and nod to a yellow-flowered *Erigeron*, a dandelion similar to one growing in our lawn at home. Birds are always an excuse for a halt. A pair of red-billed choughs, a crow-like species, probes beneath dried yak droppings for insects; a great rosefinch elicits admiration; and white-winged snow finch and desert wheatear demand definitive identification through my binoculars. Occasionally I find the skeletal remains of a Marco Polo sheep with horns to measure, and I wonder whether the animal has been killed by a wolf, died after being wounded by a hunter, or succumbed from some other cause.

Fortunately, I meet the Bekmurodi brothers, Atobek, Aidibek, and Zafar. They have a hunting concession, the Murgab Company, and we are invited to visit their camp not far from the Afghan border.

They have comfortable bungalows and even a swimming pool with water fed directly from a nearby hot spring. Guards actively patrol their concession, a large one of about 850 square miles, to prevent poaching. It's the main well-protected area in the Tajik Pamirs. We find a total of 1,044 Marco Polo sheep in only a few days. As with many ungulate species, Marco polo rams and ewes live mostly separate except around mating time. We count one herd with 183 ewes, youngsters, and a few subadult rams, and a herd with 110 rams, to give the two largest. Ever generous, the Bekmurodi brothers invite me to come back the following year. I am eager to continue the surveys, hoping to obtain a better idea of sheep numbers in Tajikistan. So far I can only guess that there might be around 15,000.

After less than a month in the field, several members of our team suddenly have most urgent business at home. I manage to squeeze in a few more days, but then I return reluctantly with my Tajik colleagues to Dushanbe. There I discuss our findings with officials in various departments and promote the idea of an International Pamir Peace Park. Tolibjon has disappeared to Khujand with the project vehicle and all equipment. When both Abdusattor and I try to retrieve anything the following year to continue our Pamir project, we are wholly unsuccessful and never see any of the items again.

AFGHANISTAN 2004

We have planned a two-month trip through the Afghan Pamirs of the kind I cherish: pack animals will be our only transport in this region without roads or even villages other than an occasional cluster of yurts. "I am afoot with my vision," to quote the poet Walt Whitman. We plan to travel up one side of the Pamirs to the so-called Little Pamir, cross a mountain range, and return down the Big Pamir to the village of Qala-i-Panja from where we came by road yesterday. We've reached the village of Sarhad, altitude 10,000 feet, far up the Wakhan Corridor where the road ends. Ahead, to the east, are the rugged mountains leading to the broad valleys of the Pamirs. A cuckoo calls. In a dip in the mountains to the south is Baroghil Pass, which I had reached from the Pakistan side three decades earlier.

Our immediate task is to repack all our gear into loads suitable for the seven donkeys and five horses we have hired. Our team consists of three persons besides me. Beth Wald is a professional photographer whom I first met in Wyoming; she has been on assignment in Afghanistan before, and, learning of my interest in the Wakhan Corridor, suggested this expedition and organized it. Sarfraz Khan, tall and calm, is a Wakhi who lives in Pakistan. At one time he was a trader in this region, and, speaking excellent English, he will be our contact with the local people. At present he also supervises the construction of schools in the Wakhan Corridor on behalf of Greg Mortenson, director of the Central Asian Institute and author of *Three Cups of Tea*. Journalist Scott Wallace, craggy, well built, and around fifty, has joined at the last moment on behalf of the National Geographic Society; he will later publish a fine article about our trip in a 2006 issue of their *Adventure* magazine.

Early the next morning, August 23, the pack animals are loaded. *Barakat*, let's go!

To get this far has been an interesting exercise in politics. In Kabul, Afghanistan's capital, we obtained our research permit from the minister of environment, Yusuf Nooristani, trained as an anthropologist at the University of Arizona. When I offered to report our findings to him later, he noted dryly, "I'll be here, or I'll be dead." (In fact, he survived and attended our 2006 workshop in Urumqi.) His mordant humor is only too well justified. Between 1992 and 1996 the mujahideen from the north showered Kabul with rockets, reducing large parts of it to rubble. Then in late 1996 a Taliban military force captured Kabul. And on October 7, 2001, the first American bombs began falling on the city.

We had flown from Kabul north to Faizabad on August 17 and there Sarfraz met us. He urged us not to linger in town because the previous night a bomb had blown up a UN vehicle. We are also advised not to drive at night up the Wakhan Corridor, that thin panhandle of Afghanistan jutting eastward. It is 225 miles to the end of the road and there might be problems. That day we traveled only as far as the town of Baharak, passing fields of wheat stubble, orchards of apple and apricot, and herds of fat-tailed sheep. Commander Khan, the warlord in charge of the Wakhan, lived nearby. Dressed in white pantaloons, a gray tunic, and flat-topped cap, he greeted us cordially and invited us to stay the night. He assured us that there was "no problem" in the region but noted that armed guards were stationed all around us. He had lived in these hills for twenty-three years, first to fight the Russians, who invaded Afghanistan in December 1979 and left in April 1989 having lost 15,000 troops, and after that he battled the Taliban. The town had a good bazaar, and we spent the following day shopping for whatever we might need during a month or more in the mountains, everything from pots and cups to rice and onions, our every move monitored by loafing, white-bearded men.

Along our route were green plots of alfalfa, wheat stacked in golden bundles, and many fields of poppy, some still in beautiful purple flower. Most seed heads had already been slashed vertically several times and the exuding pale purple latex scraped off and collected. According to the office of the Aga Khan Foundation in Baharak, 30 to 40 percent of adult Wakhi in this district use opium. The Taliban banned opium—as well as education for women, music, kite flying, pigeon keeping, and American haircuts. However, this region had remained under the control of the Northern Alliance militia that was fighting the Taliban. During a three-year drought which ended in late 2002, farmers could grow only a little wheat, the staple food of families. Most households had to mortgage their land at that time to get cash to buy wheat, the price of which had shot up. Without good crops, families had little seed to plant the following year, and without wheat straw to eat in winter their livestock starved. To pay off debts, get mortgaged land back, and enhance their meager income, farmers continued to grow poppies, rather than just grains, fruits, and vegetables.

The Panj River, gray with glacial silt, flows past the town of Ishkashim; farther upriver I had followed its course on the Tajik side the previous year. A guard at a checkpost asserted that our papers are not in order. "No power but to disrupt," murmured Sarfraz and talked our way through without having to pay a bribe. At the village of Khandud, the home of one of Sarfraz's assistants, a local warlord tried to turn us back, playing up his importance in front of a curious crowd, but a kindly local judge spoke up on our behalf. Kabul is far away and official letters count for little. The valley widened at the village of Qala-i-Panja (*qala* means "fork"), one branch going to the Little Pamir and the other to the Big Pamir. The local commander, Yakub Khan, severe in his scowl and intimidating in his uniform, checked up on us, but he was then most helpful in every way. He took us to the hunting lodge of former king Mohammad Zahir Shah, now a decrepit building. The Wakhi, he noted, resent that rich foreign trophy hunters came here in the 1970s to shoot Marco Polo sheep in the nearby Big Pamir without any of the money being given to their community. Memories are long. Another visitor, Alex Duncan, a British doctor, came by to invite us for coffee. He and his wife Eleanor, a nurse, with their three children, the youngest seven months, were here to help the Wakhi, particularly the women and children. Without medical facilities, not even a midwife, women not infrequently die in childbirth, and the mortality rate of small children is 40 percent from malnutrition, pneumonia, and other causes. I greatly admired the Duncans and other aid workers like them: they are the true and unsung heroes in this troubled country.

On leaving Sarhad, the trail follows the contours of the hills along slopes covered with stunted sage and scarred by livestock trails. After crossing two low passes, we have lunch in a narrow valley, a piece of unleavened *naan* bread and a cup of tea prepared over a fire of willow twigs. Our breakfast menu is the same, and it will remain a staple at meals throughout the trip. My legs feel heavy whereas Beth has spring in her step; she is trim and tough, like a long-distance runner, and I need to get in condition to keep up with her. We camp by a stream, and the next day we continue over ridges and up and down valleys to a cluster of five stone huts. The families are from Sarhad, here to graze their yaks, sheep, and goats from July to

September. Our host in one of the huts is Arbab, and for dinner we are served boiled rice with butter melted over it. The evening meal becomes a focus after each strenuous day, and my journal notes usually refer to it. The night is a chilly 26°F at this elevation of 13,000 feet, but already at 5:00 a.m. the women are outside milking yaks. Scott arises shivering. He has brought only a thin sleeping bag and his tent is little more than a mosquito net with a roof; his assignments are often in places like the Amazon rain forest. Today the weather is blustery with snow flurries, and I walk with eyes down to spot flowers such as wild geraniums and asters, instead of looking for ibex. That night it snows with heavy wet flakes, and I can hear Scott cursing as he bangs snow from the sagging roof of his tent. The next day our Wakhi guides prod the donkeys on, up past snowfields and glacial moraines and over a pass at 15,800 feet. Then the route descends into a long valley with good grazing and many herders. From one we beg some yak chips to cook our dinner of noodles with tomato sauce.

On the fifth day we leave terrain occupied by Wakhi for that used by Kyrgyz. The two peoples have a complex relationship, symbiotic and often acrimonious. The Wakhis are mostly agriculturalists who may also keep livestock. They are primarily Ismaili Muslims, followers of the Aga Khan, and their origin lies westward toward Iran. The Kyrgyz, by contrast, are Sunni Muslims whose flat, wide features are those of Central Asia, and are solely herders. They barter livestock for flour, tea, clothes, and other items with Wakhi traders who, we are told, often cheat them. Kyrgyz also herd Wakhi livestock on their pastures and take sheep in payment.

I like to learn about these local cultures, not only out of personal interest but also because such knowledge helps me to fit in. Every culture is full of unspoken rules that are all too easily trampled. The Kyrgyz have a strongly feudalistic society whose local leader is a khan, usually a wealthy man who makes basic decisions and is supposed to look after his people by providing the poor with food and jobs. The previous khan of the Little Pamir, Rahman Gul, was powerful and respected. In 1978, fearing a Soviet invasion, he fled with about 200 families to Pakistan where, unwanted, they crowded into scarce livestock pastures. Some families soon returned to the Little

Pamir, but most left for Turkey where they established a thriving community now numbering about 300 families, a larger total population than the 140 families in the Little Pamir and the 110 families in the Big Pamir in 2004. When the Kyrgyz departed in such numbers, two things happened: one was that the overgrazed rangelands on the Little Pamir recovered, and the other was that the Wakhis promptly occupied big chunks of formerly Kyrgyz territory, a move that still stirs animosity between the groups.

As we continue, the terrain opens to a wide valley flanked by snow-capped hills. From here the Little Pamir stretches about thirty-five miles to the east. We reach Bozai-Gumbaz, an encampment of seven yurts with more nearby. Mohammad Sadiq joins our expedition here, having just come from Pakistan. A relative of Sarfraz's, he is thirty-three years old, slight and sinewy, and he now manages our camp with great efficiency. In one of the yurts are two Afghans from the government, flown in by helicopter, to register voters for the next presidential election. The Big and Little Pamir have, they inform me, 527 voters aged eighteen years and older. Since a wedding will be held in two days, no one will want to guide us until it is over, so we might as well relax. I meet Mohammad Osman, a *hajji*—someone who has been on pilgrimage to Mecca. During the 1970s he was a guide to Ronald Petocz, a Canadian biologist who studied Marco Polo sheep here for the United Nations Development Program, specifically to provide management guidelines for trophy hunting. His study is still the best one on these sheep, and his census provides the baseline for my current survey.

Unlike the Kyrgyz in Tajikistan, households here do not want to divulge details about their life. They are afraid that the warlord in Qala-i-Panja or his deputies might be attracted by any wealth they reveal. But even some of their general comments are of interest. One man says that he works part-time for a wealthy herder; a poor family such as his receives little outside help, in his case one bottle of cooking oil this past year. We learn that the medicines destined for the Pamirs are diverted in Faizabad and resold, and he feels the Americans should build schools, hospitals, and a road in the Pamirs. I agree with him that schooling and medical help are necessary, but point out that in Tajikistan the Russians moved the Kyrgyz into villages where it was easy to provide social services, and there was an active administration. Here households are widely scattered and there is no obvious administration that deals with community matters. How would he solve that problem? He has no coherent reply.

Four phlegmatic yaks carry our luggage to the place of the wedding. Two sheep have just had their throats cut in preparation for a banquet. Several men gallop around on horseback trying to snatch a sheepskin from each other, practicing for a game of *buzkashi*. Women wear their finery, featuring a red embroidered jacket and skirt with a long white lace scarf covering a pillbox cap and draping down the back, and many silver-bead necklaces festooned with coins and medallions. In this drab landscape they look wonderfully joyous, especially compared to the men, who are either dressed in Russian camouflage or in suit jackets and pants of the kind distributed by relief agencies. The wedding itself is in the privacy of a yurt. I have given the groom a new shirt and the bride a sewing kit, comb, and lighter. Later the men gather and I am asked to say a few words. Remembering an earlier complaint that no one has profited from trophy hunts in the 1970s, I suggest, in brief, with Sarfraz translating my comments, that they should protect the sheep so that rams will grow long horns with age. Some day perhaps foreign hunters will be allowed to shoot argalis again, and I noted that such trophy hunters in neighboring Tajikistan pay $25,000 to kill a ram. If that were to happen here, the community must demand benefits such as a good percentage of the fees. In addition, tourists certainly would be excited and pay well if they were able to observe and photograph these beautiful animals. It is a responsive crowd, mumbling or nodding approval, when I compare the past with potential future benefits.

I do not discuss with these Kyrgyz the impact of heavy livestock grazing on Marco Polo sheep. The rangelands of the Wakhi areas through which we have recently passed had been seriously degraded, the slopes corrugated like a washboard along the contours with livestock trails. The Marco Polo sheep can find succulent feed high up in the summer, as I noted in Tajikistan, but when snow drives them to lower elevations in winter they find only a short, dry stubble, the pasture already devastated by livestock. Winter is the time of rut. A ewe that fails to meet her minimum nutritional requirement will lose weight and be less fertile. If she does get pregnant, her fetus will grow poorly and be born stunted; she will produce little milk and her offspring will fail to grow large and robust. All this has an eventual effect on the horn growth of rams. A ram that has a poor start in life and poor nutrition afterward will not grow the spectacularly long horns that trophy hunters seek. Not that I care in the least if an animal might make a suitable trophy. But a large ram with long horns, full of vigor because of good nutrition throughout his life, will breed earlier and produce more offspring.

We have traveled up the Little Pamir for a week and still have not seen a Marco Polo sheep. Impatient, I leave camp before the others after Sarfraz has explained the route to me. I amble across the steppe and through ravines, and stop on rises to look back, expecting to see our little caravan. But I spot only three men walking rapidly until our paths converge. *Salam aleikum*, hello. Wide smiles. Each man carries a leather satchel and nothing else. I suspect them of being opium dealers making the rounds. One speaks a few words of English. "You alone?"

"*Na, na,*" I reply in Dari, showing ten fingers and pointing back along my route.

They crowd closer. One wants to look at my binoculars, another fingers my fanny pack. "You American, Japanese?" They talk rapidly among themselves, grinning, and I leave abruptly with a wave of goodbye. It has been foolish of me to wander alone in this lawless region.

Following livestock trails, I reach eight yurts and a mud-brick hut. The three drug dealers are already there, as is a trader of cloth and Chinese shoes. The rest of our team finally arrives. The next morning, as every morning, the pack animals have to be rounded up and loads securely tied on, a slow process. Having learned my lesson, I remain with our team that day. Our route is over fine grassland along the south side of Chakmaktin Lake. In mid-afternoon we reach more yurts. There again are the same three men, and we greet like old friends. One of them is tall and stares as if in a trance, a second short with an endless grin, and the third converses pleasantly. From him we learn that three-quarters of the families here use opium, women as well as men. The traders come twice a year. Households pay one sheep to obtain three *toli* (1.9 ounces) of opium. These dealers acquire about one hundred sheep on each trip and drive them to Bakharak to sell at a good profit. Several other dealers operate here as well. Every warlord is involved in the opium business, and border guards have to be paid off to allow the trade. Though opium is *haram*—forbidden by Islam—Afghanistan produces about 90 percent of the world's supply.

Households sell their sheep for opium rather than barter them for food—and then complain that the Aga Khan Foundation and other relief organizations don't provide enough to eat. The Russians, several households note, were much more generous with food and medicines. Then the mujahideen came and they take what they want. When a family has too little livestock to subsist, it works for a wealthy herder, a *bouy*, much like a serf. It is with great sadness that I become familiar with the culture of the Little Pamir and its self-imposed suffering. For comparison I have the Kyrgyz in Tajikistan, who are also poor, but not hopelessly so at present; their literacy is high and they have options.

Also in this encampment is Mohammad Arif Kuthu with three of his nine sons. He is the son, forty-seven years old, of the previous khan, Rahman Gul, who left for Turkey. A tall, bulky man with a dissipated face, Arif talks of how backward the people are here. If, as he claims, his community is wealthy, why does it not provide mobile teachers and health workers for his people? Why has he come? The following morning the answer to this last question is evident: Arif is on his back asleep in the yurt, opium paraphernalia beside him.

It snows two inches during the night. We trudge up the valley to the encampment of the current khan, Abdul Rashid, whose permission we have to seek out of politeness to do our survey. The khan is a wizened sixty-three years, dressed in black pants and black coat. He is generally considered ineffective, an opium user, holding the title of khan for a quarter century and little else. His yurts, like those of others, are at this season on the south side of the Little Pamir. To avoid the commotion of people, dogs, and livestock, the Marco Polo sheep move to the north side—where we must now find them. Later in the year the Kyrgyz shift to their winter huts on the north side, and the Marco Polo sheep then move again. I have had a surfeit of the Kyrgyz and their problems and am more than eager to move on.

We reach the far eastern end of the Little Pamir and set up tents by a stream with good grazing for the pack animals. A cutbank protects us from an icy September wind. With us now is Arambouy, the son of Khan Abdul Rashid, a vague, dreamy man with a liking for opium. Atchee and Nasime have come to handle the yaks and horses which serve as our pack and riding animals. The previous night, Nasime had with typical Kyrgyz hospitality invited us to stay in his yurt, where he entertained us by playing his three-stringed guitar, a *kurmuz*, and singing mournful songs.

On the other side of the valley in Tajikistan is the Russian-manned border post where I spent a night the previous year. Beside the post is a high observation tower. "I bet they are watching us to see who we are and what we are doing," I say to Beth. She is an excellent traveling companion, with a cheerful laugh, uncomplaining, sensitive to local cultures, and thoroughly focused on documenting our journey with photographs. At dusk a generator stutters at the Russian post and lights blink on. "Russian generator," says Sarfraz, pointing across the valley. "Afghan generator," he says, pointing at our dung fire.

Sarfraz will leave us for two weeks at this point to check on his school construction projects. We head into the Tegermansu Valley, which juts south toward China's Chalachigu Valley. Among its silent hills and fine pastures we finally find the Marco Polo sheep. A herd of about 150, all ewes and young, bolts at the sight of us, and we spot several small herds of rams, totaling 188. This whole area has fine grassland, seldom used by herders, and I think that it would make a good small reserve. To celebrate the possibility, we open one of our carefully hoarded army rations, kindly given us by the U.S. embassy in Kabul. Chemically heated in its packaging, the macaroni and burrito with beans are delicious, and we snack on various cookies.

On the north side of the Little Pamir seven valleys project toward the Tajik border, and we begin to explore. The Birkitiyo, Andamin, Itchkeli, and other valleys each demand hikes of a day or two while searching the barren slopes and side valleys. Mohammad is already up at 5:00 a.m. brewing tea, after a night during which temperatures may have dropped to 12°F. His response to any request is "As you wish," and he then does it, whether carrying Beth's camera bag or preparing something special for dinner. We have a new helper, Nyazeli, whose main duty is to guard the camp while we are away. A languid opium user, I suspect that he sleeps as soon as we're out of sight. We find Marco Polo sheep in each of the valleys, most of them high up near 15,000 feet and all are so shy that Beth has difficulties in photographing them. My only close-up view of wildlife is a cute mouse with white belly and short, hairless tail, which Beth inadvertently squashed in her duffel. Later Abdusattor in Tajikistan identified it from the skull as *Microtus muldashi*. It takes us fifteen days to survey the seven valleys and our tally is 353 Marco Polo sheep.

When, in the 1970s, Ronald Petocz counted Marco Polo sheep in the eastern part of the Little Pamir, his total was 760. If we add the 188 animals seen in the Tegermansu Valley to the 354 on this side of the Little Pamir, our total is 541. There are probably fewer now than thirty years ago, but figures such as these are never precise; besides, the sheep can move in and out of other countries, so making surveys in those places is also necessary.

We move back across the Little Pamir to the south side, to an encampment at the mouth of the Waghjir Valley. On the way we pass remnants of a Soviet army base, mostly trenches, scrap metal, and stone huts dug into a hillside. Remnants of an empire. The Waghjir offers a major travel route over a pass into the Hunza area of Pakistan. With the borders from this part of Afghanistan to China and Tajikistan closed, traders use the Pakistan route before winter snows close the pass. At the encampment is a partially completed mud hut, and inside it is a haggard, hawk-nosed mullah with his young acolyte, flaxen-haired and snub-nosed, almost Scandinavian in appearance. They have sacks of dried cheese, probably begged from households, but apparently no money to rent transport to the lowlands. The mullah asks me for money, signaling the amount with his fingers. I signal half the amount, and he accepts this grudgingly. In a yurt are three Kyrgyz from Kyrgyzstan, yet other outsiders adrift in this remote corner of Afghanistan. They are conspicuous because each wears new North Face–brand clothing, a contrast to the tattered appearance of everyone else, including us. Their mission, they say, is to study tribal groups in Afghanistan. They speak Russian, as does Beth, and their discussion is lively; according to them, the Kyrgyz in the Little Pamir lack initiative, have a welfare mentality, and wait for the khan to think for them. No new insights for me there.

Three horses and three donkeys transport us up the Waghjir Valley. The pack animals are handled by old Bustam with watery eyes and but a few yellow teeth, and by a young assistant whose sole possession is a horse, having lost everything else to opium. The upper Waghjir is devoid of people and livestock, though some yaks graze here in winter on the lush, glacier-fed meadows. A brown bear has dug a fresh winter den, but I find no one home. A side valley takes us to the base of the pass leading to China. This area, like the eastern tip of the Little Pamir, could, I think, make a fine refuge for the Marco Polo sheep. But where are animals? We have seen only four young rams after being told that over a hundred come here. Beth still lacks good Marco Polo sheep photographs and Scott's mind is back in the United States; he calls someone almost daily on his satellite phone. Mohammad reports that we have little food left. I usually find a satellite phone in the field to be an intrusion, but it now proves its value. We phone Alam Jan Dario, Sarfraz's brother in Hunza, and ask him to bring various food items over the pass. This he generously does a few days later after a hard, hurried trip. Our diet of *naan* and instant Chinese noodles is now well supplemented; we even have chocolate bars, for me a much-desired daily addition. Scott has ordered bootlaces and to his consternation receives three cans of shoe polish instead.

The additional food buys us a little time, but we have to plan our return. Money too is running low—a yak rents for the equivalent of eleven dollars per day. Scott, a copious taker of notes, feels that he has completed his task, and his satellite phone has ceased to function. He wants to go home, but I cannot let him go alone, as he suggests, or with just a guide, given the unsettled condition of the country. I want to complete the survey by crossing the mountains to the Big Pamir, assuming that heavy snows will not strand us on the high passes. But we have to try before our expedition falls apart.

We leave with five yaks and three horses on September 30. The first pass is easy and I ride a horse part of the way. Our route takes us out of Kyrgyz territory and into land occupied by Wakhi. The following day it snows as we cross another pass, each of us drawn into ourselves, the caravan isolated and silent except for muffled hooves on snow. We reach Arbab's place in mid-afternoon where we had stayed a night in late August. We embrace the fire in his hut as well as the warmth of a bowl of noodle soup. A mere sack covers his door opening and snow swirls in. Later, in my sleeping bag, I hear the snow rustling on the tent roof. Morning brings continuing snow with dense clouds hugging the ground, marooning us for the day. Our two Kyrgyz guides want to head home, and we pay them. We also buy a sheep from Arbab and have chunks of boiled mutton for lunch. The sun appears briefly, and in the intense radiating whiteness I feel as if I'm in a microwave oven. The only sensation is of cold when the sun retreats, and then it snows heavily again. In the night's darkness, grunting yaks stumble around in the storm, and there is a questioning cry of "bear, bear" from Scott.

Arbab agrees to take us over the next pass. The five yaks plow a trail through a foot and a half of fresh snow, and we follow them across the 15,400-foot Karabili Pass into the next valley. A Wakhi family we meet has spent the summer here but soon plans to move back to Sarhad. A sagebrush fire and rice porridge with butter and milk revive us. The family agrees to rent us two yaks for riding. A yak is much more comfortable to ride, but not to guide, than a horse. Like an all-terrain vehicle, a yak glides along over bogs, up and down hillocks, and through rocky streams and snowdrifts without hesitation.

It is a short day's journey from here to the base of Garambu Pass. We are in a vast amphitheater of sheer peaks edged with snow, their contours broken by glaciers. In the center is a stone hut, just a simple shelter, among glacial moraines. Three traders with four yaks arrive on their way to the Big Pamir to exchange flour, salt, and other goods for butter to sell in the lower Wakhan. I am concerned that Sarfraz has not rejoined us, as he knows the Big Pamir well. Though the route ahead remains a somewhat daunting mystery to us, it does not deter me; I discuss possible plans with Scott and Beth. But just then Sarfraz arrives, having tracked our caravan all day. He notes that the road to Faizabad is unsafe and that flights to Kabul have been cancelled. With presidential elections near, four persons with land mines have been arrested at a polling place in Baharak, and a bomb in Faizabad has injured the governor and killed three others. Such situations change day by day, and there is nothing we can do about it here.

Our line of yaks snakes through the snow among boulders toward the pass. My riding yak overheats and simply lies down to cool off; I continue on foot. On the other side of the pass we camp in an area free of snow. Mohammad immediately starts a fire for tea. He is among the best camp managers I have ever known, including Nepali Sherpas. Ahead, on the other side of the Panj River are the hills of Tajikistan where I roamed just last year, and to the east behind a ridge is Zorkul Lake. Crossing into the Big Pamir has taken six days. Sun, wind, and cold have cracked my lips and fingertips.

We talk to herders in a nearby encampment. Their khan, Turgi Arkhum Haji, is said to be young and dynamic. The Soviets did not come to the Big Pamir, and instead the mujahideen moved in. They hunted so many Marco Polo sheep that valleys with many sheep thirty years ago have none now. Occasionally a few rams drift over from Tajikistan but usually they are shot. Here the rule, a good one, is that we must hire new pack animals at each encampment to give everyone a chance to make some money.

The route down the Big Pamir is along bleak glacial moraines. Wind blasts hard into our faces as if looking for something to slam and finding us as the only protrusions. Snow again, but this time it's a heavy, soggy snow that cakes the yaks, baggage, and us. When we stop at noon to make tea at the mouth of the Ali Su Valley, my legs are so stiff from cold that I can barely dismount. Evening brings us to another encampment. By morning there is a foot more of snow and clouds herald another storm. Women shrouded in red cloaks milk yaks wearing blankets of snow, and the yurts are little more than snow mounds, a bleak yet starkly beautiful scene. Under their quilt of snow the hills so scarred by livestock now look perfect. We cannot travel today. Nine men crowd into our yurt to chat and to look at us—a form of tourism for them.

We reach the Shikargah Valley the following day. It cuts into the heart of the Big Pamir Wildlife Reserve, 260 square miles of mountains. Once the protected hunting ground for royals and foreigners, now it is little more than a line drawn on the map, a reserve that was never legally established. The four Wakhis with us do not want to take their yaks farther up the valley: the snow is too deep, they say, and more will fall. I accept that I will not be able to complete the survey of this last corner of the Afghan Pamirs, but I beg for one more day. We have halted at four stone shelters used to store dung. Tracks of a brown bear in the snow show that it has investigated three of the huts; apparently deciding that none would provide a cozy retreat, it headed up a nearby slope. We move into the shelters instead.

One of the men spots ten Marco Polo sheep and later Sarfraz points to a herd of about fifty. On the other side of the valley we see thirty-six ibex. From this one location we have spotted more animals than at any time since mid-September. Snow has driven the animals down into pastures badly overgrazed by livestock. At noon we leave, clouds low on the slopes and heralding more snow. All we want to do now is thank Commander Yakub Khan, Ismaili leader Sha Ismail Jan, and the Duncans in Qala-i-Panja, pay off the guides and staff, and head back to Kabul.

On October 13, we reach Qala-i-Panja, fifty-four days after we left there. It has been a splendid trip. There has been a mixture of pleasure and hardship in traveling much as Marco Polo did—exposed to the elements, concerned about pack animals, uncertain of the route. I delight in silence and solitude, but we have had little of that, dependent as we were on the help of the Kyrgyz and Wakhi, who gave it with such generosity. My notebooks contain much useful information about the people, rangelands, and wildlife. We have seen 625 Marco Polo sheep, more than I had expected, and my guess is that the total population may be around a thousand. The Great Pamir Wildlife Reserve would make a convenient and spectacular place for tourists to observe wildlife in sublime mountain scenery. Local people could earn income from renting pack animals and yurts to tourists and be paid well as guides and guards. My mind is filled with possibilities.

TAJIKISTAN 2005

Atobek, stocky, ebullient and a wildlife enthusiast, had invited us to study Marco Polo sheep again at his hunting concession. In mid-February 2005 we rent a vehicle and drive to his hot-spring camp to take him up on his offer. I am eager to observe Marco Polo sheep some more in an area where they are abundant and note their physical condition at the end of a harsh winter season. Beth Wald is with me once more in quest of wildlife photographs. Snow is exceptionally deep this winter, up to three feet in places, making travel difficult both for us and for the Marco Polo sheep. Ravens and a bearded vulture alert us to a kill at one spot where three wolves have overtaken a ram as he struggled through a snowdrift. Atobek has a large balloon-tired vehicle, nicknamed Big Foot, for ease in rolling over rough terrain and snow. He and his guide Tolibek Gulbakov take us cross-country in search of Marco Polo sheep. The rut is over, but many rams are still with ewes forming large herds. One such herd numbers 490 animals and another 315, each a dramatic and memorable sight. In just a few days we count 2,200 sheep, giving us data on group size, composition, and the survival of last year's lambs. Extremely shy, the animals are a reminder that this is a hunting concession.

An international trophy hunting program began officially in Tajikistan in 1987. Basic license fees range from $22,000 to $27,000, depending on the nationality of the hunter and the size of the trophy. Most hunters are American, but there are also Russians, Germans, Frenchmen, Mexicans, and others. Some forty to sixty licenses are issued officially each year, and an unknown number unofficially. (No trophy hunting was allowed between 2008 and 2010.) A trophy-sized ram has a horn length of at least fifty-three inches, but records show that some are killed with horns as short as forty inches. Driving around in Big Foot, I can see how easy it is to shoot a sheep. Stop the vehicle when animals are low on a slope, and, with the rifle sighted at 500 to 600 yards, aim to kill.

Two trophy hunters arrive at Atobek's camp, and one of them kills a large Marco Polo ram the following day. Though shot through thigh and chest, the wounded ram still struggles and drags himself half a mile up and over a ridge, leaving a blood trail. The hunter returns to the comfort of camp while the staff tracks the ram to where it has died, hauls it off the mountain, straps it grotesquely to the back of the vehicle, and brings it back. The massive body is now placed with a serene view of mountains as background and its head propped up to display the great curve of horn. The hunter mounts the sheep like a horse for a photograph. Then, together with Atobek and Tolibek, he poses in a crouch behind it. Meanwhile the second hunter has gone out in another vehicle and bagged an ibex, its body dark brown and stocky and its knobby horns long and scimitar-shaped.

Both bodies are taken to the skinning room, and I go along to measure and weigh them. The hunters stop by for a brief glance. Statistics of the ram: age almost nine years, shoulder height 45.5 inches; horn length 59 inches; total weight of ram 294 pounds. The ibex is the same age as the Marco Polo sheep, his horns 37.5 inches long and his weight 196 pounds. Both animals are extremely lean, their bone marrow red and gelatinous, indicating body reserves depleted of fat. After the stress of the rut and a hard winter, their emaciated condition is not a surprise.

Beth accompanies the second hunter on his sheep hunt. He shoots a ram in the leg and it escapes limping. On a more positive note, Beth photographs a snow leopard walking from one rock outcrop to another. The first hunter does not get his planned ibex that day and is annoyed because he wants to leave for home. Now the hunt will have to extend to three whole days so that he can get his ibex and the staff can find the wounded Marco Polo sheep. The limping ram is tracked and shot, skinned, and its carcass left on the mountain; it has horns of fifty inches in length. The first hunter is successful, too, killing a small ibex. The interest of the two hunters seemed to be solely in the body count. It was not even armed tourism.

Both clunky vehicles keep breaking down. More hunters are due to arrive and they must have functional transport because the Marco Polo sheep are too far from camp to reach easily by foot. Beth and I are obviously superfluous now. And besides, a hunt manager, Afsunov, says that he does not want Beth around because a woman on a hunt brings bad luck. Did not Big Foot have mechanical problems, did not a ram break a horn tip. . . ? Beth feels dejected but decides to stay a few more days before crossing to the Wakhan Corridor of Afghanistan. I leave for Dushanbe to discuss a meeting concerning the establishment of an International Pamir Peace Park once again with officials. They agree that it would be a good idea, and I leave the country assured.

CHINA 2005

After two decades, I once again drive up the Karakoram highway. It is October 23 and fresh snow caps the hills. We pass the gleaming splendor of Mustagh Ata, like all such peaks alien but full of allure, and stop in Taxkorgan, grown from the large village I'd seen in 1985 to a small town. A rented house by the highway is to be our base from which to explore the Pamirs. We are interested in conducting a census of Marco Polo sheep, and to compare the status of these animals with those in the neighboring countries. There are a dozen of us, including drivers and guides. Kang Aili, my coworker on several Chang Tang trips, is here, as is Hu Zuojun of the Xinjiang Forestry Department, and Xi Zhinong, the wildlife photographer. The vagaries of politics are such that permits allow me now to survey areas closed in 1986 but not the Chalachigu Valley where I had been on that earlier trip.

Since I am not permitted there, Aili goes instead to the Chalachigu Valley with a team while I busy myself elsewhere. They count 284 Marco Polo sheep, three times as many as I did in the summer of 1986, but these include a number of large rams which appeared from somewhere for the rut due in late November. Some came perhaps from the west, from the Little Pamir in Afghanistan, over the high pass that separates the two countries. On this return visit to Khunjerab Pass, I find that China has built a double-row fence, six feet high, across the valley, and this as well as heavy truck traffic no doubt deter Marco Polo sheep from moving as freely as in the past. Five other passes provide the sheep with access to and from Pakistan, but the Khunjerab area has the most extensive high pastures. I doubt if more than 150 sheep now visit Pakistan seasonally.

For a month we explore every major valley by horse or on foot, concentrating near the western border of Tajikistan. Our guides, Gawaxia and Hudabeidi, are superb at finding animals, a few in some valleys and many in others. Numbers seem to have increased greatly after the government confiscated firearms and sent guards to patrol the Taxkorgan Nature Reserve. The animals have even recolonized areas, such as the lower slopes of Muztagh Ata. These days of tramping through snow and tracing ridge crests, tensed against cold and wind, are tiring yet rewarding, even when we see few or no Marco Polo sheep. On one occasion, a golden eagle swoops down and lands among a feeding flock of Himalayan snowcock, a chunky, six-pound relative of grouse. I expect them to flush in a panic, but instead they merely face away from the eagle, and, as if on signal, raise and fan their tails. Confronted with what looks like a phalanx of white shields, the eagle leaves. At night we sometimes stay in the flat-roofed hut of a Kyrgyz or Tajik family, where we are offered the warmth of a stove and a meal. Mats are spread on the floor for sleeping, and in the still of the night the earth draws inward as we lie long hours waiting for dawn.

One day we ascend the Tak Valley. It has snowed the previous night and the slopes bounce with light. Two large rams recline on a slope near a herd of sixty-eight ewes, yearlings, and lambs. When a red fox strolls by they flee, flowing uphill tightly bunched like an errant stream of lava defying gravity. Farther on are more ewes and several groups of rams. Hudabeidi has a hut here, empty while his livestock is at lower elevation, and we move in. I set up my spotting scope outside, and Xi Zhinong his cameras. While sipping a hot cup of tea, warming both hands and stomach in this near-zero cold, we observe the sheep. Six large rams approach several resting ewes. They stir up the ewes by kicking them with a foreleg, causing them to rise and mill around. However, the rut is still in its preliminary stages, and the rams then ignore the ewes to focus on a more immediate imperative, that of achieving dominance over each other. Two may walk parallel, displaying the size of their horns, or they push each other shoulder to shoulder until one shows submission by veering aside or acting as if grazing. Occasionally an actual fight breaks out to determine status. In unison they turn and trot twenty to thirty feet apart, wheel around to face each other, and rear up on their hind legs. They then run upright toward each other and fall forward to clash horns with a loud crack. They stand briefly as if stunned, while the ewes seemingly ignore the power and timeless beauty of the display.

Our count for the month is 2,175 Marco Polo sheep. There are about five ewes to every ram, a skewed ratio, but, as Gawaxia notes, more rams will arrive from somewhere as the rut progresses. All in all, I am pleased with the status of the sheep here, but too much livestock is denuding these hills; rangelands are in worse condition than those in Afghanistan and Tajikistan. Starvation of at least some sheep is inevitable in years of such heavy snows as there had been the previous winter.

PEACE PARK AND POLITICS, 2010–2011

I had by 2005 made extensive wildlife surveys in the Pamirs of Pakistan, China, Afghanistan, and Tajikistan. The minimum total number of Marco Polo sheep we estimated in the four countries was 20,000, enough animals to protect and manage with confidence. Much remained to be discovered about the numbers and movements of the sheep, about the impact of livestock on these upland pastures, and on other issues, but we knew enough now, I felt, to discuss details concerning the creation of an International Pamir Peace Park. I was delighted to learn that all four countries were interested in attending the 2006 workshop, to be hosted by the Wildlife Conservation Society and Xinjiang's Forestry Department, to discuss the proposal further.

The 2006 International Workshop on Wildlife and Habitat Conservation in the Pamirs, as it was officially called, ended with noble ideals and plans for the creation of a four-country International Pamir Peace Park. The next meeting, it was later decided, was to be held in December 2007 in Tajikistan.

In the meantime, the Wildlife Conservation Society in 2006 began an integrated conservation program in Afghanistan's Wakhan Corridor, funded by a grant from USAID, of the kind that should be emulated particularly in Tajikistan and China. Demographic

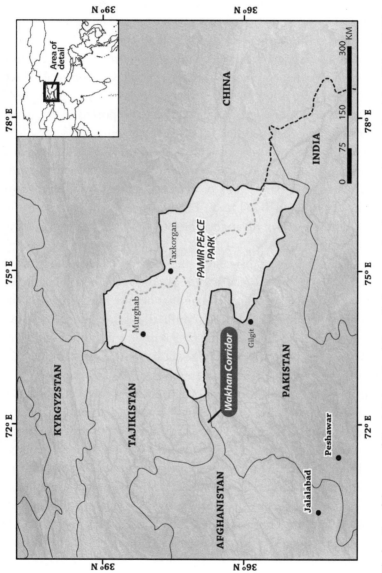

The location of the proposed Pamir International Peace Park, or trans-frontier conservation area, involving China, Tajikistan, Pakistan, and Afghanistan.

information was being collected on most Wakhi and Kyrgyz herder camps, and fifty-nine community rangers were being trained to patrol and conduct wildlife surveys. A management plan was developed for the Big Pamir Wildlife Reserve with community participation. Richard Harris of the University of Montana, Zalmai Moheb, and others collected fecal pellets of Marco Polo sheep for DNA analysis in that reserve, an area we could not census in 2004 because of deep snow. Analyzing only the pellets of ewes, they calculated a population of 172. If one adds rams and lambs, the total could reach 300, a population size similar to the 308 reported in the 1970s. Camera-trapping revealed that snow leopards remained widespread in the high valleys. Education workshops in most communities and schools were held and community members were trained to guide tourists. Two veterinary teams of Afghans, trained by the program, had soon vaccinated over 7,000 head of livestock against various diseases. This list is just an indication of the variety of initiatives in this imaginative program.

Tajikistan, however, cancelled the proposed December 2007 meeting a month before it was due to convene. The official letter, dated November 5, explained the sudden demise by saying that "the reason for this request stems from conflicts in scheduling. The Government of the Islamic Republic of Pakistan will be holding elections starting in November 2007, resulting in the installation of an interim government." Key representatives of Afghanistan were also unavailable "due to previous responsibilities." However, Tajikistan "will discuss options for a suitable date with all delegations." Nearly three years later, no "suitable date" had been proposed. Three times in 2007 the Wildlife Conservation Society had sent a representative to Tajikistan to help organize the workshop with no intimation that there might be problems. Cooperation among the four countries, as envisioned by the Action Plan, had as yet not begun, with the exception of one meeting between China and Pakistan to discuss the adjoining Taxkorgan Nature Reserve and Khunjerab National Park. What had really happened?

The peace park itself was obviously moribund. I had been busy with projects elsewhere and only monitored the situation at a distance. It taught me the lesson that someone is needed full-time on a project such as this to shuttle continually between countries and prod things along. Feeling guilty and partly responsible for the collapse of a venture to which I had devoted much fieldwork, I decided on a trip to Tajikistan in August 2010.

In both Dushanbe and Khorog, the national and provincial capitals, respectively, I visited relevant government offices and talked with members of hunting and conservation organizations. It was immediately obvious that serious misconceptions existed about the peace park, whether from ignorance or devious agendas. The Tajik officials who had attended the workshop and presumably knew the facts seemed to have gone mute on the subject. One complaint was that the boundaries of the peace park within Tajikistan were not realistic. Fine, I replied, the Tajik delegates drew them and you can change them. A peace park would expel livestock herders, it was claimed. Nothing is further from the truth, I said, pointing to the parts of the 2006 report which specifically discussed increasing household incomes and recommended that "local conservation committees should be established by communities to address management issues including rangeland management, wildlife-livestock conflicts, and other issues." Trophy hunting for Marco Polo sheep and ibex would be prohibited, I was emphatically told. Wholly untrue. The report noted that management plans for the species are needed and that they "should be managed sustainably." It further stated that "a considerable percentage of the fees derived by government from trophy hunts should be devoted to improving the livelihood of communities in the area where the animal was taken." I do not know how these and other perceptions veered so radically from reality. Unfortunately, if perception and reality clash, the former always tends to win. Perhaps Mark Twain said it best: "First get your facts; then you can distort them at your leisure."

Of course, private political agendas always roil beneath the surface of any complicated initiative, especially from those in quest of private profit. I was told that members of a Tajik trophy-hunting association had convinced the provincial governor, Kadir Kosimov, to send a letter to the country's president, Emomali Rakhmonov, opposing the peace park. This he allegedly did. No wonder it all came to a halt.

The good news was that in 2009 the Tajik government and a German donor organization made a census of Marco Polo sheep and counted a minimum of 23,711 animals, an apparent increase probably due to better protection in recent years.

It was suggested to me, and I readily agreed, that there should be a meeting of Tajik stakeholders with an interest in the proposed peace park, including everyone from community leaders, park staff, and government officials to hunting associations, scientists, and donor organizations. Such a meeting, to be held in Dushanbe during 2011, might dispel confusion and offer guidelines for cooperation in management of the natural resources of the Pamirs, thereby renewing the impetus toward the establishment of the Pamir International Peace Park, or a trans-frontier conservation area.

In September 2011, Peter Zahler and Stephane Ostrowski of the Wildlife Conservation Society, together with representatives of the United States Forest Service International Program, held consultative meetings in Tajikistan with a variety of stakeholders about the proposed conservation area, and these were followed by a two-day workshop during which problems were identified and discussed. Unfortunately, I was unable to attend because of prior commitments in Brazil. Peter Zahler told me later that everyone was in favor of trans-boundary cooperation in such matters as building capacity of local staff and sharing ideas and data. However, those holding hunting concessions or otherwise involved in trophy hunting were against the establishment of an official reserve, fearing that the government might evict them and take over the lucrative business. It also turns out that Tajikistan has no law or policy to create a reserve within which local people can continue their traditional lives. There are *zapovedniks*, strictly protected areas in which human settlement is prohibited, whereas a peace park would strive for holistic management to sustain its biological diversity as well as benefit local communities. All in all, the workshop raised awareness about the ecological importance of the Tajik Pamirs, especially among potential project donors, such as USAID, which has been a key participant in the conservation of the Wakhan Corridor in Afghanistan.

In other recent news, the six main hunting concessionaires were given the responsibility of protecting their wildlife. A total of 51 trophy permits for Marco Polo sheep were issued for the 2010–2011 season, earning the Tajik government $768,000. In an important new initiative, 60 percent of these funds are supposed to be spent on nature protection and local development in the districts where the hunts occur. (A total of 80 permits were given for the 2011–2012 season.) Also during 2011, China and Tajikistan adjusted part of their common border, with the former gaining 446 square miles of rangeland and Marco Polo sheep habitat. A new border fence has been constructed.

After a hiatus of five years since the 2006 workshop, during which progress on the peace park almost ceased, there might now be action on trans-frontier cooperation. I am tempted to write that I hope the peace park will become a reality. However, hope is all too often an indulgence or a prediction of disappointment; it is not a plan of action. With perseverance, we will ultimately succeed. Is it stubbornness or principle on my part after working toward this goal for a quarter century? Actually both. Conservation is my life and I must believe in success or I have nothing.

But to have succeeded is not to have finished. Even at the start of a project one knows that it will never be finished. Having the peace park officially designated is only the beginning. To manage the area, to adapt to increasing pressures from humans and livestock on habitats, which will shift, shrink, or be altered under the impact of climate change, will be a never-ending challenge. What is the ultimate aim of a management program under such unstable conditions? All we can do at present is strive for a balance between the needs of the local communities and the needs of Marco Polo sheep and other wildlife. And we must work ceaselessly to keep the Pamirs, this natural treasure, ecologically healthy and beautiful.

CHAPTER 13

A Bear in the House

ONE JUNE DAY IN 2011, a Tibetan arrived on a motorcycle at our field base in China's Qinghai province to tell us of the many tracks of Tibetan brown bears he'd seen around his home. Like most pastoral families, he had moved with his family and livestock to a summer tent camp and left his house empty, though on occasion he returned to check on it. We hurried to the site, about one and a half hours away by vehicle, and concealed three foot snares, baited with meat, two in a shed and one across the road from the house. We had already spent a month trying to catch brown bears to fit with satellite radio collars which would enable us to track each animal's movements. But our snares had so far yielded only an occasional stray Tibetan mastiff dog. If nothing else, our efforts to establish a bear project had so far been a glowing example of deferred pleasures in fieldwork. But we were in just the preliminary phase of a project that would require several years.

Full of anticipation, we left early the following morning to check the snares. Here at 15,000 feet the temperature was still below freezing. A scan of the shed by the house showed no movement, but by the road, watching us quietly with large dark eyes was a bear cub, the snare holding a hind foot. It was cute, like a scraggly plush toy. We thought its age was about five to six months, and its weight about twenty-five pounds. With a tan-colored face, black ears, white neck ruff, and brown body, it already looked like an adult Tibetan brown bear, if in miniature

Where was its mother? Tracks showed that she and another cub had circled the trapped cub, reluctant to abandon it. We could not radio-collar such a small cub and we hurried to release it. Wang Dajun threw a blanket over it and held the struggling, bawling animal down while Ben Jimenez took the snare off its foot, and I looked around sharply to warn the others if a furious mother suddenly appeared. Released within a minute or two, the cub ran straight toward a nearby isolated mountain massif where it would later rejoin its family.

The Tibetan brown bear represents a unique subspecies designated as *Ursus arctos pruinosus*, confined to the Tibetan Plateau where it roams from the forested eastern parts to the arid uplands in the west. Though uncommon, the bear is not considered endangered, but, like almost all wildlife species, it is protected by law in that it may not be killed or captured except by special permit. As the largest carnivore in its realm, the bear has only humankind to fear. Shot or snared by households to protect possessions or killed by hunters to provide body parts for sale as delicacies and traditional medicines, the species needs human voices to speak on its behalf; we are here to add ours.

When a species is protected by law, it often increases in number and causes unforeseen problems: more snow leopards may mean more livestock predation, and more kiang may mean more competition with domestic sheep and yaks for sparse pasture. In recent years, the Tibetan brown bear has come into frequent conflict with humans, not, it seems, because there are many more of them, but because the lifestyle of Tibetan pastoralists and the policies of the government have changed. Bears and I have had only occasional, fleeting meetings in the Chang Tang, and I was always careful to keep a respectful distance from these powerful animals. But now with the aims of mitigating bear–human conflict and investigating the bear's survival needs, I sought contact with them.

Until the late 1900s, most nomads on the Tibetan Plateau lived in traditional black yak-hair tents. They moved seasonally with their livestock to different grazing grounds within a prescribed area. Once the nomads considered themselves a brother to the bear and marmot, but the bear, as the oldest brother, was feared and shot whenever one came near a tent. The bear, or *jemu*, as people here call it, avoided the settled places in plains and valleys and retreated into the mountains. The situation began to change in the late 1980s, when the government divided rangelands into individual household plots. Most families built permanent flat-roofed, mud-brick homes, with one to three rooms and often a shed. There they spent the long winter months and grazed their livestock nearby. In about May, a family left its winter residence to live in tents on better grazing grounds until August or September.

Around the turn of the twenty-first century, the government confiscated guns from households, an action that had far-reaching and unintended consequences. The bears soon discovered that they could visit empty houses with impunity, attracted by yak bones, rags saturated with the smell of butter, dented pots with remnants of *tsampa*, plastic soft-drink bottles, and other trash that litters the yard of every house. And from inside the house came the enticing smells of nutritious meat hanging from the rafters, as well as sheep hides and sacks of flour. During the short summer months, the bears must stuff themselves with calories to survive the months without food during hibernation, a time when females also give birth and lactate. It is an easy task for a bear to push in a flimsy door of poplar wood or rip a window frame out of a mud wall. Or a bear may simply bash through a wall or claw a hole in the roof. Households tend to leave rooms in such a chaos of bedding, clothing, broken plastic containers, dismantled stove pipes, and other items when moving out for the summer that it is sometimes difficult to distinguish the people's disarray from that caused by bears. But a cupboard door torn off its hinges or a pot with tooth punctures is evidence of an ursine visitor. One bear spent several days in a house, consumed most of two sacks of commercial livestock pellets, and left as a token of its presence fifteen large, soft scat piles. Such breaking and entering is now common. The Junqu community at the eastern edge of the Chang Tang in Qinghai province, where we did much of our work, has 125 households scattered over 1,155 square miles. In August 2010, bears entered thirty-four (27 percent) of the houses at least once, in September eighteen (14 percent) of the houses, and in October, not long before hibernation, ten (8 percent) of the houses.

With bears now protected—though at least three were killed in retaliation in the nearby Yaqu community during 2010—how do households respond to invasive bears? If people are home, they yell, bang pots, and even set off fire crackers, but this has at best only a short-term effect on the bears. In a study of American black bears, it was found that after such nonlethal deterrents most bears returned to a house within forty days. Some families are so fearful of leaving home for their summer encampment that they remain all year in their house, or they move only a short distance, sometimes within sight of their house. Many simply leave the front door open to reduce damage. If livestock is kept around the winter home all year, the rangelands deteriorate, and livestock may become less productive, gain less weight, and give less milk—an interesting consequence of gun confiscation.

In a report published in a 2008 issue of the journal *Human-Wildlife Conflict*, Fiona Worthy and Marc Foggin wrote that the "costs of repairing [bear] damage have been estimated at between $700 and $2,800—an amount that far exceeds most families' annual income." Occasionally a bear enters a sheep coral and in the confusion kills a number of animals, a further loss of income. In a survey of bear damage in one Tibetan county, as described by Dawa Tsering and his coauthors in *Competition and Coexistence* (2007), it was found that 49 percent of 300 households interviewed reported bear problems in recent years, and that "204 rooms [had been] damaged by bears and a reported 94,907 kg of foodstuffs lost to animals."

The Wildlife Conservation Society and its local partners, with a grant from the European Union–China Biodiversity Programme, sought means of reducing bear damage, and I looked at a number of ransacked homes. I suggested putting glass shards and barbed wire on walls that surround some houses and along the edge of roofs, as well as placing boards with spikes by doors and beneath windows when the family leaves home—simple and cheap methods that would deter at least some bears. Dogs could be kept with sheep herds day and night instead of being uselessly tied up by the house. But the granting agency thought that the ideas were not "high-tech" enough. Instead, expensive wire fences over six feet high were constructed around 110 homes and corrals. Bear damage was reduced by 90 percent in the ensuing months. When I visited such fenced houses, it felt like being in a low-security prison. And thousands of unprotected households remain.

By the spring of 2011, when we began the bear project in Qinghai, funded by the Liz Claiborne–Art Ortenberg Foundation, homeowners were becoming increasingly intolerant of the break-ins, occurrences that would only increase as bear numbers increased. The bears should be killed, some said, or the government should do something. But I was puzzled by the fact that few households did anything to help themselves. Windows and doors were seldom reinforced, meat was stored outside on roofs or even within low mud walls covered with a tarp, and inside the houses were sacks of flour, skin bags filled with butter, and other delectable items to entice a bear. Food could readily be stored in a large bear-resistant metal container, or in a cache—in effect, a storeroom on stilts, unreachable by bears, as commonly employed in Alaska. Sheep corrals could be covered with wire netting to keep out predators (though not a determined bear), instead of merely confining sheep inside a low wall or leaving them unguarded in the open. The critical issue in stemming the tide of break-ins is obviously to keep food away from bears. Such deterrents would cost a family less than, for example, a motorcycle.

Little information about the habits of Tibetan brown bears was available. I had observed them expending considerable effort digging into burrows after pikas to obtain just a morsel of food, and their scats showed a principal diet of pikas, grass, and the scavenged remains of wild and domestic hoofed animals. It was not known, however, how often bears visit houses, whether only certain bears or all of them come into conflict with people, and how widely bears travel. With such information, it might be possible to devise means of reducing conflict. This was a major justification for our project, one strongly supported by the Qinghai Forestry Department.

After we released the snared bear cub, I did not expect the family to return soon to the site of its traumatic experience. Yet here they were the following night at 10:37, the female and her two cubs, as revealed by an infrared camera we had mounted in the shed. The cubs entered the shed, where meat and cookies served as bait, and played there, wrestling and batting at a rope suspended from the ceiling and inadvertently setting off a snare without getting caught. Meanwhile their mother climbed into the house through a window smashed during a previous visit. There she picked up a sack of flour, tore it open, and carried it from one room into the next and out an open door into the yard, leaving a white flour trail. The bears roamed around the site until sometime after midnight. By the time we checked the snares on the following morning, the bears had vanished. Since they did not return that night or the next, we dismantled the snares to prevent dogs and yaks from getting caught.

We had arrived at Junqu village, the site of this trapping effort, on May 17 to begin our bear research. The term "village" is merely an administrative term for the widely scattered households. Junqu is remote, located at the eastern edge of the Chang Tang, a twelve-hour drive northwest of the town of Yushu. As a land of plains, broad valleys, and mountain ranges, it is ideal habitat for snow leopard, bear, blue sheep, and kiang, as well as for livestock, of which Junqu has 6,000 sheep and 5,000 yaks. The area lies within the Sanji-angyuan Nature Reserve, whose 58,600 square miles cover parts of central and eastern Qinghai, including the headwaters of the Yang-tze, Mekong, and Yellow Rivers. About 50,000 people live in the reserve, over two-thirds of them pastoralists. We had selected Junqu as a study site in part because the village leadership was so interested in conservation that in 2007 Lu Zhi's Center for Nature and Society at Peking University had made an agreement through the government authorizing the village to manage its own conservation program. I had visited here the previous year and concluded that there were indeed good study opportunities. Now Party Secretary Ouzhu generously opened his home to our team.

The bear project is under the direction of the Center for Nature and Society, which had offered two of its graduate students to conduct the research. Wu Lan, tall with a wide and cheerful smile and hair reaching mid-back, will use the bear data for her PhD thesis. Whether climbing a steep mountainside or plucking apart a scat, she is full of enthusiasm for her work. Bu Hongliang, here to assist in gathering information, is the more reserved of the two but equally dedicated and very observant of nature around him. It was he, for example, who showed me a blackish slug in a pika burrow apparently eating pika feces, a good example of pika hospitality to other species. We had two drivers, Suo Cai and Ulsa, both Tibetans from this area. Suo Cai is stolid, whereas Ulsa—his name is similar to *Ursus*, the bear genus—is paunchy and bearded, resembling a jovial bear. Though designated as drivers, the two were an integral part of the team, helping with everything from interpreting Tibetan and Chinese to setting snares. Lu Zhi visited the project briefly in the beginning to help establish it with officials; Wang Dajun from the Center came for a week in mid-June bringing with him Ben Jimenez, on leave from the Montana Department of Fish, Wildlife, and Parks.

I was already familiar with the foot snares, a widely used method of capturing bears in North America, having caught both Asiatic black bears in China's Sichuan province and Gobi brown bears in Mongolia's Gobi desert. The snare can be hidden beneath a thin layer of soil or grass on a trail, or it can be concealed near bait to which an animal is attracted. When the animal inadvertently depresses the trigger and its foot sinks into a shallow hole dug beneath the snare, a spring whips the snare wire up and around the leg. With the snare attached to a log or something else heavy, the animal cannot escape. I had used simple radio collars before as well, the signal transmitted to a handheld antenna and receiver, but never satellite collars. The new equipment made me nervous; I felt complete lack of control. The satellite would send the signal to the German manufacturer, Vectronic Aerospace, which would relay the data to the Panthera office in New York. Lisanne Petracca there would convert the signals into precise locations and prepare route maps of the animals for our team. The satellite transmits a signal at a predetermined rate, every two hours in our collars. The collars are expensive—$4,200 each (with discount)—and we have three of them with us. Now all we needed was to catch a bear.

We set snares by six recommended houses, some of which had been entered by bears in previous weeks. No bears came but Tibetan mastiff dogs repeatedly triggered the snares. Most families permit their dogs to roam, especially at night, and some families had moved to town and simply abandoned their dogs to a feral existence. We had no idea how long our wait might be: a bear could show up tomorrow or in four months.

After checking snares for ten days without sign of a bear, we decided to move our effort to the village of Yaqu, over an hour's drive away. There, at the mouth of the Quirirongga Canyon is a small *gompa* consisting of a temple and several mud-walled rooms. I had stayed here before to help Li Juan with her graduate-school study of snow leopards, and I knew that bears also roamed these mountains. Only two monks were in residence now, Angye and Lu Ga Le, who greeted us cordially and invited us in. The monks care for several infrared cameras on behalf of Li Juan. One camera had been set by a rock outcrop where a side valley meets the main one. Li Juan had shown me a fascinating series of photos taken at that site. At least four snow leopards came by, stopped, rubbed a cheek on the rocks, and then swiveled around, tail looped over the back, to spray the place with scent. Other carnivores were also attracted for unknown reasons to this scent post, among them Tibetan brown bears, both red and Tibetan foxes, manul cats, and mastiff dogs, in addition to wolves, which passed but did not stop. What an intriguing world of scents from which we people are excluded!

In these mountains among narrow valleys and limestone pinnacles, we set five snares at sites where a bear might come by, and we also put two snares at empty houses. We checked snares daily, often in snow- and hailstorms, to make certain a fox had not taken the bait of meat scraps and butter. We clambered through the mountains in search of bear sign, a track or scat, but seldom found any. Occasionally we came across an old sleeping place in a rocky alcove, a shallow bowl scooped in dry soil with perhaps a little grass carried in for comfort. Snow leopard scats were easier to find, usually along the base of cliffs, and we collected these as a contribution to Li Juan's study. "I am happy when I find droppings," exclaimed Wu Lan; pleasures in the field tend to be simple. Only once did we observe a bear; it rested on a rock in the evening sun for half an hour before moving uphill among the boulders and the shadows of the hill.

Bears, snow leopards, and I like the jumble of limestone which covers some slopes and ridges, a place of strangeness and beauty. The gray and faintly pink rocks are worn smooth by the elements into congealed shapes of gargoyles and goblins. When I walk among these pinnacles, domes, and cliffs, it's like being in a strange and silent city, caves in the rocks like dark windows and doors leading into an alternate world.

I always welcome close-up meetings with predators such as snow leopard and wolf—but not with brown bear. The bear pervades my thoughts and adds tension to this wild terrain; I walk with a heightened awareness as I try to visualize the best course of action on meeting a bear at close quarters. Perhaps I might save a fraction of a second in my response time, and with it gain a little in survival. What to do when stumbling upon a bear made irascible because I awakened it from slumber? If the bear behaves aggressively out of fear or annoyance, I would have several options, such as shouting, throwing something, standing quietly, or running away, the action depending on circumstances. Stephen Herrero in *Bear Attacks* (1985) stresses that close encounters with a mother and cubs or with a bear on a kill are most likely to be an extreme provocation and thus lead to actual attack. The chance of surviving a mauling appears somewhat better if one plays dead than if one resists. But I remember looking at a huge stuffed male bear in a Xining museum the previous month. He had entered the city of Golmud in 2010 and randomly and apparently without provocation killed two people before being shot.

In a previous radio-telemetry study, I once followed a Gobi brown bear through the desert hills of Mongolia alone and on foot at night into places where a car could not follow. I walked without light to prevent the bear from noting my presence. The radio signal from the collar told me approximately where the bear was and where it was heading. The night was cool, though the rocks retained warmth after a blistering day, and silent except for the beeps of the receiver that bound me to the bear. At times the bear reversed direction and the signal approached me. My first impulse was to run somewhere, but the rational mind said "sit down quietly and wait." Listening for footsteps and imagining a shadow among the boulders lumber closer with a bear's rolling gait, I waited until the signal once more moved away.

Three weeks and again no bear had come near our snares. Ben Jimenez, who had joined us two days before we caught the bear cub, also checked snares each day with anticipation. In his mid-thirties, he was energetic, adaptable, and precise in his knowledge. He showed us how to improve the functioning of a snare. "Rub it with candle wax," he said and flicked a snare wire to show how it closed more smoothly. But we could do nothing about the weather. The snows of May and early June had given way to the downpours of the rainy season. The river by the *gompa* was in flood with brown water surging past, too dangerous to cross by car or on foot to check snares. To retrieve the snares, Ben and I waded across the river, tied together by a rope to prevent the current from sweeping us away. Our method of waiting for a bear to pass near a snare was obviously inefficient. What next?

The monk Argye was versatile. He checked our infrared cameras, cooked dinner, and performed various rituals such as blowing a sonorous conch shell every evening and blessing yak herds that passed by. And he ran what was, in effect, a roadhouse. With a shop that sold gasoline, instant noodles, and soft drinks, local Tibetans came to purchase items or just stopped by for a cup of tea or bowl of soup. At least half a dozen motorcycles and a couple of horses were often parked in front of the *gompa*. All visitors had bear stories, and Ulsa was adept at gathering them. We realized now that we needed an informant network with people notifying us promptly if a bear had invaded a house. Only then might we have a chance to capture the animal if it returned for another night raid.

On June 23 our luck finally changed. The owner of the house where we had caught the bear cub came to the *gompa* to tell us that the bear family had returned. It broke into his house on June 21. To deter bears, he had built a yak-dung fire in the yard, yet still they came back the following night. We rushed to the house to set snares again. Wang Dajun and I unfortunately had to leave for Beijing the next morning. While on the road, at 11:05 a.m., Dajun's cell phone rang. Wu Lan was on Ouzhu's satellite phone. "We got the bear," she said.

I regret not being present when the female was captured, but Hongliang sent me photographs and a detailed report which has enabled me to take part vicariously. Our team members had returned to the house early the following morning; all was quiet and from a distance they saw nothing unusual. Drawing nearer, my colleagues noted that snares had been triggered and a heavy twelve-foot wooden beam, to which snares were attached, had vanished. A drag mark headed away from the house, but of the female there was no sign. Five hundred feet away was a muddy gully, and into it both the female and the wooden beam had disappeared. When the vehicle drew close, she briefly clambered to the rim and then ducked out of sight. At 8:07 a.m., Ben shot a drug-filled dart into the muscles of the female's chest, using a sort of air pistol with pressure provided by a bicycle foot pump. Waiting out of sight for fifteen minutes, my colleagues checked on the female and found her restlessly asleep on her back; an injection of another drug quieted her. They removed the snare from her right front paw and examined her. She was around sixteen years old, judging by wear on her teeth, and was in good physical condition and still lactating—a living trophy whose satellite collar would finally provide us with detailed information. By 9:30 a.m. the female had recovered and climbed out of the gully. Spotting the vehicle, she immediately charged it and hit the back with a long-clawed paw, leaving scratch marks on the paint and my colleagues impressed and intimidated by her fury. Afterward she meandered around the area as if looking for her cubs, but she finally headed toward the nearby mountain massif where, later, mother and cubs found each other. She was given the name Troma, a commonly used designation for a woman in Tibetan.

On a hill, five miles from the *gompa*, two houses squatted near each other. In one a bear had lounged and left a lode of droppings. The two baited snares we set on June 22 were triggered by a fox, as shown by an infrared camera we had mounted at the site. Three days later, the camera revealed that a bear had come to the house at 4:00 a.m. Somehow the bear had avoided the snares when it returned at dawn the following day, but the next night it was less lucky. The snare cable was long enough to enable the bear to hide by climbing into the house through a window when the vehicle with my colleagues arrived. The massive broad head of a male then stared out at the vehicle, the snare still around his right front paw. After being darted at 10:33 a.m., it took only twelve minutes for the drug to take effect. Estimated at 160–170 kg in weight, the male was huge and difficult to drag out of the house to be collared. Shortly after midday, the bear got to his feet and half an hour later moved away into the hills. He was given the name Tashi.

The satellite collars started to transmit information immediately. Troma and her cubs remained on or around the mountain massif where they had been caught. This, we hoped, would give us a chance to observe their behavior in detail. The collars have another mode of transmitting signals, VHF (Very High Frequency), which a person can pick up with a handheld antenna and receiver. I was interested in, among other things, the interactions between mother and cubs and those between cubs, and also how the mother captured pikas, whether mostly by laborious digging or by catching them aboveground. But following bears is difficult and potentially hazardous. Liu Yanlin, who had been my coworker on the chiru calving ground in 2005 and now in late June had joined the project as part of the team from Peking University, wrote to me of a brief, tense encounter with the female and her cubs. "We walked for about 15 minutes and the bears suddenly came out from behind the rock. We were 30 to 40 meters to the bears. The mother ran to us for 10 meters for three times. . . . We underestimated the danger to follow bear with cubs."

The male Tashi, by contrast, did not tarry near where he was captured. Heading directly west along a mountain range, between July 4 and 18 he covered seventy-five miles straight distance through rugged terrain, including a spurt of forty miles in just four days. He crossed the Yangtze River into the Cuochi community, which I had visited in 2006. The mating season is in June and July, and perhaps he was searching for that scarce resource, a receptive female.

While the two bears roamed their mountains in the ensuing months, I was either deskbound at home or checking jaguar projects in Brazil and tiger projects in India. The bear team in Qinghai had taken a much-needed break at the height of the rainy season, when travel was difficult. I heard that Troma and the cubs had moved for a week into an empty house, feasting on flour while the owner was away. Lisanne Petracca continued to summarize the bear movements from the signals of the satellite collars. During the first two and a half months after being collared, Troma roamed widely around the mountain massif where we had first met her, covering a range of about 775 square miles of terrain. To the north, Tashi cruised along his mountain range, traversing terrain of 1,300 square miles. These ranges were calculated by the so-called kernel method, which calculated the 99 percent probability of the bear being in that area at any given time. Another male was photographed within his area; we would try to collar him next spring after he emerges from hibernation.

My mind often dwells on these bears and on the project. When and where will the two bears enter a winter den, something the satellite collars may pinpoint? What equipment do I need to order for next spring's work? The first few months of a project (and this chapter) are preliminary and fragmentary until we focus more on questions critical to the survival of the bears. I worry, of course, that someone will kill the animals in retribution for damage to a house or to make money from the gall bladders, a high-priced commodity in Chinese traditional medicine. Over fifty medicines contain the unique biliary acid of bear gall, and these are used to treat cancer and other ailments, as well as being a cure-all tonic. Most bear gall is produced in the notorious Chinese bear farms which house 7,000 animals or more, most of them Asiatic black bears though also some brown bears. To obtain the bile, the bear is placed on its side in an iron-barred squeeze cage, a tube is surgically inserted through its stomach wall into the gall bladder, and the bile is milked into a container. I do not know if the Tibetan brown bear in our area is caught for that purpose. But even the thought that the winsome bear cub we snared might someday be lying disheveled and uncomprehending in a squeeze cage makes me shudder.

I eagerly awaited further news about Tashi and Troma. In early November, Liu Yanlin sent me a fascinating report with information which he and his team had collected during the first four months of the project. The home ranges of the two bears remained largely separate as before, but they had enlarged considerably. Tashi wandered over 1,920 square miles (5,117 km^2) and Troma over 942 square miles (2,448 km^2). Male home ranges of bears are typically two or more times larger than those of females. The ranges of our two bears were extraordinarily large and will, no doubt, increase further over time. For comparison, in a study of grizzly bears in Canada's Yukon

Territory, A. M. Pearson found that the minimum range size of adult males was 110 square miles and adult females 33 square miles. From the Russian Far East, Ivan Seryodkin and his coworkers reported adult brown bear males with an average home range of 191 square miles and females 70 square miles.

Our two bears moved around a great deal each day. The mean daily straight-line distance, not including the inevitable meandering up and down mountains, was about six to seven miles. However, Troma and her cubs, according to Liu Yanlin's analysis, "are active all night and rest during daytime." At night they were at low elevations, digging for pikas and marmots, but in the morning they moved high up among the rocks where they were little disturbed and could find good cover. Tashi, meanwhile, showed no such pattern. Wu Lan wrote me that Troma and her cubs entered two houses and lived in each for some days in the owner's absence, and passed several other houses without entering. Tashi, on the other hand, lived in remote mountains with few homes. He was not known to have broken into any house since he was first captured in one the previous June.

The two satellite collars suddenly ceased to transmit during the last days of October, and the bears could not be located even on foot with handheld antennas. Did they enter deep into caves for their winter sleep? We will have to wait until they appear again, perhaps in March. While lumbering among the peaks, Tashi and Troma, large and powerful, were king and queen of these mountains. As they sleep, the snow leopards reign.

CHAPTER 14

The Snow Leopard

EVER SINCE I FIRST MET a female snow leopard and photographed her in northern Pakistan in 1970, the frosty eyes and smoky-gray coat of the cat has shadowed my work, sometimes as an insistent presence and at others as a vague mountain spirit. I have spent years in the realm of the snow leopard yet have seldom seen it. "Imperiled Phantom of Asian Peaks" is the title of my 1971 *National Geographic* article, and indeed *Panthera uncia* has remained a phantom. On one occasion in 1973 a snow leopard and I startled each other in a willow thicket in Nepal, but during my wide-ranging surveys for the cat in the Kunlun, Karakoram, Tian Shan, and other ranges in China between 1984 and 1986, for example, I did not encounter a single one. No doubt some observed me trudging along valleys and ridges, my eyes cast down to find at least a trace of them. When Peter Matthiessen and I trekked through northern Nepal in 1973, he did not see a snow leopard, yet like a good Zen Buddhist he said in his evocative book about the trip, *The Snow Leopard*, "Have you seen the snow leopard? No! Isn't that wonderful?" I am not quite able to achieve a similar attitude.

The snow leopard tantalized, even taunted as when it passed by me like a silver shadow one night while I slept in the open, leaving only tracks of its silent appearance. Such tracks are round and attractive, the pad about three inches across, and the four toes without visible claws. Miles spent tracking snow leopards across winter landscapes have revealed at least reminders of their presence. The cat might have stopped at the base of a cliff, or on a mountain pass, or along a ridge and made a tidy scrape in sand or gravel by raking its hind paws alternately back and forth. Occasionally a boulder with an overhang carried a pungent odor where the cat had squirted urine and scent from its anal glands, the marks communicating to others: "It's me and I passed this way." Another cat that smells the message can judge who the individual was and how long ago he or she had been there. Then it can decide whether to ignore the message, avoid the sender, or seek a meeting.

I examined each scat with special interest. A sniff gave an idea of its freshness. Picked apart, the hair and bone fragments reveal what the cat had eaten. Long, curved incisors and tan, black-tipped hairs are from marmot, brittle grayish hair from blue sheep, or curly white wool from domestic sheep, to mention just three. Sometimes I stumbled on a kill, wild or domestic. I recorded species, sex, approximate age, and physical condition, and saved the lower jaw for determining age at death more precisely from the tooth wear. Scuff marks and tracks give an indication of how the animal was ambushed, and tooth and claw marks show how it was killed. Was the body still warm? How much had been eaten?

To find out the food habits of snow leopards is of basic importance to conservation, especially because this provides information on the amount of livestock in the cat's diet. Almost nowhere, no matter how remote the alpine meadows, is the species outside the range of livestock and shepherds. It naturally kills the phlegmatic domestic animals, free and easy meals, whereas a principal cause of death of snow leopards, as well as of tiger, jaguar, and other large cats, is retaliation by the herders affected by such predation.

How extensive is livestock predation by snow leopards? One indication comes from China's Taxkorgan Nature Reserve adjoining Pakistan, where my analysis of scats revealed that 60 percent of the content was blue sheep, 29 percent marmot, 5 percent livestock, 4 percent ibex, 1 percent hare, and a little vegetation. Marmots hibernate in winter and are unavailable as prey for about five months, putting more pressure on other species during that period. To gain a clearer idea of livestock predation, we obtained community records and also interviewed families in that area. They reported an average loss of 3.3 sheep and goats and 0.3 yaks during the past twelve months, mostly to snow leopard and a few to wolf. This translates into 7.6 percent of all sheep and goats and 1.7 percent of yaks. The loss of only three sheep may not seem like much, but it represents a considerable financial burden to a family owning just fifty animals. Livestock is a family's capital, a bank account on the hoof. Understandably, a family wants to retaliate by killing the predator. And there is the added incentive to shoot, trap, or poison these cats because the luxurious pelts and bones bring a good price in the wildlife trade. The problem aroused my compassion for both snow leopards and herder families, but I had no way of providing direct help during my fleeting visits to such areas. Over the years my concern for the issue grew until it dominated my thoughts about snow leopard conservation.

Of the twelve or possibly thirteen countries of Central Asia where the snow leopard occurs, I attempted a detailed project on the species only in Mongolia. Kay and I first went there in 1989 when the country was still a satellite of the Soviet Union. There we collaborated in a snow leopard survey with Jachin Tserendeleg, the director of the Mongolian Association for Conservation of Nature and Environment and an enthusiastic proponent of fieldwork, and with the Ministry of Environment, under the leadership of Minister Zamba Batjargal. We traveled widely through the Altay and other ranges and also through the Gobi Desert, where the cats live on desolate massifs at elevations as low as 2,000 feet. We ultimately estimated a population of around 1,000 snow leopards in Mongolia, second only to 2,000 or more in neighboring China.

The following November we returned to the Uert Valley in the Burhan Budai, a subrange of the Altay, where, acting on a suggestion of Academy of Sciences biologist Gol Amarsanaa, we had found much snow leopard spoor. This time we brought with us telemetry equipment in the hope of fitting a cat or two with a radio collar and tracing movements and other activities in detail. When we arrived back in the Uert Valley, we erected our two *gers* or yurts, and I then wandered around, almost immediately finding two sets of snow leopard tracks in the snow. With luck, I thought, in the next week or two we should be able to catch a snow leopard in one of our foot snares hidden on trails.

The following morning my Mongolian colleagues and I hiked up the valley. In a gully, at the base of a slope, was a dead female ibex. And just above her, draped over a boulder, my startled eyes fixed on a male snow leopard. My companions talked loudly and pointed, and the snow leopard melted away, sliding uphill, halting briefly several times to look back at us before vanishing. The ibex had been attacked somewhere above, judging by scuff or drag marks on the barren slope. Only about a pound of meat had been eaten around the groin and the body was warm: we had interrupted a breakfast. There were no external injuries on the ibex. Dissection of the throat showed bruises and clotted blood, signs that she had been strangled. The weight of the ibex was 101 pounds, ample meat to last the snow leopard for days. Near the kill were several stout willow bushes and we tied a hind leg of the ibex to one. After a quick trip back to camp, I returned with a snare. I hid it by the body, attached with a cable, and set the spring. A small barrier of willow twigs would, it was hoped, guide the cat over the snare to the kill. We then returned to camp. At dusk, I checked the kill site and unrolled my sleeping bag nearby to spend the night. Amarsanaa, with us again this trip, preferred to sleep in camp. I asked him to return at dawn, at 7:30.

Cautiously I approached the snare at first light. The willow twigs had been scattered, but I saw nothing else until, up among the low branches, I discerned a dark mass—the snow leopard. After waiting nearly an hour for Amarsanaa, both the cat and I motionless, it was imperative that I release the animal from the snare to prevent harm to its paw. I filled a syringe with the tranquilizing drug Telazol and attached it to the end of a special six-foot aluminum pole. My approach was hesitant, worried that the animal might struggle and injure itself or react badly to the drug. The snow leopard remained crouched, growling, fiery eyes glaring, but made no move when I injected the drug with a quick jab into the thigh. Five minutes later he was asleep.

I lifted him gently from among the willow branches, holding his warm woolly body close, and placed him on the ground. Admiring the size of the paw, like that of a miniature snowshoe, I removed the snare and massaged it to get the blood circulating normally after being constricted by the snare. His fur felt sensuous as I moved one hand over his body and along the fluffy tail. He was about six feet long, nearly half of it tail. With a rope tied around his chest, I weighed him hanging from a spring scale. At 82.5 pounds, he was not particularly heavy, about the weight of an adult female, with males scaling up to 120 pounds, according to the literature. I fitted the radio collar around his neck. At 9:15 he awakened a little with a growl. After covering his eyes with a cloth to offer a peaceful recovery in darkness, I waited at a distance, binoculars trained on him to monitor his breathing. Amarsanaa finally showed up at 10:40. At 11:15 the snow leopard walked shakily uphill, stopping several times to eat snow.

The radio signals revealed that the snow leopard—we never named him—remained for four days on the mountainside above his kill. Then on each of the next four nights he returned to his ibex and ate a total of forty-six pounds of meat. In the meantime, on November 17, wildlife photographer Joel Bennett and his wife Luisa arrived to film for Survival Anglia, a British Company. With them was my son Eric, a diligent coworker even as a child, taking a break before starting post-doctoral research in molecular biology of plants at the University of Wisconsin. I was delighted to have him with me in the field again, something all too rare in recent years.

The snow leopard remained in our valley, where on occasion we saw him rest at the entrance of a cleft between two boulders. He reclined in the sun's warmth, chin on forepaws, hour after hour, sometimes shifting onto his side or licking himself. Toward dusk we returned to camp not much richer in data but so much richer in the satisfaction of having been near this rare predator at ease among the peaks. The radio transmitter had a motion sensor which indicated with rapid beeps on our receiver that the cat was active and slow beeps that it was at rest. What does this snow leopard do at night? To find out, Eric and I spent several continuous twenty-four-hour periods monitoring his activity. We'd pitched a small tent, and tucked into our sleeping bags against the 0°F cold, checked the signal every fifteen minutes, noting on a chart the letter A (active) or I (inactive). On the night of December 21, for example, the male was active from just after dark at 7:00 p.m. to midnight, and then he mostly rested until 5:00 a.m., when he began to travel steadily for three hours until daylight. His signals showed that he had been active for 53 percent of that day. Similarly, Rodney Jackson, who studied the species in Nepal during the 1980s, had found that the cats there were also busy for about half the day.

In the forty-six days between November 11, when we first saw this snow leopard, and December 27, when we left the valley, we observed him on ten days and picked up his radio signal on thirty-six days. Our male consumed an ibex and three goats during this time, eating something on thirteen of the forty-six days, for an average daily consumption of 3.7 pounds. Remarkably sedentary, he remained in the Uert Valley except for brief excursions elsewhere, using just 4.6 square miles of terrain. Of course, we had no idea about the total extent of his wandering. Rodney Jackson found that range size in Nepal varied from about five to fifteen square miles. However, in the Gobi Desert, where prey is scarce, a snow leopard may roam over 200 square miles or more, as Tom McCarthy learned in a later study. In the Uert Valley, as elsewhere, the ranges of several snow leopards overlapped. At the time we were there, the Uert Valley and its surroundings, an area of seventy-five square miles, included the ranges of eight snow leopards—two males, a female with large cub, a female with two large cubs, and an unidentified individual.

Just as in China, snow leopards preyed a great deal on livestock. In 1990, the eight households in and around the Uert Valley owned 2,990 sheep and goats, 94 horses, 59 yaks, and 13 camels. Of these, snow leopards had killed 13 sheep and goats (0.4 percent), 7 yaks (11.9 percent), and 16 horses (17.6 percent) during the past year. Yaks and horses, mostly young ones, were killed in disproportionately large numbers because they roam unattended for days in the mountains, whereas sheep and goats are herded.

Joel, a quiet and methodical person, worked long hours to obtain footage of snow leopards, ibex, and the culture of the local herder families. In the evening, sitting in the *ger* around the woodstove, we shared our day's experiences. We ate noodle and yak stew, and we drank tea, though the Mongolians preferred what they called *Ivan chi* ("Russian tea") and we called vodka, sometimes in excessive amounts. Our plan was to establish this research project, and then Amarsanaa and his Mongolian colleagues would continue it. We had obtained useful fragments of information so far but needed much more. However, I was not sufficiently familiar with attitudes toward work by many of the Academy of Sciences staff. Under the recent Soviet system, staff had been paid whether or not they did anything. Amarsanaa preferred to go home, and as a consequence the project stalled. Although Joel had obtained unique snow leopard footage, he needed more to complete his film, and I agreed to help him the following winter.

Thus, a year later in October, we were back in the Uert Valley. We filmed and collected additional information until Joel had enough to produce a fine television program, "Mountains of the Snow Leopard." Also on this trip was Tom McCarthy, a wildlife biologist who had worked in Alaska and was now determined to devote himself to snow leopards. Unable to find a suitable Mongolian, I turned the project over to him. Tom is now a world expert on the species, and twenty years later still has a project in Mongolia as well as in other countries. For several years he was affiliated with the International Snow Leopard Trust, based in Seattle, but now we are working together again out of New York, both of us with the Panthera organization.

By the early 1990s I had surveyed the distribution of snow leopards over much of Pakistan, China, and Mongolia, and the brief detailed study in Mongolia gave me an insight into the general behavior of the species. Tom McCarthy was now continuing such work, along with others in Nepal, Russia, and India. Except for a brief snow leopard survey in the Inner Mongolia province of China with my friend Wang Xiaoming in 1996, my interests drifted to other species. Besides, my enthusiasm for looking at scats and scrapes had waned.

Paradoxically, three new technological advances in the 1990s also stifled my desire to devote more intensive time to the natural history of snow leopards. Each of them has contributed greatly to the precision of studies and at the same time decreased the ostensible need to be in the field, reducing "tedious visual observations," as one report phrased it. Animals could now be tracked wearing a collar sending signals via a Global Positioning Satellite (GPS), as later we would do ourselves with Tibetan brown bears. Once the GPS is on the animal, the investigator can go home anywhere in the world, and there, cup of tea or coffee in hand, sit in front of a computer to check on where the animal is.

The camera trap was another major innovation. Set along a trail or other suitable site, the camera with its infrared sensors automatically takes photographs of any animal crossing the beam. It is an ideal way to find out which species occur in an area, especially the cryptic and rare ones. Species with distinctive markings, such as the spot pattern on a snow leopard's coat, can be accurately censused, as Ullas Karanth has shown so well with tigers in India. The camera traps, scattered over the terrain, can be checked at weekly intervals or longer and the marvelous self-portraits of animals admired. I no longer saw any point in trying to photograph snow leopards in the old, hard way, patiently waiting for hours and stalking them, ever alert, hoping for a glimpse and usually failing, but occasionally delighting in the thrill of success.

The third great advance is in DNA technology. If you want to know the number of snow leopards in a mountain area, collect scats widely. The DNA will identify the individual, and from the scat locations it is possible to plot the range without intruding on the animal's life by handling and collaring. I avail myself of such technology, but I try not to become a tool of such tools at the expense of direct immersion with nature, because I enjoy the outdoors and remote monitoring deprives me of the sight, sounds, and smells of the animal and its environment.

By the 1990s the snow leopard was considered a symbol of the mountains, a magnificent emblem of a country's natural heritage. But to a herder it remained a predator that killed livestock. My concern had been with the cat, yet I also had sympathy for the poor families which had lost their sheep and yaks. After all, why should a family strain its meager livelihood because of an obscure law protecting snow leopards so that others in some faraway city can talk about the ecological balance of the mountain ecosystem and our moral obligation to save the species? Is there a way to compensate families for loss of livestock to predators? I knew that the survival of all big cats depends in part on an adequate answer to this question.

Some predation is the result of poor herding practices. When a herder carelessly permits his charges to drift out of sight while he is asleep or busy collecting medicinal herbs, a snow leopard or wolf may well grasp the opportunity. Snow leopards commonly enter a poorly constructed or guarded corral at night and there may kill several animals. Rodney Jackson of the Snow Leopard Conservancy helped Ladakhi households build a roof of wire netting over corrals to deter entry, an effective method now used in some other areas as well. But it's not always easy to convince families to adjust herding practices, and some find it difficult to do so. When a new law in Qinghai province mandated that all children of a certain age go to school, some families lost their principal herders. But it seemed to me that households were often fatalistic about natural events, as I had also noted in Pemako when discussing tiger predation on livestock with villagers. One man complained to me about his livestock losses to snow leopard or *sa*, as the cat is known in his area. When I asked what he was doing about it, he replied, "I can do nothing. The snow leopard kills my sheep because I have somehow offended the mountain deity." One shepherd explained his worldview to journalist Lin Lan: "Nature is like a circle that includes wolves, sheep, and people." The circle must not be broken, even in defense of livestock.

Various ways of compensating herder families for losses to predators are now being tested with the hope that this might lead to greater tolerance of snow leopards, and I've followed these initiatives with great interest.

One way to reimburse households for losses is to give direct compensation for all or part of the value of the animal, with the understanding that there should be no retaliatory killing of the predator. Whether paid by private organizations or the government, this procedure can function reasonably well if payment is timely and adequate. The North American organization Defenders of Wildlife paid $1.4 million over twenty-three years to livestock owners in the United States for verified losses to wolves, and this contributed to the recovery of the species. By contrast, direct compensation schemes in various other countries, such as Bhutan, India, and China, have been largely ineffective. Bureaucracies have great inertia, claims are difficult to verify in remote places, officials may be corrupt, and false claims by households are common. In general, compensation does not lead to better herding practices and it is a steady drain on funds.

A more effective method of compensation is to establish an insurance scheme managed directly by the community and not by a far-off bureaucracy. To learn about such a venture, during the summer of 2008 I joined Yash Veer Bhatnagar and Sumanta Bagchi of the Mysore-based Nature Conservation Foundation, in the Indian Himalaya. There, at 13,500 feet in the Spiti district of Himachal Pradesh state, is the Tibetan village of Kibber. Yash Veer and his team have for years studied the rangelands and the wildlife of this area, and Pranav Trivedi has held field courses in natural history for students in Kibber and other villages. Kibber itself is an attractive village of whitewashed, flat-roofed houses on a hillside marred only by several ugly cement government buildings. There are a few fields of peas and barley, but most of the land consists of alpine pastures where livestock and ibex graze.

A small infusion of money starts the insurance program and after that it is expected to be self-supporting. It is voluntary. Each household decides which animals to insure: in Kibber it's usually just yaks and horses, which graze unattended. In the previous year, the ninety Kibber households had lost thirteen yaks and four horses to snow leopard and four donkeys to wolves. A local committee decides how much each family has to contribute, based on species, sex, and age of animals insured. If a predator kills an animal, the owners are compensated for its total market value as determined by the committee, though the dead animal must be left for the predator to eat at leisure to prevent it from immediately killing again to satisfy its hunger. On one payday I joined the six members of the committee, who sat in a circle on a meadow. The five villagers expecting payment came forward one at a time. A ledger was checked. The amount of compensation had already been calculated. After the villager had signed his name in the ledger, he received rupee notes—a straightforward and efficient system.

At the western end of the Tibetan Plateau in Ladakh, just north of Spiti, I observed another incentive program to enhance the livelihood of households and promote conservation. A family caters to tourists by offering "homestays." Instead of having to camp, trekkers can spend the night, get meals, enjoy the hospitality of a local family, and see blue sheep and other wildlife species that have been protected in the vicinity. It is a kind of bed-and-breakfast with standardized prices and amenities, with the bonus of insights into Ladakhi culture and nature. In the mid-2000s, a household offering homestays earned an average of about $230 during the four-month tourist season, a significant income supplement.

When I made one of my periodic visits back to Mongolia, I became familiar with yet another imaginative incentive program, this one initiated by Tom McCarthy. Tom and three other dedicated snow leopard researchers, Rodney Jackson, Charudutt Mishra, and Som Ale describe the basics in "Snow Leopards: Conflict and Conservation," a chapter in *Biology of Conservation of Wild Felids*:

> Snow Leopard Enterprises generates income for herder-artisans in Mongolia through handicraft development and sales, in exchange for community support of snow leopard conservation. Artisans receive training and simple tools to develop culturally appropriate woolen products which are marketable in the West. In exchange, communities sign conservation contracts stipulating a moratorium on snow leopard and wild ungulate poaching. . . . Currently 29 communities and over 400 herder families benefit from increased household incomes of nearly 40%. . . . Over US$90,000 worth of Mongolian handicrafts were sold in 2007 and further growth is expected. Proceeds from sales now cover all programme costs. . . .

Annually the artisans and communities receive a 20 percent bonus over the agreed price of the products—but the bonus is lost if there is even one case of poaching. In recent years only two ibex and one snow leopard are known to have been killed.

Shafqat Hussain from the Yale School of Forestry and Environmental Studies explained to me how several communities in Pakistan derive economic benefits through trophy hunting for ibex and the spiral-horned markhor goat. Eighty percent of the government's trophy fee, which may be as high as $25,000, goes to the community, which must in exchange patrol their area against poachers and monitor wildlife. (In an ironic twist, communities have demanded compensation when a snow leopard kills a trophy-sized animal because of potential loss of income.) In another village, Shafqat established an insurance compensation scheme similar to the one in Spiti, except that a tourist company donates supplementary cash.

Engaging pastoral communities in conservation is vital, but good protection by guards of critical areas is also essential, even if rather seldom provided. As Tom McCarthy and his coauthors wrote about snow leopards in the chapter quoted above: "Although officially fully protected in all countries such protection is rarely enforced because of lack of awareness, indifferent political will to uphold regulations, shortage of funds and trained personnel, and low priority some governments afford to biodiversity conservation." The same lament applies to the protection of all other big cat species as well.

Information about snow leopards has accumulated at a surprisingly slow pace during the past half century. A few studies have been done and it is known that the species is distributed over roughly two million square miles of which about 6 percent has been designated as reserves. But no one has checked most of that vast range in detail, a fact reflected in estimates of total snow leopard numbers in the wild. Published estimates range from 6,000 to 8,000, 4,500 to 7,500, and 3,000 to 7,000, figures so imprecise that they are little more than guesses. There is a "Snow Leopard Survival Strategy," prepared by the International Snow Leopard Trust, and several countries, including India, Nepal, Mongolia, and Pakistan, have each developed a National Snow Leopard Action Plan. In March 2008, Beijing hosted an International Conference in Range-Wide Conservation Planning for Snow Leopards. All this activity has raised awareness and provided focus. It has also emphasized how little was still known about the species.

I became involved with the snow leopard again in 2008 but this time focused more on communities and conservation than on the cat's natural history. In this work, I cooperated closely with Lu Zhi and her staff and graduate students of the two conservation centers at Peking University. Li Juan, a graduate student, planned a snow leopard study in Qinghai for her PhD degree, and we searched together for a suitable site and found one, as noted in the previous chapter on Tibetan brown bear.

I was especially interested in the southeastern part of Qinghai with its maze of limestone ridges, most of it good snow leopard terrain, as I had seen during visits in the 1980s. With a broader perspective acquired in more recent years, I felt that one should try to manage the whole landscape, not just a small reserve here and there, so that conservation will benefit all inhabitants, including the human population. I had always collected factual information, which is of course the basis for a clear assessment of what needs to be done. But I had too often neglected to translate my moral convictions into action by interacting much with communities. Now I would try to achieve a balance between the two approaches. This, in brief, is what drew me back to snow leopards.

My work in the Chang Tang had shown the importance of protecting a whole landscape, a whole ecosystem, in which even migratory species can continue to seek their destiny. Perhaps similar whole-landscape conservation, but on a smaller scale, could be achieved for snow leopards in southeastern Qinghai and extending into similar habitat in eastern Tibet and western Sichuan. Most existing protected areas are too small to maintain more than a few of the cats, and these could become extinct due to inbreeding, disease, poaching, or other causes. Instead, there is need to enlarge the concept of a protected area to a whole landscape. Such a landscape would consist of several strictly guarded core areas where animals have peace and security, connected by corridors of suitable terrain to enable species to disperse from one safe haven to another. The

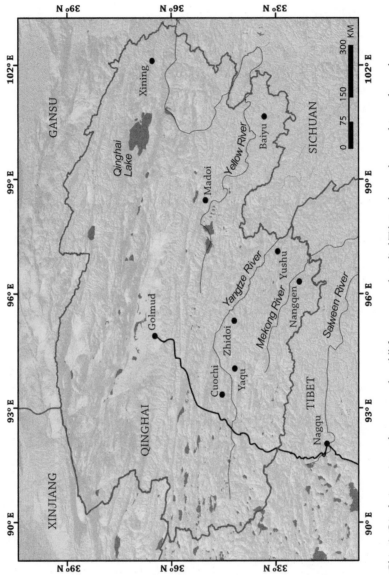

China's Qinghai province where we made wildlife surveys and studied Tibetan brown bear and snow leopard.

remaining parts of the landscape would be managed for sustainable human use in a mosaic of habitats that guarantee the livelihood of both people and other species. To think of an idyll where snow leopards, livestock, and people live in harmony may seem like a chimera but it is achievable—except that climate change lurks, ready to disrupt any plans. With time, vegetation zones will shift, and trees and brush, for example, will creep up mountainsides to engulf alpine meadows, the habitat of snow leopards, blue sheep, and marmots. All species of plants and animals will be affected by climate change, and they must adapt, move, or die. But a landscape may be large enough so that a species retains choices of where to move.

Between late 2008 and mid-2010 we made four trips through Qinghai. Various members joined our team at times, but aside from me there were three main ones. Wang Dajun, a sturdy senior researcher at Peking University's conservation centers, has had much experience with giant pandas and Asiatic black bears. Li Juan, often looking serious in her dark-rimmed glasses and straight hair framing her face, is warm and enjoyable company, a conscientious worker, and a determined climber. Zha La was officially our driver, but he was far more than that. A physically fit Tibetan with hair to his shoulders, usually tied in a ponytail, he enabled the team to function. Fluent in Chinese, he was our translator and our liaison in gaining local support. Outgoing and cheerful, he seemed to have friends and family everywhere. Zha La also cooked, purchased supplies, and joined us in the field to record observations.

We drove widely through eastern and southeastern Qinghai to look at the landscape and to interview villagers about snow leopards and wildlife, especially about problems between livestock and predators. With local guides we climbed into the mountains, up through stunted conifer forests and scrub to cliffs in search of snow leopard spoor. Often we evaluated and discussed conservation problems, both current and potential. One problem in particular drew our attention during the months of May and June.

At that season a peculiar migration occurs in the region. Schools close, villages become almost deserted, and offices barely function. Roads stream with small, tractor-pulled wagons and pickup trucks loaded high with tents, kitchen gear, bundles of clothes, bedrolls, and other household goods; the scene resembles an exodus from a war zone. Whoever can do so moves to alpine meadows, where clusters of white tents then sprout like puffballs. All this is precipitated by the caterpillar fungus, known scientifically as *Cordyceps sinensis* and in Tibetan as *yartsa gunbu*. Its lure is wealth. We wondered what impact this invasion of people has on the wildlife and the sensitive high-altitude habitat.

On many alpine meadows in the eastern part of the Tibetan Plateau, at elevations up to 16,500 feet, there lives a small drab moth of the genus *Thirtarodes*. It lays its eggs at the base of plants, and, upon hatching, the caterpillars dig into the turf and feed on roots for a year or more before emerging as a short-lived moth. Spores from a fungus invade the caterpillar and consume its insides, leaving a dead husk. The fungus grows sticklike up to four inches long from the head of the caterpillar. In spring the fungus pokes its tip up through the soil into air to shed its spores, thus beginning a new cycle. This caterpillar with its attached fungus has been used in China for medicinal purposes ever since it was first described by a Tibetan physician in the fifteenth century. Eating a caterpillar fungus or soaking it in a drink is said, for example, to alleviate symptoms of asthma, promote renal function, regulate blood pressure, and bolster the immune system. Recent tests have shown that there may be some actual benefits. To me, the caterpillar fungus lacks flavor. Fifteen or so years ago, I could buy one for the equivalent of ten to fifteen cents. Prices fluctuate but now one sells for three to four dollars, depending on size, age, and condition, or $10,000 or more a pound in China's coastal cities. The price is said to have gone up after the 2010 earthquake in the Yushu area.

Dozens of people can be seen on mountain meadows walking bent or crawling, a small hoe or knife in hand, searching for the spindly fungus tip protruding into the grass. A lucky day may lead to the discovery of ten or more. A hack of the hoe lifts a piece of sod, marring the meadow, and from it the *yartse gunbu* can be extracted without damage. An estimated 25 to 40 percent or more of local income is derived from caterpillar fungus. As Daniel Winkler wrote in a 2008 article in the journal *Economic Botany*, it is "the single most important source of cash for rural households in contemporary

Tibet," based on a harvest which "government statistics figured at 50,000 kg in 2004. . . . Among the wealthy and powerful in China, *Cordyceps* has come to rival French champagne as a status symbol at dinner parties or as a prestigious gift."

Whatever the price, the added income enables families to buy cell phones, motorcycles, and other items that are increasingly viewed as essential. Communities with uplands suitable for caterpillar fungus are annually invaded by hordes of strangers, leading at times to fights. County governments try to control the harvest by requiring a license for locals and one of higher price for outsiders, or by closing some areas to outsiders, but even with road checkpoints the fungus rush is difficult to control. The long-term impact on the moths and alpine meadows has so far not been assessed and remains a conservation issue.

In our travels we noted that every monastery has a sacred land of varying size associated with it, and many communities have a sacred mountain within their area. With hunting prohibited by local tradition within these holy sites, they represent in effect a network of small reserves, a good basis for creating a snow leopard landscape. For example, Shen Xiaoli, then a graduate student at Peking University's Center for Nature and Society, recorded 355 sacred mountains in parts of western Sichuan and eastern Qinghai. Although a sacred mountain covered on average only ten square miles, the total protected area is considerable. Given one of the basic tenets of Buddhism, that of showing compassion for all life, and given the respect which the religious community has among local people, we realized that conservation could best be achieved by involving government, communities, and monasteries all working together on behalf of the environment. But first we needed to learn more about the active interests and attitudes of monasteries toward nature. We visited seven monasteries and I describe here my impressions regarding their actual concern for nature, or, sometimes, their lack of it.

TARTHUNG

In a mountain valley about five hundred miles south of Xining, the capital of Qinghai, is the small town of Baiyu, and dominating the town is the Tarthung monastery. Among its residents is the monk Tashi Sang'e, an extraordinary individual whose reputation as naturalist had spread beyond Qinghai. As our vehicle approached Baiyu we were met by five monks. While one placed white ceremonial *katas* over our necks, others photographed the scene with digital and video cameras, a neat reversal of the usual when drab visitors and colorful locals meet.

Tashi welcomed us with a broad smile. He is about five foot seven inches tall and thirty-eight years old. One of eight children, he decided to become a monk at age thirteen, though he was always interested in watching and drawing birds. After years of the usual monk's life of prayer, ritual, and work, he decided to honor the principles of Buddhism by actively helping the environment. With several like-minded monks he started the Nianbuoyuze Environment Protection Association, named for a nearby holy mountain. The association then visited schools in Baiyu and surrounding communities to awaken interest in conservation. Tashi also began to paint seriously Qinghai's birds from life by watching, sketching, and recording them in the field. As we sat in his room by a woodstove on a chilly November day, he showed us a folder of some of his bird paintings, each species—360 so far—meticulously detailed and vivid in color.

When Tashi showed his paintings to a group of foreign birdwatchers, they recognized a sparrow-like bird with rusty back, gray chest, white eye stripe and throat, and black cap and cheeks, a Kozlov's or Tibetan bunting. Tashi did not know that it was rare and found only in this region. So he and some others turned themselves into scientists to study the distribution and nesting habits of the species. For example, Zhou Jie, a chubby, red-cheeked monk who seemed welded to his video camera, studied one nest in detail for forty-six days, from nest building to egg laying to hatching, and finally to fledging. Tashi went on to present the team's findings in 2009 at the international meeting of the Society for Conservation Biology, held that year in Beijing.

After breakfast of *tsampa*, yogurt, and tea, Tashi and three other monks—Zhou Jie, Te Ba, and Hua Ze—wanted to show us a potential area for a snow leopard study. When we reached the small Dum Co,

"Devil Lake," formed in the narrow valley by two landslides, we saw around the entrances of marmot dens sparkling necklaces of frost crystals formed by the breath of the hibernating animals. Tashi said, "My family grazed livestock here and snow leopards killed many animals. Blue sheep increased after they were better protected from hunters. Now the snow leopards kill less livestock."

We collected some dry yak droppings and built a smoldering fire. Te Ba made instant noodles which we ate quickly with hunched shoulders in icy blasts of wind. After tea was brewed, Hua Ze dipped a ladle into it and flipped a glistening arc of tea toward the sky while he chanted. He did this about twenty times to express his devotion to the land and to appease the deities. I asked why he did it so often, and the reply was, "There are many peaks here. Each has its own spirit." We then drank what little tea remained.

In the hills we showed the monks how best to classify blue sheep by age and sex, how to monitor sheep numbers, and how to identify and collect snow leopard scats and preserve them for our return. I wondered what they thought about our fascination with feces. There is a derogatory Tibetan expression: "What are you doing? Looking for feces?"

GONGYA

Our team headed south from Xining in early May 2009 toward the city of Yushu. As we sped across the high rangelands, I noted that few of the pastoralists now lived in the squat, black yak-hair tents that once were so common even a decade ago. These had been replaced by store-bought white canvas tents, light in weight and easy to move when households shift from their winter houses to summer encampments. In a sample of one hundred consecutive tents there were only six traditional ones. It was romantic nostalgia on my part, but the aura of nomadic life had changed. Yushu—polluted, noisy with traffic—had grown a great deal since I had first visited it in 1984.

We continued south to the county town of Nangqen. The county extends over 4,500 square miles of mountainous terrain to the Tibet border, and includes about 300 monasteries. A short way south of town is the Gongya monastery, crowded like a medieval village on the lower slopes of a mesa-like plateau. After introducing ourselves, we were assigned a room. As I wandered around, a vehicle drew alongside me and a monk leaned out of the window and said in English, "How are you? Where are you going?" I was somewhat startled because most monks speak only Tibetan, not even Chinese and certainly not English. It turned out to be Namgyal Pachiy, a manager of the monastery, who like Tashi had a deep interest in conservation. He was particularly keen to receive advice from our team member Zhaduo, who had been with us on the 2006 traverse of northern Tibet and who had established a conservation organization based in Yushu; Namgyal wanted advice on how to formally establish a similar organization at the monastery.

Namgyal described the conservation efforts the monastery had initiated here on its own. Five nearby communities and two across the border in Tibet were part of the monastery program. On the fifth of every month, several monks visit these communities to stress the need to care for the land; twenty persons from each community assist with protecting wildlife, collecting garbage, and reporting items of interest. The plateau behind the monastery is sacred land where not even livestock is supposed to graze. About a dozen of the monastery's 400 monks are always on patrol, living in simple shelters. But as Namgyal noted, the monks lack government authority to expel trespassers and poachers so they can only use their moral strength. Aware of climate change, the monks also monitor vegetation at several sites by photographing it at intervals with digital cameras.

We explored the plateau for several days in small groups led by the monks, but one morning I went alone. Already at dawn old women, bent with arthritis and supported by their canes, were spinning prayer wheels and mumbling incantations as they circled the periphery of Gongya, which is marked by hundreds of small, white *chortens*, or stupas. I passed them on my way climbing toward a herd of blue sheep. But monastery dogs raced past me, intent on catching and killing a blue sheep, and the latter retreated to the safety of a cliff. I continued upward, using the low *Potentilla* shrubs for handholds on the steep slope, until I reached the top of the plateau. A herd of thirty-seven blue sheep grazed there. I collected some of their fresh pellets for later analysis of intestinal parasites. A magpie landed near me to find out what I was doing and gave a harsh *kek kek*. Hours of searching revealed no snow leopard scats, tracks, or scrapes, but Wang Dajun and Li Juan reported the tracks of a female with large cub. A herder noted that snow leopards here were less of a problem than wolves, yet "if you kill a wolf they will come back in greater numbers."

GAER

Descending through a valley flanked by slopes partially covered by junipers, we reached Gaer, a blue-roofed temple with a village of mud huts around it. Above were limestone cliffs and ahead a broad valley. The head lama, the Rinpoche, now lived in the United States; the second one in the hierarchy had moved to Taiwan; and the third-ranking one was sick in Xining. Their absence, a monk confided, expressed itself in lax religious and temporal management. Gaer looked like a construction camp, as do many monasteries, with piles of timber and stones and workers hauling and hammering as they erected an imposing new building. Zhaduo talked to several villagers about wildlife around here. Most herders had given up on sheep and goats because they were too much work to tend and predators, mainly wolves, killed them too easily, whereas yaks could usually take care of themselves. Poaching gangs hunted blue sheep and musk deer in valleys away from the monastery. Four snow leopards had been found dead nearby in past months, probably poisoned. I was shown the skin-covered head of one, a prime adult. With hunting and logging officially banned in the country, households complained of lost income. We soon left the monastery, not much liking its atmosphere of minimal interest in conservation.

DA NA

Southwest of Yushu, over many miles of dismal road under construction, is Da Na, the Horse's Ear, so named for a distinctive limestone outcrop. The monastery is ramshackle, its buildings mostly of mud brick, but there was new construction as well. As a woman,

Li Juan was by tradition not allowed to stay within the main monastery compound. Interviews with the monastery managers provided a little information: blue sheep had been tame until harassed by more and more dogs, and a snow leopard had recently killed a yak calf. A monk patrol was occasionally sent out to check on the area, but there was no special commitment to conservation as at Tarthung and Gongya.

The monks showed us the gloomy interior of their temple. Three monks sat side by side chanting and beating drums in the soft glow of butter lamps, emanating a feeling of calm and well-being. I happened to glance up and my eyes were met by a floating, flying menagerie of crudely stuffed animals. A bearded vulture glided on outstretched wings, an argali sheep treaded air with dangling legs and so did a small brown bear. Of two snow leopards stalking the air, one had been killed by village dogs two or three years previously. I identified a Tibetan fox, a badger, and an eagle owl among the animals, all of them sooty and dusty. I had the eerie feeling of being surrounded by hidden malevolent spirits.

Da Na's interest in wildlife protection seemed minimal, and the stuffed animals reminded me that many Tibetans have no aversion to killing. Although Buddhism is opposed to intentional killing, such as by hunting, this has never prevented many Tibetans from pursuing animals for subsistence and profit. As with any religion, there is a contradiction between the ideal and actual practice. Indeed, as Toni Huber pointed out in his chapter "The Chase and the Dharma" in *Wildlife in Asia: Cultural Perspectives* (2004), antihunting laws inspired by Buddhist teachings did not appear in Tibet until the fifteenth century. At that time, animals were given the "gift of fearlessness," places where they did not have to fear for their lives, refuges protected by "sealing the hills and the valleys." These are the holy mountains and sacred lands of which there are many today holding considerable potential for conservation. As Toni Huber wrote, "It would appear that localized prohibitions, such as the Tibetan Buddhist innovation of "sealing the hills and sealing the valleys" around individual monastic communities or discrete natural landscapes (such as holy mountains), were far more effective against hunting than blanket prohibitions issued by the state."

JABRA

The Jabra monastery is located on a slope overlooking the Mekong River, its waters at this season swift and rust-brown. We were given a room in a large, newly built guesthouse. Two managers, Zamla and Nyima, told us that their biggest problem was dogs, five hundred of them, the same as the number of monks. Most of these dogs were Tibetan mastiffs, large and powerful, and recently so fashionable among Han Chinese that prices had reached $5,000 or more for some animals. To cash in, herder households bred them, and it was common to see half a dozen or more tied to stakes around a hut. Then the dog bubble burst. Households could not afford to feed many of these large beasts, so they disposed of them. Some were let loose in the mountains, where they formed feral packs that hunted wildlife for subsistence and killed livestock—deaths which were then often blamed on wolves. Others were released in monasteries. Packs now roamed the alleys of Jabra, attacking and sometimes eating each other and harassing people. We might want to carry a big stick for protection, it was suggested. The monks did not want to kill the dogs and government officials ignored the matter. What to do? There were puppies everywhere and the situation would get worse. I suggested castrating every male, but this was not enthusiastically endorsed.

On the other side of the Mekong River is Nagin, a holy mountain, a good place to check for snow leopard spoor. It was also the site of a gorge, a gorge of death. The willows by a stream were draped with the possessions of the dead—bags of clothes, coats, a monk's hat, amulets, prayer beads, a strangled cat and mastiff puppy hanging by the neck, and much else. Pilgrims doing the *kora*, or circumambulation, of Nagin blessed the dead as they passed. High on the slope of Nagin we visited a monk named Gama Zhaxi, aged seventy-one, in his tiny smoke-blackened room. Two months ago, he told us, he watched a snow leopard walk past as he stood in the doorway.

We heard that in the mountains not far away lived Cinchen Tashin, a famous lama with magic powers who had convinced people to stop hunting, smoking, and drinking. We followed a single track that snaked up the mountainside until it became too rough for a vehicle, and we then walked to an ochre *gompa* tucked against a cliff. A monk led us into the dark interior and up a staircase, two hundred years back in time, and into a room. *Thangkas*, religious scroll paintings, hung on the wall, bags of *tsampa* were stacked in a corner, butter lamps burned, and the air was heavy with incense. Cinchen Tashin sat in a corner in a high wooden chair with armrests; above him was a poster of the Karmapa, the young head of the Kagyu sect. A massive man with stubbly gray hair, Cinchen had a smile of greeting that rippled like wavelets across his face from mouth to forehead. He wore a light-tan skirt and vest, an orange sash, and a bead necklace. Cinchen told us, Zhaduo translating, that he had lived here alone for ten years, three of them in total seclusion. It was peaceful then, he said, as he gestured toward the window with its view across the vast mountains. Snow leopards had walked past and blue sheep grazed around the *gompa*. But livestock, dogs, and motorcycles had driven the wildlife away.

In our conversations, Cinchen stressed that we must show benevolence to all forms of life, to value kindness. He kneaded a fist-sized ball of butter tea and *tsampa* for each of us and urged us to eat it. To do so would bring good luck. Zhaduo explained in greater detail why we were here and what we wanted to accomplish, and Cinchen repeatedly exclaimed "*ooya, ooya*" in assent. In late afternoon, Cinchen invited us to stay the night. A nun in the downstairs kitchen gave us tea and noodle soup. Our beds consisted of thin mattresses spread on the floor of Cinchen's room, and we slept in our clothes. Cinchen remained sitting in his chair all night, motionless, wrapped in a tan sheet with even his face covered, looking like a mummy in the wan light of the moon.

The following morning, Li Juan, Lu Zhi, and I traced the base of a cliff. I found a fresh scrape of snow leopard with a squirt of pungent urine and was immediately alert. Farther on we saw above us a cave with a wide and high entrance. From my journal: "Li Juan is ahead a little and climbs into the cave opening. 'There is a body in here,' she calls.

"'What kind of a body?' I respond, thinking it might be a Tibetan.

"'I think it's a goat,' she calls back."

Lu Zhi and I walked closer. There was a thump—and a large snow leopard bounded from the cave, crashed through a clump of barberry shrub, and streaked uphill before trotting out of sight over a ridge. Li Juan had passed the snow leopard seated on a ledge near the entrance without seeing it. Feeling itself unnoticed, the snow leopard remained motionless even when Li Juan shouted but a dozen feet away. With our approach it fled. Li Juan was somewhat shaken, her mind imagining an attack, but I reassured her that snow leopards are kindly unless provoked. The body she had seen was that of a young female blue sheep, her forelegs encrusted with thick, gray, and bloody sarcoptic mange. The meat of one hind leg and part of the other had been eaten. Drag marks suggested that the kill had been made at the cave entrance. A close look showed that the blue sheep had been strangled, with one canine tooth puncturing a jugular.

Cinchen's large ball of *tsampa* did bring us luck, just as he had prophesized.

XIA RI

On April 14, 2010, at 7:20 a.m. an earthquake of 6.9 magnitude shook Yushu and surrounding areas and killed an estimated 3,000 people. When we drove through the city a month later, devastation was everywhere. Some large concrete buildings were mere shells, the interiors collapsed, and a few had wholly crumbled. Most of the small mud-brick houses and shops had turned to rubble; city block after block had only an occasional decapitated *chorten*, or stupa, rising above the desolation. The government had with remarkable swiftness supplied thousands of padded blue tents, about eight by ten feet in size, marked with four large Chinese characters: "Aid for the Earthquake." Refugee camps at the edge of the city consisted of a sea of these blue tents and a bedlam of barking mastiffs. With many shops demolished, business was now conducted from tents along the streets. Major relief efforts were under way, houses were already being rebuilt, and teams of police and military patrolled the streets.

We drove northeast toward the town of Zhidoi, up a long valley devastated by the earthquake. Whole villages had been flattened and the town of Longbao remained only as skeletal walls and rubble, as if after a bombing raid. A side road not far from Zhidoi took us through mountains to the upper Yangtze River, spanned by a newly built bridge. From there the track climbed into a small basin and the Xia Ri monastery. Its main temple and half of the houses around it had collapsed in the earthquake, leaving many of its sixty monks homeless. They had moved into a nearby row of blue tents, and we too found a home in them during our visit. The monastery was said to be 800 years old. Destroyed during the Cultural Revolution, it was rebuilt only to crumble again. The Shan Shui Conservation Center had already begun work on a conservation plan for the site. To assist with this, two of its staff members, Yin Hang and Bu Hongliang, had joined us. The government wanted to promote tourism here to bring in money for rebuilding the monastery, something possible now with the new bridge. The site is indeed attractive with its patches of juniper forest, the curve of the Yangtze below, and snow peaks all around. The monks did not view the advent of tourism with enthusiasm, however, rightly afraid that it would disrupt their isolation and peace.

Several senior monks called a meeting to inform us of their "ecological regulations," which had been neatly typed on a sheet. These included prohibitions against littering; using cell phones, radios, and computers; playing music; veering off designated tracks in vehicles; and harming plants and animals. I was bemused by how loosely the regulations were followed. Plastic bottles and other litter were scattered about; the monks had a satellite phone and used a computer; the "Living Buddha," eighty-three years old, had a TV set; and village visitors on motorcycles roared cross-country, their boom boxes blaring music. We did, however, have stimulating discussions about the inevitable influx of tourists and how to manage them. Tourists, we agreed, should be allowed to camp only at designated sites after paying a standard fee. Only guided tours along specific trails should be allowed. Some monks should be trained as guides and should develop a familiarity with natural history. To help us with the conservation efforts, the monks agreed to monitor wildlife and keep good records of their observations.

The blowing of a conch shell at 8:00 a.m. the next morning announced breakfast. It was May 15 on the Tibetan calendar (June 26 on mine), the date on which the monastery held an annual festival to pray for nature at a traditional site in the mountains. We walked miles up a valley on a new gravel road, the last section yet to be finished, an expensive road to nowhere serving only three herder households. Along the way we tallied herds of blue sheep high on the slopes, a total of about 150. After a three-hour walk the road ended abruptly at a glacial moraine. A steep climb from there took us over alpine meadows sparkling with yellow violets, blue gentians, and white edelweiss to a small glacial lake at 15,500 feet. About fifteen monks and some villagers had already gathered there. Together they erected a *damdong*, a pole topped with a trident, which symbolizes a wrathful protector spirit. A pile of rocks at the base held the pole upright, as did strings of prayer flags radiating outward from the top and anchoring the pole in a festive circle. More strings of flags were then attached horizontally to create a pyramid of color rustling in the breeze. But moving toward us was a black cloud, and a bone-chilling wind whipped into the glacial basin. Eight of the monks chanted as they sat in a tight row facing the lake and the snow peaks. Two ruddy shelducks called in answer from the lake. A rain squall hit but the monks continued chanting. An hour later when shafts of sun streamed through cloud the monks stopped. Everyone, including me, celebrated by joyfully throwing small paper prayer flags in the traditional colors of white, green, blue, red, and yellow into the wind. Each had an image of the wind horse, the *lungta*, printed on it to assure a swift delivery of our message, a blessing to nature.

On our last day at Xia Ri, the old Rinpoche, the Precious One, emerged from his tent, a large chunk of butter in one hand and a knife in another. As if on signal, griffon vultures came from all directions, running over the ground and plummeting from the sky to land with a whoosh of wings. They crowded and pushed against the Rinpoche and the monks near him, squabbling over the bits of butter thrown to them. The monks and vultures were at ease and trusting with each other—these great, gray birds and the monks in burgundy robes—a vision of nature and humankind as one.

I was reminded of the words of the eleventh-century Tibetan saint and hermit Milarepa:

Snow, rock, and clay mountains are my hermitages.
Snow and glacial rivers are my drinking water.
Deer, gazelle, and blue sheep are my livestock.
Lynx, wild dog, and wolf are my guards.
Langur, monkey, and brown bear are my playmates.
Thrush, snow-cock, and griffon are my garden birds.
If this appeals to you, please join me.

YAQU

In June 2010 we returned to the Yaqu *gompa*, which stands at 14,600 feet at the mouth of the Quirirongga canyon. It is a small *gompa* of just one single-story building which houses the temple, kitchen and communal room, a couple of bedrooms, and a storeroom. The *gompa* is a three-hour drive northwest of Zhidoi at the edge of the upland plain, an outstation of the huge Gongsa monastery near Zhidoi. There are usually about seven monks here, and seven mastiffs, led by elderly Angye. I had been here briefly twice before—and would return in 2011 for a study of Tibetan brown bear (see Chapter 13)—and been impressed with the relaxed hospitality of the monks and their keen interest in helping Li Juan with a snow leopard study. In fact, the monks now wanted to establish their own conservation organization. Blue sheep were quite abundant—we counted 406 in one five-mile drive along the canyon—and snow leopard spoor was easy to find among the limestone cliffs. Wang Dajun and Li Juan had selected this site as the one for their intensive study. After we had visited various monasteries and potential snow leopard areas their choice did indeed seem the best one; it would be the first detailed project on the cat in China.

The monks beamed at our arrival and greeted us with hugs as old friends. On a previous visit we had given them several camera traps and showed them how and where to set these. A young monk, Trangwen, in charge of the cameras, had done a splendid job. Now in the communal room the monks crowded around us to proudly show us their camera-trap photos of snow leopards. There were about ninety photographs, some fuzzy, some showing only a tail or rump, but a few startlingly evocative. Li Juan would now compare the spot patterns of the animals to find out how many lived in this area. Lu Gala handed us a camera with deep canine indentations in the metal: a Tibetan brown bear had tested the camera as a potential snack. After a dinner of noodle soup with chunks of yak, the team slept on the benches that line three walls of the communal room; I was given a mattress in the storeroom with a butchered yak dangling from the ceiling.

The monks enjoyed leading us into the field, where they bounded up and down slopes like blue sheep in spite of their ankle-length skirts. They showed us the places where they had set the camera traps and we looked for wildlife—as always, alert for brown bear. But on this trip we also had another task. With us were David Lai and Kathy Yin, a husband and wife film team from Tianjin TV International, here to produce a half-hour documentary on our cooperative work in China. They were a pleasure to have in the field as we climbed among the mountains and discussed conservation issues.

I was content with our recent journeys in Qinghai. Snow leopards were still widespread and so were blue sheep and marmots, the leopards' principal wild prey. Li Juan had settled into a good study area. Panthera and the International Snow Leopard Trust had signed an agreement with the Shan Shui Conservation Center to cooperate on this and other projects. Four of the seven monasteries we had visited—Thartung, Gongya, Xia Ri, and Yaqu—were, to my delight, happy to see the message of their scriptures translated into actual conservation efforts. The enthusiasm of some monks for protecting the natural world uplifted my spirit. If we could stimulate all the monasteries on the Tibetan Plateau, those of all the Kagyu, Gelugpa, Nyingma, and other Buddhist sects, to collaborate with one another, as well as with the government and communities, then whole landscapes could be managed for the benefit of all living beings. I knew that this was a vision for the future. Different sects in a religion, whether Buddhist, Muslim, or Christian, tend to be self-contained, but I also knew that, for this vision to prevail, the first tentative steps must be taken. The Yushu Prefecture government, shaken by the earthquake, is in the planning stage of creating a special ecological zone for the region with conservation a priority. An environmental conscience is here beginning to permeate individuals throughout society. The snow leopard and all other species which share its realm will, I feel assured, survive if we grant them tolerance, respect, and compassion. Like an invisible deity, the snow leopard can help to assure a healthy and harmonious mountain environment, if only we will treasure its existence.

During my travels around the Tibetan Plateau to gather information about the status of wildlife, I have all too often noted the heavy human hand on the landscape. Pastures are degraded by too many livestock, snow leopards are killed in retribution for preying on sheep, poachers slaughter chiru for quick profit, illegal gold mines devastate valleys, and pikas are mindlessly poisoned. To resolve the conflicting demands of an ever-increasing human population for resources and to conserve the diversity of life are the main challenges of this century. As I became aware of the rapid changes on the Tibetan Plateau in recent years, I have been preoccupied with thoughts about how to convert my natural history information into effective conservation. To challenge conventional perceptions, a Buddhist dictum urges, go to the most difficult places. I have certainly done that.

The Buddha, in one of his sutras, provided this wise commentary: "Do not put faith in traditions, even though they have been accepted for long generations and in many countries. Do not believe a thing because many repeat it. . . . Believe nothing merely on the authority of your teacher or of the priests. After examination, believe that which you have tested for yourselves and found reasonable, which is in conformity with your well-being and that of others." The Buddha exhorts us to think for ourselves. He urges us not to study philosophy from books but to go out among the flowers and spacious mountains. Be aware and seek oneness with nature and learn from the ecological community.

The spiritual beliefs of Buddhism are ideally suited to serve as a basis upon which to practice conservation on the Tibetan Plateau. Although conservation must be scientifically grounded, it is actually a moral issue of beauty, ethics, and spiritual values. Religion has here enlarged its boundaries beyond humans to embrace all animals and plants into one community. This confers individual responsibility for the land on everyone. I have met a number of Tibetans, both layman and monk, as described in this book, who have taken this ethical relationship to heart.

A difficult challenge now is to instill the population as a whole, everyone, with a conservation ethic. Ecologists have developed concepts remarkably similar to those of Buddhism. Aldo Leopold, a professor of wildlife management at the University of Wisconsin, spoke of a "land ethic." He published in 1949 a slim volume entitled *A Sand County Almanac*, still the most eloquent and influential book on conservation. Here are two of his elegant insights: "When we see land as a community to which we belong, we may begin to use it with love and respect," and "A thing is right when it tends to preserve the integrity, stability, and beauty of the biotic community. It is wrong when it tends otherwise."

The Buddhist precepts and Leopold's concepts have meaning far beyond the words. They convey that we are wholly dependent on nature for survival. They are a reminder of our moral obligation to discard self-indulgence and to protect life on Earth. They state that every species has intrinsic worth, the right to exist. And they make us look deeply into ourselves.

Religion and science have taught us what we must do to save the environment. Ignorance is no longer an excuse. The protection of nature requires, of course, acceptance by people based on their values. Such values, or at least awareness and appreciation of nature, are already part of Tibetan society. But more than that is needed, much more; there is still too much casual indifference, too many conflicting interests. Everyone from official and trader to shopkeeper and pastoralist needs to change habits and expectations.

We don't have two planets, one to treasure and one to squander. Using common sense, we must do the rational thing—protect and restore. We must work together, all of us, rich and poor, with passion, persistence, and an everlasting commitment to assure all living beings a future. There must be a covenant with the land that decries compulsive consumption, waste, and needless destruction. We have to adapt to an era of limits. We have to arouse everyone by addressing their needs and values, whether moral, esthetic, religious, or nationalistic. Conservation must also reach the emotions, the heart, not just the mind: it must stimulate people into action. We must make this a century of environmental enlightenment, one that expresses its loyalty to the earth with all its wonder and variety, the only home we shall ever have.

To behold a snow leopard is to understand the beauty of nature, to treasure it, and to fight for its survival.

Selected References

BOOKS

Hundreds of books and reports have been written about the Tibetan Plateau and adjacent areas during the past 150 years, and a few appeared even earlier. Many of these are accounts of travel and exploration or historical descriptions of a region that has experienced so much territorial and political turmoil. I have included a few references, old and recent, to serve as background on topics which I treat only lightly or not at all. Most references here, though, concern places and subjects that are of direct relevance to this book, and they include the sources of direct quotations used in the text.

Baker, Ian. *The Heart of the World.* New York: Penguin Press, 2004.

Balf, Todd. *The Last River.* New York: Crown Publishing, 2000.

Beckwith, Christopher. *The Tibetan Empire of Central Asia.* Princeton, NJ: Princeton University Press, 1987.

Bernier, François. *Travels in the Mogul Empire.* 1646. Reprint edition. Westminster, UK: Archibald Constable, 1891.

Bessac, Frank, and Susanne Bessac. *Death on the Chang Tang.* Missoula, MT: University of Montana Printing and Graphic Services, 2006.

Bonvalot, Gabriel. *Across Tibet.* New York: Cassell Publishing Co., 1892.

Brander, Dunbar. *Wild Animals of Central India.* London: Edward Arnold, 1927.

Canfield, Michael, ed. *Field Notes on Science and Nature.* Cambridge, MA: Harvard University Press, 2011.

Clark, James. *The Great Arc of the Wild Sheep.* Norman, OK: University of Oklahoma Press, 1964.

Coggins, Chris. *The Tiger and the Pangolin: Nature, Culture, and Conservation in China*. Honolulu, HI: University of Hawaii Press, 2003.

Cunningham, Alexander. *Ladak*, 1854. Reprint edition. New Delhi: Sagar Publications, 1970.

Farrington, John, ed. *Impacts of Climate Change on the Yangtze Source Region and Adjacent Areas*. Beijing: China Meteorological Press, 2010.

Fossey, Dian. *Gorillas in the Mist*. Boston: Houghton Mifflin, 1983.

Garretson, Martin. *The American Bison*. New York: New York Zoological Society, 1938.

Geist, Valerius. *Mountain Sheep*. Chicago: University of Chicago Press, 1971.

Goldstein, Melvyn. *A History of Modern Tibet, 1913–1951*. Berkeley, CA: University of California Press, 1989.

Goldstein, Melvyn, and Cynthia Beall. *Nomads of Western Tibet: The Survival of a Way of Life*. Berkeley, CA: University of California Press, 1990.

Gopinath, Ravindran, Riyaz Ahmed, Ashok Kumar, and Aniruddha Mookerjee. *Beyond the Ban*. New Delhi: Wildlife Trust of India / International Fund for Animal Welfare, 2003.

Grenard, Fernand. *Tibet: The Country and Its Inhabitants*, 1903. Reprint edition. Delhi: Cosmo Publishers, 1974.

Harcourt, Alexander, and Kelly Stewart. *Gorilla Society*. Chicago: University of Chicago Press, 2007.

Harris, Richard. *Wildlife Conservation in China*. Armonk, NY: M. E. Sharpe Publishers, 2008.

Hedin, Sven. *Trans-Himalaya*. 2 vols. New York: Macmillan, 1909.

———. *Southern Tibet*, 1922. Reprint edition, 4 vols. Delhi: B R Publications, 1991.

Hiuen Tsiang (Xuan Zang). *Si-Yu-Ki: Buddhist Records of the Western World*, 1906. Reprint edition, 2 vols. London: Adamant Media Corporation, 2005.

Hoogland, John. *The Black-Tailed Prairie Dog*. Chicago: University of Chicago Press, 1995.

Hopkirk, Peter. *Trespassers on the Roof of the World*. Los Angeles: J. P. Archer, 1982.

Huber, Toni. "The Chase and the Dharma: The Legal Protection of Wild Animals in Premodern Tibet." In *Wildlife in Asia: Cultural Perspectives*, edited by J. Knight. London: Routledge Curzon, 2003.

International Fund for Animal Welfare and Wildlife Trust of India. *Wrap Up the Trade: An International Campaign to Save the Endangered Tibetan Antelope.* Yarmouth Port, MA: International Fund for Animal Welfare / Wildlife Trust of India, 2001.

Jackson, Rodney, Charudutt Mishra, Thomas McCarthy, and Som Ale. "Snow Leopards: Conflict and Conservation." In *Biology and Conservation of Wild Felids,* edited by David MacDonald and J. Loveridge, 417–30. Oxford: Oxford University Press, 2010.

Kaye, Roger. *Last Great Wilderness: The Campaign to Establish the Arctic National Wildlife Refuge.* Fairbanks, AK: University of Alaska Press, 2006.

Keay, John. *When Men and Mountains Meet.* London: John Murray, 1977.

Kingdon-Ward, Frank. *Riddle of the Tsangpo Gorges,* 1926. Reprinted as *Frank Kingdon Ward's Riddle of the Tsangpo Gorges: Retracing the Epic Journey of 1924–25 in South-East Tibet,* ed. Kenneth Cox. Suffolk, UK: Antique Collector's Club, 2001.

Leopold, Aldo. *A Sand County Almanac.* Oxford, UK: Oxford University Press, 1949.

Lindburg, Donald, and Karen Baragona, eds. *Giant Pandas: Biology and Conservation.* Berkeley, CA: University of California Press, 2004.

Liu Wulin. *Tibetan Antelope* (in Chinese). Beijing: China Forestry Publishing House, 2008.

Matthiessen, Peter. *The Snow Leopard.* New York: Viking Press, 1978.

Maxwell, Neville. *India's China War.* New York: Pantheon, 1970.

McCue, Gary. *Trekking in Tibet.* Seattle, WA: Mountaineers Books, 2010.

McRae, Michael. *The Siege of Shangri La.* New York: Broadway Books, 2002.

Meyer, Karl, and Shareen Blair Brysac. *Tournament of Shadows: The Great Game and the Race for Empire in Central Asia.* Washington, DC: Counterpoint, 1999.

Middleton, Robert, and Huw Thomas. *Tajikistan and the High Pamir.* Hong Kong: Odyssey Books and Guides, 2008.

Moorcroft, William, and George Trebeck. *Travels in the Himalayan Provinces of Hindustan and the Punjab,* 1841. Reprint edition, 2 vols. New Delhi: Sagar Publications, 1971.

Mortenson, Greg, and David Relin. *Three Cups of Tea.* London: Penguin Books, 2007.

Omani, Bijan, and Matthew Leeming. *Afghanistan: A Companion Guide.* Hong Kong: Odyssey Books and Guides, 2005.

Padel, Ruth. *Tigers in Red Weather.* New York: Walker and Company, 2006.

Peacock, John. *The Tibetan Way of Life, Death, and Rebirth.* London: Harper Collins, 2003.

Prejevalsky [Przewalski], Nikolai. *Mongolia, the Tangut Country, and the Solitudes of Northern Tibet.* 2 vols. London: Sampson, Low, Marston, Searle, and Rivington, 1876.

Public Employees for Environmental Responsibility. *Tarnished Trophies: The Department of Interior's Wild Sheep Loophole.* White Paper No. 7. Washington, DC: Public Employees for Environmental Responsibility (PEER), 1996.

Rawling, C. G. *The Great Plateau.* London: Edward Arnold, 1905.

Richardson, Hugh. *Tibet and Its History.* Boulder, CO: Shambhala Books, 1994.

Ridgeway, Rick. *The Big Open.* Washington, DC: National Geographic Society, 2004.

Rizvi, Janet. *Trans-Himalayan Caravans.* New Delhi: Oxford University Press, 1999.

Rockhill, William. *The Land of the Lamas.* New York: Century Company, 1891.

Rowell, Galen. *In the Throne Room of the Mountain Gods.* San Francisco: Sierra Club Books, 1977.

Schaller, George. *The Mountain Gorilla.* Chicago: University of Chicago Press, 1963.

———. *The Year of the Gorilla,* 1964. Reprint edition with a new postscript. Chicago: University of Chicago Press, 2010.

———. *Golden Shadows, Flying Hooves.* New York: Alfred Knopf, 1973.

———. *Mountain Monarchs: Wild Sheep and Goats of the Himalaya.* Chicago: University of Chicago Press, 1977.

———. *Stones of Silence: Journeys in the Himalaya.* New York: Viking Press, 1980.

———. *The Last Panda.* Chicago: University of Chicago Press, 1993.

———. *Tibet's Hidden Wilderness.* New York: Harry N. Abrams, 1997.

———. *Wildlife of the Tibetan Steppe.* Chicago: University of Chicago Press, 1998.

Shahrani, M. Nazif. *The Kirghiz and Wakhi of Afghanistan.* Seattle, WA: University of Washington Press, 2002.

Sinclair, A. R. E., and Michael Norton-Griffith. *Serengeti: Dynamics of an Ecosystem.* Chicago: University of Chicago Press, 1979.

Sinclair, A. R. E., and Peter Arcese. *Serengeti II: Dynamics, Management, and Conservation of an Ecosystem.* Chicago: University of Chicago Press, 1995.

Stein, Aurel. *On Ancient Central Asian Tracks*, 1933. Reprint edition. Chicago: University of Chicago Press, 1964.

Thapar, Valmik. *Tiger: The Ultimate Guide*. New York: CDS Books, 2004.

Tilson, Ronald, and Philip Nyhus. *Tigers of the World*. Amsterdam: Elsevier/Academic Press, 2010.

Tsering, Dawa, and J. Farrington. *Competition and Coexistence*. Lhasa: WWF–China Program, 2007.

Wellby, M. S. *Through Unknown Tibet*. London: T. Fisher Unwin, 1898.

Wiener, Gerald, Han Jianlin, and Long Ruijun. *The Yak*. Bangkok: Food and Agriculture Organization of the United Nations, 2003.

Wright, Belinda, and Ashok Kumar. *Fashioned for Extinction*. New Delhi: Wildlife Protection Society of India, 1997.

ARTICLES

The text of this book contains references to a number of articles in magazines and scientific journals; the full citation for each of these is given here.

Bagchi, Sumanta, Tsewang Namgail, and Mark Ritchie. "Small Mammalian Herbivores as Mediators of Plant Community Dynamics in the High-Altitude Arid Rangelands of Trans-Himalaya." *Biological Conservation* 127 (2006): 438–42.

Bailey, F. M. "Exploration on the Tsangpo or Upper Brahmaputra." *Geographical Journal* 44, no. 4 (1914): 341–64.

Brantingham, Oliver, John Olsen, and George Schaller. "Lithic Assemblages from the Chang Tang Region, Northern Tibet." *Antiquity* 73 (2001): 319–27.

Bunch, Thomas, Richard Mitchell, and Alma Maciulis. "C-banded Chromosomes of the Gansu Argali (*Ovis ammon jubata*) and Their Implications in the Evolution of the *Ovis* Karyotype." *Journal of Heredity* 81 (1990): 227–30.

Bunch, T., S. Wang, R. Valdez, R. Hoffmann, Y. Zhang, A. Liu, and S. Lin. "Cytogenetics, Morphology, and Evolution of Four Subspecies of Giant Sheep Argali (*Ovis ammon*) of Asia." *Mammalia* 64, no. 2 (2000): 199–207.

Corax, Janne. "Into the Unknown: A Traverse of the Chang Tang." *Japanese Alpine Journal*, (2007): 78–84.

Dura, Iveraldo, Jurgen Dobereiner, and Aires Souza. "Botulismo em bovines de cort e leite alimentados com cama de frango." *Pesquisa Veterinária Brazileira* 25, no. 2 (2005): 115–19.

Fox, Joseph, Kelsang Dhondrup, and Tsechoe Dorji. "Tibetan Antelope *Pantholops hodgsonii* Conservation and New Rangeland Management Policies in the Western Chang Tang Nature Reserve, Tibet: Is Fencing Creating an Impasse?" *Oryx* 43, no. 2 (2009): 183–90.

Gyaltsen, Nyima. "The Lost World of the Wind Horse." In *Man and the Biosphere* (Special issue edited by Zhang Hong, 2010): 34–41, 60–63, 89–91.

Kingdon-Ward, Frank. "Caught in the Assam-Tibet Earthquake." *National Geographic* 51, no. 3 (1952): 404–16.

Lin Lan. "Entering the Black Tents." In *Man and the Biosphere* (Special issue edited by Zhang Hong, 2010): 10–27, 42–55, 64–81.

Moeller, Robert, Birgit Puschner, Richard Walker, Tonie Rocke, et al. "Determination of the Medium Toxic Dose of Type C Botulinum Toxin in Lactating Dairy Cows." *Journal of Veterinary Diagnostic Investigation* 15 (2003): 523–26.

Pech, Roger, Jiebu, Anthony Arthur, Zhang Yanming, and Lin Hui. "Population Dynamics and Responses to Management of Plateau Pikas (*Ochotona curzoniae*)." *Journal of Applied Ecology* 44 (2007): 615–24.

Schaller, George. "Imperiled Phantom of Asian Peaks." *National Geographic* 140, no. 5 (1971): 702–7.

———. "Wildlife in the Middle Kingdom." *Defenders* 60, no. 3 (1985): 10–15.

Schaller, George, Lu Zhi, Wang Hao, and Su Tie. "Wildlife and Nomads in the Western Chang Tang Reserve." *Memorie della Società Italiana di Scienze Naturali e del Museo Civico di Storia Naturale di Milano* 33, no. 1 (2005): 59–67.

Smith, Andrew, and Marc Foggin. "The Plateau Pika (*Ochotona curzoniae*) Is a Keystone Species for Biodiversity on the Tibetan Plateau." *Animal Conservation* 2 (1999): 235–40.

Wallace, Scott. "The Megafauna Man." *Adventure*, December 2006–January 2007, 66–72, 108.

Williams, Ted. "Open Season on Endangered Species." *Audubon*, January 1991, 26–35.

Worthy, Fiona, and J. Marc Foggin. "Conflicts between Local Villagers and Tibetan Brown Bears Threaten Conservation of Bears in a Remote Region of the Tibetan Plateau." *Human-Wildlife Conflict* 2, no. 2 (2008): 200–5.

Yang Yongping. "Connecting Cultures." In *Man and the Biosphere* (Special issue edited by Zhang Hong, 2010): 92–96.

Zhang Endi, George Schaller, and Lu Zhi. "Tigers in Tibet." *Cat News (IUCN)* 33 (2000): 5–6.

Zhang Hong, ed. *Man and the Biosphere* (Special issue, 2010). Beijing: Chinese National Committee for Man and the Biosphere.

Index

About Island Press

Since 1984, the nonprofit Island Press has been stimulating, shaping, and communicating the ideas that are essential for solving environmental problems worldwide. With more than 800 titles in print and some 40 new releases each year, we are the nation's leading publisher on environmental issues. We identify innovative thinkers and emerging trends in the environmental field. We work with world-renowned experts and authors to develop cross-disciplinary solutions to environmental challenges.

Island Press designs and implements coordinated book publication campaigns in order to communicate our critical messages in print, in person, and online using the latest technologies, programs, and the media. Our goal: to reach targeted audiences—scientists, policymakers, environmental advocates, the media, and concerned citizens—who can and will take action to protect the plants and animals that enrich our world, the ecosystems we need to survive, the water we drink, and the air we breathe.

Island Press gratefully acknowledges the support of its work by the Agua Fund, Inc., The Margaret A. Cargill Foundation, Betsy and Jesse Fink Foundation, The William and Flora Hewlett Foundation, The Kresge Foundation, The Forrest and Frances Lattner Foundation, The Andrew W. Mellon Foundation, The Curtis and Edith Munson Foundation, The Overbrook Foundation, The David and Lucile Packard Foundation, The Summit Foundation, Trust for Architectural Easements, The Winslow Foundation, and other generous donors.

The opinions expressed in this book are those of the author(s) and do not necessarily reflect the views of our donors.